# POLICE OFFICER EXAM

# POLICE OFFICER ▶ EXAM

## 4th Edition

LEARNINGEXPRESS®

NEW YORK

Library of Congress Cataloging-in-Publication Data:
Police officer exam.—4th ed.

Police officer exam : the complete preparation guide. — 4th ed.
    p. cm.
 Includes bibliographical references and index.
 ISBN-13: 978-1-57685-740-3 (alk. paper)
 ISBN-10: 1-57685-740-9 (alk. paper)
 1. Police—United States—Examinations, questions, etc. 2. Police—Vocational guidance—United States.
I. LearningExpress (Organization)
 HV8143.P635 2010
 363.2076—dc22
                    2009051164

Printed in the United States of America

9 8 7 6 5 4 3 2

Fourth Edition

ISBN: 978-1-57685-740-3

**Regarding the Information in This Book**

We attempt to verify the information presented in our books prior to publication. It is always a good idea, however, to double-check such important information as minimum requirements, application and testing procedures, and deadlines with your local law enforcement agency, as such information can change from time to time.

For more information or to place an order, contact LearningExpress at:
 2 Rector Street
 26th Floor
 New York, NY 10006

Or visit us at:
 www.learnatest.com

# Contents ▶

# CONTENTS

# CONTENTS

# LIST OF CONTRIBUTORS

The following individuals contributed to the content of this book:

**Dorothy Moses Schulz, PhD** is a professor at John Jay College of Criminal Justice (CUNY), in New York City. She is a retired captain with the Metro-North Commuter Railroad Police Department and its predecessor railroad, Conrail. She was the first woman to hold a management rank in both departments. She is a life member of the International Association of Chiefs of Police (IACP) and other police and history associations and speaks frequently at police and academic gatherings. Dr. Schulz is the author of two books on women in law enforcement, *Breaking the Brass Ceiling: Women Police Chiefs* (Praeger Publishers, 2004) and *Their Paths to the Top* and *From Social Worker to Crimefighter: Women in United States Municipal Policing* (Praeger Publishers, 1995), has contributed to two Learning Express books on policing, and has published numerous articles on a number of historical and current police topics, particularly in areas concerning transit and railroad police and women in law enforcement.

**Elizabeth Chesla** is an adult educator and curriculum developer. She is the author of *TOEFL Exam Success* and coauthor of *ACT Exam Success*, as well as many other writing and reading guides and test-preparation books. She lives in South Orange, New Jersey.

**Lieutenant Raymond E. Foster**, LAPD (ret.), MPA, is a 24-year veteran of policing. Currently, he is a university lecturer and the author of several books, including *Police Technology, Leadership: Texas Hold 'em Style*, and *From LAPD to NYPD: An Introduction to Policing*.

**Mary Hesalroad**, a police officer for the Austin, Texas, Police Department, has many years of experience as a police recruiter.

**Rebecca LaTourneau** is a writer and researcher who lives in Forest Lake, Minnesota.

**Mary E. Masi** is the author and coauthor of several professional books, including *Firefighter Career Starter* and *EMS Essentials Glossary*.

**Judith N. Meyers** is director of the Two Together Tutorial Program of the Jewish Child Care Association in New York City.

**Judith F. Olson** is chairperson of the language arts department at Valley High School in West Des Moines, Iowa, where she also conducts test-preparation workshops.

**Judith Robinovitz** is an independent educational consultant and director of Score at the Top, a comprehensive test preparation program in Vero Beach, Florida.

**Judith Schlesinger**, PhD, is a writer and psychologist whose background includes years of working with police officers in psychiatric crisis interventions.

**Jay Smith** is an exercise physiologist and Director of Physical Fitness and Health Maintenance Programs for the Massachusetts Criminal Justice Training Council.

# 1 ▶ WHAT POLICE OFFICERS DO

## *CHAPTER SUMMARY*

Television and films present a portrait of policing that is quite different from the reality. This chapter provides you with an overview of what police officers actually do on a regular basis, as well as the different types of police agencies, facts and figures about the numbers of police officers, their salaries and benefits, and information on the numbers and types of positions that will be available in the future.

**A**nyone who has ever watched a television program or seen a movie about police officers thinks he or she knows everything there is to know about the job, including that cops often refer to policing as "the job." Knowing some small pieces of insider terminology, however, doesn't mean you really know what the job is all about.

The best thing about television shows and movies is that they make the job very exciting and make people want to be cops. On the other hand, the worst thing about these shows and movies is that... they make the job very exciting and make people want to be cops. From the inside, policing looks very different from what it appears from the outside. In fiction, cops—mostly detectives rather than uniformed officers—are portrayed as running from one major crime to another. When they are not working, their lives are either too exciting to be believed or too troubling to be believed. Their cases get solved within an hour or two. There is lots of action, car chases, frequent "shoot 'em ups," and more cursing than most people hear in many months. Sometimes love scenes are interspersed; the hero or heroine always seems to find time for romance. No wonder so many people want to become police officers!

The fact, though, is that the real draws of the job are more likely to be a) the opportunity to help people and be of service to the community, while b) receiving an excellent salary and benefit package, combined with c) an option to retire at a younger age than most other working professionals. Not as glamorous, but just as enticing!

## What You Can Really Expect

Although detectives and CSI personnel get the most media attention, they actually constitute the smallest percentages of personnel in most police departments—and almost all such personnel began their careers as uniformed officers, as did nearly *all* police officers. Only a handful of police officers have never served in uniform or did not begin their careers on patrol. These few may have been selected for an undercover assignment immediately upon graduating the police academy, or even while still in the academy, because they met a very special need the department had at that time. One such example is of a very young-looking police officer being assigned in plainclothes to a high school where serious drug dealing is believed to be taking place. Other rare examples might be an officer with unique language skills or highly specialized knowledge whose talents fit immediately into an ongoing investigation. However, do not join a police department expecting to be chosen for such a role. You should expect to spend the early years of your career in uniform on patrol—whether in a vehicle or on foot—responding to a variety of types of situations. The vast majority of police officers spend most—if not all—of their careers in uniform. Even if you are promoted to higher rank, your assignment might still very likely be in uniform. Even in large departments with many special bureaus and assignments, the overwhelming majority of personnel in the agency are assigned to patrol.

As a uniformed police officer, you will most likely be assigned to patrol in a marked police car or other motorized vehicle, answering what are termed "calls for service." Generally, this means a member of the public has called your department's dispatching center to report some problem. Your job will be to solve that problem—or at least to provide a temporary solution that permits you to leave the scene and go on to respond to other problems for which a police officer has been requested. This is both the blessing and the curse of your job. The blessing is that you have an opportunity to help many people, to make decisions on your own, and to do many different types of things within a day. The curse is that you are often called to situations with no popular, immediate, or long-term answers; you rarely have time to do something beyond applying a quick-fix; and you do not usually learn the final disposition of the problems you have confronted.

Police officers tend to refer to the job with a variety of clichés. Some call it a front-row seat to the greatest show on earth because of the varied things they see. Others call it an adventure, because each day brings situations that can be totally different from yesterday's problems. You might often hear that you can go from literally hours of boredom to moments of sheer excitement and terror. Each cliché has an element of truth.

How can this be? Part of the reason is that the job of patrol involves two kinds of work—self-initiated, which means you look for things to do on your own, or dispatched, which means you are sent to a location where someone has called your police department for assistance. The reasons a member of the public calls the police are too numerous to list. One sociologist who studied the police for most of his lifetime called the police "the people others call when they want something done and they want it done now." If something can wait until tomorrow, it is very likely it will not be the police who are called. Members of the public call the police when they are frightened, have been victimized, have been injured, are trying to help someone else in similar circumstances, or simply cannot solve a problem themselves. Police officers are called when people lock themselves out of their homes or cars, even though they are not locksmiths. All too often, people call the police when they fight with friends or relatives, even though police officers are not trained counselors, mediators, or social workers. Although police officers may be specifically trained in any of these careers, they fulfill these and hundreds of other roles on a regular basis. Police officers must truly be Jacks and Jills of all trades!

Even an officer for a specialized agency may respond to a wide and unpredictable variety of calls. For instance, if you are a campus police officer, you might receive a call to respond to a classroom for a sick or injured faculty member; an administrative office where a theft has been discovered or a student who is being expelled has threatened violence; the gym, where someone may have become injured or discovered property missing from a locker; a parking facility where a crime has occurred or someone has forgotten where he left his vehicle; or a dormitory for any of the same reasons you would be called to a private residence.

Similarly, as a transit officer, you might be sent to answer a request in someone's office, on a bus or train or a platform, in a station, or along the transit route (known as the right-of-way). The request might be for something as ordinary as a passenger who has taken the wrong bus or train or who discovers that her wallet is missing, to a domestic dispute where people have gotten into a fight no different from what might occur in their living room, or to something as tragic as someone having fallen from the platform and been hit by a moving train. Airport police officers receive similar requests; the call could involve a theft, an injury, a fight, or someone who has panicked over missing an important flight.

## How the Police Officer Exam Tests Job Readiness

Many of these requests for service do not involve any laws having been violated; this is why so many of the questions on the Police Officer Exam test for judgment and not for knowledge of specific laws or ordinances. You are not expected to know about criminal law, vehicle and traffic law, or any other type of law or procedures. Rather, you will be given brief situations that could occur and then given a series of multiple-choice questions to gauge your reading and comprehension skills and also your judgment. *Reading and comprehension* is self-explanatory— were you able to read the words and understand either the situations described or the questions you were asked? This means having a sufficient vocabulary to know what the words mean and being able to put the words together so as to understand what you read and what you are being asked to answer. *Judgment* means your ability to make reasonable choices based on being able to consider a situation and its possible outcomes. These types of questions are discussed in greater detail in Chapter 10, but here are two sample questions that give you a preview of what the exam writers consider judgment questions.

### Sample Judgment Questions

1. Officer Smyth's patrol area has recently been the subject of complaints about drug dealing during daylight hours. Which area of his beat should Officer Smyth probably be least concerned about in addressing this problem?
   a. a day-care center staffed by childcare workers from 7 A.M. to 5 P.M.
   b. a vacant lot that has remained undeveloped for the past three years
   c. a transit right-of-way that is unfenced and not visible from the local streets
   d. a bridge underpass where homeless individuals and truant teenagers are known to congregate

**1. a.** Choice **a** is fairly obvious because it is the least likely place for a daytime drug deal to take place. Does it mean a drug deal would never take place there? No, but in answering a judgment question, you must be careful to consider what is likely to occur. In this question, it was also important that you immediately recognized the word *least*. Had you missed this, and assumed you were being asked for the *most* likely place, you might have become confused because it seemed that three of the four answers could have been correct. If you had become confused due to poor reading of the questions, you would have lost points not on judgment but on improperly reading the question. Remember that all the questions on the exam, regardless of how they are labeled, rely on reading and comprehension skills.

**2.** You are the first officer to arrive in response to an anonymous call to your dispatcher of a possible burglary in Apartment 7J of a large apartment building in a quiet, residential neighborhood. When you arrive, you knock on the apartment door. An approximately 60-year-old woman opens the door and says that she is the resident, she did not call the police, and there is no problem. As the woman closes the door, your best initial course of action is:

**a.** to push the door open and enter the apartment to look around.

**b.** to put your foot in the doorway so the woman cannot close the door.

**c.** to push the door open and frisk the woman for weapons.

**d.** to wait for backup officers and to investigate further by questioning neighbors and the building management about the resident.

**2. d.** Choice **d** is correct because you are not simply accepting the resident's word but will investigate further. Choices **a** and **c** are incorrect because since the caller was anonymous and with no other indications of a crime, you would not be justified in using force. Choice **b** is incorrect because you would be endangering yourself by placing your foot where it could be pinned.

## Traffic Enforcement and the Police Officer Exam

Another entirely different area of responsibility for police officers might entail enforcing traffic regulations and investigating roadway accidents. State troopers in particular spend a large percentage of their time on these activities, but most officers on patrol can expect to be involved in traffic control.

Traffic enforcement is a key element of maintaining public safety and takes up a large portion of an officer's responsibilities. Even in agencies with a dedicated traffic bureau, all patrol officers are expected to participate in traffic enforcement activities. These activities are far broader than merely writing citations. They may involve patrolling or controlling traffic in work zones, directing traffic at major arteries or at accident scenes, and maintaining checkpoints for drivers who are intoxicated or high on drugs. A study released in 2009 by the National Highway Traffic Safety Agency (NHTSA) found that while in 2007 the percentage of people driving while intoxicated on weekend nights had dropped from 2005, more than 16% of the drivers had traces of drugs in their systems. While the actual percentage may have been surprising, the finding itself was not. The NHTSA was prompted to start its research on drug use by drivers because police officers had been reporting increasing numbers of encounters with drivers who seemed to be impaired but did not test positive for alcohol, leading to the suspicion that they might have used drugs.

Traffic fatalities are a major cause of death in the United States; in 2006, according to the NHTSA, more than 42,000 people died and more than 2.5 million were injured in traffic accidents. The NHTSA estimated that same year that the nation incurred more than $230.6 billion in economic loss as a result of traffic accidents. The 2006 figures were a slight drop from 2005, attributed in part by the NHTSA to safety features in vehicles (including greater compliance with seat belt regulations), and attributable also in part to police enforcement through a variety of national campaigns, including "Click It or Ticket," which has increased awareness of the dangers of driving without a seat belt. The high number of traffic fatalities and accidents leads directly to another major traffic-related activity of police officers, investigating these events. Accident investigation can involve a task like reporting to the scene of a minor fender-bender, where the officer's major job is to assure that those involve exchange information to report to their insurance carriers.

Most police agencies, in addition to expecting uniformed officers to respond to traffic situations, have specialized traffic and accident squads. Accident reconstruction is highly specialized and requires considerable math skills. But traffic and transit fatalities can leave an indelible mark on an officer's memory; the scene to which you are asked to respond might involve major injuries or dead bodies. These observations are not meant to discourage you in pursing a career in law enforcement, but they are a reminder of the importance of taking seriously the Police Suitability Test in Chapter 3 so that you get a sense of whether a career with such ups and downs is meant for you.

Traffic enforcement leads to an area of policing most often seen in movies and on TV—namely, police pursuits of automobiles. Vehicle pursuits are a standard feature of police films, where cars and trucks get knocked around like in video games. No one ever seems to get killed; in fact, rarely do they receive even a finger scratch. In real world policing, departments are doing all they can to limit police pursuits. Vehicle pursuits result in police being the ones who often are driving too fast, ignoring traffic signals, or running through stop or yield signs. Studies have shown that most pursuits start with a traffic violation that occurs at night and generally comes to involve at least two police cars. Although these pursuits end without an accident more than 70% of the time, the other 30% are often lethal, with serious injuries or deaths to the police, to those chased, or to innocent victims who are hit by one of the vehicles involved in the chase. To minimize danger, bad publicity, and costly lawsuits, departments discourage officers from chasing routine traffic violators.

Because traffic enforcement is a major role of the police, a number of judgment questions on your exam may be based on traffic-related situations. Here are two examples of such questions:

## Sample Traffic-Related Judgment Questions

1. To achieve the goals of traffic law, the most effective way for a police agency to enforce traffic laws is
   a. to ensure that summonses are issued for all violations.
   b. to concentrate only on the most serious violations.
   c. to encourage the public's voluntary compliance with the traffic laws.
   d. to raise as much revenue as possible.

1. **c.** Choice **c** is correct; the traffic system requires the public's cooperation and voluntary compliance. Choice **a** is incorrect because there could never be a sufficient number of officers available to issue summonses for every violation. Choice **b** is incorrect because officers should not ignore less serious violations when they are committed in their presence. Choice **d** is incorrect because revenue is not the primary consideration.

2. A police officer patrolling a major intersection observes a motorist pass a steady red light. The officer should issue a summons in all of the following circumstances, except if
   a. the motorist did not intentionally drive through the light.
   b. the motorist appears to be an upstanding, law-abiding citizen.
   c. the motorist intentionally drove through the light but had looked both ways before.
   d. the motorist carefully drove through the light because of an emergency.

2. **d.** Choice **d** is the best answer because all laws are qualified by the need to act in genuine emergencies. Choice **a** is incorrect because traffic laws apply to all violators regardless of whether their acts are intentional or due to negligence or carelessness. Choice **b** is incorrect because traffic laws are enforced against all citizens to encourage them to drive carefully. Choice **c** is incorrect because looking both ways does not excuse the violation.

## Memory Questions

Some questions that pertain to recognizing and remembering numbers may have traffic considerations. Although these examples are more complex than most states' license plate designations, you should immediately see that the formats are similar. In many tests, these are labeled as memory questions; other memory questions may involve looking at a series of photos or street scenes and answering questions about what you saw or read in relation to the visuals.

## Sample Memory Questions Based on Numbers and Letters in Series

1. Choose the answer below that contains the exact sequence of numbers, letters, and characters that appear in the follwing example.

   **BIG DAWG2**

   a. IG, DA, G2
   b. BIGDAWG2
   c. BIG DAWG 2
   d. None of these

1. **d.** None of the choice contain only the letters and numbers exactly as they appear in the sequence.

**2.** Choose the answer below that contains the exact sequence of numbers, letters, and characters that appear in the following example.

**IU, 6, JR, 14**

a. IU, 6, 6JR, 14
b. IU, 6, JR, 14
c. IU6, 6J, R1, 4
d.1U, 6, JR, I4

**2. b.** Only choice **b** is an exact copy of the numbers and letters that appear in the question. Note that choice **d** calls for a close reading, because it changes the placements of *1* and *I* in the series.

Some of these question types may rely on more complex number and letter series. For instance:

**3.** Choose the answer that contains numbers and letters that appear in the same order as they appear in the following sequence.

**N 7 O P 4 X 2 Y 2**

a. N, 7, O, P, 4
b. O, 4, 3, 2, Z
c. P, X, 2, Z, 2
d. None of these

**3. a.** Only choice **a** contains all of at least some of the numbers and letters which appear in the same order as they appear in the question.

**4.** Select the choice that contains only numbers and letters that appear in the following example.

**46 GT 89 L W 68 26 X**

a. 9, 6, 8, 9
b. 26, W, 78, X
c. LW, 4, 6, 26
d. None of these

**4. d.** None of the choices contain only letters and numbers that appear in the sequence.

As you see, these questions can be quite tricky. You must look carefully at the letter and number combinations, the spacing between them, and exactly what the question is asking. All of the numbers and letters? The exact order? To practice this on your own, if you travel with family or friends, look at their license plate numbers and then see if you recall them correctly once you are inside the vehicle. You will soon see that it is not as easy to remember numbers and letters in series as it would first appear to be.

### First Aid Situations

Most police academies train officers in basic first aid techniques and some encourage officers to become EMTs or paramedics through advanced training or by offering salary differentials to those who have obtained these certifications. Even if you have only basic knowledge of first aid, you can expect that your dispatcher will send you to assignments where you will be expected to render medical aid or assist those with more training in this area. You may also be sent to a situation that may look like a criminal matter, but upon arrival you will determine that the problem is more likely a social or medical one. These types of calls are often referred to by police as *aided cases* because the officer is expected to render assistance rather than to take legal action. Police officers also frequently encounter mentally ill persons who may be unable to care for themselves. Many large cities have established homeless outreach units which assign officers to work with social workers in joint efforts to get homeless people into sheltered living arrangements. Some judgment questions on the police officer exam might delve into you understanding and handling of such matters.

## Judgment Handling Aided Cases Sample Questions

**1.** At approximately 1 A.M. you are dispatched to respond to a call by a nightclub security officer who reported that an elderly woman is standing in the rain in front of the club's entrance. You respond and question the woman, who appears disoriented. Your best course of action is to
   **a.** send her on her way, presuming she is slightly intoxicated.
   **b.** determine if she is aware of her surroundings.
   **c.** call a taxi cab company in an attempt to have her driven home.
   **d.** call for your supervisor.

**1. b.** Choice **b** recognizes that elderly people wandering at night are often suffering from memory loss or are disoriented. Choice **a** is incorrect; it is unlikely she is intoxicated and if she were, it would be irresponsible to send her on her way to possible danger. Choice **c** is merely an attempt to make the problem disappear. Calling a supervisor (choice **d**) to the scene of a call when the officer should be able to make the decision is not the best option.

**2.** During his routine patrol at about 10 P.M. on Sunday night, a campus police officer drives through the main campus parking lot checking for vehicles with their lights on. Shining his flashlight toward what looks like a pile of discarded clothing, he observes that the pile is a man lying facing down between two cars. He approaches the man, who is breathing. Next to him are drug paraphernalia, including a hypodermic needle. The offcer is unable to awaken the man. His best of course of action is to
   **a.** presume the man is asleep, move him from between the cars so he does not get hit, and resume his patrol.
   **b.** continue to try to wake the man so he can place him under arrest.
   **c.** call for an ambulance to have the man transported to a medical facility.
   **d.** call for another officer who he knows to be a paramedic.

**2. c.** Whether due to drugs or other causes, the man on the ground is ill and requires medical attention. Choice **a** is irresponsible; choice **b** fails to recognize that human life takes precedence over an arrest, and choice **d** takes valuable time from getting the man appropriate medical attention and places responsibility on another officer rather than the reporting officer exercising his own judgment.

## Enforcing the Law and How it Relates to the Police Officer Exam

By now you may be wondering if you will ever have a chance to actually enforce the law or make arrests of those who appear to have violated the law. While certainly police officers can and do make arrests, the number of arrests you make will depend on a number of circumstances—some that you can influence and some that are out of your control. The type of agency you work in will influence your arrest activity, as will the type of neighborhood you patrol.

Studies of police officers are not only used to figure out what they do when they are patrolling, but also influence both the written and physical agility exams. To ensure that these tests are job-related, they are based in large part on studies of the knowledge, skills, and abilities that police use on a regular basis. In the human resources field, this is known as a job analysis, and is used to determine what activities employees are engaging in during the course of their work routine.

Job analyses conducted in large, municipal agencies found that police officers received more calls regarding criminal or potentially criminal matters than in small, suburban agencies. In these smaller, non-urban agencies, calls tend to be for service-related or traffic-related matters. Even in large agencies, many calls to report crimes come in to the dispatcher well after the crime has been committed. In these cases, the officer's role is primarily to take a report and do a preliminary investigation that may be turned over to detectives for further review and action. Studies also point to large amounts of what has come to be called "uncommitted time"—the time when officers are patrolling by either driving or walking around or are waiting to be given assignments by their dispatchers.

Since the terrorist attacks of September 11, 2001, some of police officers' uncommitted time has been focused more directly on preventing similar activities.

Police departments have strengthened their ties with federal law enforcement agencies, often assigning officers to joint-terrorist task forces; increased patrols around landmarks, places of worship, power plants, ports, terminals, and transit facilities; added training in emergency response for all officers; and increased outreach efforts to minority and immigrant populations.

## Why the Exam Tests Communication Skills

Whatever police officers are assigned to do, oral and written communications are an important part of their success at resolving situations. This helps to explain the focus on reading, writing, spelling, and grammar on police applicant written exams. It is also why more and more departments are adding an interview phase to the applicant selection process.

### Oral Communication

Think about the many situations in which police must speak with people. Each of these situations might involve people from all walks of life in a variety of emotional states. Oral communication can make a difference when an officer is understanding the dispatcher, other police officers, and supervisors who may provide additional instructions via radio or at the scene; talking with members of the public, whether victims, suspects, witnesses, or those in need of general assistance; mediating disputes between family members, friends, or strangers; providing information to those in distress; comforting upset persons; advising individuals of their options in complex situations; or providing assistance to or requesting assistance from other agencies. Certain specialized assignments require even greater communication skills, such as working as a school or community resource officer or representing the department at public forums and meetings. In conjunction with arrest situations, officers must explain the charges to those arrested and also to local prosecutors. Sometimes they must later testify in court, convincing a judge or jurors that what they observed and what they did made sense and followed the letter of the law. Officers may also be called on to brief the media on a high-profile case.

### Written Communication

Written communications are required for almost all activities in which a police officer participates. Active police officers complain regularly about the amount of paperwork they must complete, but a clear and complete record is essential in allowing any police department to function. Upon completion of any call to which an officer is dispatched, he or she must write a report of the events. Citations and arrests require additional paperwork. Errors can result in lawsuits against the officer or the department and in court cases being dismissed solely on the basis of an officer's report.

This brief summary of what officers may be called upon to do was meant to give you a better idea of a police officer's responsibilities than what the media portrays. The skills you will need to be successful to pass the entry exam and then to work as a police officer are the same skills you will need throughout your career. Whether your long-term goals are to remain a patrol officer, move into specialized units, or achieve higher rank, your comprehension skills, communications skills, and judgment will continue to play a role in your success. The more knowledge, skills, and abilities you gain in these areas during your career preparation period, the easier it will be for you to fulfill your next set of goals. Thus, the time you spend studying for the entry exam will have not only the short-term benefit of helping you obtain a position as a police officer, but will also pay longer-term benefits throughout your career.

## A Breakdown of the Law Enforcement Universe

By now, you probably know more about policing than you did when you first decided to select it as your career. You also probably have gathered that it is a complicated field that defies easy description. In fact, in addition to the many roles filled by police, there are many different types of agencies where you can put your skills to use. In the United States, there are more police agencies than anywhere else in the world, and there are many different types of agencies that we call "police." The major categories of police agencies include *local police*; *county police*; *county sheriffs' offices*; *state police*; *special jurisdiction police* (which might include airports, parks, transit systems, and campus and school districts), or even more specialized agencies enforcing professional licensing regulations. These last agencies are distinct from federal law enforcement, which is a different category altogether with different requirements and application procedures. There are also parts of the country where civilian agencies employ a small number of police or where city or county prosecutors employ their own law enforcement personnel.

Law enforcement is generally divided into *federal* (which is not included in this book) and *state and local*, which includes municipal police, county police, sheriffs' offices, special jurisdiction agencies, and constable/marshal agencies. Even the term "law enforcement" can be confusing, because for many people the term expands to include private security officers and others who provide enforcement services but are not police officers. However, when individuals refer to "police" or "police officers" they usually mean members of law enforcement agencies with full powers of arrest and the right to carry a firearm.

The term "police department" is usually reserved for state and local agencies. Although it may it may seem hard to believe, there are almost 18,000 such state and local agencies around the country. They range in size from the New York City Police Department (NYPD)—with a sworn officer staff complement that has recently been reduced to "only" 35,000 compared to about 40,000 in 2001—to departments of only one officer. According to figures published in 2007 by the Department of Justice's Bureau of Justice Statistics, in 2004 (the latest year for which complete figures were available), state and local law enforcement agencies employed more than one million people on a full-time basis, about 750,000 of whom were sworn officers. These figures translate into about one sworn law enforcement officer for every 400 to 500 people in the nation. However, different jurisdictions have very different ratios of police to population. Although it might seem logical that cities with more crime try to have a lower ratio (meaning more police per citizen) the ratio is more likely influenced by a jurisdiction's ability to fund a particular size police department in relationship to other requirements. The result is often that cities with less crime and a higher tax base will have more officers per capita than a poorer, more crime-prone jurisdiction.

## Small-Town Policing

Although more than 93,000 sworn full-time officers work for the ten largest police departments, there are more than 10,000 police departments with ten or fewer employees. And more than 85 percent of U.S. police departments have 25 or fewer officers, a figure that includes all ranks within those departments. Although they are located in rural areas and serve small communities, their law enforcement problems may be large. Many rural areas are faced with serious violence stemming from methamphetamine labs and gang vio-

lence. Additionally, guns are common and officers are spread far apart, with available backup often 100 miles away. Officers in rural communities also face the stress of having to police among their friends and families without being able to rely on the benefits of maintaining a psychological distance from victims and suspects—and a physical distance by being able to live away from the communities they police.

## Big-City Policing

At the other extreme are the urban police departments that receive the most media attention (and where TV dramas most often tend to be set). They are portrayed as representative of U.S. policing, but they certainly are not. The sizes of even the large departments vary considerably. Following the NYPD is the Chicago Police Department, which is not even half as large with slightly more than 13,000 sworn employees. The next largest municipal agencies are Los Angeles (about 9,000), Philadelphia (more than 6,800), and Houston (about 5,000). About one of every six full-time local police officers works for one of these five largest agencies.

## County Sheriffs' Offices and County Police Departments

If your interests are in county law enforcement, there are two very different types of agencies for you to consider—*county sheriffs' offices* or *county police departments*. The stereotypical view of rural sheriffs' offices that was portrayed in such early TV shows as "The Andy Griffith Show" is not at all realistic. From 1960 to 1968, Andy played the good-natured sheriff of Mayberry; his Aunt Bee and small son, Opie, spent as much time in the office as he did and seemed to be as involved in law enforcement as he and his comical deputy Barney Fife. The truth, though, is somewhat different.

There are about 3,000 sheriffs' offices in the United States, almost all led by an elected county sheriff. Three states (Alaska, Connecticut, and Hawaii) and the District of Columbia are the only areas of the United States that do not elect or appoint sheriffs. Sheriffs' offices pre-date police departments; the office of sheriff is the oldest law enforcement position in the nation. The vast majority of sheriffs' offices have some patrol functions similar to police departments, but many concentrate more of their efforts on civil matters. Where deputies (the entry-level rank equivalent to police officers) do patrol, it is generally in the unincorporated areas of a county or in areas where there are no or very small local police departments. Since deputies have countywide jurisdiction, they may routinely assist or work alongside town police or may wait to be called for assistance. In addition, deputies have a number of non-patrol responsibilities: They serve criminal and civil court documents including summonses and subpoenas, maintain county jails, and provide court security.

In 2004, about 11% of sheriffs' office employed at least 100 sworn personnel and only a dozen employed more than 1,000 officers. But, like police departments, their sizes range considerably. The largest sheriff's department, in Los Angeles County, employed more than 8,000 full-time sworn personnel. The next four largest agencies were Cook County (IL), with about 5,500 officers; Broward County (FL), with about 3,000; Harris County (TX), with about 2,500; and Orange County (CA), with just over 2,000. They are also representative of the different roles of sheriffs' offices; only about 500 of Cook County's deputies patrol the unincorporated areas of the county (a highly urbanized one in which Chicago is located), while the Broward County Sheriff's Office operates very much like a large, full-service police department, with marine, airborne, and airport units and a vast array of specialist positions. Regardless of size of their department, sheriffs, particularly in the south and west, are considered the chief law enforcement officers of their counties and are generally treated with deference by area police chiefs.

*County police departments* are completely different from county sheriffs' offices. They are more similar to local police departments than to sheriffs' offices but for reasons of geographic or local political development, the country has absorbed many traditional local policing functions. Two of the five largest county police agencies are in New York; Suffolk County (more than 2,500 officers) and Nassau County (smaller than Suffolk by only about 100 officers). The other three are Miami-Dade County, FL (about 3,000 officers), Las Vegas-Clark County, NV (about just under 2,700 officers), and Baltimore County, MD (about 1,800 officers). Because a number of county departments are located in some of the fastest growing portions of the nation, if you live in their jurisdictions or are willing to consider relocating for a position, you should investigate these departments, which may offer you opportunities you had not considered.

## State Law Enforcement Agencies

Most of the officers employed with a particular state work for municipal and county agencies—the number of officers employed directly by highway patrol agencies and state police is considerably smaller. State police agencies employ slightly fewer than 60,000 full-time officers. For a number of reasons (some historical, some having to do with strenuous physical requirements, and some having to do with residential police academies in rural parts of their states), state police agencies have lower percentages of women and minority officers than other police agencies. Many, though, are actively recruiting to diversity their ranks.

There are two types of uniformed state law enforcement agencies. *State police departments* that combine patrol, investigation, and provide support services to local police departments are considered the centralized, full-service model of state policing. *Highway patrol agencies*, the most visible of the decentralized state police agencies, have more limited responsibilities, although they are rarely assigned only to traffic-related matters. States with a highway patrol rather than a full-service state police department generally have a non-uniformed statewide investigative agency with different responsibilities and selection standards than the state police departments or highway patrols. The scope of an agency's responsibilities is not necessarily related to its size. The largest state law enforcement agency is California's Highway Patrol, with about 7,000 officers. The two largest full-service state police departments are in the northeast; the New York State Police employs about 4,600 sworn officers and the Pennsylvania State Police about 4,200. Statewide uniformed agencies, whether full-service or highway patrol departments, generally have entry standards similar to local police but are very likely to place greater emphasis on physical agility and fitness.

## Special Jurisdiction Police Agencies

Although they are far less well-known than state police, special jurisdiction police agencies employ almost as many officers. According to the Bureau of Justice Statistics (BJS), in 2004 there were more than 1,500 police agencies that served special geographic areas or had specialized enforcement responsibilities that together employed more than 85,000 people. The BJS groups these agencies into five categories; public buildings and facilities, natural resources and parks and recreation, transportation systems and facilities, criminal investigations, and special enforcement.

The largest group of special enforcement police is the approximately 500 *campus police departments* serving four-year public institutions, which employ more than 10,000 officers nationwide. About 90% of these are armed, fully-sworn and trained police officers. Two-year colleges and public school districts employed about 5,000 additional officers.

Campus policing is a growing area of policing and has been particularly successful in attracting large numbers of women and minority candidates to its ranks, possibly because many colleges may be more actively working to diversity their work forces overall along with their student and staff populations. Public institutions are more likely to employ fully-commissioned police officers than are private colleges. Also, the larger the campus, the more likely the officers will have full police status, will be armed, and will have attended a state-certified police academy. Most campus departments have no more than 100 officers, but many are larger and better equipped than local police serving the campus' surrounding community.

Beginning in the 1990s, a number of campus police agencies developed their own Special Weapons and Tactical (SWAT) teams rather than rely on the local police. Today such specializations as SWAT, canine, bomb disposal, and other high-profile assignments are available in campus police departments, although there is still a focus on working closely with the college community, which provides considerable opportunities in crime prevention, alcohol, drug, and sexual assault prevention programs, and a variety of other community-based specialties. Campus police tend to recruit less aggressively than local police; if your interests lie in this area, check the websites of colleges whose departments interest you or try to schedule an appointment with the chief or deputy chief of a local college department to learn more about entering this field.

*Transportation policing* has also seen considerable growth, particularly since the September 11, 2001, and subsequent attacks on transit systems around the world showed many nations how vulnerable their transit arteries were. Approximately 9,000 officers are employed by about 130 agencies; most protect airports, but they also work for mass transit systems, maritime ports, and bridges and tunnels. Transportation police protect both people and property. The components of the transit system and the infrastructure are itself potential targets, and many transit agencies have developed specialized units that include community outreach, emergency response, and canine units for both drug and explosive detection, and they participate actively in area terrorist task forces. Like campus police, many transportation agency police departments do not recruit actively, although two of the largest ones in the New York-New Jersey-Connecticut metropolitan areas, the Metropolitan Transportation Authority (MTA) Police and the Port Authority of New York and New Jersey (PANYNJ) Police, have selection processes that are similar to local police. If the transportation agencies in your area are small, consider requesting an interview to learn more about job opportunities.

*Parks and recreation police departments* are also quite varied; some are local but many are county or state agencies. These positions are particularly suited to those who enjoy being outdoors and who enjoy interacting with the public. Some may include overseeing licensing of hunting and fishing enthusiasts as well as enforcing seasonal or poaching regulations. Some involve more basic patrol of recreation facilities, which, in addition to parks, may include lakes, pools, beachfront, or any recreational facility that you can imagine.

### Federal Law Enforcement

Although not the focus of this book, federal law enforcement is just as decentralized as the other areas of the profession. Some agencies are far better known than others, including the Federal Bureau of Investigation (FBI), the Drug Enforcement Agency (DEA), the Marshals Service and Secret Service, and Customs and Border Protection (CBP), but there are more

than 50 other federal law enforcement agencies, including a few with uniformed officers and some such as the Offices of Inspectors General that are heavily involved in fraud investigations. In total, almost 60,000 people work in some form of federal law enforcement. The majority—but not all—federal law enforcement agencies require applicants to have a four-year college degree, but other requirements may be similar to those explained here. If your interests are primarily in federal law enforcement, begin your employment search by visiting the websites of the agencies that interest you.

## Benefits of a Law Enforcement Career

The benefits of a policing career vary from agency to agency, and may include salary, fringe benefits (medical, dental, college tuition payments or reimbursement), and retirement and pension options. Law enforcement careers offer all of these. Benefits can also refer to non-tangible items, such as helping people, having an interesting or exciting career, or fulfilling a lifelong dream.

### Salary

Salary is often a candidate's first consideration in taking a job. Although police agencies tend to offer excellent fringe benefits, many candidates—particularly the youngest ones—don't think as much about the future as much as older candidates or those who have had the bad luck of being unemployed. The U.S. Department of Labor Statistics found in 2007 that entry-level police and sheriffs' officers had a median annual earnings of $47,460. Although one might expect that the largest departments pay the highest salaries, this is not always true. Since police salaries are based on a combination of the local jurisdiction's ability to pay and how strong the police union might be, smaller, wealthier suburban areas often pay their police officers far more than large urban departments. Starting salaries and other benefits are featured on agency recruitment websites; the frequently asked questions (FAQs) will generally answer most of your questions in these areas.

Detectives and criminal investigators, who are most often selected from among the police officer ranks, had median annual earnings of $58,260. Supervisors—virtually all of whom likewise begin their careers as police officers and move through the ranks based on written exams and related factors similar to entry-level selection standards—had median annual earnings of more than $69,000. These are generally base salaries that do not include extra pay for working holidays, nights, or overtime.

## Fringe Benefits

Included in the definition of fringe benefits are paid vacations; sick leave; life, medical, dental, and disability insurance (for you and your dependents), tuition assistance or refund programs; a uniform allowance or possibly having your uniform provided by your agency, and retirement and pension benefits. While not every agency offers all these benefits, police departments tend to offer some of the most generous packages of public agencies. Often officers are eligible to retire after 20 or 25 years of service regardless of their age; other departments extend the 20-year retirement to those who have reached the age of 50 or 55. Either way, you may literally receive your retirement benefits for more years than you worked for them. These retirement benefits may be quite generous; it is not unknown for officers to receive at least half their final salaries as a retirement benefit and, depending on contractual agreements, far more than half if pension payouts are based on the final three or five years of salary.

## A Rundown of Working Conditions

The working conditions for police officers are a two-edged sword. What many see as the benefits are exactly what others see as the detriments. Among those are primarily working alone or with only one partner who may be assigned to you for eight to 12 hours a day. You might be bored sometimes and filled with terror at other times, sometimes within a span of just a few minutes. You can expect to work holidays and weekends, when many of your friends or family members may be having a good time and you may be unavailable to celebrate many family events and occasions. Although you may receive generous vacation benefits, as a newly hired officer you will probably be assigned vacation during times your family or friends might consider inconvenient.

Can you follow rules closely and accept having a large amount of freedom (discretion) but also having a number of supervisors and managers critiquing those decisions after they have been made? Although police departments are moving away from describing themselves as "para-military" organizations, they are certainly top-down organizations. This means that rank and position are very important. As one of the newest officers, what police officers call a "rookie," you will be expected to do what many people tell you to do. This will include, in addition to supervisors and managers, those who hold the same rank as yours but have more experience and seniority.

Are you able to work with people who are not like you? This might include your colleagues but also will most likely include many of the people you will be asked to help. If you are a woman or member of a minority group, you may discover that you are one of only a few members of your group within the department. While this does not mean that you will be harassed or isolated, it does mean that unfortunately you and your actions will stand out and may be subject to closer scrutiny than the behavior of those who are members of the majority group. As a woman or a member of a minority group, you may have already experienced tokenism, but you may be unprepared to accept that your peers look at you differently and may initially see you as someone with whom they do not feel comfortable.

On a more physical note, are you prepared to work in all weather conditions; are you prepared to accept danger; are you prepared to consider that someone may try to take your life and that you might have to take the life of another person? Some of these events may be rare—the majority of police officers never fire their weapons except on the practice range—but there are no guarantees that such events will not occur during your career.

Many of the working conditions are the primary reasons individuals choose to become police officers, are also associated with the stressors of the job. Scholars—and police officers themselves—differ as to exactly how stressful policing is, but it is generally listed as one of a number of highly stressful occupations. Some of the stress comes from exposure to antisocial, violent, and mistrustful members of society. Other stress comes from the need to exercise discretion in volatile situations. Could I have made a better decision? Could I have avoided making an arrest, issuing a summons, getting injured, or having to injure someone else? These are questions that officers may ask themselves after a situation has been resolved.

The role of supervisors and managers who often assess an officer's handling of a situation after the fact can also be stressful, particularly when supervisors were not at the scene and make a decision based on an incomplete picture of events or with political pressure being exerted from higher ranks, community

members, or local politicians. It is for these reasons that officers frequently cite the internal management of their agency as the most stressful aspect of their job, particularly when the need to document everything and write voluminous reports is included in the definition.

What about death or serious physical injury? Many police candidates worry whether injury and—under extreme conditions—death is an ever-present condition of being a police officer. Certainly deaths and serious injuries of police officers, particularly when they occur during the handling of incidents, receive wide local publicity, but studies of policing indicate they are not as common as newspaper accounts would have you believe. The major cause of injuries to police officers is accidents, particularly traffic accidents. The National Law Enforcement Officers Memorial Fund (NLEOMF), in conjunction with Concerns of Police Survivors (C.O.P.S) found that line-of-duty deaths among law enforcement officers nationwide rose 20% during the first six months of 2009. But the percentages are more frightening than the numbers; preliminary statistics showed 66 officer deaths between January 1 and June 30, 2009, compared with 55 during the same period of 2008, while 35 died in accidents, mostly traffic-related.

In any discussion of working conditions, remember that one person's minuses are another person's pluses. If you enjoy having to make decisions on your own and doing different things on different days of the week, and if you generally dislike sitting at a desk all day, policing will help you meet those conditions. In addition, the police environment is also conducive to making very close friends. In fact, one of the criticisms of police by outsiders is their clannishness and their happiness at being almost solely with other police officers.

## Job Outlook

Whatever your reason for pursuing a law enforcement career, the current, cooled-down economic situation may make it more difficult to follow your dream. It has been an employment reality since the Great Depression of the 1930s that in times of economic instability people seek government jobs. Because policing is one of the most desirable government jobs (and in most locales is among the highest paid), competition intensifies when private industry jobs are less available and riskier.

In the period from about 2005 to 2008, many police agencies were unable to recruit a sufficient number of candidates to fill existing vacancies. Many offered signing bonuses to new officers; others began to recruit farther and farther from home. Since the nation's economic downturn, the situation has turned around dramatically. Departments are flush with applicants; departments in Connecticut, for instance, reported in mid-2009 that they were receiving up to 50 applications a month where a year earlier they were lucky to receive three or four. Police chiefs see this as wonderful news; many have reported a noticeable upturn in not only the quantity, but also the quality of applicants who see policing as a secure job with benefits and a career ladder. What the chiefs see as wonderful, though, means that the competition has intensified. Your written exam score—the first major step toward your career—will become more important than ever to open the door to your career. Do not be discouraged, though; by reading this book, you have taken an important step in preparing yourself to achieve a high test score to place yourself among the more competitive candidates for these sought-after police positions.

The number of police in the nation has grown significantly since 1990 (in part due to the 1994 Violent Crime Control Act, which provided federal funds for hiring 100,000 new officers). By 2000, there were about 78,000 more sworn officers than in 1990, an increase of about 21%. If funds remain available, and even a small fraction of these officers begin to retire at the 20-year mark, replacement positions will become available as early as 2014—which, as you will see after reviewing the hiring process, is not as far away as it might seem. Although the majority of police officers remain for a full career, there is attrition of those leaving the field. Police departments generally have an average attrition rate of about 5%, but this figure has recently increased due to vacancies that have existed for the years police departments had difficulties recruiting candidates. More recently, in mid-2009, the COPS Hiring Recovery Program awarded almost $1 million to more than 1,000 police agencies to fund close to 5,000 officers.

The U.S. Bureau of Law Statistics, in its Occupational Outlook Handbook for 2008-2009, estimated that employment of police would grow 11% between 2006 and 2016, and termed the job prospects *excellent* for those able to meet the stringent qualifications. This demand is fueled by increases in population, the movement of people into areas where smaller police agencies are growing to meet population demands, and the overall fear of crime that continues despite falling crime rates. The BLS estimated that by 2016 there would be almost 100,000 police officers employed around the country, the vast majority of them employed by municipal, state, and special jurisdiction departments. By starting your career planning now, and undertaking a study regimen before your written exam, you are enhancing your chances to be one of those officers.

## Additional Resources

*Becoming a Police Officer.* (New York: LearningExpress, 2009).

*State Trooper Exam, 2nd Edition.* (New York: Learning-Express, 2010.)

CHAPTER

# 2 ▶ HOW POLICE OFFICERS ARE SELECTED

### *CHAPTER SUMMARY*
This chapter provides a preview of the application process for becoming a police officer. It includes a discussion the basic applicant requirements, what to expect when you take the written exam, and explanations of the steps in the hiring process that take place after you have passed the written exam.

**N**ow that you have a more realistic idea of what police officers actually do, you need to know the steps you must take if you want to follow this career path. Just as the job of a police officer may differ depending on the agency, so will the steps to becoming an officer.

## A Step-by-Step Rundown

While police officers earn high salaries and generally have benefits that exceed those of other government employees, the many steps involved in the hiring process can make the finish line seem very far away indeed. That is why it is so important for you to prepare for the **written test**. If you do not pass the written exam, you will rarely have the opportunity to continue on the route to becoming a police officer. For this reason, some consider exam preparation *the* most important step.

The step prior to the written exam will generally be to complete the **application** for the agency of your choice. Passing scores differ for different agencies; you may receive your exact exam score, sometimes carried out to two decimal places, or you might receive a whole-number score. If you did not pass, you might receive your specific numerical score or just a notice that you did not pass.

Once you are advised that you have passed the exam, the length of time until you are called in for additional processing could be as soon as a few weeks or as long as a few years. Since a major portion of the second phase of the hiring process will involve the **physical agility test**, if you know you are not in good condition, you should immediately begin a fitness regimen. Remember to check the website of your agency or to contact the human resources division of the agency or of the municipality. There is an excellent chance that the requirements for the physical agility test will be available; this will help you to learn what you need to practice and may also provide you with tips on passing particular parts of the exam.

At some point you will be notified to complete the forms on which your **background investigation** will be based. The questions will be far more detailed than in your original application form. This is a crucial part of your application process; everything you write will be checked for accuracy, and any falsehoods may immediately disqualify you, regardless of how minor they might seem to you.

Your background investigation may overlap with being scheduled for **psychological and medical evaluations**. The psychological examination will likely begin with you taking paper-and-pencil personality tests and will be followed by an interview with a psychologist or psychiatrist. It is possible to study for the written exam, but not for the psychological exam. There are numerous questions—some exams provide you with literally hundreds of questions to answer. Because the questions are interrelated in ways that do not seem obvious, the questions are meant to catch you in lies. It is almost impossible to cheat on these personality tests, and even if you are able to fool the automatic scoring machine, you will be unlikely to fool the psychologist or psychiatrist.

It is also unlikely that you can outsmart the medical exam; in addition to testing for general well-being,

you will be tested for visual acuity, colorblindness, and auditory ability. While almost all departments permit you to have less-than-perfect vision and even less-than-perfect hearing, colorblindness, very poor vision (even if correctable through glasses or contact lenses), and hearing that requires physical correction will automatically disqualify you from continuing in the employment process. While this may seem harsh, the regulations today are considerably more lax than in pervious generations, when any vision that was not 20-20 or 20-40 was an automatic disqualification.

After passing each of these steps, you may receive what is called a **conditional offer of employment**. A conditional offer of employment means that if your background investigation is completed without uncovering any disqualifying factors and you successful complete any additional steps in the hiring process, you will be placed on an eligibility list from which candidates will be selected for employment. Or it may mean that you will be informed of a hiring date after completing the unfinished steps. Depending on the jurisdiction, these steps might include other physical agility, psychological, and medical tests. These tests were previously completed earlier in the process, but due to various interpretations of the Americans with Disabilities Act (ADA), they may be administered after a conditional offer of employment. Depending on the size and type of agency, you may be expect to have an interview with the chief or with an oral board comprised of members of the department and, sometimes, members of the community.

Even after all these steps, depending on the number of names on your agency's eligibility list, how high or low you are on that list, and how many officers your agency plans to hire, you might remain on the list for quite some time. Most lists established under a civil service system remain active for years, generally between two and five. This information should be available on your agency's website or from the government entity's human resources department.

Although some factors other than your written test score may affect your place on the list—such as whether you are a veteran, a college graduate, a resident of the jurisdiction, or other factors that some agencies provide extra score points for—the major factor will be your written test score. Any extra perks you receive will be added to your test score; only in very few jurisdictions do the extra points determine whether you are list-eligible.

Some departments maintain separate lists of test scores, including for minority group members or women. Whatever you may have read about the way hiring lists are established for the agency you hope to join, your best course of action is to work toward achieving the highest possible test score. This will help to ensure that you are one of the first candidates selected to begin your academy training.

You may have noticed that in describing the hiring process, words such as "generally," "usually," and "may" appear frequently. This is because not every department follows the same steps or does things exactly the same way. As you saw in Chapter 1, policing in the United States is one of the most local of all public services. While generalizations can be made, it is very important for you to learn the policies and procedures of each of the departments to which you are applying. Never assume that the selection standards and procedures for Department B are the same as those for Department A.

Although agencies may arrange the hiring process somewhat differently, virtually all agencies will include the following steps:

1. completing the written application (possibly online)
2. successfully passing the written exam
3. passing the physical agility (or fitness) tests
4. passing the background investigation
5. passing the medical and psychological examinations

Depending on your agency, you might be asked to participate in an interview with an individual or a panel, and you might be scheduled for a polygraph exam. Drug screening (generally a urinalysis but sometimes a hair analysis) will also be administered, either at the physical agility or fitness test site or during the medical exam. Whatever the order determined by your agency, it is customary that you must pass each step to be permitted to move on to the next phase of the applicant process.

Follow the instructions of your agency or agencies of choice. Some agencies may ask for letters of recommendation; others are very clear that they do not want such letters unless they specifically ask for them. Some agencies may ask for a traditional resume, while others will toss these in the trash because they expect you to provide all required information on the application or background investigation form.

Agencies that accept military service in lieu of educational requirements or that offer veterans' preference points will ask you to provide a non-returnable copy of the Certificate of Release or Discharge from Active Duty (Form DD-214, Member 4 copy). If you are applying while still an active duty member of the military, there are other requirements you must fulfill, which are generally available on the agency's website or obtainable by a telephone call or email to the recruitment section.

## Minimum (or Basic) Qualifications

Although agencies differ in their minimum qualifications to be a police officer, all have some of the same basic requirements. Minimum (or basic) qualifications mean just that—they are the least you can present and still be considered for employment. Most of them pertain to age, level of education, lack of arrests and/or convictions for serious or certain categories of crimes, and U.S. citizenship, although in a few jurisdictions resident alien status or a pending citizenship application may be accepted at the time you apply for the written exam. Other areas of your life that will be closely examined are your driving record, your credit history, and whether you have been involved in incidents of domestic or family violence.

## Citizenship

Until recently, U.S. citizenship was one of the only universal requirements to become a police officer. But as a way to encourage applicants new to the United States, a few departments no longer require citizenship and many are considering changing their present requirements. As of 2009, the only state that permitted permanent resident aliens who have applied for citizenship to become police officers was California. A few cities around the country have instituted similar regulations, including Lakewood, CO; El Paso, TX; Honolulu, HI; Portland, OR; and Chicago, IL. Because this is an area that is changing frequently, if you are not a citizen it would be wise to check the websites of any departments you are considering applying for. If you have a green card, have served in any branch of the U.S. military, and are awaiting expedited citizenship, you may also be eligible to apply to some police agencies.

## Residency Requirements

Residency requirements are not the same as U.S. citizenship; they pertain to where you actually live. Residency requirements outlining where you have to live and how long you are required to live there may differ among agencies. Some agencies require that you be a resident of the state, county, or municipality up to a year before filing your test application; others ask only that the requirement be met at the time of appointment (generally defined as when you enter the police academy), and others give you a certain amount of time (usually no more than one year) to relocate into the required living areas.

Where you must live once you are employed also differs from agency to agency. Some municipal departments require that you live within the city limits; others specify that you must live within the county in which the city is located, and others permit you to live in a number of surrounding counties. Residency requirements are often subject to litigation, primarily because many police unions view them as infringing on the rights of employees. The history of residency requirements is complex; today many of the issues revolve around the costs of housing in some urban areas, the availability of housing and good schools in those areas, and the desires of many officers to live away from their place of employment. Although a number of courts have ruled against the maintenance of residency requirements, in 2009 about half of municipal departments that employed 100 or more officers had some sort of residency policy, although of these, only about 25% demanded that officers live only in the city of county of employment. For instance, the New York City Police Department has residency regulations that permit living in a number of counties in and near the city.

Many young officers are unconcerned with these rules when they begin their careers, but find the regulations restrictive once they marry and have a family. Whatever your plans for the future might be, your present concern as an applicant is to understand the requirements, particularly if they apply to whether or not your application will be accepted or if they become effective immediately upon appointment.

## Age

The minimum age at which you may apply to the police department can be as confusing as where you must live. Many agencies permit you to apply at a much younger age than when you can actually be appointed. In policing, the term "appointed" is used to designate when you actually begin your career in a police department. Thus, when police officers refer to their "appointment date," they are talking about the first day they began their employment.

Exceedingly few—if any—agencies will appoint you before you turn 18; most require you to be 20 or 21 before permitting you to begin academy training. Despite this prohibition, many departments not only permit, but actually encourage, candidates to apply for and to take the written exam in advance of the age at which they can be appointed.

Some departments, in an effort to encourage a wider selection of applicants, allow you to complete an application as young as 16. Many departments believe that early testing would encourage young people who knew they had passed the test to maintain a healthy and lawful lifestyle so that they would not jeopardize their career possibilities. Also, in many parts of the country, the list of eligible candidates who have passed the written exam might be used for up to three or more years. Knowing the length of time that can pass from initial application to the actual hiring date, agencies realize that even if candidates took the test well before the age of appointment, most would be old enough to become officers once they completed the entire hiring process. Whatever the age restrictions, make sure you understand the differences between the age at which you are eligible to apply, the age at which you are eligible to take the written test, and the age at which you are eligible to be appointed as a police officer.

### The Older Applicant

Not everyone decides to become a police officer at a young age. What if you are an older applicant? Maybe becoming a police officer was a dream you deferred. Maybe changes in your current profession have led you to consider a career in policing. If you are in good physical condition and meet the other requirements, your age is no longer a barrier to employment. The vast majority of non-federal law enforcement agencies today have no maximum age limit. After a number of laws and lawsuits, departments eventually altered their requirements so that

if you are able to pass the physical agility and medical tests and complete the physical requirements of the police academy, you are eligible to join the department. Older recruits still attract media attention, though; many recruits in their 40s, 50s, and even a handful in their early 60s will be the subject of local newspaper stories. If you are an older-than-average applicant, you should learn as much as you can about your agency of choice to get a sense of whether you will be comfortable in a situation where not only your peers, but the majority of your supervisors, may be much younger than you are.

### Education

A high school diploma or General Equivalency Diploma (GED) remains the most common educational requirement to begin a law enforcement career. According to DOJ, more than 80 percent of departments require either a high school diploma or a GED, although the majority of federal law enforcement agencies require a college education. Of the non-federal agencies that require more than a high school diploma or GED, only 1 percent require a four-year college degree; the others require some combination of either a two-year (associate's) degree or a minimum number of college credits, usually about 60 (which is generally equal to a college-level junior). Where college credits are required, two years of military experience can often be substituted if you were discharged honorably.

This does not mean you should neglect getting an education. The same DOJ study found that many police officers have educational levels in excess of what is required. Also, some departments require additional education for promotion. Having these added credits or a degree before you join the department will permit you to apply for promotion at the earliest possible opportunity. If you are still in school, becoming a police officer before earning your degree can have financial benefits, since, according to DOJ, more than 30 percent of local departments offer either incentive pay or tuition reimbursement to officers.

## The Application Process

Even if you have carefully reviewed the basic requirements for becoming a police officer, the application process can be confusing. Because the application process differs among departments, you should carefully consider how many agencies you want to apply for.

### Picking a Location

If you have your heart set on one department, your initial thought might be to apply only to that one agency. But if you are more interested in being a police officer in general than in being a member of a particular department, you should consider applying to more than one agency. In some parts of the country, you can take a county-wide written exam and become eligible to be hired by any of the departments within the county. This could be a large number of departments—some counties in relatively urban areas adjacent to large cities might have more than 50 police departments within the county's borders. How applicants are hired from county-wide lists may vary. In some areas, any department that is ready to hire officers may use the list and must call the applicants based on their test scores. In other areas, departments may or must select residents of their particular town regardless of their place on the eligibility list, as long as the applicant received a passing score. Many agencies find the civil service rules pertaining to eligibility lists as limiting and as confusing as applicants do. In mid-2009, for instance, the Westchester County and the New York State police chiefs associations asked the legislature to consider a bill that would permit local departments to recruit more women and minority candidates by going outside local lists to find a wider selection of candidates.

Large city and state police departments generally give their own written tests and do not share their lists with other agencies. In these instances, if you are interested in more than one department, you must take a different written test for each one. This is true even if your departments of choice are in the same geographic area. In the New York metropolitan area, for instance, this can be quite complicated. In addition to the NYPD, two large area transportation agency police departments—the MTA and the PANYNJ—test separately. Depending on the needs of these individual agencies, entry tests could be years apart or could occur within months of one another.

Even if the departments you want to test for are many miles apart, you may not have to travel far to test for them. Since the 1990s, many departments have offered their exams in locations far from their cities, often at colleges with criminal justice programs, where they anticipate finding a large number of applicants. The reasons were two-fold. One, even if they did not require college, many departments were eager to employ those working towards their degrees. The second reason may be less true in times of economic woe; until recently, many departments lacked a sufficient number of applicants and traveled to where the applicants were. The option of these away-from-home tests are another reason for you to continue your education while pursuing your career goals.

Obviously, if a department gives its entry exam far from home, it cannot expect you to fulfill an applicant residency requirement right away, but the agency might expect you to establish residency prior to entering its police academy or immediately upon graduation. You should find out where you will be expected to complete the hiring process if you pass the written exam. To expedite processing applicants from around the country, some departments provide almost instant test scores, and a few set up the other applicant steps on-site over the course of weeks to save time and travel expenses. If such opportunities do not exist, traveling to a nearby city or state at your own expense once or twice might be possible if you feel you have a good chance of receiving a job offer; traveling across the country might be less attractive unless you are seriously interested in relocating to the area where the job will be.

- Neatness and accuracy are critical.
- Make a photocopy of the application.
- Read all directions before you complete the application.
- Use the photocopy to make a practice application first. Then, complete the real application in neat block letters, or better yet, type it.
- Keep a photocopy of the application. (Later in the employment screening process, you will complete other forms that will ask for the same information.)
- Do NOT send a resume in place of an application. Civil service rules will most likely require the application form.
- If you mail the application, be sure to include all required supporting documentation and double-check the address.
- If you download the application from the Internet, make sure your printer produces a good, clear copy. Also, if you complete the form online and print a copy, use the spell-check feature and have somebody else proofread it.

## Completing the Application

The easiest way to learn the basic qualifications and the requirements to apply for a position with any police agency is to visit its website. Many departments now permit you to file your application online so that you can be notified when an exam is scheduled. If there is a civil service newspaper in your area, you will find exam announcements published regularly. Some police agencies advertise in local newspapers and post notices in areas where they expect potential applicants might congregate, including military bases, gyms and health clubs, and college campuses. If you are interested in a more specialized agency, you may have to do more advance work to find whether openings exist.

Campus police, park and natural resources, airport, rail, transit, and marine port police are less likely to advertise; many receive inquiries from local police officers who are aware of their existence and who are looking for a change in careers. Although some of these agencies may give preference to experienced officers, very few agencies hire only transfer candidates. Although lateral entry (where officers from another agency are given preference in hiring) may limit your chances of winning a job, it does not mean you have no chance of being employed. If there is a special jurisdiction police agency that interests you, contact either its police force or its human resources office directly to find out about the hiring process.

There is no limit to the number of departments to which you can apply. Although some require a filing fee, many do not charge for you to fill out an application, particularly if you are able to do so online. Many also do not charge for entry into the written test site. It is wise to consider more than one department, but do not apply to departments thoughtlessly. Even an online application can be time consuming, and spreading yourself too thin will prevent you from concentrating your efforts on the agencies that really interest you and for which you are a good fit. Also, although written exams test for similar skills, not all are identical. If you apply to too many departments, you may find yourself jumping from one set of requirements to another without having sufficient time to work toward getting the best possible score that you are capable of obtaining.

- Gather as much information as you can about the exam in advance. Some agencies will issue study guides, while others hold study sessions. If your agency has a website, you may find sample test questions online.
- Practice, practice, practice! Review the material in the instructional chapters of this book, which offer tips on how to improve in each skill area on your exam.
- Take all the applicable practice police exams in this book.
- Listen carefully to any and all directions given by the person who administers the test.
- Budget your time during the exam. Don't spend too much time on any one question.
- Read through the entire question before answering it, and make sure you carefully read each answer before choosing the correct one.
- When you read questions, look for words that modify such as *not*, *never*, and *only*.
- Stop to check every now and then to make sure you are filling in the correct bubble or blank for each answer. You don't want to fail the test because of misplaced marks!
- If there is time left after you are finished, go back and double-check your answers.

## The Written Exam

Once again, know that the written exam may be the most important step in your path to becoming a police officer. It is generally the first screening device in the selection process. It is your first opportunity to show that you have the skills and abilities to become a police officer—and unfortunately, if you do not pass the exam, it may be your last opportunity. Under most circumstances, you will not be permitted to continue in the selection process unless you receive a passing score on the written exam. This is by design; agencies rely on the written exam as their first elimination step because it is easy and inexpensive to administer. In the nation's largest cities, literally thousands of applicants might take the written exam at the same time at schools or auditoriums throughout the area.

How do you make sure you will stand out and that your score will help you to be among the first applicants invited to move onto the next steps in the screening process? The written exam is almost always a multiple-choice exam; *although not all exams are identical, they will most frequently follow the formats of the practice exams in this book.* Although some agencies

may send you study material or a fact sheet about the exam, you are *not* expected to have knowledge of police procedures or rules or to know the laws of your state. Those are the topics you will learn and be tested on when you attend the police academy after successfully completing the screening process.

If the written exam is not based on police knowledge, what is it all about? The exam tests for many of the abilities you see in the headings of the chapters of this book. Questions will evaluate your ability to reason; to understand and answer questions about reading passages, pictures, and maps; and to select actions you would take based on a given fact pattern. There will also likely be a section on grammar, spelling, and selecting the correct word to complete a sentence or idea. Finally, there will be math-type questions that may ask you to add, subtract, multiple, and divide, and to pick up number patterns.

You may not see the connections to policing in these types of questions, but the format tests whether you have the ability to master the complex sets of rules and procedures and laws that you will study in the police academy, and whether your vocabulary and language is sufficient enough to read and understand material that will be presented to you and to speak with people and write accurate reports detailing your activities.

To discern your ability to grasp police-like situations, many of the questions and fact patterns that will presented to you will be similar to what you would be asked to do while working. For example, you might read a passage that explains the difference between two legal concepts and then answer a series of questions about those concepts or about how you would apply them in a situation that will be described. Similarly, you might read a passage written in the same style a police procedures manual would be and asked to answer questions that indicate whether you understood what you read. Or you might be given a common police situation and asked questions about how you would write the follow-up report.

## Sample Police Situation Report Question

*Instructions: Answer the next two questions based on the following information.*

Officers Biddle and Barron were dispatched in response to a 911 call regarding an automobile accident. At the scene, they obtained the following information:

| | |
|---|---|
| Date of accident: | July 18, 2008 |
| Type of accident: | Hit and run |
| Victim: | Bob Sellis, a pedestrian |
| Type of car: | Ford |
| Color of car: | Green |
| Driver of car: | Unknown male |

1. Officer Barron is writing up the crime report. Which of the following expresses the relevant information most clearly and accurately?
   a. On July 18, 2008, pedestrian Bob Sellis was the victim of a hit and run accident when he was struck by a green Ford, driver unknown.
   b. The hit and run victim, pedestrian Bob Sellis, was struck by an unknown male driver of a green Ford.
   c. A green Ford hit and ran from Bob Sellis, a pedestrian on July 18, 2008.
   d. Bob Sellis, a pedestrian, was hit and run by a man driving a green Ford.

1. a. Choice **a** is the only one that contains information provided in the question. Choices **b** and **d** imply that Sellis was struck by a driver rather than by a car; choice **c** creates an illogical category of "hit and ran."

2. Which of the following is a correct assumption based on the material provided?
   a. Bob Sellis was exiting his vehicle when he was struck.
   b. The man driving the green Ford was talking on a cell phone.
   c. Bob Sellis was seriously injured when he was hit.
   d. Bob Sellis was not killed by the unknown male driver.

2. d. Since there is no mention of anyone other than Bob Sellis talking to the police, it must be assumed he provided the information and must therefore be alive. Choices **a**, **b**, and **c** contain information that is not provided in the fact pattern.

Memory and map-reading questions might present you with wanted posters that you will then have to answer questions about, without looking back at the pictures. The maps might ask you to select the best way to get from one location to another.

The math questions on the exam might also be related to law enforcement responsibilities. An example of this could be a description of a burglary scene that required you to total the value of missing or stolen property. Some of the numbers in series or patterns might resemble what a state's license plates look like, as shown in the samples in Chapter 1.

## Sample Math Questions

*Instructions: Based on the information provided in the following descriptive paragraph, answer the next three questions.*

You are dispatched to take a report of a burglary at Tom's Tire Store. Tom is convinced that someone drove a truck up to his store to take the tires because a large number have been taken. According to Tom, six Silver Edition touring tires, six Pathfinder Truck/SUV tires, and four each of the All Season Regular and All Season Ultra tires were stolen.

The tires are valued at:

Silver Edition touring tires $66 each
Pathfinder Truck/SUV tires $111 each
All Season Regular tires $41.99 each
All Season Ultra tires $83.99 each

1. What is the total value of the Pathfinder Truck SUV tires reported by Tom?
   a. $600.00
   b. $666.00
   c. $444.00
   d. $396.00

1. b. You calculated 6 × 111. Choice a is an incorrect multiplication; choice c is probably based on recalling four rather than six tires having been taken, and choice d is the value of only the Silver Edition tires.

2. What is the total value of the All Season Ultra tires reported by Tom?
   a. $600.00
   b. $666.00
   c. $503.94
   d. $335.96

2. d. You calculated 4 × $83.99. Choice a is an incorrect multiplication; choice b is the value of the Pathfinder Truck SUV tires, and choice is c is most likely based on recalling six rather than four tires having been taken.

3. What is the total value of all the tires reported by Tom?
   a. $1,565.92
   b. $1.655.96
   c. $1,230.00
   d. $899.96

3. a. Choice a is the sum of all the values calculated (6 × 66) + (6 × 111) + (4 × 41.99) + (4 × 83.99). Choice b reverses numbers and results in an addition error; choice c omits the value of the All Season Ultra Tires, and choice d omits the value of the Pathfinder Truck/SUV tires.

As these samples illustrate, each question tests more than one thing. Judgment, reading, and the ability to do math are combined in the samples. You were required to do more than merely add up numbers; you had to note not only what was missing and how much each cost, but also how many of each were missing.

## Preparing for the Written Test

Not every question will have a policing angle, but many will. While it is difficult to study for an exam that does not test specific facts you learned in school or at a job, there are ways to improve your score on this type of an exam. You have begun your study routine by purchasing this book with sample tests. When you take the sample tests, create a situation that matches the conditions under which you will take the actual written exam. This usually means you will be given about two hours to take the exam and you will not be permitted to leave the room once the exam booklets are distributed.

To get the best effect of the sample tests, create a test situation identical to the real thing. Go to a quiet place; turn off your phone, music, or television; sharpen two or three pencils; and take the exam just as you would if it were the real thing. This not only prepares you for the type of questions and the atmosphere, it provides you with insight into your own behavior. Do you need to practice sitting still in a quiet atmosphere? Are you able to maintain your attention span for two hours while concentrating on only one task? If you grab your cell phone or feel the need to get up and walk around, you will need to stop yourself from doing those things.

All of the questions will in some way test your reading and memory abilities, whether they are labeled that way or not. If you know you do not read as much as you should, begin to read regularly. Reading a newspaper is an excellent way to improve your reading and your comprehension skills. Test passages are generally written at the same skill level as a daily newspaper. A newspaper also introduces you to places and names that are unfamiliar; after you read an article, test yourself to see how well you recall what you read. After reading, ask yourself some questions that are similar to those in the practice tests. This will help you to learn to focus and to remember what you have read Think

about what happened, to whom it happened, and who reported the events. Each of these questions is similar to creating a police report, and also to what you will be asked to do on the written exam.

Learn to read carefully and to pick out key words. Does the passage say "always," "never," "often," or "sometimes"? These words are important for answering the questions that follow. Look for negatives; if a sentence has the word *not* and you miss it, the meaning will be lost on you. "I did not pass the written exam" is exactly the opposite of "I did pass the written exam," but only one word separates the two realities. To make sure the second sentence pertains to you, learn to read carefully without skipping over important words.

If you come across words you are not familiar with, use a dictionary to learn their meanings. It can be fun to guess at the meaning of a word based on another word it looks like, but you can be tricked. Since the roots of many English words come from a variety of languages, two words that look similar often have very different definitions. Knowing the meanings of words will help you answer not only the actual vocabulary questions, but *all* the questions. If you think a word means something different from what it does mean, you are likely to misinterpret a reading passage. If the passage is followed by four or five questions, you could lose all those points just because there was one key word you did not understand.

Some questions may ask you to rephrase sentences that are awkward or are not grammatically correct. One way to prepare for this is to improve your own speech patterns. Do you use slang or speak in incorrect sentences? If so, when faced with sentences that need to be corrected, you might see nothing wrong with them. (Using standard English and avoiding slang will also serve you well when you meet your background investigator or if your agency requires an interview prior to being hired).

For additional tips on the written exam, review the material that explains specific test sections in later chapters of this book.

The rest of this chapter outlines the steps after you pass the written test. Depending on the agency to which you have applied and your score on the exam, it may be only months before you are called to the next step in the selection process or it may be years. In many jurisdictions, your next hurdle will be the physical agility test.

## The Physical Agility Test

One of the first very first things to know about this test is that different agencies have different terms for it. Whether it is called the *physical agility test*, the *physical ability test*, the *physical performance test*, or the *fitness test*, it is an attempt to measure your ability to perform the duties of a police officer or, at least, to be sufficiently agile to complete the training to perform those duties.

To accommodate the entry of women and smaller applicants into policing, many physical agility tests were modified in the 1970s. In some agencies, applicants are permitted to show these competences at the end of academy training rather than prior to acceptance into the academy. While physical agility requirements differ across types of agencies and geographic areas, state police and some federal agencies generally place a higher priority on physical agility tests than other agencies. You may be permitted to enter the academy conditionally if you have not passed these tests, but don't let that prevent you from preparing for them. Any agency may change its rules if the pass rates on the physical agility exam increase, or may group applicants in such a way that a lower score places you in a second-tier entry group.

The physical agility test will measure your abilities through such exercises as sit-ups, push-ups, running a specified distance within a specified time, lifting or dragging something that simulates the size and weight of a person or common object, and similar tasks that can be compared to what police officers may be asked to do during their work day. Some agencies, particularly state police agencies and many police departments in California, have retained a six-foot wall climb as part of the physical agility test. Although many candidates find this the most intimidating of the physical requirements, departments that retain it as part of the test have shown that candidates who prepare sufficiently are consistently able to pass.

Departments use somewhat different exercises and different cutoff scores to indicate passing. Some departments also permit different cutoff scores based on age (called age-norming) or sex (called gender-norming). A few departments, most notably the New Jersey State Police, maintain that all officers must achieve and maintain the same level of fitness because people challenging or running away from an officer do not first determine the age or sex of the officer before deciding whether to stay or to flee and, if to flee, how fleet of foot they must be to escape. In cases where norming is used, it is based on extensive physiological testing to ensure fairness in the selection process.

Sometimes in addition to (but also in some cases in place of) the physical agility test, departments include in the selection process a *general fitness test*. The fitness tests require less physical exertion and are, in some ways, more similar to the medical exam than to a physical agility test. The fitness exam, rather than have you actually participate in physically exerting activities, measures your body composition, aerobic capacity, muscular strength and endurance, and flexibility. Using a variety of tests and medical technology, your height and weight will be measured to see if they are proportionate, your body-fat content will be measured, and your breathing techniques may also be considered. The fitness test involves far less running, jumping, and pushing and pulling, but is viewed by

- Begin a rigorous fitness program and stick with it. Work on your upper body strength, reaction time, cardiovascular endurance, and flexibility. Make sure you include daily stretches in your routine.
- Don't forget exercises that strengthen your legs. Strong legs can help you surpass other applicants because most practical physical ability tests (like pulling a dummy, pushing a car, or scaling a wall) involve the use of legs as much as, if not more than, the upper body.
- Maintain a healthy diet; lay off the junk food!
- On the day of your exam, eat lightly and don't overdo the caffeine. You want to be clearheaded, energetic, and calm.

many departments as a better predictor of your ability not only to complete physical tasks but to complete them without becoming injured or disabled.

Agencies that process large numbers of candidates schedule the physical agility test fairly early in the application process. Like the written test, it can be administered to a large number of candidates at the same time—making it a cost-effective and efficient way to determine the number of candidates who will remain in the selection pool.

Agility tests are often scheduled in gyms, field houses, or similar facilities. When you are notified to appear, you will also be advised of what clothing to bring or to wear to the test facility. Generally you will be advised to bring a warm-up suit, sweat pants and shirt, shorts and a T-shirt, and sneakers. Although the test differs from meeting your background investigator or participating in an oral interview, it's still best to maintain a professional image. Your wisest course of action is to rely on plain sweats or shorts and a single-color T-shirt without any writing or photos. You may be asked to place masking tape with your name written on it on your gym clothing, another reason that unadorned outfits are best.

Do not bring extra gear or food and liquid refreshment unless you receive instructions to do so, although bringing a towel and a change of clothing for the trip home would be sensible. Bring a few sheets of paper and pencils or pens; you may be given information that you want to write down for retention. Since so much of police work involves taking notes and writing reports, you will almost never be faulted for thinking ahead that a paper and pen are amongst your most important tools of the trade.

As fewer young people play sports competitively and more are involved in sedentary activities in front of their computer screens, the physical agility test has become a serious obstacle for many applicants. To increase the number of candidates who pass, many departments post the entire test on their websites. Many also provide exercises and tips to assist candidates in preparing for the exams. Few of the tasks are based on brute strength; most involve learning a particular technique—including the much feared wall.

Whatever the specifics, each agility test requires you to be physically fit to pass it. Whether or not you are now physically fit, you should begin a physical fitness regimen as early as possible, based on what you can learn about your agency's testing style. Some agencies offer the opportunity to practice for the agility exam under the direction of their physical fitness instructors. This training will give you unique insights into how to pass the physical exam. If it is impossible for you to attend agency-sponsored training, find out if you can receive a copy of the training program to participate on your own or to set up a study group with other candidates. Particularly if you are attending a school with a criminal justice program, others may be

## Sample Physical Fitness Exam

Here is an example of an actual physical fitness exam used by a police department to screen potential candidates.

1. Sit-ups. The candidate lies flat on the back, knees bent, heels flat on the floor, fingers interlaced and placed behind the head. The monitor holds the feet down firmly. In the up position, the candidate should touch elbows to knees and return with shoulder blades touching floor. A passing score depends on your age and gender. For example, a 21-year-old female must do 32 sit-ups in one minute to pass the test.

2. Flex. The candidate removes shoes, sits down with legs extended, and places the feet squarely against a box with feet no wider than eight inches apart. Toes are pointed directly toward ceiling; knees remain extended throughout the test. With hands placed one on top of the other, the candidate leans forward without lunging or bobbing and reaches as far forward as possible. The hands must stay together and the stretch must be held for one second. Three attempts are allowed with the best of the three recorded to the nearest $\frac{1}{4}$ inch to determine whether the candidate passed/failed.

3. Push-ups. The hands are placed slightly wider than shoulder width apart, with fingers pointing forward. The monitor places one fist on the floor below the candidate's chest. (If a male monitor is testing a female candidate, a 3-inch sponge will be placed under the sternum to substitute for the fist.) Starting from the up position (elbows extended), the candidate must keep the back straight at all times and lower the body to the floor until the chest touches the monitor's fist. The candidate then returns to the up position. This is one repetition. The candidate's score will consist of the number of correct repetitions performed without a break (i.e., failing to extend the elbows, one or both knees touching the floor, hitting the floor, remaining on the floor, or stopping). A 22-year-old male must do 29 push-ups in one minute to achieve a passing score.

4. One-and-a-half-mile run. The 1.5-mile run will be administered on a track. The candidate will be informed of his/her lap time during the test. A 31-year-old female must be able to complete the 1.5-mile run within 15 minutes and 57 seconds to achieve a passing score.

interested in forming a physical training study group, which should motivate you to continue until the actual testing period.

What else can you do to prepare for the physical agility test? This is not the type of test you can cram for; you need to start immediately upon learning that you passed the written exam, or even earlier. Even if you change your mind and decide not to become a police officer, getting in better shape than you are now is never a waste of effort. Aside from an organized physical education program, if you know you are overweight, begin a weight reduction program. Improve your aerobic capacity by becoming more active; think about places you could walk to or ride a bicycle to rather than jumping into a car. Could you take up swimming, ice or roller skating, rowing, hiking, jogging, or simply walking?

If the funds or time for joining a gym cause problems for you, think of activities that are totally free. Most of the callisthenic activities you will be tested on can be done at home or in a park. Jumping jacks, squats, sit-ups, push-ups, and stomach crunches help build the strength and flexibility you will need to pass the physical agility exam. How many times do you take an elevator or escalator? Think about walking up and down the stairs next time. Dancing is also an aerobic activity!

FITT stands for Frequency, Intensity, Type, and Time. FITT simplifies your training by helping you plan what to do, when, how hard, and for how long. Because the four FITT variables are interrelated, you need to be careful in how you exercise. For example, intensity and time have an inverse relationship: As the intensity of your effort increases, the length of time you can maintain that effort decreases. A good rule of thumb when adjusting your workout variables to achieve optimum conditioning is to modify one at a time, increasing by five to ten percent. Be sure to allow your body time to adapt before adjusting up again.

The following presents some FITT guidelines to help you plan your training program.

**Frequency**
- 3-5 times a week

**Intensity**
- Aerobic training—60–85% of maximum effort
- Resistance training—8–12 repetitions
- Flexibility training—Just to slight tension

**Type**
- Aerobic—Bike, walk, jog, swim
- Resistance—Free weights, weight machines, calisthenics
- Flexibility—Static stretching

**Time**
- Aerobic—20–60 minutes
- Resistance—1–3 sets, 2–4 exercises/body part
- Flexibility—Hold stretched position 8–30 seconds

Once you set up a workout schedule, stay with it even after you pass the physical portion of the selection process. Remember that the tasks you will be asked to perform will also be part of your academy training, and if you start to exercise regularly and work it into your lifestyle, you will remain fit throughout your career.

## Background Investigation

Your background investigation will be based on the information you supply to your investigator. You provide the information through what is commonly called a **personal history statement**.

You will be asked to provide many details of your entire life, possibly including every school you ever attended; any address you lived at for the last 15 years; any jobs you had for the same period of time and whether you were ever fired from a job; whether you served in the military and what type of discharge you received; information on your driving record and any vehicles you own; other property in your name; your credit history; whether you have ever been arrested; whether you have used drugs at all or alcohol to excess... you get the idea. Questions may also pertain to parents, step-parents, or guardians; past and present spouses; and siblings (including step-siblings).

In addition to answering questions and being photographed and fingerprinted, you will be required to sign release forms that permit your investigator to gain access to your personal records. You will also be required to submit a number of documents, most which will have to be certified as accurate by their sources or by a notary public. These documents might include your educational records; employment records; military history and discharge papers; driving record and vehicle insurance forms; mortgage or other loan forms; and any papers pertaining to arrests or a criminal history.

You are likely to be asked to include up to three references who are not family members. Do not forget to ask these individuals whether you may use their names; if they agree, make sure their addresses and contact information are correct. If your investigator cannot contact your references, this will show up as an incomplete portion of your investigation and may lead to delays or even termination of your application.

Each of your answers and documents will be checked by your investigator, often a police officer already employed by the department. You will be interviewed about your responses by your investigator, particularly about any that are incomplete or do not seem to match with the timeline of your life.

There are two iron-clad rules to follow for getting through your investigation. One is to *start putting together your documentation as soon as you know you have made it to this step*: Collect your paperwork; ask parents or guardians for earlier residence addresses if you were too young to remember them; be sure of your replies (now is not the time for guessing); and think about who you will ask to serve as personal or professional references.

The second bit of advice is even more important—*do not lie about anything in your past*. Not everyone has made it to adulthood without something they would rather not talk about or have publicly known. When you decided to become a police officer, you signed away those secrets. But police departments are not comprised only of perfect people. Whatever you may have been told, not everyone who gets hired is without any small blemishes. Certain youthful indiscretions may not disqualify you if you can explain the circumstances, but falsehoods will assuredly eliminate you from further consideration.

Rarely will two agencies conduct the background investigation exactly the same way, so rather than making yourself tense trying to provide all the information and all the documents that comprise the background investigation, you may decide that concentrating on the agencies where you sincerely want to work is a better use of your time and efforts.

Some departments also include the Law Enforcement Candidate Record (LECR), a 185-question exam that asks about your personal experiences, your education, your work history and habits, your relationships with family members and friends, and your feelings or attitudes on a variety of aspects of your life. Like the psychological exam, there are no "right" or "wrong" answers and your best course of action is to be truthful. Many of the questions may seem to repeat earlier questions in slightly different ways. This is intentional; it is meant to catch you if you are dishonest because the test is based on the premise that eventually you will forget to lie and will answer truthfully.

Each of these types of tests, whether the LECR or a psychological or behavioral test, departments use these to develop a profile of your personality and attitudes and compare this with statistical analyses of successful officers. These statistical profiles help departments determine where you fit on the continuum of officers they have hired.

## Ready for Action

So, you are as prepared as you can be. You've made your decision on where you are applying, and let's even assume you are at the point in the application process where you've received the personal history statement. Before you set pen to paper, make a copy of the form. Do not write on it, breathe on it, or set it down on the coffee table without making a copy first. After you have a copy, put away the original for now. (You will be using the photocopy as a working draft and a place to make mistakes.) Eventually you will transfer all the information you have on your practice copy onto the original. And then you'll be making a copy of your original. You may be spending lots of time on this project and using more than a few dimes in the copy machine before this is all over, but it will be time and money well spent. Especially if the unthinkable happens:

> Your phone rings. It's your recruiter. "Gee, this is Officer Jones at Friendly P.D. recruiting and I have a little bad news. We can't seem to find that application you sent. Could you make us a copy from the one you have at home and send it out right away?"

Be sure to make copies of your completed personal history statement and accompanying documentation you submit and keep them in a safe place. Hold on to these copies! You need to review this document before the oral board contacts you, not to mention the possibility that you may need this information to complete other applications years down the road.

Personal history statements vary from department to department, but the questions most applicants ask about filling out these tedious documents have not changed over the years. The following are a few questions and comments made by actual applicants as they went through application processes across the United States. The responses to and comments about these questions will allow you to learn from someone else's mistakes, thereby giving you an advantage over the competition—and having an advantage in this highly competitive field can never hurt!

## "What do you mean you don't accept resumes? It took me four hours to get this one done!"

A formal resume like the one you may prepare for a civilian job may not be much good to a law enforcement agency. Although criminal justice instructors in many colleges suggest that their students prepare a resume, it's always best to call and ask a recruiter whether or not to bother. Why go to the trouble if the agency is going to throw away the resume upon receipt? Most agencies rely upon their personal history statements to get the details of your life, education, and experience, so save yourself the time and money when you can. Some departments do, however, request that you submit a resume. They use it as an additional screening element. So it's always best to ask first.

## "I didn't realize the personal history statement would take so long to complete, and the deadline for turning it in caught me by surprise. I got in a hurry and left some things blank."

The letter this applicant received in the mail disqualifying her from further consideration probably caught her by surprise as well. As you know from reading this chapter so far, a personal history statement requires planning, efficiency, and attention to detail. Most police departments demand accuracy, thoroughness, and timeliness. There are entirely too many applicants who have taken the necessary time to properly fill out an application for a busy background investigator to bother with an applicant who has left half of the form blank and isn't quite sure what should go in the other half. In fact, many departments will tell you in their application instructions that failing to respond to questions or failure to provide requested information will result in disqualification.

### "I read *most* of the instructions. I didn't see the part that said I had to print."

Read all of the instructions. Every sentence. Every word. And do so before you begin filling out your practice copy of the personal history statement. In fact, you should read the entire document from the first page to the last page before you tackle this project. Have a notepad next to you, and as you read, make notes of everything you do not understand. You will be making a phone call to your recruiter after reading the entire document to ask questions. It's important to read the whole document because the questions on your pad may be answered as you read along.

### "No one is going to follow up on all this stuff anyway. It'd take way too long and it's way too involved."

A good background investigator will be thorough in following up on the details of your life. That's his or her job. When all is said and done, the investigator must sign his or her name at the bottom of the report documenting the investigation. It's not wise to assume someone will put their career at risk by doing a sloppy job on your background investigation. A thorough investigator will take as much time as it takes to do a good job. The good news is that you can earn brownie points by making that investigator's job as simple as possible. Give as much information as you possibly can and make sure that information is correct. When you write down a phone number, make sure it's current. For example, if you worked at Jumpin' Jack's Coffee Parlor four years ago and you still remember the phone number, call that number to make sure it's still in service before you write it down. Nothing is more irritating to a busy investigator than dialing wrong number after wrong number. If that's the only number you have and you discover it's no longer in service, make a note of this so the investigator doesn't assume you are being sloppy.

When you turn in a personal history statement, you are building on the reputation you began forming from the moment you first made contact with the recruiting staff. An application that is turned in on time, is filled out neatly and meticulously, and has correct, detailed information—that is easily verified—says a lot about the person who filled it out. Not only will an investigator have warm fuzzy thoughts for anyone who makes his or her job easier, he or she will come to the conclusion that you will probably carry over these same traits into your police work.

The investigator, the oral board, and the staff psychologist all will be looking at how you filled out the application as well as what information is contained in the application. Police officers will build a case for hiring you (or not hiring you) based on facts, impressions, and sometimes even intuition. With this in mind, every detail is worth a second look before you call your personal history statement complete. Ask yourself:

- Is my handwriting as neat as it can be?
- Did I leave off answers or skip items?
- Do my sentences make sense?
- Is my spelling accurate?
- Are my dates and times consistent?
- Did I double-check the telephone numbers?
- Did I double-check the ZIP codes?

### "I figured you could find out that information more easily than I could. That's why I didn't look up that information. After all, you're the investigator."

And this applicant is probably still looking for a job. The personal history statement is a prime opportunity for you to showcase your superb organizational skills, attention to detail, and professionalism. Do as much of the work as you can for the background investigator. For example, let's say you worked for Grace's Record Store. The business went under after a few months, and you moved on to other employment. You're not sure what happened to Grace, your immediate supervisor and the owner of the business, but you do know a friend of hers. Contact that friend, find out Grace's address and phone number, and give this information to your investigator. Going the extra mile shows initiative, and you are going to get the extra credit points.

It's not uncommon for a major police department to get thousands of applications per year. Most of the applicants have the same credentials to offer as you do. Do all you can do to stand out from the crowd by showing your efficiency, professionalism, and accuracy.

**"I know I got disqualified, but it's only because I misunderstood the question. I didn't want to ask about it because I didn't want to look dumb."**

If you do not understand a question, ask someone. By not making sure you know how to properly answer a question, you run the risk of answering it incorrectly, incompletely, or not at all. Any one of these mistakes can lead to your disqualification if an investigator thinks that you are not telling the truth, or that you are unwilling to provide the information requested. Don't take chances when a simple question can clear up the problem.

**"You know, I didn't have any idea what that question meant, so I just guessed."**

Never guess. Never assume. This advice can never be repeated too often—if you don't know, find out. Answering your questions is part of the job for recruiters or background investigators.

**"I lied because I thought if I told the truth, I'd look bad."**

Never lie about anything. As far as police departments are concerned, there is no such thing as a harmless lie. Supervisors don't want people working for them who cannot tell the truth; other officers don't want to work with partners whom they can't trust; and communities

expect criminals to lie—not police officers. Your credibility must be beyond reproach.

Let's look at an example. One applicant told his recruiter that the reason he didn't admit to getting a ticket for an unregistered car was because he thought the department would think he wasn't organized and couldn't take care of business. Which would you prefer for a potential employer to know about you—that you lie instead of admitting to mistakes, or that you make mistakes and admit to them readily? Telling the truth is crucial if you want to do police work.

**"I listed John Doe as a personal reference because he's the mayor and I worked on his campaign. Why did my investigator call me and ask me to give him another reference?"**

Choose your personal references carefully. Background investigators do not want to talk to people because they have impressive credentials. They want to talk to them so they can understand you are a little better. Investigators will know within minutes whether or not a reference knows you well. Personal references are important enough to warrant their own in-depth discussion later in this chapter, so read on.

## How to Read and Answer Questions

Reading questions and instructions carefully is critical to successfully completing the personal history statement. Certain words should leap off the page at you. These are the words you should key in on:

- all
- every
- any
- each

If you see these words in a question, you are being asked to include all the information you know. For example, you may see the following set of instructions in your personal history statement:

List **any** and **all** pending criminal charges against you.

This doesn't mean to list only the charges facing you in Arizona, but not the ones from that incident in Nevada last week. This department wants to know about every single criminal charge that may be pending against you, no matter what city, county, parish, village, country, or planet may be handling the case(s). Do not try to dodge instructions like these for any reason. If your fear is that the information you list might make you look bad, you may have some explaining to do. And you may have perfectly good explanations. If you lie to try to make yourself look good, though, chances are you'll be disqualified in short order and no one will get the opportunity to consider your explanations.

Another question you may see is:

Have you **ever** been arrested or taken into police custody for **any** reason?

The key words here are *ever* and *any*. This department means at any time in your life. If you don't know what is meant by the word *arrested*, then call your recruiter or investigator and ask. When in doubt, list any situation you think has a ghost of a chance of falling into the category you are working on. The best advice, though, is to ask if you don't know.

Here's a request for information that includes several eye-catching words.

List **all** traffic citations you received in the past five (5) years, in this or **any** other state (moving and nonmoving), **excluding** parking tickets.

In this example, the department leaves little doubt that what you should do here is make a complete list of every kind of violation you've been issued a citation for, no matter where you got it and no matter what the traffic violation was for, within the past five years. They even let you know the one kind of citation they don't need to know about—parking tickets. If you aren't sure what a moving violation is or what a non-moving violation is, call the department and have them explain. Keep in mind that if an officer issued you a citation on a single piece of paper, you may have been cited for more than one violation. Most citations have space for at least three violations, sometimes more. For example, say that last year you were pulled over for speeding. The officer discovered you had no insurance and your license plates were expired. She told you she was writing you three tickets for these violations, but handed you only one piece of paper. Did you get one ticket or three? You got three.

Once again, ask if you don't know. No one will make fun of you if you are unfamiliar with terminology such as *moving violation*.

Here are some sample questions taken from actual personal history statements:

List all traffic citations ever received, including the date, place, and full details of each incident.

Submit seven-year driving history from each state in which you have ever held a driver's license.

List all moving and nonmoving traffic citations, excluding parking tickets (e.g., speeding, running a red light, expired registration, no insurance), that you have received in the past five (5) years, starting with the most recent citation. List the month and year each was issued, the type of violation, and the issuing agency.

## Personal References

Your personal references are the people who will be able to give the background investigator the best picture of you as a whole person. Some personal history statements ask you to list up to six people as references, and some ask for only three. You also may be given a specific time limit for how long you may have known these people before listing them. Your instructions may direct you to list only those individuals whom you've known for a minimum of two years, for example. Pay close attention to the instructions for this section, if there are any. Selecting the people for this section is not something you should take lightly for many reasons.

Earlier, you read that by making the investigator's job easier you make your investigation run smoother, you get brownie points, and your background is finished quickly. The personal references section is one area where you really want to make it easy. You'll want the investigator to talk to people who know you well, who can comment on your hobbies, interests, personality, and ability to interact with others. Try to choose friends who will be honest, open, and sincere. When an investigator calls a reference and figures out quickly that the person he or she is talking to barely has an idea of who you are, the red flags will come shooting up. The investigator will wonder why you listed someone who doesn't know you well. Are you trying to throw him or her off track? Are you afraid someone who knows you too well will let out information you don't want known? This is how an investigator will look at the situation. And, at the very least, you will get a phone call requesting another reference because the one you listed was unsatisfactory.

Most investigators expect that you will notify your personal references and tell them that they will be getting a phone call or a personal visit from the investigating agency. Get the right phone numbers, find out from your references what times they are most accessible, and especially find out if they have any objections to being contacted. You don't need a reluctant personal reference. He or she will probably do more harm than good.

Tell your references how important it is for them to be open and honest with the investigator. It's also wise to let them know that there are no right or wrong answers to most of these questions. Investigators do not want to have a conversation with someone who is terrified about saying the wrong thing. And that's what your personal references should expect to have with an investigator—a conversation, not an interrogation. Your goal here is to let the investigator see you as a person through the eyes of those who know you best.

Here are sample requests for references taken from actual personal history statements:

CHARACTER REFERENCES (do not include relatives, former employers, or persons living outside the United States or its Territories). List only character references who have definite knowledge of your qualifications and fitness for the position for which you are applying.
Do not repeat names of job supervisors. List a minimum of three (3) character references. Give each person's name, the number of years known, street address, and phone number.

Provide three (3) references (not relatives, fellow employees, or school teachers) who are responsible adults of reputable standing in their communities, such as heads of households, property owners, business or professional men or women, who have known you well during the past five (5) years. List each one's name, home and business phone numbers, street address, and occupation.

Additionally, provide three (3) social acquaintances who have known you well during the past five (5) years. (These must be different people from the three references listed above.)

Additionally, provide contact information for three (3) of your neighbors.

## Before You Turn It In

You've filled out the practice copy you made of the personal history statement, made all your mistakes on that copy, answered all the questions, and filled in all the appropriate blanks. Now you're ready to make the final copy.

Part of the impression you will make on those who make the hiring and firing decisions will come from how your application looks. Is your handwriting so sloppy that investigators pass your work around to see who can read it? Did you follow the instructions directing you to print? Were you too lazy to attach an additional sheet of paper, and instead you wrote up and down the sides of the page? Did you spell words correctly? Do your sentences make sense to the reader? (A good tip here is to read your answers aloud to yourself. If it doesn't make sense to your ear, then you need to work on what you wrote.)

Every time you contact the hiring agency, you make an impression. The written impression you make when you turn in your personal history statement is one that can follow you through the entire process and into the academy. In fact, it can have a bearing on whether or not you even make it into the academy because most departments have a method of scoring you on the document's appearance.

Here are some items you might find useful as you work on your application and prepare it for submission.

- a dictionary
- a grammar handbook
- a good pen (or pencil—whatever the directions tell you to use)

Make sure that you check your work, check it again, and have someone you trust check it yet again before you make your final copy.

You now have the information you need to make the personal history statement a manageable task. This is not a document to take lightly, especially when you are now aware of the power this document has over your potential career as a police officer. Remember, it's important that you:

- follow instructions and directions
- be honest and open about your past and present
- provide accurate information
- choose excellent personal references
- turn in presentable, error-free documentation
- submit documents on time

A recruiting department can ask for nothing better than an applicant who takes this kind of care and interest in the application process.

### Polygraph Exam

Departments that include a polygraph exam, often in conjunction with the background investigation, do so to encourage honesty. If your only experience with a polygraph is what you have seen in the media, you may be surprised at how one is conducted. You will be questioned by an experienced examiner who will begin by asking you a series of basic questions including your name and address. This is to set you at ease and to establish how you respond to factual questions. Questions will then move to areas where dishonesty could seriously affect your chances for employment, including questions about prior criminal history, drug use, thefts, vehicle accidents, or domestic violence incidents. As with your background questionnaire and interview, always answer truthfully to the best of your knowledge. If you are asked something about your youth, for instance, and you honestly do not remember, say so rather than try to make up something you think the polygraphist or the machine wants to hear.

Show the board how much you want this job. They will check to see when you arrived for your board. An early arrival means you planned ahead for emergencies (flat tires, wrong turns, and so on), that you arrived in enough time to prepare yourself mentally for what you are about to do, and that you place a value on other people's time as well as your own.

## The Interview

An interview with a member of the department or with a panel has become prevalent in the police officer selection process. Similar to the background investigation and the polygraph exam, the worst thing you can do during the interview is to lie or to try to create a persona that is different from whom you are. The interview may take many forms; for instance, you might be asked questions that are based on your personal history statement. In another style of interview, you might be asked to describe a past personal or work-related situation that caused you stress, or to describe your best and worst traits. You might be given a typical policing situation, a "hypothetical," and asked what you would do. In some interviews, the content of your answers is of primary importance, in others, the questioners are more interested in how you present yourself, and whether you are able to maintain your composure in a stressful situation.

The majority of police departments include an oral interview in the hiring process. If you are under consideration by a department that does not conduct an interview, it would be wise to treat your background investigator as you would a formal interviewer. How you present yourself, dress, and react to questions may become part of your background write-up by your investigator. Although your investigator is there to help you become a police officer, do not think of this person as a confidant to whom you can show negative traits or towards whom you can act in an unprofessional way. For your initial visit with your investigator, you should dress just as you would for a formal interview; even if

the interviewer tells you that you need not wear business attire to subsequent visits, do not go the informal route of showing up in jeans and a T-shirt or shorts and flip-flops. You may have seen active police officers dress casually when they are off-duty, but this is not the impression you want to make before your career has even begun.

Aim for a neat, conservative appearance at your interview. This includes having your hair neatly styled (women might consider pinning up or back long hair so it is not a distraction) and wearing only makeup that is minimal and natural-looking. Too much jewelry can also be a distraction; both men and women should limit jewelry and keep what they wear to small, discreet items. Men and women who choose to wear pant suits should make sure that their clothing is clean, fits well, and is free of wrinkles; women wearing skirt and blouse combinations or a dress should wear nude hosiery without runs or snags. Applicants should be sure their shoes are polished and heels not run down.

The interview is costly in time and money because each candidate must be individually scheduled to appear before a panel of three to five people, often active police officers but sometimes community leaders, too. In small agencies and in many sheriffs' offices, the interview may be with the chief or the sheriff, particularly if agency policy permits hiring outside civil service regulations. In these instances, the chief or sheriff has the authority to select the candidate in large part on his or her individual discretion. At the other extreme, interviews can be highly formalized, including

- Be respectful, courteous, and pleasant throughout the process. Always keep your cool.
- Answer all questions honestly and to the best of your ability. Sincerity counts!
- Listen carefully to the questions. Don't distract yourself by thinking too much about how you might look or what they might be thinking about you. Stay in the moment. If you have to pause and think for a moment before you answer a question, that's okay. It's better than rushing yourself through the process.
- Have a question or two ready for when the board invites you to ask them. This shows your genuine interest in the job.
- Make sure you are on time! Better yet, arrive early.
- Dress conservatively, and go light on jewelry or makeup.
- Don't drink too much caffeine beforehand—you want to be able to relax.

being taped for later review or in the event you do not do well and request an appeal.

The interview is intended to test what written and agility tests cannot measure. In addition to your answers, the panel is watching your posture, your body language, and your poise as you formulate your responses. They notice whether you make eye contact with panel members and generally how you react to unanticipated questions and situations. In addition to how you dress, remember to make eye contact with the questioner; use their names or titles when answering. Listen to the question and answer what you are asked. If you did not understand the question at all, ask that it be repeated rather than risk providing an incorrect or inappropriate answer. If you know you are uncomfortable in interview situations, try to get friends, family, co-workers, or faculty members to help you by asking you sample questions and measuring the quality of your responses. Did you answer what was asked? Could your voice be heard, or was it too low or too loud? Did you answer without too many, "um"s, "like"s, "you know"s, and similar verbal distractions? These are things you can practice without knowing what the questions will be. Remember, although the interview may actually be quite short—probably well under one hour—it can seem like a lifetime if you do not prepare yourself.

### The Interview Board Members

If you are like most people, you've had some experience asking someone for a job. So, it's not unrealistic to expect that the police oral interview board will be similar to a civilian oral interview—is it? Yes and no. There are a few similarities: Both prospective civilian and police employers are looking for the most qualified person for the job—reliable, honest men and women who will work hard and be there when they are needed.

Civilian employers expect applicants to show up on time for their interviews, to dress professionally, and to show off their best manners, as do police employers. When you step into a police oral interview board, however, you will realize that the people who are interviewing you have more than a surface interest in you and your past experiences. And the board will have more than a one- or two-page resume in their hands when the interview begins.

Exactly who is going to be using the details of your personal and professional life to interview you? More than likely it will be a panel of two or more individuals with one purpose in mind: to get to know you well. The board members will most likely be supervisory-level police officers who have several years' experience on the force. Some departments use civilian personnel specialists to sit on their boards, but most interview boards will be made up of experienced police officers.

These board members will be using information you have provided on your personal history statement and information investigators discovered during your background investigation. Investigators will provide board members with a detailed report on your past and present life history. Yes, you will be asked questions when board members already know the answers and when they don't know the answers. You will be asked to explain why you've made the decisions you've made in your life—both personal and professional. You will also be asked questions that don't have correct or incorrect answers. In short, you can expect an intense grilling from men and women who don't have the time or patience for applicants who walk into their interviews unprepared.

### What Is the Interview Board Looking For?

Today's departments expect officers to attend neighborhood meetings, get to know the people living and working in their patrol areas, and be accessible to the public. This concept is known as community policing. Community policing is being embraced by most medium to large police agencies and is designed to get the officers out of the squad car and back into the community. The days of riding around in a car waiting for the next call to come out are over for most officers.

Officers nationwide feel that community policing is simply a return to the basic idea behind policing—public service. Therefore, oral interview boards are faced with the formidable task of hiring men and women with the skills and talents equal to the demands of modern policing.

The men and women most highly sought after by police departments are those who can handle the demands placed on them by advanced technology and changes in policing concepts. Computers are here to stay—in the office and in the patrol car. If you haven't already, now's the time to brush up on your typing skills and sign up for a computer class.

Then there's the liability issue. Lawsuits and threats of lawsuits have law enforcement agencies scurrying to find applicants who have specific qualities and skills that will keep them out of the headlines and civil courtrooms will be most competitive.

Yes, law enforcement agencies want it all: motivated, versatile candidates who are ready to take on the challenges of police work. You will be most competitive if you can convince the board you have the following qualities:

- maturity
- common sense
- good judgment
- compassion
- integrity
- honesty
- reliability
- the ability to work without constant supervision

These qualities aren't ranked in order of importance because it would be hard to say which should come first. They are all of importance in the eyes of the board, and your task in the oral interview is to convince them you possess these qualities. You will do your convincing through how and what you say when you respond to questions.

### Youth and Inexperience— Plus or Minus?

The question here is, will an oral board think you have enough life experience for them to be willing to take a chance on hiring you? Law enforcement agencies have never been as liability conscious as they are today. Incidents like the Rodney King trial and the subsequent Los Angeles riots have heightened the awareness of city legal departments around the country.

This concern ripples straight through the department and eventually arrives to haunt recruiters, background investigators, oral boards, and everyone who has anything to do with deciding who gets a badge. The first question you hear when trouble hits a police department is, "How did that person get a job here anyway?" As a result, police departments are scrutinizing applicants more closely than ever before, and they are clearly leaning toward individuals who have proven track records in employment, schooling, volunteer work, and community involvement.

Youth and inexperience are not going to disqualify you from the process. You should be aware that if you are 21 years old and have never held a job, you will have a more difficult time getting hired on your first try at a larger police department than someone who is older, has job references to check, and is able to demonstrate a history of reliability, responsibility, and community involvement.

Maturity is a huge concern with police departments. They cannot hire men and women who are unable to take responsibility for their actions or the actions, in some cases, of those around them. Although maturity cannot be measured in the number of years an individual has been alive, departments will want to see as much proof as possible that you have enough maturity and potential to risk hiring you.

### Get Out in the World

Make it as easy as possible for the oral board to see how well you handle responsibility. Sign up for volunteer work if you don't have any experience dealing with people. If you are still living at home with parents, be able to demonstrate the ways in which you are responsible around the home. If you are on your own, but living with roommates, talking to the board about this experience and how you handle conflicts arising from living with strangers or friends will help your case.

You may want to work extra hard on your communication skills before going to the board. The more articulate you are, the better you will be able to sell yourself.

### Older and Wiser Can Pay Off

Being older certainly is not a hindrance in police work. Oral boards are receptive to men and women who have life experience that can be examined, picked apart, and verified. Maturity, as has been mentioned before, is not necessarily linked with how old you are. Older applicants can be either blessed or cursed by the trail they have left in life. Many applicants have gone down in flames because they were unable to explain incidents in their past and present that point to their immaturity and inability to handle responsibility.

Applicants of any age who have listed numerous jobs and have turned in personal history statements too thick to run through a stapling machine should be extra vigilant about doing homework before the oral board stage. If you fall into this category, you should carefully pore over the copy of the application your background investigator used to do your background check. Be fully aware of the problem areas and consider what you will most likely be asked to explain. And decide now what you are going to say. Prepare, prepare, prepare.

### Don't Leave the Meter Running

The longer your history, the longer you can expect to sit before an oral board. If a board is not required to adhere strictly to time limits, you may be required to endure a longer session than other applicants simply because there's more material to cover. The more you know about yourself and the more open you are about your life, the more smoothly your interview will run. This advice holds true for all applicants.

## The Types of Questions You Will Be Asked

*What kind of questions are they going to ask?* Isn't that what everyone is really worried about when they are sitting in the chair outside of the interview room? You will hear all kinds of questions—personal questions about your family life, questions about your likes and dislikes, your temperament, your friends, and even a few designed to make you laugh so you will get a little color back into your face. Don't look for many questions that can be answered with simply "yes" or "no," because you won't get that lucky. Let's look at the types of questions you are likely to be asked.

## Open-Ended Questions

The open-ended question is the one you are most likely to hear. Here's an example of an open-ended question:

Board Member:   "Mr. Jones, can you tell the board about your Friday night bowling league?"

Board members like these questions because it gives them an opportunity to see how articulate you can be, and it gives them a little insight into how you think. This is also a way for them to ease into more specific questions. For example:

Board Member:   "Mr. Jones, can you tell the board about your Friday night bowling league?"

Jones:   "Yes ma'am. I've been bowling in this league for about two years. We meet every Friday night around 6 P.M. and bowl until about 8:30 P.M. I like it because it gives me something to do with the friends that I might not get to see otherwise because everyone is so busy. This also gives me time to spend with my wife. We're in first place right now, and I like it that way."

Board Member:   "Oh, congratulations. You must be a pretty competitive bowler."

Jones:   "Yes ma'am, I am. I like to win and I take the game pretty seriously."

Board Member:   "How do you react when your team loses, Mr. Jones?"

That one question generates enough information for the board to draw a lot of conclusions about Mr. Jones. They can see that he likes to interact with his friends, he thinks spending time with his wife is important, and that competition and winning are important to him. Mr. Jones's answer opens up an avenue for the board to explore how he reacts to disappointment, how he is able to articulate his feelings and reactions, and they'll probably get a good idea of his temperament.

Open-ended questions allow the board to fish around for information, but this is not a negative situation. You should seize these opportunities to open up to the board and give them an idea of who you are as a person.

## Obvious Questions

This is the kind of question boards ask when everyone in the room already knows the answer. For example:

Board Member:   "Ms. Rasheed, you were in the military for four years?"

Rasheed:   "Yes sir, I was in the Marines from 1992 until 1996."

Board Member:   "Why did you get out?"

The obvious question is used most often as a way to give the applicant a chance to warm up and to be aware of what area the board is about to explore. It's also a way for the board to check up on the information they've been provided. Board members and background investigators can misread or misunderstand information they receive. Understanding this, board members will usually be careful to confirm details with you during the interview.

Interview boards ask two other types of ice-breaker questions for which you should be prepared. They may ask you something like, "What have you done to prepare yourself to become a police officer?" Or, you may be asked, "Why do you want to become a police officer?" These icebreakers are your opportunity to impress the board with your qualifications for the job, so be prepared to answer them.

Why do you want to become a police officer? You should be thinking about this question now. A good candidate will often answer that he or she likes working with and helping people and solving problems, and is attracted to the idea of facing different challenges on a daily basis. A good candidates may answer that he or she prepared for the oral and the job by interviewing other police officers, working as a volunteer, or reading books and websites on police work.

## Fishing Expeditions

The fishing expedition is always a nerve-racking kind of question to answer. You aren't certain why they are asking or where the question came from, and they aren't giving out clues. For example:

Board Member:  "Mr. Yang, in your application, you stated that you've never been detained by police. You've *never* been detained?"

If your nerves aren't wracked by this kind of questioning, someone probably needs to check you for a pulse. In the example above, if the applicant has been detained by police and failed to list this on his application, then he'll be wondering if the board knows this happened. The odds are high that the board does know the answer before asking the question. If the applicant has never been detained, then paranoia is certain to set in. Did someone on his list of references lie to the background investigator? Did someone on the board mis-read his application? These questions race through his mind as the board scrutinizes him.

Chances are, the board is simply fishing to see what he will say. In any event, don't let these questions cause you a dilemma because if you are honest there can be no dilemma. You simply must tell the truth at all times in an oral board. Your integrity is at stake, your reputation, and, not least of all, your chance to become a police officer is at stake. Don't try to guess at why the board is asking a question. Your job is to answer truthfully and openly.

## Situational/Ethics Queries

Who doesn't dread these? You hear the words, "What would you do if . . ." and your heart pounds wildly. For example:

Board Member:  "Ms. Peterson, assume you are a police officer and you are on your way to back up an officer who is on the scene of a burglary alarm at a clothing store. You walk in just in time to see him pick up a small bottle of men's cologne and put it into his pocket. What do you do?"

Some oral boards almost exclusively ask one situational question after another. Other departments may ask one, then spend the rest of the interview asking you about your past job history. Your best defense here is to decide ahead of time what your ethics are and go with how you honestly feel. The only possible right answer is your answer. If the board doesn't like what they hear, then you may be grilled intensely about your answer; however, you cannot assume that you've given the incorrect answer if the board does begin questioning you hard about your answers. Boards have more than one reason for challenging you, and it's never safe to assume why they are doing it.

Keep in mind, too, that it's not uncommon on police boards for one board member to be assigned the task of trying to get under an applicant's skin. The purpose is to see if the applicant rattles easily under pressure or loses his or her temper when baited. The person assigned this task is not hard to spot. He or she will be the one you thoroughly detest after you've had to answer such questions as, "Why in the world would we want to hire someone like you?"

Expect boards to jump on every discrepancy they hear and to pick apart some of your comments—all because they want to see how you handle pressure. Not all departments designate a person to perform this function, but someone is usually prepared to slip into this role at some point in the interview.

## Role-Play Situations

Answering tough questions is stressful enough, but doing it under role-play conditions is even tougher. Many departments are using this technique more and more frequently in the oral board setting. A board member will instruct you to pretend you are a police officer and ask you to act out your verbal and/or physical responses. For example:

Board Member:  "Mr. Patel, I want you to pretend that you are a police officer and you are chasing a fleeing suspect. The suspect is running from you now and I want you to stand up and instruct him to stop by yelling, "Freeze! Police!"

Board members may set up more elaborate role-playing scenes for you. Try to enter into these situations with a willingness to participate. Most people are aware that you are not a professional actor or actress, so they are not looking for Academy Award performances. Do the best you can. Role-playing is used heavily in almost all police academies and training situations today, so expect to do a lot of role-playing during your career as a law enforcement professional. Shy, reserved people may have difficulty working up enthusiasm for this kind of interaction. Practice how you'd handle this scene, and prepare yourself mentally as best you can.

## Highly Personal Questions

The members of the oral board can indeed ask you just about any question that comes to mind. Applying for a job in public safety puts you in a different league than the civilian sector applicant. Yes, federal and state laws may prohibit civilian employers from seeking certain information about their applicants. But law enforcement agencies are allowed more freedom of movement within the laws for obvious reasons.

For example, you will rarely find a space for an applicant's birth date on an application for employment in private industry. This is the result of age discrimination litigation. Law enforcement agencies, as well as other agencies dealing with public safety, need such information to perform thorough background investigations and do not have many of the same restrictions. You will be expected to provide your date of birth and identify your race and your gender before you get very far in the application process for any police department. You are applying for a sensitive public safety job and must expect information you may consider highly personal to come to light.

In short, law enforcement agencies can ask you any question that may have a bearing on your mental stability, ability to do the physical tasks common to police work, integrity, honesty, character, and reputation in the community. There's not much left to the imagination after all of this is covered. If some of the questions are probing and perhaps even offensive, it is because you are being held to a higher standard by both the courts that allow these questions to be asked and the departments that want to hire you to protect life and property.

## Answers—How Many Are There?

While you are sitting in the interview hot seat, you may feel like only two kinds of answers exist—the one you wish you had given and the one you wish you could take back. Most law enforcement officers in uniform today have war stories about the one thing they wish they hadn't brought up in the oral interview board. And this is to be expected. Nerves and pressure often conspire at the most inappropriate times. To help you be on guard for these moments, let's look at the mysterious wrong and right answers.

### The Wrong Answer

The wrong answer to any question is the answer you think you should say because that's what you've been told the board wants to hear. Do not take well-meant advice from friends or officers who haven't been before an oral board recently. Boards will often overlook answers they don't like if they feel you have good reasons for what you say and if you are being honest with them.

If the board fails you, it will not be because you gave the wrong answer. It will be because you are not the kind of person they are looking for, or there are some things about your life or yourself you need to work on. The board just feels you need some time to work on these matters before they consider you for a job in law enforcement.

### The Right Answer

The answers the board wants to hear are the ones only you can give. They want your opinion, your reasons, your personal experiences, and they want to know what you would do under certain circumstances. No one else matters but you and how you present yourself in the oral interview. If you try to say what you think the board wants to hear, you will almost certainly give them a shallow, unsatisfying response to their question.

## What Do I Say?

It's not so much what you say as how you say it. The best way to answer any question is with directness, honesty, and brevity. Keep your answers short, but give enough information to fully answer the question. The board won't be handing out prizes for conserving words, but they also don't want to have to pull answers out of you just so that they can get enough information.

Avoid skirting the issue when answering questions. For example:

Board Member: "Ms. Abdul, I see you've been arrested once for public intoxication while you were in college? Is that true?"

Abdul: "No, sir."

Board Member: "Really? That's odd. It says here on page seven that you were arrested and spent the night in the city jail."

Abdul: "Yes, well, I wasn't exactly *arrested* because the officer didn't put handcuffs on me."

Don't play word games with the board. You won't win. In this case, the applicant clearly knows that the board is aware of her arrest record, but she's trying to downplay the incident by ducking the question.

You should also elaborate as much as as possible when answering questions so you don't come across as difficult. For example:

Board Member: "Mr. O'Malley, tell the board why you left the job you held at Tread Lightly Tire Shop."

O'Malley: "I was fired."

Board Member: "Why were you fired?"

O'Malley: "Because the boss told me not to come back."

Board Member: "Why did the boss tell you not to come back?"

O'Malley: "Because I was fired."

Board Member: "What happened to cause you to be fired?"

O'Malley: "I was rude."

Board Member: "Rude to whom and under what circumstances?"

You get the picture. This question could have been answered fully when the board member asked O'Malley why he left the tire shop job. The board would prefer that you not rattle on and on when you answer questions, but they would also appreciate a complete answer. An oral board's patience is usually thin with an applicant who uses this answering technique.

Make sure you are answering the question the board is asking you. Try to avoid straying from the topic at hand. For example:

Board Member: "Well, Ms. Goldstein, we know about some of the things you are good at, now tell us something about yourself that you'd like to improve."

Goldstein: "I'm really good with people. People like me and find it easy to talk to me for some reason. I guess it's because I'm such a good listener."

If she is a good listener, Ms. Goldstein didn't demonstrate this quality with her answer. It's important to listen to the question and answer directly. If you duck the question then the board will assume you have something to hide or you are not being honest. If you don't understand how to answer the question, tell the person who asked it what you don't understand. They will be happy to rephrase the question or explain what they want. Be specific and above all, answer the question you are asked, not the one you wish they had asked instead.

## Sample Interview Scenarios

By now, you should have a reasonable idea of what an oral board is looking for and how best to not only survive the experience, but come out ahead on your first oral interview. You've had a lot of material to absorb in this chapter. Read the following scenarios illustrating the wrong way and the right way to tackle an oral interview. As you read, try to put yourself in the shoes of the oral board member who is asking the questions.

### Scenario #1

Marie Garcia is sitting before the St. James Police Department oral interview board. She is wearing a pair of black jeans, loafers without socks, and a short-sleeved cotton blouse. As the questions are being asked, she is tapping her foot against the table and staring at her hands.

Board Member: "Ms. Garcia, can you give the board an example of how you've handled a disagreement with a coworker in the past?"

Garcia: "Nope. I get along with everybody. Everyone likes me."

Board Member: "I see. So, you've never had a disagreement or difference of opinion with anyone you've ever worked with."

Garcia: "That's right."

Board Member: "Well, I see by your application that you were once written up by a supervisor for yelling at a fellow employee. Can you tell us about that situation?"

Garcia: "That's different. It was his fault! He started talking to a customer I was supposed to wait on so I told him off."

Now read the second situation.

## Scenario #2

Marie Garcia is sitting before the Friendly Police Department oral interview board dressed in a gray business suit. She is sitting still with her hands folded in her lap and is looking directly at the person asking her a question.

| | |
|---|---|
| Board Member: | "Ms. Garcia, can you give the board an example of how you've handled a disagreement with a coworker in the past?" |
| Garcia: | "Yes sir. I can think of an example. When I was working at Pools by Polly I had an argument with a coworker over which one of us was supposed to wait on a customer. I lost my cool and yelled at him. My boss wrote me up because of how I handled the situation." |
| Board Member: | "I see. How do you think you should have handled the situation?" |
| Garcia: | "If I had it to do over again, I'd take James, my coworker, aside and talk to him about it in private. If I couldn't work something out with him, I would ask my supervisor to help out." |
| Board Member: | "What have you done to keep this sort of thing from happening again?" |
| Garcia: | "I've learned to stop and think before I speak and I've learned that there is a time and place to work out differences when they come up. I haven't had a problem since that incident." |

So, which scenario makes the better impression? In scenario #1, the applicant is obviously unwilling to accept responsibility for her actions, she isn't showing any evidence that she is mature, and she isn't honest with herself or the board members when she says everyone likes her and she's never had disagreements with coworkers.

On the other hand, in scenario #2, the applicant is able to admit her mistakes and take responsibility for her part in the incident. Although she may have wished she could present herself in a better light, she did illustrate maturity by being honest, open, and straightforward in talking about the disagreement. In scenario #2, the applicant may have had to endure a long, hard interview in order to sell herself, but she was able to articulate what she did to correct a fault.

On the other hand, you can bet she had a very short interview and a "We're not interested, but thanks" from the board in scenario #1. Differences in the applicant's appearances and mannerisms would also affect the board's perception of their levels of professionalism.

These two situations may seem exaggerated, but applicants all over the country are making these same mistakes.

## Medical and Psychological Evaluations

The medical evaluation is not the same as the physical agility test. Physical agility testing measures your ability to perform tasks associated with the police role, while a medical evaluation assesses your medical fitness to perform those tasks. For instance, if you have a heart condition, you might be able to run and jump successfully during the physical agility test, but the medical evaluation would reveal that you might be prone to collapse immediately after performing strenuous activity.

The medical evaluation will measure your height and weight (primarily to ensure they are in a healthy balance); your vision (including a test for colorblindness); and your hearing. You may be tested on a treadmill or other device for cardiovascular-pulmonary health; your blood may also be tested; and you will definitely be tested for drugs in your system. Not all of the evaluations will result in automatic disqualification, but some will. If you are colorblind, show a history of drug use, have a heart condition, or are considerably overweight, you should expect to be disqualified. While some medical decisions can be appealed, failing other parts of the evaluation is considered too serious to permit you to move on in the selection process. If you fail a portion of the medical evaluation that can be rectified in some way (for instance, being overweight), you may be offered a set time period to lose the weight and appear for retest.

The psychological test is another one for which you cannot study. It is generally administered in two parts. The first is a paper-and-pencil test that is similar to any other multiple-choice test. In this one, however, the questions are personal. They ask you about your personal attitudes and to describe yourself in many ways. Answer honestly; the questions are intended to pick up in the scoring whether you have tried to trick the test. Some questions are what you might anticipate—asking if you used drugs, if you get depressed easily, or similar queries—but others may be unexpected for this sort of test. You can be sure that the questions are intended to get at issues you might not recognize. If your score indicates no personality traits that would prevent you from becoming a police officer, you will be scheduled to meet with a psychologist or psychiatrist who will interview you to further determine your adaptability to the police profession. Based on the assessment of the interviewer, your agency will determine whether you will continue on in the application process.

This chapter has taken you through the most common steps in the hiring process. With this knowledge, your task now is to prepare for the written exam with the goal of obtaining a high enough score to become a viable applicant. Taking the practice exams and studying the tips provided in the review chapters will go a long way toward helping you reach your goal.

## Now What?

You have taken all the tests, so what next? Waiting is usually the answer, because the results of the tests may take a while. So might the recommendations from the oral board, the psychologist, and the background investigator.

### Wait Patiently

You may have several weeks, months, or more to practice patience while waiting to find out how you did on your exams. Even if you are tempted, don't pester the department with phone calls, asking if you made it to the eligibility list or how much longer it will be before you find out your results. For one thing, when you call the department, you will most likely be talking to a receptionist who cannot give you that information anyway. For another, even if you did get through to a higher official, you would be making an impression you don't want to make—that of a pest! They can't indulge the concerns of every new applicant who wants to know how he or she did on a test.

However, you don't have to sit around and do nothing while waiting to find out whether you have been selected. In fact, it will work in your best interest if you actively pursue activities that will help to further your new career. Volunteer somewhere in the community. Work hard at your physical fitness training. Learn more about the law. Even if a problem comes up this time around, you can always try again later or at a different department. Decide now to be successful. Get out there and shine!

# Some Final Words of Advice

Dr. Rick Bradstreet is a 20-year veteran psychologist for the Austin Police Department in Austin, Texas. He holds a law degree from Stanford University and a PhD in counseling psychology from the University of Texas at Austin. His specialty is communication skills and conflict resolution. Throughout his career with APD, Dr. Bradstreet estimates that he's sat on about 250 to 300 oral interview boards and has had plenty of opportunity to observe applicants in oral interviews. He offers the following advice to those who see an oral board in their future.

- Make eye contact. Applicants who fail to make eye contact with interviewers can expect a negative reaction from the board. Making eye contact makes the speaker feel like what he or she is saying is being heard and is being taken seriously.

- Sit erect in your chair, but not too stiff. You should not have the same posture that you would have if you were sitting at home in your living room, yet you want to appear somewhat relaxed and alert.

- Keep your hands in your lap if you have a tendency to wring your hands together when agitated. Wringing hands are generally perceived as signs of nervousness.

- Try not to drum your fingers on the table. Although this behavior is most often interpreted more as a sign of someone who has excess energy and is not necessarily seen as nervous behavior, it can be distracting to those around you.

- Feel free to shift positions periodically. It's perfectly natural to move around as you speak and is expected during normal conversation. An oral board is not meant to be an interrogation, so you are not expected to sit frozen in place for the duration.

- Speak up. If a board member lets you know you are mumbling, then project your voice. Speaking in a voice so soft that no one can hear you does nothing to enhance the image you want to project—that of a self-confident, take-charge person who knows what you want.

- Focus on explaining how you are as a person; do not respond to questions defensively. Once again, this is not an interrogation. Try to have a normal, respectful conversation with the board members and your body language will take on a more natural, confident look.

- Get out of the self-conscious mode. Your goal is to let the board see you and your experiences as unique. Do not try to mold your experiences and answers to questions according to what you think the board may want.

- Read over your application and any other written material you have submitted to the department to refresh your memory of events in your past that you described. You may be asked a number of questions about each event, so be prepared ahead of time.
- Be confident when you walk into the room, and greet the psychologist with a firm handshake.
- Focus on answering each question clearly, but try not to draw out your answers into lengthy stories. You want to answer the questions, but not supply unrelated additional information.
- Try not to get defensive if the psychologist seems to be getting too personal. Just be honest and remember that he or she is just doing his or her job.

## If You Get Bad News

The selection process for police officers is a rigorous one. If you fail one or more of the steps, take time for some serious self-evaluation. The good news is that many police officers on the job today initially failed one or more portions of the test. However, the reason they are on the job is because they, like you, learned from their experience, practiced many of the techniques and tactics in this book, and went on to become police officers.

**If you fail the written test**, look at the reasons you didn't do well. Was it just that the format was unfamiliar? Well, now you know what to expect.

Do you need to brush up on some of the skills tested? There are lots of books out there to help with reading, writing, and mathematics. Enlist a teacher or a friend to help you, or check out the basic reading and writing courses offered by local high schools and community colleges.

Many cities allow you to retest after a waiting period—a period you can use to improve your skills. If the exam isn't being offered again for years, consider trying another police department.

**If you fail the physical agility test**, your course of action is clear. Increase your daily physical exercise until you know you can do what is required, and then retest or try another police department.

**If you fail the oral board**, try to determine what the problem was. This could be a little trickier to figure out, since you probably won't be told specifics about what exactly the problem was. However, going back over the interview in your mind should provide some clues. How did you feel during the interview? Did you have a hard time expressing yourself? Were you fidgety or inattentive? Were there moments when you lost your temper or found yourself answering questions in a defensive manner?

Practice improving your communication skills. Take a course or read books about effective communication. Talk to other police officers and find out what kinds of answers they gave during their interviews. Go online and visit discussion boards where others are talking about their own oral board interview experiences. Take a look at your opinions and beliefs about the law and the use of force. Are you overly eager to respond aggressively to chaotic situations? Police department officials are looking for candidates with cool heads and sound judgment. They don't want a loose cannon among their new recruits.

**If the medical exam eliminates you**, you will usually be notified as to what condition caused the problem. Is the condition one that can be corrected? See your doctor for advice. A few minor conditions can eliminate you in one department but be acceptable in another. Contact the recruiting officer at a nearby police department to see if you can apply there.

**If you don't make the list and aren't told why**, the problem might have been the oral board or, more likely, the psychological evaluation or the background investigation. Did past drug use eliminate you? Different jurisdictions have different criteria when judging the past drug use of an applicant. Some have a zero tolerance policy where they don't allow applicants to have had any previous drug use whatsoever. However, most jurisdictions are more lenient about past drug use and will put a time constraint on their policy, such as no drug use in the past three to five years. Other departments have a rule that says you may have used drugs as a juvenile but not as an adult. If past drug use turns out to be a problem for you in the police department you are applying to, it may not be in another jurisdiction. However, if you have had a consistent pattern of drug or alcohol abuse, especially if it is recent, you will most likely have a problem wherever you apply.

If the problem isn't drug use, can you think of anything else in your past that might lead to questions about your fitness to be a police officer? Could any of your personal traits or attitudes raise such questions? Get the opinions of others you know, especially those who are not emotionally connected to you, such as a former teacher or employer. Ask them if there is anything they can think of that might work against you in a psychological evaluation. Encourage them to be honest, and explain why you wish to know.

And then the hard question: Is there anything you can do to change these aspects of your past or your personality? If so, you might have a chance when you reapply or apply to another police department. If not, it may be time to think about another field.

If you feel you were wrongly excluded, most departments have appeals procedures if the rejection was on the basis of a psychological evaluation or background check. However, that word *wrongly* is very important. The psychologist or background investigator almost certainly had to supply a rationale in recommending that the department not hire you. Do you have solid factual evidence that you can use in an administrative hearing to counter such a rationale? If not, you would be wasting your time and money, as well as the police department's, by making an appeal. Move carefully and get legal advice before you take such a step.

## Still Waiting?

If you make the eligibility list, go through the waiting game, and still aren't selected, don't despair. Think through all the steps of the selection process, and use them to do a critical self-evaluation.

Maybe your written, physical, and oral board scores were high enough to pass but not high enough to put you near the top of the list. At the next testing, make sure you are better prepared so you can achieve higher scores.

Maybe you had an excellent score that should have put you at the top of the list, and you suspect that you were passed over for someone lower down on the list. That means someone less qualified was selected while you were not, right? Maybe, maybe not.

There were probably a lot of people on the list, and a lot of them may have scored high too. One more point on the written test might have made the difference, or maybe the department had the freedom to pick and choose on the basis of other qualifications. Maybe, in comparison with you, a lot of people on the list had more education or job-related experience. Maybe there was a special need for people with particular skills, like proficiency in Spanish or Cantonese or training in photography. Or maybe the department is focusing on recruiting a specific group or gender to which you don't belong.

What can you do? You may have heard or read about lawsuits being brought against law enforcement agencies about their selection processes, particularly in large cities. That's a last resort, a step you would take only after getting excellent legal advice and thinking through the costs of time, money, and energy. You would also have to think about whether you would want to occupy a position you got as the result of a lawsuit, and whether you would be hurting your chances of being hired somewhere else.

If you are not selected for the exact position you applied for, in the area you wanted to be hired in, this does not mean you should give up altogether. Most people are better off simply trying again. And don't limit your options. There are lots of police departments all over the country, and there are other careers available in law enforcement as well. Do your research. Find out what's available. Find out who's hiring. Consider applying to smaller agencies in small towns or rural agencies, to sheriff's departments, to the state police, or a federal agency. Being turned down by one police department need not be the end of your law enforcement career.

## When You Are Selected

Congratulations! The end of the waiting game for you is notification that you have been selected. What happens next, in most cases, is that you'll go to the police academy. Then you are on your way to a career in law enforcement.

In most jurisdictions, you will be hired as a police recruit. You will be paid to go to the academy, usually at a lower rate than you will make when you actually become a member of the force. Academies typically run between 12–30 weeks and include physical and firearms training as well as courses in the laws you will be expected to enforce and in police techniques and procedures. In many jurisdictions, the academy is followed by a period of field training in the jurisdiction that hired you.

After your field training is complete, many states require you to pass a certification exam. This exam is usually based on the same curriculum you studied at the academy, so you should know exactly what to expect. The exam is tough, but the department has already invested a lot of time and money in you and will be sure to prepare you sufficiently beforehand. They want you to succeed!

Once the certification exam is passed, you have passed the finish line. Your hard work and dedication have paid off, and you can stand tall and proud at your swearing-in ceremony, in full dress uniform, as you vow to protect the lives and property of the citizens of your community.

# 3 ▶ THE POLICE OFFICER SUITABILITY TEST

## CHAPTER SUMMARY
The desire to be a police officer is one thing; being suited for it is something else. This chapter provides you with a quiz to help you decide whether you and policing are a good match.

**B**y now you know that becoming a police officer takes study, effort, and time. You may also have realized for the first time that the process may involve years of your life. This does not mean you will be busy every day being a police applicant, but it does mean that the time you first apply to take a police exam until you are hired by a police department may span anywhere from a few months to a few years. If you have read this far, you probably are willing to put forth the effort required to do well on the exam and wait for this rewarding career.

It might still be a wise idea to get a better idea of whether you and a police career are a good fit. To do this, take the following Police Officer Suitability Test. This is another tool in your arsenal to help you decide whether you want to invest the effort and time it will take you to pursue a career in policing. While it might appear to be the career of your dreams, possibly the job is not really for you. Maybe something else would better fit your personality and your abilities. It is better to find this out sooner rather than later.

Remember that there is no such thing as a police personality—there is not only one type of person who makes a good police officer. Despite that, it is equally true that there are some people who are not the best fit with the job. Cops are not all alike; just like some are men and some are women, some are short and some are tall, their personalities can be as different as their demographics and their sizes.

Despite all the possible differences, there do seem to be some abilities and personalities that fit policing better than others and that seem to predict who will be successful and satisfied in this varied career. Remember that these personality traits are not related to your intelligence or dedication; they are more likely to indicate more about what you like to do and how you interact with the world around you.

These *suitability factors* were developed from the large body of research about police and from discussions with police psychologists and applicant screeners across the country. The factors fall into five groupings; each has ten questions spaced throughout the test.

The LearningExpress Police Officer Suitability Test is not a formal psychological test. For one thing, it is not nearly long enough. The Minnesota Multiphasic Personality Inventory (MMPI) test used in most psychological assessments has 11 times more items than you will find in this test. For another, it does not focus on your general mental health.

You should view this test as an informal guide to help you decide whether being a police officer is a job you would enjoy and that would suit you. If it turns out you decide against pursuing a career in law enforcement, this test may provide you with the chance to understand yourself better and to lead you to a career that is more in keeping with your personality. Either way, you have gained self-knowledge.

## The Police Officer Suitability Test

### Directions

You will need about 20 minutes to answer the following 50 questions. It's a good idea to answer all of the questions in one sitting—scoring and interpretation can be done later. For each question, consider how often the attitude or behavior applies to you. You have a choice between Never, Rarely, Sometimes, Often, and Always; write the number for your answer in the space after each question. To score your answers, see the table below. How the numbers add up will be explained later. If you try to outsmart the test or figure out the "right" answers, you won't get an accurate picture at the end. So just be honest.

Don't read the scoring sections before you answer the questions, or you will defeat the whole purpose of the exercise!

**How often do the following statements sound like you? Choose only one answer for each statement.**

| NEVER | RARELY | SOMETIMES | OFTEN | ALWAYS |
|-------|--------|-----------|-------|--------|
| 0 | 5 | 10 | 20 | 40 |

1. I like to know what's expected of me. _____

2. I am willing to admit my mistakes to other people. _____

3. Once I've made a decision, I stop thinking about it. _____

4. I can shrug off my fears about getting physically injured. _____

5. I like to know what to expect. _____

6. It takes a lot to get me really angry. _____

7. My first impressions of people tend to be accurate. _____

8. I am aware of my stress level. _____

9. I like to tell other people what to do. _____

**10.** I enjoy working with others. _____

**11.** I trust my instincts. _____

**12.** I enjoy being teased. _____

**13.** I will spend as much time as it takes to settle a disagreement. _____

**14.** I feel comfortable in new social situations. _____

**15.** When I disagree with a person, I let that person know about it. _____

**16.** I'm in a good mood. _____

**17.** I'm comfortable making quick decisions when necessary. _____

**18.** Rules must be obeyed, even if you don't agree with them. _____

**19.** I like to say exactly what I mean. _____

**20.** I enjoy being with people. _____

**21.** I stay away from doing exciting things that I know are dangerous. _____

**22.** I don't mind when a supervisor tells me what to do. _____

**23.** I enjoy solving puzzles. _____

**24.** The people I know consult me about their problems. _____

**25.** I am comfortable making my own decisions. _____

**26.** People know where I stand on things. _____

**27.** When I get stressed, I know how to make myself relax. _____

**28.** I have confidence in my own judgment. _____

**29.** I make my friends laugh. _____

**30.** When I make a promise, I keep it. _____

**31.** When I'm in a group, I tend to be the leader. _____

**32.** I can deal with sudden changes in my routine. _____

**33.** When I get into a fight, I can stop myself from losing control. _____

**34.** I am open to new facts that might change my mind. _____

**35.** I understand why I do the things I do. _____

**36.** I'm good at calming people down. _____

**37.** I can tell how a person is feeling even when he or she doesn't say anything. _____

**38.** I can take criticism without getting upset. _____

**39.** People follow my advice. _____

**40.** I pay attention to people's body language. _____

**41.** It's important for me to make a good impression. _____

**42.** I remember to show up on time. _____

**43.** When I meet new people, I try to understand them. _____

**44.** I avoid doing things on impulse. _____

**45.** Being respected is important to me. _____

**46.** People see me as a calm person. _____

**47.** It's more important for me to do a good job than to get praised for it. _____

**48.** I make my decisions based on common sense. _____

**49.** I prefer to keep my feelings to myself when I'm with strangers. _____

**50.** I take responsibility for my own actions rather than blaming others. _____

# Scoring

Attitudes and behaviors can't be measured in units, like distance or weight. Besides, psychological categories tend to overlap. As a result, the numbers and dividing lines between score ranges are approximate, and numbers may vary about 20 points either way. If your score doesn't fall in the optimal range, it doesn't mean a failure—only that an area needs more focus.

It may help to share your test results with some of the people who are close to you. Very often, there are differences between how we see ourselves and how we actually come across to others.

## Group 1—Risk Questions

**Add up scores for questions 4, 6, 12, 15, 21, 27, 33, 38, 44, and 46.**

**TOTAL = _____**

This group of questions evaluates your tendency to be assertive and take risks. The ideal is in the middle, somewhere between timid and reckless: You should be willing to take risks, but not seek them out just for excitement. Being nervous, impulsive, or afraid of physical injury is an undesirable trait for a police officer. This group also reflects how well you take teasing and criticism, both of which you may encounter every day as a police officer. And as you can imagine, it's also important for someone who carries a gun not to have a short fuse.

- A score between 360 and 400 is rather extreme, suggesting a short temper that could be dangerous in the field.
- If you score between 170 and 360, you are on the right track.
- If you score between 80 and 170, you may want to think about how comfortable you are with the idea of confrontation.

- A score between 0 and 80 indicates that the more dangerous and stressful aspects of the job might be difficult for you.

## Group 2—Core Character Traits

**Add up scores for questions 2, 8, 16, 19, 26, 30, 35, 42, 47, and 50.**

**TOTAL = _____**

This group reflects such basic traits as stability, reliability, and self-awareness. Can your fellow officers count on you to back them up and do your part? Are you secure enough to do your job without needing praise? In the words of one police psychologist, "If you're hungry for praise, you will starve to death." The public will not always appreciate your efforts, and your supervisors and colleagues may be too busy or preoccupied to pat you on the back.

It is crucial to be able to admit your mistakes and take responsibility for your actions, to be confident without being arrogant or conceited, and to be straightforward and direct in your communication. In a job where lives are at stake, the facts must be clear. Having control of your moods is also very important. While we all have good and bad days, someone who is depressed much of the time is not encouraged to pursue police work; depression affects one's judgment, energy level, and the ability to respond and communicate.

- If you score between 180 and 360, you are in the ballpark. A score of over 360 may indicate that your answers were unrealistic.
- A score of 100–180 indicates that you should look at the questions again and evaluate your style of social interaction.
- Scores between 0 and 100 suggest you may not be ready for this job yet.

## Group 3—Judgment Questions

**Add up scores for questions 3, 7, 11, 17, 23, 28, 37, 40, 43, and 48.**

**TOTAL =** _____

This group of questions evaluates how you make decisions. Successful police officers are sensitive to unspoken messages, can detect and respond to other people's feelings, and are able to make fair and accurate assessments of a situation, rather than being influenced by their own personal biases and needs. Once the decision to act is made, second-guessing can be dangerous. Police officers must make their best judgments in line with accepted practices, and then act upon these judgments without hesitancy or self-doubt. Finally, it's important to know and accept that you cannot change the world single-handedly. People who seek this career because they want to make a dramatic individual difference in human suffering are likely to be frustrated and disappointed.

- A score over 360 indicates you may be trying too hard.
- If you scored between 170 and 360, your style of making decisions, especially about people, fits with the desired police officer profile.
- Scores between 80 and 170 suggest that you think about how you make judgments and how much confidence you have in them.
- If you scored between 80 and 170, making judgments may be a problem area for you.

## Group 4—Authority/Leadership Questions

**Add scores for questions 1, 10, 13, 18, 22, 25, 31, 34, 39, and 45.**

**TOTAL =** _____

This group assesses the essential attributes of respect for rules and authority—including the personal authority of self-reliance and leadership—and the ability to resolve conflict and work with a team. Once again, a good balance is the key. Police officers must accept and communicate the value of structure and control without being rigid. And even though most decisions are made independently in the field, the authority of the supervisor and the law must be obeyed at all times. Anyone on a personal mission for justice or vengeance will not make a good police officer and is unlikely to make it through the screening process.

- A score between 160 and 360 indicates you have the desired attitude toward authority—both your own and that of your superior officers. Any higher may indicate that you were trying too hard to give the "right" answers.
- If you scored between 100 and 160, you might think about whether a demanding leadership role is something you want every day.
- With scores between 0 and 100, ask yourself whether the required combination of structure and independence would be comfortable for you.

## Group 5—Personal Style Attributes

**Add up scores for questions 5, 9, 14, 20, 24, 29, 32, 36, 41, and 49.**

**TOTAL = \_\_\_\_**

This is the personal style dimension, which describes how you come across to others. Moderation rules here as well: Police officers should be seen as strong and capable, but not dramatic or heavy-handed; friendly, but not overly concerned with whether they are liked; patient, but not to the point of losing control of a situation. A good sense of humor is essential, not only in the field, but also among one's fellow officers. Flexibility is another valuable trait—especially given all the changes that can happen in one shift—but too much flexibility can be perceived as weakness.

- A score between 160 and 360 is optimal. If you scored over 360, you may be trying too hard.
- Scores between 80 and 160 suggest that you compare your style with the preceding description and consider whether anything needs to be modified.
- If you scored between 0 and 80, you might think about the way you interact with others and whether you would be happy in a job where people are the main focus.

## Summary

The Police Officer Suitability Test reflects the fact that being a successful police officer requires moderation rather than extremes. Attitudes that are desirable in reasonable amounts can become a real problem if they are too strong. For example, independence is a necessary trait, but too much of it could result in an officer taking the law into his or her own hands. Going outside accepted police procedure is a bad idea; worse, it can put other people's lives in jeopardy.

As one recruiter said, the ideal police officer is "low key and low maintenance." In fact, there's only one thing you can't have too much of, and that's common sense. With everything else, balance is the key. Keep this in mind as you look at your scores.

# 4 ▶ THE LEARNINGEXPRESS TEST PREPARATION SYSTEM

### CHAPTER SUMMARY

Taking the police officer written exam can be tough. It demands a lot of preparation if you want to achieve a top score. Your rank on the eligibility list may be determined largely by this score. The LearningExpress Test Preparation System, developed by leading test experts, gives you the discipline and attitude you need to be a winner.

This chapter can help you take control of the entire test preparation process. It clearly explains the steps you need to take to achieve a top score on the written exam. Do not underestimate the importance of doing well on the written exam: Your future career in law enforcement depends on it. This chapter will help you to

- become familiar with the format of the exam.
- overcome excessive test anxiety.
- prepare gradually for the exam instead of cramming.
- understand and use vital test-taking skills.
- know how to pace yourself through the exam.
- learn how to use the process of elimination.
- know when and how to guess.
- be in tip-top mental and physical shape on the day of the exam.

The purpose of this chapter is to ensure that you are in control of the test-prep process. You do not want the exam to control you.

The LearningExpress Test Preparation System puts you in control. In just nine easy-to-follow steps, you will learn everything you need to know to make sure that you are in charge of your preparation and your performance on the exam. Other test takers may let the test get the better of them; other test takers may be unprepared or out of shape, but not you. You will have taken all the steps you need to take to get a high score on the police exam.

Here's how the LearningExpress Test Preparation System works: Nine easy steps lead you through everything you need to know and do to get ready to master your exam. The time listed next to each of the steps includes both reading about the step and one or more activities. It's important that you do the activities along with the reading, or you won't be getting the full benefit of the system. Each step tells you approximately how much time that step will take you to complete.

We estimate that working through the entire system will take you approximately three hours, though it's perfectly okay if you work faster or slower than the time estimates assume. If you can take a whole afternoon or evening, you can work through the whole LearningExpress Test Preparation System in one sitting. Otherwise, you can break it up, and do just one or two steps a day for the next several days. It's up to you—remember, you are in control.

| Nine Steps to Success | Time |
| --- | --- |
| Step 1. Get Information | 30 minutes |
| Step 2. Conquer Test Anxiety | 20 minutes |
| Step 3. Make a Plan | 50 minutes |
| Step 4. Learn to Manage Your Time | 10 minutes |
| Step 5. Learn to Use the Process of Elimination | 20 minutes |
| Step 6. Know When to Guess | 20 minutes |
| Step 7. Reach Your Peak Performance Zone | 10 minutes |
| Step 8. Get Your Act Together | 10 minutes |
| Step 9. Do It! | 10 minutes |
| **Total** | **3 hours** |

## Step 1: Get Information

**Time to complete: 30 minutes**
**Activities: Read Chapter 2, "How Police Officers Are Selected"**

Knowledge is power. The first step in the LearningExpress Test Preparation System is finding out everything you can about your police officer written exam. If you have access to the Internet, you can perform a search on any basic search engine to find out if the police department you want to apply to has a website. Or you can check out a site that contains a long list of links to police departments around the country: www.policeone.com/careers. If you find that your targeted police department has a website, review it carefully to see if it contains any information about the written exam. If not, contact the police department you want to apply to and ask for the personnel office. In larger cities, you will be referred to a recruiting unit or to the human resources department. In smaller towns, you may speak to someone right there in the department. Request a position announcement, find out if an exam bulletin is available, and ask when the next written exam is scheduled. If the department issues an exam bulletin, then you'll get a brief outline of what skills will be tested on the written exam.

### What You Should Find Out

The more details you can find out about the written exam, either from the bulletin online or from speaking with a recruiter, the more efficiently you'll be able to study. Here's a list of some things you might want to find out about your exam:

- What skills are tested?
- How many sections are on the exam?
- How many questions does each section have?
- Are the questions ordered from easy to hard, or is the sequence random?

- How much time is allotted for each section?
- Are there breaks in between sections?
- What is the passing score and how many questions do you have to answer correctly in order to get that score?
- Does a higher score give you any advantages, like a better rank on the eligibility list?
- How is the test scored: Is there a penalty for incorrect answers?
- Are you permitted to go back to a prior section or move on to the next section if you finish early?
- Can you write in the test booklet or will you be given scratch paper?
- What should you bring with you on exam day?

### What's on Most Police Officer Exams

The skills that the police officer written exam tests vary from city to city. That's why it's important to contact the recruiting office of your police department to find out exactly what skills are covered. Below are the most commonly tested subjects:

- reading comprehension
- grammar
- vocabulary and spelling
- math
- judgment
- map reading
- memory and observation
- number and letter recall
- personal background

If you haven't already done so, stop here and read Chapter 2 of this book, which gives you an overview of the entire police officer selection process. Then move on to the next step to find out how you can get a handle on test anxiety.

## Step 2: Conquer Test Anxiety

**Time to complete: 20 minutes**
**Activity: Take the Test Stress Test**

Having as much information as possible about the exam is the first step in getting control of the exam. Next, you have to overcome one of the biggest obstacles to test success: test anxiety. Test anxiety cannot only impair your performance on the exam itself, but it can even keep you from preparing! In Step 2, you'll learn stress management techniques that will help you succeed on your exam. Learn these strategies now, and practice them as you work through the exams in this book, so they will be second nature to you by exam day.

### Combating Test Anxiety

The first thing you need to know is that a little test anxiety is a good thing. Everyone gets nervous before a big exam—and if that nervousness motivates you to prepare thoroughly, so much the better. It's said that Sir Laurence Olivier, one of the foremost British actors of the twentieth century, was ill before every performance. His stage fright didn't impair his performance; in fact, it probably gave him a little extra edge—just the kind of edge you need to do well, whether on a stage or in an examination room.

### Stress Management before the Test

Stress is the difference between your capabilities and the environment. The more prepared you are to handle the examination, the greater your capabilities and the less stress you feel. Preparation for the written exam, oral board, and physical agility test is the only surefire way to increase your score and reduce stress-related anxiety.

If you feel your level of anxiety rising in the weeks before your test, here is what you can do to bring the level down again:

- **Get prepared.** There's nothing like knowing what to expect and being prepared for it to put you in control of test anxiety. That's why you are reading this book. Use it faithfully, and remind yourself that you are better prepared than most of the people who will be taking the test.
- **Practice self-confidence.** A positive attitude is a great way to combat test anxiety. This is no time to be humble or shy. Stand in front of the mirror and say to your reflection, "I'm prepared. I'm full of self-confidence. I'm going to ace this test. I know I can do it." If you hear it often enough, you will believe it.
- **Fight negative messages.** Every time someone starts telling you how hard the exam is or how it's almost impossible to get a high score, fight back by telling them your self-confidence messages above. If the someone with the negative messages is you, telling yourself *you don't do well on exams, you just can't do this*, don't listen. Listen to your self-confidence messages instead.
- **Visualize.** Imagine yourself reporting for duty on your first day of police academy training. Think of yourself wearing your uniform with pride and learning the skills you will use for the rest of your life. Visualizing success can help make it happen—and it reminds you of why you are doing all this work in preparing for the exam.
- **Exercise.** Physical activity helps calm your body down and focus your mind. Being in good physical shape can actually help you do well on the exam, as well as prepare you for the physical agility test. So, go for a run, lift weights, go swimming—and do it regularly.

### Stress Management on Test Day

There are several ways you can bring down your level of test anxiety on test day. They will work best if you practice them in the weeks before the test, so you know which ones work best for you.

# Test Stress Test

You need to worry about test anxiety only if it is extreme enough to impair your performance. The following questionnaire will provide a diagnosis of your level of test anxiety. In the blank before each statement, write the number that most accurately describes your experience.

0 = Never  1 = Once or twice  2 = Sometimes  3 = Often

___ I have gotten so nervous before an exam that I simply put down the books and didn't study for it.

___ I have experienced disabling physical symptoms such as vomiting and severe headaches because I was nervous about an exam.

___ I have simply not showed up for an exam because I was scared to take it.

___ I have experienced dizziness and disorientation while taking an exam.

___ I have had trouble filling in the little circles because my hands were shaking too hard.

___ I have failed an exam because I was too nervous to complete it.

___ **Total: Add up the numbers in the blanks above.**

## Your Test Stress Score

Here are the steps you should take, depending on your score. If you scored

- **below 3,** your level of test anxiety is nothing to worry about; it is probably just enough to give you that little extra edge.
- **between 3 and 6,** your test anxiety may be enough to impair your performance, and you should practice the stress management techniques listed in this section to try to bring your test anxiety down to manageable levels.
- **above 6,** your level of test anxiety is a serious concern. In addition to practicing the stress management techniques listed in this section, you may want to seek additional, personal help. Call your local high school or community college and ask for the academic counselor. Tell the counselor that you have a level of test anxiety that sometimes keeps you from being able to take an exam. The counselor may be willing to help you or may suggest someone else you should talk to.

- **Deep breathing.** Take a deep breath while you count to five. Hold it for a count of one, then let it out on a count of five. Repeat several times.
- **Move your body.** Try rolling your head in a circle. Rotate your shoulders. Shake your hands from the wrist. Many people find these movements very relaxing.
- **Visualize again.** Think of the place where you are most relaxed: lying on the beach in the sun, walking through the park, or wherever is most comforting to you. Now close your eyes and imagine you are actually there. If you practice in advance, you'll find that you need only a few seconds of this exercise to experience a significant increase in your sense of well-being.

When anxiety threatens to overwhelm you right there during the exam, there are still things you can do to manage the stress level:

- **Repeat your self-confidence messages.** You should have them memorized by now. Say them silently to yourself, and believe them!
- **Visualize one more time.** This time, visualize yourself moving smoothly and quickly through the test, answering every question right and finishing just before time is up. Like most visualization techniques, this one works best if you have practiced it ahead of time.
- **Find an easy question.** Skim over the test until you find an easy question, and answer it. Getting even one circle filled in can get you into the test-taking groove.
- **Take a mental break.** Everyone loses concentration once in a while during a long test. It's normal, so you shouldn't worry about it. Instead, accept what has happened. Say to yourself, "Hey, I lost it there for a minute. My brain is taking a break." Put down your pencil, close your eyes, and do some deep breathing for a few seconds. Then you'll be ready to go back to work.

Answer the questions on the Test Stress Test to learn more about your level of test anxiety.

## Step 3: Make a Plan

**Time to complete: 50 minutes**
**Activity: Construct a study plan**

One of the most important things you can do to get control of yourself and your exam is to make a study plan. Too many people fail to prepare simply because they fail to plan. Spending hours the day before the exam poring over sample test questions not only raises your level of test anxiety, but it also is simply no substitute for careful preparation and practice over time.

| Police Officer Exams | Study Chapters |
|---|---|
| Exam 1, Chapter 5<br>Exam 4, Chapter 11<br>*These exams test your basic reading and writing skills.* | 7. Reading Text, Tables, Charts, and Graphs<br>8. Grammar<br>9. Vocabulary and Spelling |
| Exam 2, Chapter 6<br>Exam 5, Chapter 12<br>*These exams test job-related skills, such as memory and observation.* | 7. Reading Text, Tables, Charts, and Graphs<br>10. Math<br>11. Judgment<br>12. Map Reading<br>13. Memory and Observation |
| Exam 3, Chapter 7<br>Exam 6, Chapter 13<br>*These exams are similar to the Law Enforcement Candidate Record (LECR) exam.* | 9. Vocabulary and Spelling<br>14. Number and Letter Recall<br>15. Personal Background |

Don't fall into the cram trap. Take control of your preparation time by mapping out a study schedule. There are four sample schedules on the following pages, based on the amount of time you have before the exam. If you are the kind of person who needs deadlines and assignments to motivate you for a project, here they are. If you are the kind of person who doesn't like to follow other people's plans, you can use the suggested schedules here to construct your own.

An important aspect of a study plan is flexibility. Your plan should help you, not hinder you, so be prepared to alter your study schedule once you get started, if necessary. You will probably find that one or more steps will take longer to complete than you had anticipated, while others will go more quickly.

In constructing your study plan, you should take into account how much work you need to do. If your score on the first practice test wasn't what you had hoped, consider taking some of the steps from Schedule A and fitting them into Schedule D, even if you have only three weeks before the exam.

You can also customize your study plan according to the information you gathered in Step 1. If the exam you have to take doesn't include memory questions, for instance, you can skip that section of Chapter 10 and concentrate instead on some other area that *is* covered. The table on page 70 lists all the chapters you need to study for each exam.

Even more important than making a plan is making a commitment. You can't improve your skills in reading, writing, and judgment overnight. You have to set aside some time every day for study and practice. Try for at least 20 minutes a day. Twenty minutes daily will do you much more good than two hours on Saturday.

If you have months before the exam, you are lucky. Don't put off your study until the week before the exam! Start now. Even ten minutes a day, with half an hour or more on weekends, can make a big difference in your score—and in your chances of making the force!

## Schedule A: The Leisure Plan

If no test has been announced yet in your city, you may have a year or more in which to get ready. This schedule gives you six months to sharpen your skills. If an exam is announced in the middle of your preparation, you can use one of the later schedules to help you compress your study program. Study only the chapters that are relevant to the type of exam you will be taking.

| Time | Preparation |
|---|---|
| 6 months before the test | Take one of the exams from Chapters 3, 4, 5. Then study the explanations for the answers until you know you could answer all the questions right. Start going to the library once every two weeks to read books or magazines about law enforcement, or browse through police-related websites. |
| 5 months before the test | Read Chapter 8 and work through the exercises. Use at least one of the additional resources listed in the chapter. If possible, find other people who are preparing for the test and form a study group. |
| 4 months before the test | Read Chapter 9 and work through the exercises. Use at least one of the additional resources for the chapter. Start making flash cards of vocabulary and spelling words. |
| 3 months before the test | Read Chapter 10 and work through the exercises. Practice your math by making up problems from everyday events. Exercise your memory by making note of people and places you see each day. Continue to read and work with your flash cards. |
| 6 weeks before the test | Take one of the sample tests in Chapters 11, 12, or 13. Use your score to help you decide where to concentrate your efforts. Go back to the relevant chapters and use the extra resources listed there, or get the help of a friend or teacher. |
| 1 week before the test | Review both of the sample tests you took. See how much you've learned in the past months. Concentrate on what you have done well and resolve not to let any areas where you still feel uncertain bother you. |
| 1 day before the test | Relax. Do something unrelated to police exams. Eat a good meal and go to bed at your usual time. |

# Schedule B: The Just-Enough-Time Plan

If you have three to six months before your exam, that should be enough time to prepare for the written test, especially if you score above 70% on the first sample test you take. This schedule assumes four months; stretch it out or compress it if you have more or less time, and study only the chapters that are relevant to the type of exam you will be taking.

| Time | Preparation |
|---|---|
| 4 months before the test | Take one practice exam from Chapters 3, 4, or 5 to determine where you need the most work. Read Chapter 7 and work through the exercises. Use at least one of the additional resources listed in the chapter. Start going to the library once every two weeks to read books about law enforcement, or visit police-related websites online. Also, make flash cards of vocabulary and spelling words. |
| 3 months before the test | Read Chapter 8 and work through the exercises. Use at least one of the additional resources for each chapter. Continue to read and work with your flash cards. |
| 2 months before the test | Read Chapter 9 and work through the exercises. Exercise your memory by making note of people and places you see each day. Practice your math by making up problems from everyday events. |
| 1 month before the test | Take one of the sample tests in Chapters 11, 12, or 13. Use your score to help you decide where to concentrate your efforts. Go back to the relevant chapters and use the extra resources listed there, or get the help of a friend or teacher. |
| 1 week before the test | Review both of the sample tests you took. See how much you have learned in the past months. Concentrate on what you have done well, and resolve not to let any areas where you still feel uncertain bother you. |
| 1 day before the test | Relax. Do something unrelated to police exams. Eat a good meal and go to bed at your usual time. |

# Schedule C: More Study in Less Time

If you have one to three months before the exam, you still have enough time for some concentrated study that will help you improve your score. This schedule is built around a two-month time frame. If you have only one month, spend an extra couple of hours a week to get all these steps in. If you have three months, take some of the steps from Schedule B and fit them in. Study only the chapters that are relevant to the type of exam you will be taking.

| Time | Preparation |
|------|-------------|
| 8 weeks before the test | Take one sample test from Chapters 3, 4, or 5 to find your weakest subjects. Choose the appropriate section(s) from among Chapters 8–10 to read in these two weeks. When you get to those chapters in this plan, review them. |
| 6 weeks before the test | Read Chapter 7 and work through the exercises. |
| 5 weeks before the test | Read Chapter 8 and work through the exercises. |
| 4 weeks before the test | Read Chapter 9 and work through the exercises. |
| 2 weeks before the test | Take one of the second sample tests in Chapters 11, 12, or 13. Then score it and read the answer explanations until you are sure you understand them. Review the areas where your score is lowest. |
| 1 week before the test | Review Chapters 8–10, concentrating on the areas where a little work can help the most. |
| 1 day before the test | Relax. Do something unrelated to police exams. Eat a good meal and go to bed at your usual time. |

# Schedule D: The Fast Track

If you have three weeks or less before the exam, you really have your work cut out for you. Carve half an hour out of your day, *every day*, for study. This schedule assumes you have the whole three weeks to prepare in; if you have less time, you'll have to compress the schedule accordingly. Study only the chapters that are relevant to the type of exam you will be taking.

| Time | Preparation |
| --- | --- |
| 3 weeks before the test | Take one practice exam from Chapters 3, 4, or 5. Then read the material in Chapters 8–9 and work through the exercises. |
| 2 weeks before the test | Read the material in Chapter 10 and work through the exercises. Take one of the sample tests in Chapter 11, 12, or 13. |
| 1 week before the test | Evaluate your performance on the second sample test. Review the parts of Chapters 8–10 where you had the most trouble. Get a friend or teacher to help you with the section you found to be the most difficult. |
| 2 days before the test | Review both of the sample tests you took. Make sure you understand all of the answer explanations. |
| 1 day before the test | Relax. Do something unrelated to police exams. Eat a good meal and go to bed at your usual time. |

## Step 4: Learn to Manage Your Time

**Time to complete: 10 minutes to read, many hours of practice!**

**Activities: Practice these strategies as you take the sample tests in this book**

Steps 4, 5, and 6 of the LearningExpress Test Preparation System put you in charge of your exam by showing you test-taking strategies that work. Practice these strategies as you take the sample tests in this book, and then you will be ready to use them on test day.

First, you will take control of your time on the exam. The first step in achieving this control is to find out the format of the exam you're going to take. Some police exams have different sections that are each timed separately. If this is true of the exam you'll be taking, you'll want to practice using your time wisely on the practice exams and trying to avoid mistakes while working quickly. Other types of exams don't have separately timed sections. If this is the case, just practice pacing yourself on the practice exams, so you don't spend too much time on difficult questions.

- **Listen carefully to directions.** By the time you get to the exam, you should be familiar with how all the sections work, but listen to the person who is administering the exam just in case something has changed.
- **Pace yourself.** Glance at your watch every few minutes, and compare the time to how far you've gotten in the sections. When one-quarter of the time has elapsed, you should be a quarter of the way through the sections, and so on. If you're falling behind, pick up the pace a bit.
- **Keep moving.** Don't spend too much time on any one question. If you don't know the answer, skip the question and move on. Circle the number of

the question in your test booklet in case you have time to come back to it later.

- **Keep track of your place on the answer sheet.** If you skip a question, make sure you skip that space on the answer sheet too. Check yourself every 5–10 questions to make sure the question number and the answer sheet number are still the same.
- **Don't rush.** Though you should keep moving steadily through the test, rushing won't help. Try to keep calm and work methodically and quickly.

## Step 5: Learn to Use the Process of Elimination

**Time to complete: 20 minutes**

**Activity: Complete worksheet on Using the Process of Elimination**

After time management, your next most important tool for taking control of your exam is using the process of elimination wisely. It's standard test-taking wisdom that you should always read all the answer choices before choosing your answer. This practice helps you find the right answer by eliminating wrong answer choices. And, sure enough, that standard wisdom applies to your exam, too.

Let's say you're facing a vocabulary question that goes like this:

13. "Biology uses a <u>binomial</u> system of classification." In this sentence, the word *binomial* most nearly means
    a. understanding the law.
    b. having two names.
    c. scientifically sound.
    d. having a double meaning.

If you happen to know what *binomial* means, of course, you don't need to use the process of elimination, but let's assume that, like many people, you don't. So you look at the answer choices. "Understanding the law" sure doesn't sound very likely for something having to do with biology. So you eliminate choice **a**—and now you have only three answer choices to deal with. Mark an **X** next to choice **a** so you never have to read it again.

On to the other answer choices. If you know that the prefix *bi-* means *two*, as in *bicycle*, flag answer **b** as a possible answer. Mark a check mark beside it, meaning "good answer, I might use this one."

Choice **c**, "scientifically sound," is a possibility. At least it's about science, not law. It could work here, although, when you think about it, having a "scientifically sound" classification system in a scientific field is kind of redundant. You remember the *bi* thing in *binomial*, and probably continue to like answer **b** better. But you are not sure, so you put a question mark next to **c**, meaning "well, maybe."

Now, choice **d**, "having a double meaning." You are still keeping in mind that *bi-* means *two*, so this one looks possible at first. But then you look again at the sentence the word belongs in, and you think, "Why would biology want a system of classification that has two meanings? That wouldn't work very well!" If you are really taken with the idea that *bi* means *two*, you might put a question mark here. But if you are feeling a little more confident, you'll put an **X**. You already have a better answer picked out.

Now your question looks like this:

**13.** "Biology uses a <u>binomial</u> system of classification." In this sentence, the word *binomial* most nearly means
  X **a.** understanding the law.
  ✔ **b.** having two names.
  ? **c.** scientifically sound.
  ? **d.** having a double meaning.

You have just one check mark, for a good answer. If you are pressed for time, you should simply mark choice **b** on your answer sheet. If you have the time to be extra careful, you could compare your check-mark answer to your question-mark answers to make sure that it's better. (It is: The *binomial* system in biology is the one that gives a two-part genus and species name like *homo sapiens*.)

It's good to have a system for marking good, bad, and maybe answers. We're recommending this one:

**X** = bad
**✔** = good
**?** = maybe

If you don't like these marks, devise your own system. Just make sure you do it long before test day—while you are working through the practice exams in this book—so you won't have to worry about it during the test.

Even when you think you're absolutely clueless about a question, you can often use the process of elimination to get rid of at least one answer choice. If so, you're better prepared to make an educated guess, as you will see in Step 6. More often, the process of elimination allows you to get down to only two possibly right answers. Then you're in a strong position to guess. And sometimes, even though you don't know the right answer, you can find it simply by getting rid of the wrong ones, as you did in the last example.

Try using your powers of elimination on the questions in the worksheet entitled Using the Process of Elimination that begins page 78. The answer explanations there show one possible way you might use the process to arrive at the right answer.

The process of elimination is your tool for the next step, which is knowing when to guess.

# Using the Process of Elimination

Use the process of elimination to answer the following questions.

**1.** Ilsa is as old as Meghan will be in five years. The difference between Ed's age and Meghan's age is twice the difference between Ilsa's age and Meghan's age. Ed is 29. How old is Ilsa?
   **a.** 4
   **b.** 10
   **c.** 19
   **d.** 24

**2.** "All drivers of commercial vehicles must carry a valid commercial driver's license whenever operating a commercial vehicle." According to this sentence, which of the following people need NOT carry a commercial driver's license?
   **a.** a truck driver idling his engine while waiting to be directed to a loading dock
   **b.** a bus operator backing her bus out of the way of another bus in the bus lot
   **c.** a taxi driver driving his personal car to the grocery store
   **d.** a limousine driver taking the limousine to her home after dropping off her last passenger of the evening

**3.** Smoking tobacco has been linked to
   **a.** increased risk of stroke and heart attack.
   **b.** all forms of respiratory disease.
   **c.** increasing mortality rates over the past ten years.
   **d.** juvenile delinquency.

**4.** Which of the following words is spelled correctly?
   **a.** incorrigible
   **b.** outragous
   **c.** domestickated
   **d.** understandible

## Answers

Here are the answers, as well as some suggestions as to how you might have used the process of elimination to find them.

**1. d.** You should have eliminated choice **a** off the bat. Ilsa can't be four years old if Meghan is going to be Ilsa's age in five years. The best way to eliminate the other answer choices is to try plugging them into the information given in the problem. For instance, for choice **b**, if Ilsa is 10, then Meghan must be 5. The difference in their ages is 5. The difference between Ed's age, 29, and Meghan's age, 5, is 24. Is 24 two times 5? No. Then choice **b** is wrong. You could eliminate choice **c** in the same way and be left with choice **d**.

**2. c.** Note the word *not* in the question, and go through the answers one by one. Is the truck driver in choice **a** "operating a commercial vehicle"? Yes, idling counts as "operating," so he needs to have a commercial driver's license. Likewise, the bus operator in choice **b** is operating a commercial vehicle; the question doesn't say the operator has to be on the street. The limo driver in **d** is operating a commercial vehicle, even if it doesn't have passenger in it. However, the cabbie in choice **c** is not operating a commercial vehicle, but his own private car.

**3. a.** You could eliminate choice **b** simply because of the presence of the word *all*. Such absolutes hardly ever appear in correct answer choices. Choice **c** looks attractive until you think a little about what you know—aren't *fewer* people smoking these days, rather than more? So how could smoking be responsible for a higher mortality rate? (If you didn't know that *mortality rate* means the rate at which people die, you might keep this choice as a possibility, but you'd still be able to eliminate two answers and have only two to choose from.) And choice **d** seems seems unlikely, so you could eliminate that one, too. And you're left with the correct choice, **a**.

**4. a.** How you used the process of elimination here depends on which words you recognized as being spelled incorrectly. If you knew that the correct spellings were *outrageous, domesticated,* and *understandable,* then you were home free.

## Step 6: Know When to Guess

**Time to complete: 20 minutes**
**Activity: Complete worksheet on Your Guessing Ability**

Armed with the process of elimination, you're ready to take control of one of the big questions in test taking: Should I guess? Unless the exam has a guessing penalty, you have nothing to lose and everything to gain from guessing. The more complicated answer depends both on the exam and on you—your personality and your guessing intuition.

Most police officer written exams don't use a guessing penalty. The number of questions you answer correctly yields your score, and there's no penalty for wrong answers. So most of the time, you don't have to worry—simply go ahead and guess. But if you find that your exam does have a guessing penalty, you should read this section to find out what that means to you.

### How the Guessing Penalty Works

A guessing penalty really works only against *random* guessing—filling in the little circles to make a nice pattern on your answer sheet. If you can eliminate one or more answer choices, as outlined previously, you're better off taking a guess than leaving the answer blank, even on the sections that have a penalty.

Here's how a guessing penalty works: Depending on the number of answer choices in a given exam, some proportion of the number of questions you get incorrect is subtracted from the total number of questions you got correct. For instance, if there are four answer choices, typically the guessing penalty is one-third of your wrong answers. Suppose you took a test of 100 questions. You answered 88 of them correctly and 12 incorrectly.

If there's no guessing penalty, your score is simply 88. But if there's a one-third point guessing penalty, the scorers take your 12 incorrect answers and divide by 3 to come up with 4. Then they subtract that 4 from your correct-answer score of 88 to leave you with a score of 84. Thus, you would have been better off if you had simply not answered those 12 questions that you weren't sure of. Then your total score would still be 88, because there wouldn't be anything to subtract.

### What You Should Do about the Guessing - Penalty

That's how a guessing penalty works. The first thing this means for you is that marking your answer sheet at random doesn't pay. If you're running out of time

The following are ten really hard questions. You're not supposed to know the answers. Rather, this is an assessment of your ability to guess when you don't have a clue. Read each question carefully, just as if you did expect to answer it. If you have any knowledge at all of the subject of the question, use that knowledge to help you eliminate wrong answer choices. Use this answer grid to fill in your answers to the questions.

1. ⓐ ⓑ ⓒ ⓓ    5. ⓐ ⓑ ⓒ ⓓ    9. ⓐ ⓑ ⓒ ⓓ
2. ⓐ ⓑ ⓒ ⓓ    6. ⓐ ⓑ ⓒ ⓓ   10. ⓐ ⓑ ⓒ ⓓ
3. ⓐ ⓑ ⓒ ⓓ    7. ⓐ ⓑ ⓒ ⓓ
4. ⓐ ⓑ ⓒ ⓓ    8. ⓐ ⓑ ⓒ ⓓ

**1.** September 7 is Independence Day in
   **a.** India.
   **b.** Costa Rica.
   **c.** Brazil.
   **d.** Australia.

**2.** Which of the following is the formula for determining the momentum of an object?
   **a.** $p = mv$
   **b.** $F = ma$
   **c.** $P = IV$
   **d.** $E = mc^2$

**3.** Because of the expansion of the universe, the stars and other celestial bodies are all moving away from each other. This phenomenon is known as
   **a.** Newton's first law.
   **b.** the big bang.
   **c.** gravitational collapse.
   **d.** Hubble flow.

**4.** American author Gertrude Stein was born in
   **a.** 1713.
   **b.** 1830.
   **c.** 1874.
   **d.** 1901.

**5.** Which of the following is NOT one of the Five Classics attributed to Confucius?
   **a.** *I Ching*
   **b.** *Book of Holiness*
   **c.** *Spring and Autumn Annals*
   **d.** *Book of History*

**6.** The religious and philosophical doctrine that holds that the universe is constantly in a struggle between good and evil is known as
   **a.** Pelagianism.
   **b.** Manichaeanism.
   **c.** neo-Hegelianism.
   **d.** Epicureanism.

**7.** The third chief justice of the Supreme Court was
   **a.** John Blair.
   **b.** William Cushing.
   **c.** James Wilson.
   **d.** John Jay.

**8.** Which of the following is the poisonous portion of a daffodil?
   **a.** the bulb
   **b.** the leaves
   **c.** the stem
   **d.** the flowers

**9.** The winner of the Masters golf tournament in 1953 was

  **a.** Sam Snead.

  **b.** Cary Middlecoff.

  **c.** Arnold Palmer.

  **d.** Ben Hogan.

**10.** The state with the highest per capita personal income in 1980 was

  **a.** Alaska.

  **b.** Connecticut.

  **c.** New York.

  **d.** Texas.

## Answers

Check your answers against the correct answers below.

  **1. c.**

  **2. a.**

  **3. d.**

  **4. c.**

  **5. b.**

  **6. b.**

  **7. b.**

  **8. a.**

  **9. d.**

**10. a.**

## How Did You Do?

You may have simply gotten lucky and actually known the answers to one or two questions. In addition, your guessing was more successful if you were able to use the process of elimination on any of the questions. Maybe you didn't know who the third Chief Justice was (question 7), but you knew that John Jay was the first. In that case, you would have eliminated choice **d** and, therefore, improved your odds of guessing correctly from one in four to one in three.

According to probability, you should get $2\frac{1}{2}$ answers correct by guessing, so getting either two or three correct would be average. If you got four or more correct, you may be a really terrific guesser. If you got one or none correct, you may not be a very strong guesser.

Keep in mind, though, that this is only a small sample. You should continue to keep track of your guessing ability as you work through the practice questions in this book. Circle the numbers of questions you guess on as you make your guess, or, if you don't have time while you take the practice exams, go back afterward and try to remember which questions you guessed at. Remember, on a test with four answer choices for each question, your chances of getting a right answer is one in four. So keep a separate "guessing" score for each exam. How many questions did you guess on? How many did you get correct? If the number you got correct is at least one-fourth of the number of questions you guessed on, you are at least an average guesser, maybe better—and you should go ahead and guess on the real exam. If the number you got correct is significantly lower than one-fourth of the number you guessed on, you should not guess on exams where there is a guessing penalty, unless you can eliminate a wrong answer. If there's no guessing penalty, however, you would be safe in guessing anyway.

on an exam that has a guessing penalty, you should not use your remaining seconds to mark a pretty pattern on your answer sheet. Take those few seconds to try to answer one more question right.

But as soon as you get out of the realm of random guessing, the guessing penalty no longer works against you. If you can use the process of elimination to get rid of even one incorrect answer choice, the odds stop being against you and start working in your favor.

Sticking with our example of an exam that has four answer choices, eliminating just one incorrect answer makes your odds of choosing the correct answer one in three. That's the same as the one-out-of-three guessing penalty—even odds. If you eliminate two answer choices, your odds are one in two—better than the guessing penalty. In either case, you should go ahead and choose one of the remaining answer choices.

But what if you're not much of a risk-taker, *and* you think of yourself as the world's worst guesser? Complete the Your Guessing Ability worksheet to get an idea of how good your intuition is.

## Step 7: Reach Your Peak Performance Zone

**Time to complete: 10 minutes to read; weeks to complete!**
**Activity: Complete the Physical Preparation Checklist**

To get ready for a challenge like a big exam, you have to take control of your physical, as well as your mental, state. Exercise, proper diet, and rest will ensure that your body works with, rather than against, your mind on test day, as well as during your preparation.

### Exercise

If you don't already have a regular exercise program, the time during which you're preparing for your writ-ten exam is an excellent time to start one. You'll have to be in shape to pass the physical agility test and to make it through the first weeks of basic training anyway. And if you're already keeping fit—or trying to get that way—don't let the pressure of preparing for the written exam be an excuse for quitting now. Exercise helps reduce stress by pumping wonderful good-feeling hormones called endorphins into your system. It also increases the oxygen supply throughout your body, including your brain, so you'll be at peak performance on test day.

A half hour of vigorous activity—enough to raise a sweat—every day should be your aim. If you're really pressed for time, every other day is okay. Choose an activity you like and get out there and do it. Jogging with a friend always makes the time go faster, or take a radio.

But don't overdo it. You don't want to exhaust yourself so much that you can't study. Moderation is the key.

### Diet

First of all, cut out the junk food. Go easy on caffeine, and try to eliminate alcohol and nicotine from your system at least two weeks before the exam. Promise yourself a celebration the night after the exam, if need be.

What your body needs for peak performance is simply a balanced diet. Eat plenty of fruits and vegetables, along with protein and complex carbohydrates. Foods that are high in lecithin (an amino acid), such as fish and beans, are especially good brain foods.

### Rest

You probably know how much sleep you need every night to be at your best, even if you don't always get it. Make sure you do get that much sleep, though, for at least a week before the exam. Moderation is important here, as well. Too much extra sleep could just make you groggy.

If you're not a morning person and your exam will be given in the morning, you should reset your internal clock so that your body doesn't think you're taking an exam at 3 A.M. You have to start this process well before the exam. The way it works is to get up half an hour earlier each morning, and then go to bed half an hour earlier that night. Don't try it the other way around; you'll just toss and turn if you go to bed early without having gotten up early. The next morning, get up another half an hour earlier, and so on. How long you will have to do this depends on how late you're used to getting up.

## Step 8: Get Your Act Together

**Time to complete: 10 minutes to read; time to complete will vary**
**Activity: Complete Final Preparations worksheet**
You're in control of your mind and body; you're in charge of test anxiety, your preparation, and your test-taking strategies. Now it's time to take charge of external factors, like the testing site and the materials you need to take the exam.

### Find out Where the Test Is and Make a Trial Run

The exam bulletin or notice the recruiting office sent you will tell you when and where your exam is being held. Do you know how to get to the testing site? Do you know how long it will take you to get there? If not, make a trial run, preferably on the same day of the week at the same time of day. Make note, on the Final Preparations worksheet, of the amount of time it will take you to get to the exam site. Plan on arriving 10–15 minutes early so you can get the lay of the land, use the bathroom, and calm down. Then figure out how early you will have to get up that morning, and make sure you get up that early every day for a week before the exam.

### Gather Your Materials

The night before the exam, lay out the clothes you will wear and the materials you have to bring with you to the exam. Plan on dressing in layers; you won't have any control over the temperature of the examination room. Have a sweater or jacket you can take off if it's warm or put on if the air conditioning is on full blast. Use the checklist on the Final Preparations worksheet on page 86 to help you pull together what you will need.

### Don't Skip Breakfast

Even if you don't usually eat breakfast, do so on exam morning. A cup of coffee doesn't count. Don't eat doughnuts or other sweet foods, either. A sugar high will leave you with a sugar low in the middle of the exam. A mix of protein and complex carbohydrates is best: Cereal with milk or eggs with toast will do your body a world of good.

# Physical Preparation Checklist

During the week before the test, write down (1) what physical exercise you engaged in and for how long and (2) what you ate for each meal. Remember, you're trying for at least a half an hour of exercise every other day (preferably every day) and a balanced diet that's light on junk food.

**7 Days before the Exam**

Exercise: _____ for _____ minutes

Breakfast: _____

Lunch: _____

Dinner: _____

Snacks: _____

**6 Days before the Exam**

Exercise: _____ for _____ minutes

Breakfast: _____

Lunch: _____

Dinner: _____

Snacks: _____

**5 Days before the Exam**

Exercise: _____ for _____ minutes

Breakfast: _____

Lunch: _____

Dinner: _____

Snacks: _____

**4 Days before the Exam**

Exercise: _____ for _____ minutes

Breakfast: _____

Lunch: _____

Dinner: _____

Snacks: _____

**3 Days before the Exam**

Exercise: _____ for _____ minutes

Breakfast: _____

Lunch: _____

Dinner: _____

Snacks: _____

**2 Days before the Exam**

Exercise: _____ for _____ minutes

Breakfast: _____

Lunch: _____

Dinner: _____

Snacks: _____

**1 Day before the Exam**

Exercise: _____ for _____ minutes

Breakfast: _____

Lunch: _____

Dinner: _____

Snacks: _____

# Step 9: Do It!

**Time to complete: 10 minutes, plus test-taking time**
**Activity: Ace the Police Officer Written Exam!**
Fast forward to exam day. You're ready. You made a study plan and followed through. You practiced your test-taking strategies while working through this book. You're in control of your physical, mental, and emotional state. You know when and where to show up and what to bring with you. In other words, you're better prepared than most of the other people taking the exam with you.

Just one more thing. When you're done with the police officer written exam, you will have earned a reward. Plan a celebration. Call up your friends and plan a party, or have a nice dinner for two—whatever your heart desires. Give yourself something to look forward to.

And then do it. Go into the exam, full of confidence, armed with the test-taking strategies you've practiced till they're second nature. You're in control of yourself, your environment, and your performance on the exam. You're ready to succeed. So do it. Go in there and ace the exam. And look forward to your future career in law enforcement!

## Final Preparations

### Getting to the Exam Site

Location of exam: _____

Date of exam: _____

Time of exam: _____

Do I know how to get to the exam site?   Yes ____   No ____ (If no, make a trial run.)

Time it will take to get to exam site: _____


### Things to Lay out the Night Before

Clothes I will wear        ____

Sweater/jacket             ____

Watch                      ____

Photo ID                   ____

Admission card             ____

4 No. 2 pencils            ____

_____    _____

_____    _____

# 5 ▶ POLICE OFFICER PRACTICE EXAM 1

### CHAPTER SUMMARY
The first practice exam gives you an example of a police officer exam based primarily on your basic reading and writing skills. It is similar to tests used by many police departments around the nation. Remember that all test questions rely on reading comprehension and English skills, so mastering these skills is very important for all types of entry exams.

**M**any police departments use exams similar to this one to test police applicants. This kind of exam primarily tests your reading and writing skills. The police agency wants to know whether you have the basic skills to enable you to succeed in the academy, during field training, and throughout your career. This multiple-choice exam is divided into four parts:

- Part One: 30 reading comprehension questions
- Part Two: 25 grammar questions
- Part Three: 25 vocabulary questions
- Part Four: 20 spelling questions

To get the maximum benefit from this practice test, treat it as if it were the real thing. Get out your sharpened number 2 pencils and give yourself two hours to take this exam. Put away your electronic devices, find a quiet place sitting in a straight-backed chair at a desk or table, and concentrate only on the exam.

The answer sheet is on the next page; make a copy or neatly tear it out of the book, and fill it in just as you would at an actual test site. Following the answer sheet is the exam itself, which is followed by the answers and explanations. The last section of this chapter is an explanation of how to score your exam.

Good luck!

## Police Officer Practice Exam 1

| | | | | | | | | | | | | | |
|---|---|---|---|---|---|---|---|---|---|---|---|---|---|
| 1. | ⓐ | ⓑ | ⓒ | ⓓ | 36. | ⓐ | ⓑ | ⓒ | ⓓ | 71. | ⓐ | ⓑ | ⓒ | ⓓ |
| 2. | ⓐ | ⓑ | ⓒ | ⓓ | 37. | ⓐ | ⓑ | ⓒ | ⓓ | 72. | ⓐ | ⓑ | ⓒ | ⓓ |
| 3. | ⓐ | ⓑ | ⓒ | ⓓ | 38. | ⓐ | ⓑ | ⓒ | ⓓ | 73. | ⓐ | ⓑ | ⓒ | ⓓ |
| 4. | ⓐ | ⓑ | ⓒ | ⓓ | 39. | ⓐ | ⓑ | ⓒ | ⓓ | 74. | ⓐ | ⓑ | ⓒ | ⓓ |
| 5. | ⓐ | ⓑ | ⓒ | ⓓ | 40. | ⓐ | ⓑ | ⓒ | ⓓ | 75. | ⓐ | ⓑ | ⓒ | ⓓ |
| 6. | ⓐ | ⓑ | ⓒ | ⓓ | 41. | ⓐ | ⓑ | ⓒ | ⓓ | 76. | ⓐ | ⓑ | ⓒ | ⓓ |
| 7. | ⓐ | ⓑ | ⓒ | ⓓ | 42. | ⓐ | ⓑ | ⓒ | ⓓ | 77. | ⓐ | ⓑ | ⓒ | ⓓ |
| 8. | ⓐ | ⓑ | ⓒ | ⓓ | 43. | ⓐ | ⓑ | ⓒ | ⓓ | 78. | ⓐ | ⓑ | ⓒ | ⓓ |
| 9. | ⓐ | ⓑ | ⓒ | ⓓ | 44. | ⓐ | ⓑ | ⓒ | ⓓ | 79. | ⓐ | ⓑ | ⓒ | ⓓ |
| 10. | ⓐ | ⓑ | ⓒ | ⓓ | 45. | ⓐ | ⓑ | ⓒ | ⓓ | 80. | ⓐ | ⓑ | ⓒ | ⓓ |
| 11. | ⓐ | ⓑ | ⓒ | ⓓ | 46. | ⓐ | ⓑ | ⓒ | ⓓ | 81. | ⓐ | ⓑ | ⓒ | ⓓ |
| 12. | ⓐ | ⓑ | ⓒ | ⓓ | 47. | ⓐ | ⓑ | ⓒ | ⓓ | 82. | ⓐ | ⓑ | ⓒ | ⓓ |
| 13. | ⓐ | ⓑ | ⓒ | ⓓ | 48. | ⓐ | ⓑ | ⓒ | ⓓ | 83. | ⓐ | ⓑ | ⓒ | ⓓ |
| 14. | ⓐ | ⓑ | ⓒ | ⓓ | 49. | ⓐ | ⓑ | ⓒ | ⓓ | 84. | ⓐ | ⓑ | ⓒ | ⓓ |
| 15. | ⓐ | ⓑ | ⓒ | ⓓ | 50. | ⓐ | ⓑ | ⓒ | ⓓ | 85. | ⓐ | ⓑ | ⓒ | ⓓ |
| 16. | ⓐ | ⓑ | ⓒ | ⓓ | 51. | ⓐ | ⓑ | ⓒ | ⓓ | 86. | ⓐ | ⓑ | ⓒ | ⓓ |
| 17. | ⓐ | ⓑ | ⓒ | ⓓ | 52. | ⓐ | ⓑ | ⓒ | ⓓ | 87. | ⓐ | ⓑ | ⓒ | ⓓ |
| 18. | ⓐ | ⓑ | ⓒ | ⓓ | 53. | ⓐ | ⓑ | ⓒ | ⓓ | 88. | ⓐ | ⓑ | ⓒ | ⓓ |
| 19. | ⓐ | ⓑ | ⓒ | ⓓ | 54. | ⓐ | ⓑ | ⓒ | ⓓ | 89. | ⓐ | ⓑ | ⓒ | ⓓ |
| 20. | ⓐ | ⓑ | ⓒ | ⓓ | 55. | ⓐ | ⓑ | ⓒ | ⓓ | 90. | ⓐ | ⓑ | ⓒ | ⓓ |
| 21. | ⓐ | ⓑ | ⓒ | ⓓ | 56. | ⓐ | ⓑ | ⓒ | ⓓ | 91. | ⓐ | ⓑ | ⓒ | ⓓ |
| 22. | ⓐ | ⓑ | ⓒ | ⓓ | 57. | ⓐ | ⓑ | ⓒ | ⓓ | 92. | ⓐ | ⓑ | ⓒ | ⓓ |
| 23. | ⓐ | ⓑ | ⓒ | ⓓ | 58. | ⓐ | ⓑ | ⓒ | ⓓ | 93. | ⓐ | ⓑ | ⓒ | ⓓ |
| 24. | ⓐ | ⓑ | ⓒ | ⓓ | 59. | ⓐ | ⓑ | ⓒ | ⓓ | 94. | ⓐ | ⓑ | ⓒ | ⓓ |
| 25. | ⓐ | ⓑ | ⓒ | ⓓ | 60. | ⓐ | ⓑ | ⓒ | ⓓ | 95. | ⓐ | ⓑ | ⓒ | ⓓ |
| 26. | ⓐ | ⓑ | ⓒ | ⓓ | 61. | ⓐ | ⓑ | ⓒ | ⓓ | 96. | ⓐ | ⓑ | ⓒ | ⓓ |
| 27. | ⓐ | ⓑ | ⓒ | ⓓ | 62. | ⓐ | ⓑ | ⓒ | ⓓ | 97. | ⓐ | ⓑ | ⓒ | ⓓ |
| 28. | ⓐ | ⓑ | ⓒ | ⓓ | 63. | ⓐ | ⓑ | ⓒ | ⓓ | 98. | ⓐ | ⓑ | ⓒ | ⓓ |
| 29. | ⓐ | ⓑ | ⓒ | ⓓ | 64. | ⓐ | ⓑ | ⓒ | ⓓ | 99. | ⓐ | ⓑ | ⓒ | ⓓ |
| 30. | ⓐ | ⓑ | ⓒ | ⓓ | 65. | ⓐ | ⓑ | ⓒ | ⓓ | 100. | ⓐ | ⓑ | ⓒ | ⓓ |
| 31. | ⓐ | ⓑ | ⓒ | ⓓ | 66. | ⓐ | ⓑ | ⓒ | ⓓ | | | | | |
| 32. | ⓐ | ⓑ | ⓒ | ⓓ | 67. | ⓐ | ⓑ | ⓒ | ⓓ | | | | | |
| 33. | ⓐ | ⓑ | ⓒ | ⓓ | 68. | ⓐ | ⓑ | ⓒ | ⓓ | | | | | |
| 34. | ⓐ | ⓑ | ⓒ | ⓓ | 69. | ⓐ | ⓑ | ⓒ | ⓓ | | | | | |
| 35. | ⓐ | ⓑ | ⓒ | ⓓ | 70. | ⓐ | ⓑ | ⓒ | ⓓ | | | | | |

# Police Officer Practice Exam 1

## *Part One: Reading Comprehension*

*Answer questions 1-6 based on the following passage.*

In order for our society to make decision about the kinds of punishments we will impose on convicted criminals, we must understand why criminals are punished. Some people believe that retribution is the purpose of punishment and that, therefore, the punishment should in some direct way fit the crime. This view is based on the belief that a person who commits a crime should be punished. Because the punishment should fit the specific crime, the theory of retribution allows a sentencing judge to consider the circumstances of each crime, criminal, and victim when imposing a sentence.

Another view, called the deterrence theory, promotes punishment as a way to discourage the commission of future crimes—whether by the same criminal or by others. In this view, punishment does not have to relate directly to the crime committed, because the aim of punishment is to deter both the specific criminal and the general public from committing crimes in the future, knowing that they will be punished. However, punishment must be uniform and consistently applied so that members of the public understand what the punishment for a particular crime will be. Laws setting mandatory sentences are based on the deterrence theory and do not permit a judge to consider the specifics of the crime, criminal, or victim when imposing sentence.

Sentencing guidelines, which may permit a range of punishments, provide the judge with some opportunities to consider more than just the crime itself, but the sentence cannot be higher or lower than the guidelines recommend.

1. According to the passage, punishment
   a. is rarely an effective deterrent to future crimes.
   b. must fit the crime in question.
   c. is imposed solely at the discretion of a judge.
   d. may be imposed for differing reasons.

2. The retribution theory of punishment
   a. is no longer considered valid.
   b. holds that the punishment should fit the crime committed.
   c. applies only to violent crimes.
   d. allows a jury to recommend the sentence that should be imposed.

3. Sentencing guidelines
   a. permit the judge to decide the sentence totally on his or her own.
   b. mandate exactly what the sentence should be.
   c. provide a range of sentences a judge may select from.
   d. allow the jury to recommend a sentence to the judge.

4. A good title for this passage would be
   a. Sentencing Reform: A Modest Proposal.
   b. More Criminals Are Sentenced.
   c. Punishment: Deterrent or Retribution?
   d. The Arguments for Sentencing Guidelines

5. A person who believes that the punishment should fit the crime is most closely stating
   a. retribution theory.
   b. deterrence theory.
   c. crime control theory.
   d. none of the above.

**6.** The theories described in the passage differ in
  **a.** the amount of leeway they would allow judges in determining sentences.
  **b.** the number of law enforcement professionals who espouse them.
  **c.** their concern for the rights of the accused.
  **d.** the types of crimes they apply to.

*Answer questions 7–12 based on the following passage.*

DNA is a powerful investigative tool because no two people have the same DNA. The only exception scientists have found to this is identical twins. The sequence, or order, of the DNA building blocks is different in particular regions of the cell, making each person's DNA unique. Because of this, DNA evidence collected at the scene of a crime can link a suspect to the crime or can eliminate someone from suspicion. DNA is similar to fingerprints, but has been considered more accurate for the past decade. DNA can also link evidence to a victim by using DNA of relatives if the victim's body cannot be found. For example, if technicians have a biological sample from the victim, such as a bloodstain found at the crime scene, the DNA taken from that bloodstain can be compared with DNA from the victim's biological relatives to determine whether the bloodstain came from that particular victim. When a DNA profile developed from evidence at one crime scene is compared with a DNA profile developed from evidence found at another crime scene, the crimes can be linked to each other or to the same suspect, making it possible to link crimes committed at a distance from one another.

Although many forensic scientists had begun to think of DNA as a miracle identifier, in 2009, scientists for the first time found that it was possible to fabricate DNA evidence from a person other than the donor of the blood or the saliva. This means that someone could plant another person's DNA at a crime scene, causing the person whose DNA was found to be considered a prime suspect in a case. While this does not mean that DNA evidence will no longer be important, it reinforces that solving crimes must continue to rely on more than science to find a guilty party.

**7.** What is the primary purpose of this paragraph?
  **a.** to show that DNA is a powerful investigative tool
  **b.** to illustrate how the unique characteristics of DNA make different types of comparisons and eliminations possible
  **c.** to teach the reader that identical twins have the same DNA
  **d.** to show how laboratory technicians develop DNA profiles

**8.** All of the following are true EXCEPT
  **a.** everyone, except for identical twins, has different DNA.
  **b.** the sequence of DNA building blocks is the same in particular regions of the cell, making comparisons possible.
  **c.** DNA can be used for comparisons or eliminations of offenders from different states.
  **d.** DNA from relatives can be used to identify victims.

**9.** According to the passage, DNA should be collected from a crime scene because
  **a.** it is better than fingerprints.
  **b.** there is DNA left at every crime scene.
  **c.** it can be used to eliminate potential suspects.
  **d.** DNA is a new investigative tool.

**10.** Which of the following conclusions can be drawn from the paragraph?
   **a.** DNA can be collected from sources other than blood.
   **b.** DNA can be collected only from bloodstains.
   **c.** DNA cannot be collected from bloodstains.
   **d.** DNA can connect crime scenes only if it is taken from bloodstains.

**11.** The recent scientific finding that DNA evidence can be fabricated is most likely to result in
   **a.** discontinuing any efforts to collect DNA at a crime scene.
   **b.** the field of forensic science losing its current popularity.
   **c.** renewed efforts to find evidence other than DNA at crime scenes.
   **d.** the end of innocent people being freed from prison on the basis of DNA evidence.

**12.** According to the passage, DNA structures for different people depend on
   **a.** the region where they reside.
   **b.** their age.
   **c.** their race.
   **d.** none of the above

*Answer questions 13–17 based on the following passage.*

Adolescents are at risk of being both victims and perpetrators of violence. Although they make up only 14% of the population age 12 and over, 30% of all violent crimes—1.9 million—are committed against them. Because crimes against adolescents are likely to be committed by offenders of the same age, sex, and race, preventing violence among and against adolescents is a twofold challenge. New violence-prevention programs in urban middle schools have helped reduce the crime rate by teaching both the victims and the perpetrators conflict resolution skills. Conflict resolution involves applying reason to disputes to prevent misunderstandings that can lead to violence. It also involves changing adolescents' belief that they must achieve respect through violence and that they must always retaliate against any actions or words they view as disrespectful to them. These programs provide a safe environment for students to discuss their conflicts and, therefore, may decrease the numbers of students at risk of being the victims or the offenders of violent acts.

**13.** What is the main idea of the passage?
   **a.** Adolescents are more likely to commit crimes than older people and must therefore be taught nonviolence in order to protect society.
   **b.** Middle school students appreciate the conflict resolution skills they acquire in violence-prevention programs.
   **c.** Middle school violence-prevention programs are designed to help to lower the rate of crimes against adolescents.
   **d.** Violence against adolescents is increasing.

**14.** Which of the following is NOT mentioned in the passage as a skill taught by middle school violence-prevention programs?
   **a.** keeping one's temper
   **b.** settling disputes without violence
   **c.** avoiding the need for vengeance
   **d.** being reasonable in emotional situations

**15.** According to the passage, which of the following statements about adolescents is true?

  **a.** Adolescents are disproportionately likely to be victims of violent crime.

  **b.** Adolescents are more likely to commit violent crimes than other segments of the population.

  **c.** Adolescents are the victims of 14% of the nation's violent crimes.

  **d.** Adolescents are reluctant to attend violence-prevention programs.

**16.** According to the passage, preventing violence against adolescents is a "twofold challenge" because?

  **a.** they are twice as likely to be victims of violent crimes as members of other age groups.

  **b.** they must be prevented from both perpetrating and being victimized by violent crime.

  **c.** they must change both their violent behavior and their attitudes towards violence.

  **d.** they are vulnerable yet reluctant to listen to adult advice.

**17.** According to the passage, crimes against adolescents are most likely to be committed by

  **a.** their guardians.

  **b.** their parents.

  **c.** their teachers.

  **d.** other adolescents.

*Answer questions 18–22 based on the following passage.*

In 1966, the Supreme Court issued a decision in the case of *Miranda v. Arizona* that resulted in police officers having to advise suspects of their Fifth Amendment right against self-incrimination. The decision led to what has become commonly known as the Miranda warnings. In its decision, the Supreme Court outlined two general principles to guide the behavior of police officers, stating that if a suspect was in custody and the police were going to ask accusatory questions, the suspect must be given the Miranda warnings. Police officers were very negative toward the *Miranda* decision. They believed it would result in suspects refusing to answer any questions posed by the police, but this did not turn out to be a serious problem. Later Supreme Court decisions have added situations in which the warnings must be given, including during in-field detentions, transportation, arrest, and booking as part of the definition of custody. Each of these additions stemmed from later cases but did not acquire names of their own; they came to be considered part of the Miranda warnings. Each added restrictions on how and when police officers may question suspects. One thing that has remained unchanged is that police officers are permitted to ask non-accusatory questions, such as a suspect's name, without giving the individual the Miranda warnings.

**18.** The best title for this passage would be

  **a.** How to Interrogate Suspects.

  **b.** When to Interrogate Suspects.

  **c.** Police and the Supreme Court.

  **d.** *Miranda* and Police Interrogations.

**19.** Based on the information in the passage, which statement is correct?

  **a.** Police officers may not ask suspects any questions other than their name.

  **b.** Police officers must always read suspects the Miranda warnings.

  **c.** The Supreme Court used the *Miranda* case to regulate police behavior.

  **d.** Changes in the Miranda warnings are difficult for police officers to understand.

**20.** Which of the following is an NOT an example of a non-accusatory question?
 **a.** the suspect's name
 **b.** the suspect's address
 **c.** the suspect's alibi
 **d.** the suspect's date of birth

**21.** Based on the information in the passage, which statement is incorrect?
 **a.** The Miranda warnings must only be given in Arizona.
 **b.** The Miranda warnings guide when police may question suspects.
 **c.** The Supreme Court considered the Fifth Amendment in its *Miranda* decision.
 **d.** None of the above; all the statements are correct.

**22.** How did police officers think the *Miranda* decision would affect them?
 **a.** It would mean more work for them.
 **b.** Suspects would refuse to answer any questions.
 **c.** Lawyers would be flooding police stations.
 **d.** They would have to learn to think like lawyers.

*Answer questions 23–26 based on the following passage.*

Many people confuse education and training, but they are not the same thing. Education is knowledge-based and is defined as a body of academic knowledge that is most often learned in a classroom setting. Training is coaching to become proficient in particular behaviors or actions. Sometimes the two are confused because many training experiences, like a police academy, often involve many hours of classroom instruction. Such institutions combine elements of education and training, but the differences between the two remain. Knowledge is theoretical. Using a law enforce-

ment example, you can study the laws of arrest without ever having to arrest anyone, but you need to be trained in handcuffing techniques if you will be expected to actually take someone into custody. Similarly, you can study laws and court cases pertaining to deadly physical force without ever having to fire a weapon. Training, on the other hand, is skills-based. It covers what you need to do, as much as what you need to know, in order to perform a task or group of tasks. Learning when or why is not the same as learning how.

**23.** The best title for this passage would be
 **a.** When or Why Is Not the Same As How.
 **b.** Education versus Training.
 **c.** The Benefits of Studying Case Law.
 **d.** The Importance of Handcuffing Techniques.

**24.** The main idea of the passage is that
 **a.** education and training are different.
 **b.** education and training are the same.
 **c.** people often confuse education and training.
 **d.** training is ineffective without the foundation of education.

**25.** Based on the passage, the activity most likely to be defined as training is
 **a.** studying for a graduate school entrance exam.
 **b.** learning the firearms laws in your state.
 **c.** learning how to fire a shotgun.
 **d.** learning a foreign language.

**26.** Based on the passage, the activity most likely to be defined as education is
 **a.** learning how to drive.
 **b.** learning the firearms laws in your state.
 **c.** learning handcuffing techniques.
 **d.** studying for the police entrance exam.

*Answer questions 27–30 based on the following passage.*

In many police departments, detectives who want to move up the detective rank structure must spend an extended period of time working in the internal affairs division. Many officers do not consider this a popular assignment because the majority of officers feel uncomfortable investigating their peers. Even officers with high personal levels of integrity find that, because the police culture and relationships with police colleagues is so strong, the act of rooting out officers who go astray is considered an unpopular assignment.

Yet officers assigned to internal affairs not only become well versed in investigating police misconduct, but also become familiar with the circumstances and attitudes out of which such misconduct might arise. Assignment to internal affairs is believed to reduce the possibility that a commanding officer might be too lenient in investigating or disciplining a police colleague. The transfer to internal affairs also separates a detective for his or her precinct or squad, reducing the prospect of cronyism. Finally, it familiarizes the detective with the responsibilities of serving in a supervisory capacity.

**27.** According to the passage, detectives are transferred to internal affairs in order to
   **a.** enable them to identify situations that might lead to police misconduct.
   **b.** familiarize them with the laws regarding police misconduct.
   **c.** ensure that they are closely supervised.
   **d.** increase the staff of the internal affairs division.

**28.** Who, according to the passage, must spend an extended period working for the internal affairs division?
   **a.** detectives interested in police misconduct
   **b.** all detectives
   **c.** detectives interested in advancement
   **d.** officers who want to become detectives

**29.** The internal affairs requirement is apparently intended to
   **a.** teach detectives how to conduct their own police work properly.
   **b.** demonstrate to the community that the police department takes internal affairs seriously.
   **c.** strengthen the internal affairs unit.
   **d.** make supervisors more effective in preventing police misconduct.

**30.** According to the passage, officers do not like to work in internal affairs because
   **a.** they are uncomfortable investigating other officers.
   **b.** the assignment involves working nights and weekends.
   **c.** they resent being taken from their other assignments.
   **d.** they have to work with too many higher-ranking officers.

## Part Two: Writing

*Answer questions 31–55 by choosing the sentence that is correct in both grammar and punctuation.*

**31. a.** The search took place without incident. Except for a brief argument between two residents.
   **b.** The search took place. Without incident except for a brief argument between two residents.
   **c.** The search, took place without incident except, for a brief argument between two residents.
   **d.** The search took place without incident, except for a brief argument between two residents.

**32. a.** They finished their search, left the building, and return to police headquarters.
   **b.** They finished their search, left the building, and returns to police headquarters.
   **c.** They finished their search, left the building, and returned to police headquarters.
   **d.** They finished their search, left the building, and returning to police headquarters.

**33. a.** Searching for evidence, police officers, must be mindful of the Fourth Amendment.
   **b.** Searching for evidence. Police officers must be mindful of the Fourth Amendment.
   **c.** When searching for evidence. Police officers, must be mindful of the Fourth Amendment.
   **d.** When searching for evidence, police officers must be mindful of the Fourth Amendment.

**34. a.** The evidence had been improperly gathered, the case was dismissed.
   **b.** Because the evidence had been improperly gathered, the case was dismissed.
   **c.** Because the evidence had been improperly gathered. The case was dismissed.
   **d.** The evidence had been improperly gathered the case was dismissed.

**35. a.** Officer Alvarez was able to search the suspect's car, where she found $200,000 worth of cocaine. Because she had a warrant.
   **b.** $200,000 worth of cocaine was found. The result of a search by Officer Alvarez of the suspect's car, because she had a warrant.
   **c.** Because of a warrant and a search of the suspect's car. $200,000 worth of cocaine was found by Officer Alvarez.
   **d.** Because Officer Alvarez had a warrant, she was able to search the suspect's car, where she found $200,000 worth of cocaine.

**36. a.** The guard, like the prisoners, were tired of the radios constantly blaring in the recreation room, and yesterday he went to the warden and complained.
   **b.** The guard, like the prisoners, was tired of the radios constantly blaring in the recreation room, and yesterday he goes to the warden and complains.
   **c.** The guard, like the prisoners, was tired of the radios constantly blaring in the recreation room, and yesterday he went to the warden and complained.
   **d.** The guard, like the prisoners, were tired of the radios constantly blaring in the recreation room, and yesterday he goes to the warden and complained.

**37. a.** Mr. Lowell felt it was time to move away from the crime-ridden neighborhood, but he could not afford to do so.
   **b.** Mr. Lowell felt it was time to move away from the crime-ridden neighborhood, he could not afford to do so.
   **c.** Mr. Lowell felt it was time to move away from the crime ridden neighborhood he could not afford to do so.
   **d.** Mr. Lowell felt it was time to move away. From the crime-ridden neighborhood, but he could not afford to do so.

**38. a.** Lieutenant Wells did not think the prisoner could be capable to escape.
   **b.** Lieutenant Wells did not think that the prisoner capable of escaping.
   **c.** Lieutenant Wells did not think the prisoner capable of escape.
   **d.** Lieutenant Wells did not think that the prisoner capable to escape.

**39. a.** The gunman ordered the passengers to remove their watches and jewelry and lie down on the station platform with a growl.

   **b.** The gunman ordered the passengers to remove their watch and jewelry with a growl and lie down on the station platform.

   **c.** The gunman ordered with a growl the passengers to remove their watches and jewelry and lie down on the station platform.

   **d.** With a growl, the gunman ordered the passengers to remove their watches and jewelry and lie down on the station platform.

**40. a.** Of all the dogs in the K-9 Corps, Zelda is the most bravest.

   **b.** Of all the dogs in the K-9 Corps, Zelda is the bravest.

   **c.** Of all the dogs in the K-9 Corps, Zelda is the braver.

   **d.** Of all the dogs in the K-9 Corps, Zelda is the more brave.

**41. a.** When her workday is over, Officer Hernandez likes to watch TV, preferring sitcoms to police dramas.

   **b.** When her workday is over. Officer Hernandez likes to watch TV, preferring sitcoms to police dramas.

   **c.** When her workday is over, Officer Hernandez likes to watch TV. Preferring sitcoms to police dramas.

   **d.** When her workday is over, Officer Hernandez likes to watch TV, preferring sitcoms. To police dramas.

**42. a.** All day the exhausted volunteers had struggled through snake-ridden underbrush. In search of the missing teenagers, who still had not been found.

   **b.** All day the exhausted volunteers had struggled through snake-ridden underbrush in search of the missing teenagers, who still had not been found.

   **c.** All day the exhausted volunteers had struggled through snake-ridden underbrush in search of the missing teenagers. Who still had not been found.

   **d.** All day the exhausted volunteers had struggled through snake-ridden underbrush. In search of the missing teenagers. Who still had not been found.

**43. a.** My partner Rosie and I, we did not like each other at first, but now we get along fine.

   **b.** My partner Rosie and I did not like each other at first, but now her and I get along fine.

   **c.** My partner Rosie and me did not like each other at first, but now she and I get along fine.

   **d.** My partner Rosie and I did not like each other at first, but now we get along fine.

**44. a.** A sharpshooter for many years, Miles Johnson could shoot a pea off a person's shoulder from 70 yards away.

   **b.** Miles Johnson could shoot a pea off a person's shoulder from 70 yards away, a sharpshooter for many years.

   **c.** A sharpshooter for many years, a pea could be shot off a person's shoulder by Miles Johnson from 70 yards away.

   **d.** From 70 yards away, a sharpshooter for many years, Miles Johnson could shoot a pea off a person's shoulder.

**45. a.** Sergeant Cooper was the most toughest commander we had ever had, yet she was also the fairest.
 **b.** Sergeant Cooper was the toughest commander we had ever had, yet she was also the most fair.
 **c.** Sergeant Cooper was the toughest commander we had ever had, yet she was also the most fairly.
 **d.** Sergeant Cooper was the tough commander we had ever had, yet she was also the most fair.

**46. a.** Officer Chen thought they should call for backup; moreover, Officer Jovanovich disagreed.
 **b.** Officer Chen thought they should call for backup; meanwhile, Officer Jovanovich disagreed.
 **c.** Officer Chen thought they should call for backup; however, Officer Jovanovich disagreed.
 **d.** Officer Chen thought they should call for backup; furthermore, Officer Jovanovich disagreed.

**47. a.** The TV show *Colombo* is said to have been inspired in part of the classic Russian novel *Crime and Punishment.*
 **b.** The TV show *Colombo* is said to have been inspired in part by the classic Russian novel *Crime and Punishment.*
 **c.** The TV show *Colombo* is said to have been inspired in part off of the classic Russian novel *Crime and Punishment.*
 **d.** The TV show *Colombo* is said to have been inspired in part from the classic Russian novel *Crime and Punishment.*

**48. a.** Corky and Moe, respected members of the K-9 Corps, has sniffed out every pound of marijuana in the warehouse.
 **b.** Corky and Moe, respected members of the K-9 Corps, sniffs out every pound of marijuana in the warehouse.
 **c.** Corky and Moe, respected members of the K-9 Corps, sniffing out every pound of marijuana in the warehouse.
 **d.** Corky and Moe, respected members of the K-9 Corps, sniffed out every pound of marijuana in the warehouse.

**49. a.** When ordered to be removing their jewelry and lying down on the floor, not a single bank customer resisted.
 **b.** When ordered to have removed their jewelry and to have lain down on the floor, not a single bank customer resisted.
 **c.** When ordered to remove their jewelry and lie down on the floor, not a single bank customer resisted.
 **d.** When ordered to remove their jewelry and be lying down on the floor, not a single bank customer resisted.

**50. a.** Recession, like budget cuts, is hard on the beat cop.
 **b.** Recession and budget cuts is hard on the beat cop.
 **c.** Recession, like budget cuts, are hard on the beat cop.
 **d.** Budget cuts, like the recession, is hard on the beat cop.

**51.**
**a.** Jury members become impatient with both prosecution and defense when they were sequestered for months.
**b.** When jury members are sequestered for months, they are becoming impatient with both prosecution and defense.
**c.** Jury members became impatient with both prosecution and defense when they are sequestered for months.
**d.** When jury members are sequestered for months, they become impatient with both prosecution and defense.

**52.**
**a.** Sergeant Falk believes that neither suspect Hamm nor suspect Kozorez is responsible for the theft.
**b.** Sergeant Falk believes that neither suspect Hamm nor suspect Kozorez are responsible for the theft.
**c.** Sergeant Falk believes that suspect Hamm and suspect Kozorez is not responsible for the theft.
**d.** Sergeant Falk believes that both suspect Hamm and suspect Kozorez is not responsible for the theft.

**53.**
**a.** Of the two dogs in the K-9 Corps, Major is the bravest.
**b.** Of the two dogs in the K-9 Corps, Major is the most bravest.
**c.** Of the two dogs in the K-9 Corps, Major is the braver.
**d.** Of the two dogs in the K-9 Corps, Major is the more braver.

**54.**
**a.** Officer DeAngelo phoned his partner every day when he was in the hospital.
**b.** When his partner was in the hospital, Officer DeAngelo phoned him every day.
**c.** When in the hospital, a phone call was made every day by Officer DeAngelo to his partner.
**d.** His partner received a phone call from Officer DeAngelo every day while he was in the hospital.

**55.**
**a.** Some of the case transcripts I have to type are very long, but that doesn't bother one if the cases are interesting.
**b.** Some of the case transcripts I have to type are very long, but that doesn't bother you if the cases are interesting.
**c.** Some of the case transcripts I have to type are very long, but it doesn't bother a person if the cases are interesting.
**d.** Some of the case transcripts I have to type are very long, but that doesn't bother me if the cases are interesting.

## Part Three: Vocabulary

*Answer questions 56–80 by choosing the correct definition of the underlined word.*

**56.** Special equipment is required to find <u>latent</u> fingerprints.
**a.** obvious
**b.** hidden
**c.** human
**d.** mammal

**57.** As soon as the Department of Corrections' recommendations for prison reform were released, the department was <u>inundated</u> with calls from people who said they approved.
a. provided
b. bothered
c. rewarded
d. flooded

**58.** Sergeant Jones has often been described as <u>eccentric</u>. Based on this description, his behavior could also be described as
a. normal.
b. boisterous.
c. fussy.
d. peculiar.

**59.** An <u>obedient</u> pet is one who is submissive and easy to care for.
a. vicious
b. docile
c. high-strung
d. small

**60.** These unfortunate changes would result in the <u>elimination</u> of five positions in the department.
a. addition
b. reversal
c. removal
d. recall

**61.** The warning stated that a terrorist attack was <u>imminent</u>, and we should immediately take precautions.
a. soon
b. powerful
c. unlikely
d. distant

**62.** The police department assigned Officer Long to the records section because he was <u>proficient</u> in the use of computers.
a. rigorous
b. helpful
c. pretentious
d. skilled

**63.** Sergeant Kohler has been assigned to the public affairs office based on her ability to <u>articulate</u> the department's philosophy and communicate with the public easily.
a. express
b. translate
c. verify
d. hide

**64.** A day after returning from vacation, Police Officer Doyle seemed <u>lethargic</u>.
a. enthusiastic
b. tired
c. curious
d. obnoxious

**65.** The Adamsville Police Department's computer system was <u>outmoded</u>.
a. worthless
b. unusable
c. obsolete
d. unnecessary

**66.** The <u>integrity</u> of the entire department was jeopardized by one officer's ill-advised actions.
a. data
b. honesty
c. information
d. facts

**67.** We found the suspect's explanation for her presence at the crime scene to be <u>credible</u>.
  **a.** fantastic
  **b.** believable
  **c.** insufficient
  **d.** outrageous

**68.** The officer testified in court that the suspect's actions were <u>overt</u> and that there was no question she was the guilty party.
  **a.** open
  **b.** hidden
  **c.** closed
  **d.** known

**69.** Mayor Owly regarded budget cuts as a <u>panacea</u> for all the problems faced by the police department.
  **a.** cure
  **b.** result
  **c.** cause
  **d.** necessity

**70.** The attorney's <u>glib</u> remarks irritated the judge.
  **a.** angry
  **b.** superficial
  **c.** insulting
  **d.** dishonest

**71.** The store clerk's account of how shoes were stolen from his store seemed <u>plausible</u>.
  **a.** untrue
  **b.** credible
  **c.** insufficient
  **d.** hilarious

**72.** Joe's <u>spiteful</u> remarks about other officers he had worked with made others in the precinct careful about what they said in front of him.
  **a.** malicious
  **b.** jealous
  **c.** dishonest
  **d.** crafty

**73.** There was no <u>precedent</u> for the city council's shocking actions.
  **a.** vote
  **b.** tax
  **c.** support
  **d.** example

**74.** The terrorist group's <u>ideologies</u> seemed to be downright evil and contradicted all decency and common sense.
  **a.** technologies
  **b.** beliefs
  **c.** members
  **d.** inadequacies

**75.** One of the duties of a captain is to <u>delegate</u> responsibility.
  **a.** analyze
  **b.** respect
  **c.** criticize
  **d.** assign

**76.** Warrantless searches are allowed under some <u>exigent</u> circumstances.
  **a.** serious
  **b.** written
  **c.** verbal
  **d.** ordinary

**77.** Officer Albaghadi was called upon to <u>articulate</u> the philosophy of her entire department.
   **a.** trust
   **b.** refine
   **c.** verify
   **d.** express

**78.** After the party in his honor, he was in an <u>expansive</u> mood.
   **a.** outgoing
   **b.** relaxed
   **c.** humorous
   **d.** grateful

**79.** The ruling proved to be <u>detrimental</u> to the investigation.
   **a.** decisive
   **b.** harmful
   **c.** worthless
   **d.** advantageous

**80.** According to the code of conduct, "Every officer will be <u>accountable</u> for his or her decisions."
   **a.** applauded
   **b.** compensated
   **c.** responsible
   **d.** approached

## Part Four: Spelling

*Answer questions 81–100 by choosing the correct spelling of the word that belongs in the blank.*

**81.** In many states, road tests require _____ parking.
   **a.** paralel
   **b.** paralell
   **c.** parallal
   **d.** parallel

**82.** The paramedics attempted to _____ the victim.
   **a.** stablize
   **b.** stableize
   **c.** stableise
   **d.** stabilize

**83.** Prosecutors argued that testimony concerning the past behavior of the accused was _____.
   **a.** irelevent
   **b.** irelevant
   **c.** irrelevant
   **d.** irrelevent

**84.** The mayor pointed to the _____ drop in crime rate statistics.
   **a.** encouredging
   **b.** encouraging
   **c.** incurraging
   **d.** incouraging

**85.** The mentally ill suspect will have a _____ hearing on Friday.
   **a.** commitment
   **b.** committment
   **c.** comittment
   **d.** comitment

**86.** The prisoner's alibi seemed _____ from the outset.
   **a.** rediculous
   **b.** rediculus
   **c.** ridiculous
   **d.** ridiculus

**87.** It was a _____ day for the department's annual picnic.
a. superb
b. supperb
c. supurb
d. sepurb

**88.** The first time Officer Lin drove the squad car into town, all his old friends were _____.
a. jellous
b. jealous
c. jealuse
d. jeolous

**89.** When we were halfway up the hill, we heard a _____ explosion.
a. teriffic
b. terriffic
c. terific
d. terrific

**90.** If elected, Deputy Gana will make a fine _____.
a. sherrif
b. sherriff
c. sherif
d. sheriff

**91.** Catching the persons responsible for the fire has become an _____ for Officer Beatty.
a. obssession
b. obsessian
c. obsession
d. obsessiun

**92.** Officer Alvarez would have fired her weapon, but she did not want to place the hostage in _____.
a. jeoperdy
b. jepardy
c. jeapardy
d. jeopardy

**93.** Although the scenery around Lake Susan is _____, police officers who are on patrol have little time to enjoy it.
a. magniffisent
b. magnificent
c. maggnifisent
d. magnifisent

**94.** From inside the box came a strange _____ whirring sound.
a. mechinical
b. mechanical
c. mechenical
d. machanical

**95.** The community was shocked when Cindy Pierce, the president of the senior class, was arrested for selling _____ drugs.
a. elicitt
b. ellicit
c. illicit
d. illicet

**96.** There will be an immediate _____ into the mayor's death.
a. inquiry
b. inquirry
c. enquirry
d. enquery

**97.** Dimitry Mansky was subject to a lawsuit after he attempted to _____ his contract.
a. termenate
b. terrminate
c. termanate
d. terminate

**98.** Ben Alshieka feels that he is being _____ for his religious beliefs.
a. persecuted
b. pursecuted
c. presecuted
d. perrsecuted

**99.** The warehouse exuded a _____ odor.
a. peculior
b. peculiar
c. peculliar
d. puculior

**100.** Sergeant Chin gave his _____ to Lt. Brown that the report would be completed by the end of the work day.
a. assurance
b. insurance
c. assurrance
d. insurrence

# Answers

## Part One: Reading Comprehension

**1. d.** The passage presents two reasons for punishment. The second sentence notes a view that *some people* hold; the first line of the second paragraph indicates *another view*.

**2. b.** This is the main idea expressed in the first paragraph.

**3. c.** This idea is expressed in the last paragraph.

**4. c.** The first sentence indicates that the passage is about punishment. The first paragraph is about retribution; the second is about deterrence.

**5. a.** This idea is expressed in the first paragraph.

**6. a.** This must be inferred from the first and second paragraphs.

**7. a.** This choice most completely summarizes the primary purposes of the paragraph. The other choices are all supporting details in the passage.

**8. b.** This statement is expressed in the second sentence.

**9. c.** The passage states that DNA collected from crime scenes can either link or eliminate a suspect.

**10. a.** The statement *if technicians have a biological sample from the victim, such as a bloodstain* enables you to infer that DNA is collected from biological samples, of which bloodstains are one example.

**11. c.** This idea can be found in the last paragraph.

**12. d.** There is no discussion of any of these factors in the passage.

**13. c.** The other choices, though mentioned in the passage, are not the main idea.

**14. a.** While keeping one's temper is probably an aspect of the program, it is not explicitly mentioned in the passage.

**15. a.** This idea can be found in the second sentence.

**16. b.** This idea is stated in the fourth sentence.

**17. d.** The passage tells you that crimes against adolescents are most likely to be committed by offenders of the same age.

**18. d.** The passage begins with an explicit reference to the Supreme Court and then outlines how Supreme Court and other court decisions have influenced police interviewing and interrogation techniques.

**19. c.** This idea is stated in the third sentence.

**20. c.** Choice **a** is specifically mentioned as a non-accusatory question, so you must infer that similar questions are also non-accusatory. Asking for an alibi infers that the questioner believes the individual did something wrong and is, therefore, accusatory.

**21. a.** The passage does not mention where the warnings must be given; in this instance, the name of the court case tells you only where it originated, not where it is applicable.

**22. b.** This is stated in the fifth sentence.

**23. b.** This best summarizes the overall theme of the passage.

**24. a.** This best summarizes the totality of the passage; choice **c**, while seemingly correct, covers only one specific aspect of the passage.

**25. c.** It is the only one that is skills-based.

**26. b.** The choice can be inferred from the passage's description of studying laws and court cases as education.

**27. a.** See the second sentence of the passage.

**28. c.** See the first sentence of the passage.

**29. d.** This reason is implied throughout the passage.

**30. a.** This reason is stated in the first paragraph of the passage.

## Part Two: Writing

**31. d.** Choices **a** and **b** contain sentence fragments; choice **c** uses commas incorrectly.

**32. c.** The words *returned*, *finished*, and *left* are all in the past tense; this is the only sentence that uses proper parallel structure.

**33. d.** Choices **b** and **c** contain sentence fragments.

**34. b.** Choices **a** and **d** are run-on sentences; choice **c** contains a sentence fragment.

**35. d.** Each of the other choices includes a sentence fragment.

**36. c.** The verb should be singular, *was*, to agree with *the guard*. The verbs in the second half of the sentence should also be in the past tense.

**37. a.** It is the only complete sentence; choice **b** misuses the comma; choice **c** is a run-on sentence, and choice **d** contains a sentence fragment.

**38. c.** Choice **c** uses the correct preposition, *of*.

**39. d.** The modifier *with a growl* should be placed next to the *masked gunman*.

**40. b.** *Bravest* is the correct form of the adjective; it is the superlative (brave, braver, bravest).

**41. a.** The other choices contain sentence fragments.

**42. b.** The other choices contain sentence fragments.

**43. d.** The correct pronoun case forms are used; choice **a** contains a redundant subject (*My partner Rosie and I, we...*); choices **b** and **c** contain incorrect pronoun case forms.

**44. a.** This is the only choice in which the modifier *sharpshooter for many years* is clear and correctly placed.

**45. b.** This is the only choice that contains the correct forms of the adjectives *tough* and *fair*.

**46. c.** *However* is the clearest and most logical transition word.

**47. b.** The correction preposition is *by*; choices **a**, **c**, and **d** contain incorrect prepositions.

**48. d.** The correct form of the verb is *sniffed*.

**49. c.** *To remove* and *lie* are the correct forms of these verbs.

**50. a.** The subject *recession* agrees in number with its verb *is*; choices **b**, **c**, and **d** present subjects and verbs that do not agree.

**51. d.** The verbs *are sequestered* and *become* are both present tense; choices **a**, **b**, and **c** present unnecessary shifts in tense.

**52. a.** The *neither...nor* construction always takes a singular verb; *both...and* always takes a plural verb.

**53. c.** This is the choice that does not contain an unnecessary shift in person.

**53. c.** Unlike question 40, in this case you must use a comparative, not a superlative, because only two dogs are being compared.

**54. b.** This is the only choice in which the pronoun is not ambiguous; choice **c** also contains a misplaced modifier.

**55. d.** This is the only choice that does not contain unnecessary shifts in person.

## Part Three: Vocabulary

**56. b.** *Latent* means something that is hidden or unseen but is capable of being exposed or revealed.

**57. d.** To be *inundated* means to be flooded.

**58. d.** To be *eccentric* is deviate from the norm, to be unconventional or peculiar.

**59. b.** *Docile* means obedient or submissive.

**60. c.** To *eliminate* something is to remove or erase it.

**61. a.** Something that is *imminent* is ready to take place; it will happen soon.

**62. d.** *Proficient* most nearly means skilled.

**63. a.** *Express* most nearly means articulate.

**64. b.** *Lethargic* most nearly means tired.

**65. c.** When something is *outmoded*, it is out-of-date or obsolete.

**66. b.** *Integrity* is a strong adherence to a set of values; it most closely means honesty.

**67. b.** *Credible* most nearly means believable.

**68. a.** *Overt* means open and observable; it is the opposite of closed or hidden.

**69. a.** A *panacea* is a remedy or a cure-all.

**70. b.** A *glib* remark is one that is quick or fluent but may seem insincere.

**71. b.** *Plausible* most nearly means believable or credible.

**72. a.** A *spiteful* person is malicious and intends harm.

**73.** A *precedent* is a prior example that often serves to authorize subsequent actions.

**74. b.** *Ideologies* are a set of rigid believes held by specific groups.

**75. d.** To *delegate* something is to assign it to someone else.

**76. a.** Something that is *exigent* requires immediate attention or action because it is of a serious nature.

**77. d.** To *articulate* an idea is to express it clearly.

**78. a.** An *expansive* mood is one that is open and outgoing.

**79. b.** Something that is *detrimental* is damaging.

**80. c.** To be held *accountable* is to be held responsible or answerable.

## Part Four: Spelling

If you are unsure of why your answers to Part Four were incorrect, consult a dictionary for the specific word or a grammar text for a review of general spelling rules.

**81. d.**

**82. d.**

**83. c.**

**84. b.**

**85. a.**

**86. c.**

**87. a.**

**88. b.**

**89. d.**

**90. d.**

**91. c.**

**92. d.**

**93.**

**94. b.**

**95. c.**

**96. a.**

**97. d.**

**98. a.**

**99. b.**

**100. a.**

## Scoring

Most U.S. cities require a score of at least 70% to pass a police officer exam. Because this exam has 100 questions, the number you answered correctly is your percentage: If you got 70 questions correct, your score is 70%.

What you should do next depends not only on how you score, but also on whether the city you're applying to uses your written score to help determine your rank on the eligibility list. Some cities use other factors, such as your performance in an oral board or interview, to decide whether or not to hire you. In that case, all you need to do is to pass the written exam in order to make it to the next step in the process, and a score of at least 70% is good enough. In other cities, however, your written score, either by itself or in combination with other factors, is used to place you on the eligibility list. The higher your score, the more likely you are to be hired.

Use this practice exam as a way to analyze your performance. Pay attention to the areas in which you miss the most questions. If most of your mistakes are in the reading comprehension questions, then you know you need to practice your reading skills. Or perhaps you had difficulty with the spelling section. Once you see where you need help, then your mission will be to study the chapters in this book on the relevant skills to develop your test-taking strategies.

To help you see where your trouble spots are, break down your scores according to the four sections below:

Part One: _____ questions correct
Part Two: _____ questions correct
Part Three: _____ questions correct
Part Four: _____ questions correct

Write down the number of correct answers for each section, and then add up all three numbers for your overall score. Each question is worth one point and the total you arrive at after adding all the numbers is also the percentage of questions that you answered correctly on the test.

And now forget about your total score; what's more important right now is your score on the individual sections of the exam.

Below is a table that shows you which of the instructional chapters correspond to the three parts of the exam. Your best bet is to review all of the chapters carefully, but you'll want to spend the most time on the chapters that correspond to the kind of question that gave you the most trouble.

| EXAM PART | CHAPTER |
|---|---|
| One | 9 |
| Two | 8 |
| Three | 8 |
| Four | 8 |

Remember, reading and writing skills are important not only for the exam, but also for your job as a police officer. So the time you spend improving those skills will pay off—not only in higher exam scores, but also in career success.

After you've read the relevant chapters, take the second exam of this type, in Chapter 11, to see how much you've improved.

# 6 ▶ POLICE OFFICER PRACTICE EXAM 2

## CHAPTER SUMMARY

The practice exam in this chapter is an example of the kind of job-related exam used by many police departments around the country. It tests skills police officers actually use on the job—not only basic skills like math and reading, but also map reading, memory, and good judgment and common sense.

**A**s you did with Practice Exam 1, you should treat this exam as if it were the real thing. There is a new answer sheet for this exam; once again, make a copy or neatly tear it out so you can fill it in as you would during the actual test. Following the answer sheet is the exam, followed by the correct answers and explanations of why they are correct. The last section of the chapter is an explanation of how to score your exam.

Practice Exam 1 was an example of a police exam that tested your reading and writing skills. This practice exam is different. In addition to testing for the same skills as the first exam, it also tests your ability to memorize pictures and written material, your map-reading skills, your ability to do simple math, and your ability to use judgment to solve situations that occur frequently in police work. To create realistic test conditions, give yourself $2\frac{1}{2}$ hours to complete the test *in addition to* the 15 minutes you spend memorizing.

The 100 questions on Practice Exam 2 are divided into three sections:

- Part One: Memorization and Visualization consists of a set of pictures and text that you have to study and then a set of questions that you must answer based on the visuals and the text. You will not be allowed to look back at the material as you respond to these questions.
- Part Two: Reading covers map reading and reading comprehension.
- Part Three: Judgment and Problem Solving gives you questions that test deductive and inductive reasoning, your ability to apply good judgment and common sense in specific situations, and your ability to solve problems involving numbers (math word problems).

For best results, approach this exam as if it were the real thing. Find a quiet place where you can take the exam, and arm yourself with a few sharp number 2 pencils. Give yourself 15 minutes to study the memory material at the beginning of the exam. Then start the practice test, which begins with questions about what you memorized. Give yourself two and a half hours to complete the test, in addition to the 15 minutes you spent memorizing.

After the exam is an answer key complete with explanations of why the correct answer is the best choice. An explanation of how to interpret your test score follows the answer key.

## Police Officer Practice Exam 2

1. (a) (b) (c) (d)
2. (a) (b) (c) (d)
3. (a) (b) (c) (d)
4. (a) (b) (c) (d)
5. (a) (b) (c) (d)
6. (a) (b) (c) (d)
7. (a) (b) (c) (d)
8. (a) (b) (c) (d)
9. (a) (b) (c) (d)
10. (a) (b) (c) (d)
11. (a) (b) (c) (d)
12. (a) (b) (c) (d)
13. (a) (b) (c) (d)
14. (a) (b) (c) (d)
15. (a) (b) (c) (d)
16. (a) (b) (c) (d)
17. (a) (b) (c) (d)
18. (a) (b) (c) (d)
19. (a) (b) (c) (d)
20. (a) (b) (c) (d)
21. (a) (b) (c) (d)
22. (a) (b) (c) (d)
23. (a) (b) (c) (d)
24. (a) (b) (c) (d)
25. (a) (b) (c) (d)
26. (a) (b) (c) (d)
27. (a) (b) (c) (d)
28. (a) (b) (c) (d)
29. (a) (b) (c) (d)
30. (a) (b) (c) (d)
31. (a) (b) (c) (d)
32. (a) (b) (c) (d)
33. (a) (b) (c) (d)
34. (a) (b) (c) (d)
35. (a) (b) (c) (d)
36. (a) (b) (c) (d)
37. (a) (b) (c) (d)
38. (a) (b) (c) (d)
39. (a) (b) (c) (d)
40. (a) (b) (c) (d)
41. (a) (b) (c) (d)
42. (a) (b) (c) (d)
43. (a) (b) (c) (d)
44. (a) (b) (c) (d)
45. (a) (b) (c) (d)
46. (a) (b) (c) (d)
47. (a) (b) (c) (d)
48. (a) (b) (c) (d)
49. (a) (b) (c) (d)
50. (a) (b) (c) (d)
51. (a) (b) (c) (d)
52. (a) (b) (c) (d)
53. (a) (b) (c) (d)
54. (a) (b) (c) (d)
55. (a) (b) (c) (d)
56. (a) (b) (c) (d)
57. (a) (b) (c) (d)
58. (a) (b) (c) (d)
59. (a) (b) (c) (d)
60. (a) (b) (c) (d)
61. (a) (b) (c) (d)
62. (a) (b) (c) (d)
63. (a) (b) (c) (d)
64. (a) (b) (c) (d)
65. (a) (b) (c) (d)
66. (a) (b) (c) (d)
67. (a) (b) (c) (d)
68. (a) (b) (c) (d)
69. (a) (b) (c) (d)
70. (a) (b) (c) (d)
71. (a) (b) (c) (d)
72. (a) (b) (c) (d)
73. (a) (b) (c) (d)
74. (a) (b) (c) (d)
75. (a) (b) (c) (d)
76. (a) (b) (c) (d)
77. (a) (b) (c) (d)
78. (a) (b) (c) (d)
79. (a) (b) (c) (d)
80. (a) (b) (c) (d)
81. (a) (b) (c) (d)
82. (a) (b) (c) (d)
83. (a) (b) (c) (d)
84. (a) (b) (c) (d)
85. (a) (b) (c) (d)
86. (a) (b) (c) (d)
87. (a) (b) (c) (d)
88. (a) (b) (c) (d)
89. (a) (b) (c) (d)
90. (a) (b) (c) (d)
91. (a) (b) (c) (d)
92. (a) (b) (c) (d)
93. (a) (b) (c) (d)
94. (a) (b) (c) (d)
95. (a) (b) (c) (d)
96. (a) (b) (c) (d)
97. (a) (b) (c) (d)
98. (a) (b) (c) (d)
99. (a) (b) (c) (d)
100. (a) (b) (c) (d)

# Police Officer Practice Exam 2

## Study Booklet

You have 15 minutes to study the memory material at the beginning of the exam before starting the practice test, which begins with questions about what you have memorized.

The memory questions are divided into two distinct forms of memorization. The first part contains wanted posters, and the second part is an article on the police procedure known as a Terry stop. After reviewing the posters and reading the article for a total of 15 minutes for both sections, turn the page and answer the test questions about the study material. To create the same conditions as the actual test, **do not refer back to the study booklet to answer the questions.**

### MISSING
### Valeria Linda Velez

**DESCRIPTION:**

    **Age:** 15
    **Race:** Hispanic
    **Height:** 5'3"
    **Weight:** 110 lbs.
    **Hair:** black, straight, shoulder-length, orange streak from center part on left-hand side
    **Eyes:** greenish gray
    **Skin:** light brown

**IDENTIFYING SCARS OR MARKS:** None
**REMARKS:** Last seen in the company of a middle-aged Hispanic man in front of Sweet Things Candy Shop in the Adventure Mall in Westville on Saturday, May 21, at 3 P.M. wearing red slacks, red-and-white striped polo shirt, with her hair hanging loose; braces on top front teeth.
**IF LOCATED:** Call Westville, CT, Police Department, Missing Persons Unit, at 344-555-1220.

## WANTED
### Michael Hagan Finan

**ALIASES:** Robbie Hagan
**WANTED BY:** Hoboken, NJ, Police Department
**CHARGES:** Drug Possession and Sales
**DESCRIPTION:**

> **Age:** 24
> **Race:** White
> **Height:** 6'3"
> **Weight:** 195 lbs.
> **Hair:** Dirty blond
> **Eyes:** Green
> **Facial Hair:** Moustache and small, rounded beard, both are darker than hair color

**IDENTIFYING SCARS OR MARKS:** Tattoo on inner right bicep of black peace symbol.
**REMARKS:** Rides a black Honda 750cc with a cracked headlight and a red hawk painted on the tank. Last seen in Hoboken, NJ, and believed to reside in Camden, NJ, with girlfriend.

## WANTED
### Lin Yang

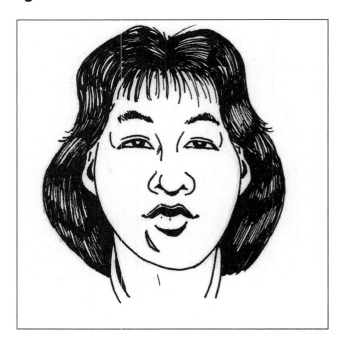

**ALIASES:** Lisa Yang, Linda Yang
**WANTED BY:** North Dakota State Police
**CHARGES:** Burglary
**DESCRIPTION:**

> **Age:** 36
> **Race:** Asian
> **Height:** 5'2"
> **Weight:** 110 lbs.
> **Hair:** Black
> **Eyes:** Brown

**IDENTIFYING SCARS OR MARKS:** Scar on chin.
**REMARKS:** Last seen at 3 Elks Casino in Grand Forks, North Dakota. Yang may be headed for Fresno, California, driving a white Firebird.

# WANTED
## Louis Robert Hart

**ALIASES:** Heartbreak Kid, LR, Blackjack Luis
**WANTED BY:** FBI
**CHARGES:** Bank Robbery
**DESCRIPTION:**

  **Age:** 45
  **Race:** Black
  **Height:** 6'3"
  **Weight:** 255 lbs.
  **Hair:** Black
  **Facial Hair:** Black moustache
  **Skin:** Light-skinned, often mistaken for Hispanic
  **Eyes:** Brown

**REMARKS:** Hart is a known gambler and card-shark who frequents casinos in Atlantic City, NJ, often in the company of women considerably younger than he and flashily dressed.

**CAUTION ADVISED:** Hart is known to carry a switchblade knife and, on occasion, a diving knife, either strapped to his left leg. He is not known to carry a firearm.

## WANTED
## Thomas Tankle

**ALIASES:** Thomas the Tank, Tommieboy

**WANTED BY:** Amtrak Railroad Police

**CHARGES:** Criminal mischief, tampering, theft of railroad property

**DESCRIPTION:**

> **Age:** 45
>
> **Race:** Caucasian
>
> **Height:** 6'0"
>
> **Weight:** 195 lbs.
>
> **Hair:** None; subject is bald
>
> **Facial hair:** None, subject is clean-shaven
>
> **Eyes:** Green

**IDENTIFYING SCARS OR MARKS:** Wears a black patch over right eye; may shave head rather than be naturally bald; pinky finger is missing from knuckle to nail.

**REMARKS:** Last seen in Philadelphia; previously worked for Conrail Railroad prior to being terminated for drug and alcohol use. Is familiar with railroad terminology and the layout of rail yard facilities; frequents bars in the area of 30th Street Station; drives a green Subaru with New Jersey license plates. Place of residence unknown.

**CAUTION ADVISED:** Tankle is known to carry various tools, including wire cutters, pliers, and screwdrivers, that could be used as weapons. His familiarity with railroad terminology and facilities makes it easy for him to explain his presence on railroad property if confronted by employees. He is not known to carry a firearm.

## Police Procedure—Making a Terry Stop

Often in the course of routine patrol, a police officer needs to briefly detain an individual for questioning without specific probable cause, and possibly to frisk that individual for weapons. Probable cause is defined as a reasonable belief that a person has committed a crime, is committing a crime, or is about to commit a crime. A frisk occurs when a police officer runs his or her hands rapidly over the clothing or through the pockets of a suspect. Although the officer may decide not to take an individual into custody an individual who has been stopped and frisked for weapons, this type of stop is considered a form of detention. It is known as a Terry stop, based on the 1968 U.S. Supreme Court case *Terry v. State of Ohio* that authorized such stops. In that case, the Court determined that a Terry stop does not violate a person's right to be free from unreasonable search and seizure as long as certain procedures are followed by the police.

The Supreme Court ruled that first, the person who is stopped must be behaving in some manner that arouses the police officer's suspicion. Second, the officer must believe that immediate action is required to prevent a crime from being committed or to prevent a suspect from escaping. Thirdly, the officer must have a reasonable belief that the individual is armed and dangerous to make the frisk permissible.

In determining whether an individual is acting in a suspicious manner, a police officer must rely on training and experience. Circumstances in each case will be different, but an officer must be able to explain what it was about the person's behavior that aroused suspicion, including whether it was one particular action or a series of actions taken together. For instance, it may not be unusual for shoppers in a store to wander up and down the aisles looking at merchandise; however, it may be suspicious if a person does this for a very long period of time, seems to be checking the locations of surveillance cameras, is wearing loose clothing that would facilitate shoplifting, or in a number of ways does not "match" the area being searched. An example of the latter would be a youthful looking male spending time in the women's or children's clothing department looking more at other shoppers than at the merchandise. Similarly, a person wearing sweat pants and a T-shirt running through a residential neighborhood may not arouse suspicion, but a person dressed in similar clothing running very quickly, frequently hiking up his sweat pants, and turning around to see if he is being chased could be considered to be acting suspiciously. A person who simply appears out of place based on how he or she is dressed or who appears different from others on the street or in the store, parking facility, etc., is not sufficient cause for suspicion to permit an officer to make a Terry stop.

In addition to the behavior that arouses the officer's attention, the officer must believe that immediate action is required to prevent the commission of a crime or to prevent a suspect from escaping. Although an officer may take action under *Terry* even if there is no immediate danger to the officer or to others in the area, an important element of whether an officer should undertake a Terry stop or wait for additional information is based on safety considerations. This is an example of a police officer's exercise of discretion based on experience and the totality of the circumstances.

A good example of when a Terry stop is provided by the facts of the case that led to the decision. In fall 1963, while on a downtown beat he had been patrolling for many years, a Cleveland police officer observed two men taking turns walking back and forth along an identical route, pausing to stare in the same store window after which they discussed something on the corner. They repeated this for a total of a dozen trips, after which they were joined by a third man who left after a brief conversation. Suspecting the two men of planning to rob the store, the detective followed them and saw them rejoin the third man a few blocks away in front of another store. The officer approached the three, identified himself as a police officer, and asked their names. Their answers were unclear; the officer spun Terry around, patted down his outside clothing, and felt a pistol in his overcoat pocket. He reached inside the overcoat pocket, but was unable to remove the gun. The officer ordered the three into the store. He removed Terry's overcoat, took out a revolver, and ordered the three to face the wall with their hands raised. He patted down the outer clothing of the other two men and seized a revolver from the outside overcoat pocket of one of them. He did not put his hands under any of their outer garments until he felt the guns. Two, including Terry, were subsequently charged with carrying concealed weapons. The case that went to the Supreme Court centered on whether the officer's search was legal.

As shown in the facts of the Terry case, once an officer has made the decision to detain someone, the next decision is whether or not to frisk that individual.

As with the initial decision to detain, the decision will be based on the officer's training and experience. If the officer feels the detainee poses a threat to the officer's safety, or the safety of others, the detainee should be frisked. For example, although there are exceptions, a person detained under suspicion of shoplifting is less likely to be armed with a weapon than someone detained under suspicion of being about to commit a robbery. The detainee's body movements prior to being detained may also be taken into consideration; for instance, someone observed frequently checking his or her waistband or hiking up trousers may be exhibiting behavior indicating carrying a firearm, as might be someone wearing a heavy coat on an 80-degree day. If a person's behavior seems to indicate the person is waiting to produce a weapon and threaten the safety of the officer or those nearby, this should go into the officer's decision to make a Terry stop and conduct a subsequent frisk.

## Part One: Memorization and Visualization

*Answer the following questions based on the wanted posters you have just studied. Do not refer back to the study material to answer these questions.*

1. How old is Valeria Linda Guerra?
   a. 15
   b. 20
   c. 30
   d. 36

2. How old is Lin Yang?
   a. 15
   b. 20
   c. 30
   d. 36

3. Who is described as participating in gambling?
   a. Lin Yang and Luis Robert Hart
   b. Michael Hagan Finan and Thomas Tankle
   c. Lin Yang and Michael Hagan Finan
   d. Thomas Tankle and Luis Robert Hart

4. Identifying scars or marks on Thomas Tankle include which of the following?
   a. a tattoo on his right bicep
   b. a scar on his chin
   c. track marks from drug injections on his left inner arm
   d. none of the above

5. Which of the wanted persons is described as possibly mistaken for Hispanic?
   a. Michael Hagan Finan
   b. Luis Robert Hart
   c. Valeria Linda Guerra
   d. Thomas Tankle

6. Who was described as possibly armed?
   a. Luis Robert Hart and Thomas Tankle
   b. Michael Hagan Finan and Thomas Tankle
   c. Michael Hagan Finan and Luis Robert Hart
   d. Lin Yang and Thomas Tankle

7. When last seen, Valeria Linda Guerra was
   a. being kidnapped.
   b. in the company of a middle-aged Hispanic man.
   c. buying a candy bar.
   d. with her mother.

8. Luis Robert Hart is wanted for
   a. drug possession and sales.
   b. burglary.
   c. bank robbery.
   d. none of the above

9. Lin Yang is wanted for
   a. drug possession and sales.
   b. burglary.
   c. bank robbery.
   d. none of the above

10. Valeria Linda Guerra is wanted for
    a. drug possession and sales.
    b. burglary.
    c. bank robbery.
    d. none of the above

11. Michael Hagan Finan has a tattoo on his right arm depicting a
    a. peace symbol.
    b. red hawk.
    c. motorcycle.
    d. ace of spades.

**12.** Who is described as often in the company of flashily dressed women?
  **a.** Thomas Tankle
  **b.** Lin Yang
  **c.** Michael Hagan Finan
  **d.** Luis Robert Hart

**13.** Who is wanted on charges that could be described as related to past employment?
  **a.** Thomas Tankle
  **b.** Lin Yang
  **c.** Michael Hagan Finan
  **d.** Luis Robert Hart

**14.** Who is wanted by a state police department?
  **a.** Thomas Tankle
  **b.** Lin Yang
  **c.** Michael Hagan Finan
  **d.** Luis Robert Hart

**15.** Who is described as having facial hair?
  **a.** Michael Hagan Finan and Thomas Tankle
  **b.** Luis Robert Hart and Thomas Tankle
  **c.** Michael Hagan Finan and Luis Robert Hart
  **d.** Luis Robert Hart and the Hispanic man seen with Valeria Linda Velez

*Answer the following questions based on the reading on Terry stops. Do not refer back to the study material to answer these questions.*

**16.** According to the passage, a police officer may stop a person
  **a.** for any reason at all.
  **b.** if the person's behavior has aroused the officer's suspicion.
  **c.** if a person is younger than everyone else in a store.
  **d.** none of the above

**17.** As described in the passage, probable cause is best defined as
  **a.** a reasonable belief a person has committed a crime.
  **b.** a reasonable belief that a person is in the act of committing a crime.
  **c.** a reasonable belief that a person is about to commit a crime.
  **d.** all of the above

**18.** A Terry stop is
  **a.** an arrest for robbery.
  **b.** an arrest for shoplifting.
  **c.** the brief detention and questioning of a suspicious person.
  **d.** an officer's frisking of a suspect for drugs.

**19.** Based on the passage, in which situation would a Terry stop be most appropriate?
  **a.** A man is walking through the women's section of a department store.
  **b.** A woman is walking through the men's section of a department store.
  **c.** Two women are pacing back and forth in front of small dress shop in a mall and frequently checking their skirts' waistbands.
  **d.** Two men are sitting on a bench in front of a small dress shop in a mall with shopping bags clustered around them.

**20.** A frisk can be defined as
  **a.** police officers running their hands over a person's outer garments.
  **b.** police officers stopping a person to search for drugs.
  **c.** police officers chasing a suspect who has dropped drugs on the street.
  **d.** police officers tackling a person running away from them.

**21.** The case *Terry v. State of Ohio* was decided by
   **a.** a Cleveland municipal judge.
   **b.** an Ohio state court.
   **c.** the United States Supreme Court.
   **d.** none of the above

**22.** According to the passage, the determination that a person appears suspicious
   **a.** means someone looks out of place.
   **b.** depends on the circumstances of each situation.
   **c.** pertains only to dangerous crimes.
   **d.** is something only a police officer can judge.

**23.** In the case that led to the ruling in *Terry v. State of Ohio*, the officer
   **a.** was a rookie.
   **b.** was an experienced officer.
   **c.** was off-duty shopping.
   **d.** was off-duty working as a security officer.

**24.** In the case that led to the ruling in *Terry v. State of Ohio*, the suspects were
   **a.** trying to purchase a firearm.
   **b.** walking back and forth, staring, and conferring in the area near a store.
   **c.** accosting women coming out of a store.
   **d.** walking out of a store hurriedly as if they had stolen something.

**25.** Which category of officer would be likely to have the most credibility in making a Terry stop?
   **a.** A newly-hired police officer working on a new beat.
   **b.** An experienced officer working a new beat.
   **c.** An officer of the same race and sex as the suspect.
   **d.** An experienced officer working a regular beat.

**26.** According to the passage, an officer may make a Terry stop to
   **a.** discourage loitering.
   **b.** prevent a crime from being committed or a suspect from escaping.
   **c.** find out if a person is carrying a concealed weapon.
   **d.** rule out suspects after a crime has been committed.

**27.** You are on foot patrol in a downtown mall when you observe two men standing a street corner and then walking slowly past a store selling expensive children's shoes. They repeat their activities three or four more times. Another person stops, talks to them, and walks past the store two times. You would be justified in making a Terry stop for any of the following reasons, except
   **a.** their actions appeared that they might be planning to rob the store.
   **b.** one of them appeared to be wearing an ankle holster.
   **c.** they were loitering in the mall.
   **d.** their actions appeared that they might be planning to kidnap one of the children.

**28.** If you were asked to categorize the area of law that a Terry stop pertains to, your best choice would be
   **a.** police officer training requirements.
   **b.** search and seizure.
   **c.** racial profiling.
   **d.** patrol practices.

**29.** While just beginning your patrol of the Eastview bus station at the start of your 4 P.M. to midnight shift, you notice a young woman sitting across from a bank that closes at 5 P.M. She is checking her watch frequently and making eye contact with a young man who appears to be in line waiting for an outgoing bus. When the young man leaves the line and sits down next to the young woman, you believe they may be planning to rob the bank just as it closes. You should

   **a.** immediately begin to question the two suspects.

   **b.** go into to bank, warn the employees, and announce that the customers must leave immediately.

   **c.** ask the bank security officer to call your dispatcher to request backup while you keep the suspects in view.

   **d.** clear the area around the bench on which the suspects are sitting.

**30.** Which of the following activities might best be perceived as suspicious enough to warrant a Terry stop?

   **a.** Youths standing around a park basketball court watching a pick-up game.

   **b.** A person carrying an unboxed television in a residential neighborhood and frequently turning around as if concerned he is being followed.

   **c.** Three young women standing in front of a jewelry store and pointing at a display of rings.

   **d.** Four individuals standing in front of a movie theater ticket window arguing with the clerk about the posted time of the film.

## Part Two: Reading Skills

*Answer questions 31–35 based on the following passage.*

While patrolling in their marked vehicle, on May 19, 2007, Officers Hernandez and Elmsford received a call from their dispatcher at 4:10 A.M. to respond to a report of a burglary at 945 Elm Street at D & D Deli. They arrived at the location, a convenience grocery store and gas station, approximately 10 minutes later. The officers noted that the store's large window to the right of the front door was completely smashed but that a window to the left of the front door appeared intact. Exiting the patrol car, Officer Hernandez immediately radioed to the dispatcher to request additional officers to assist in searching the location. She waited in front on the side of the store near the intact window while Officer Elmsford started down an alley on the left-hand side of the store, intending to watch the back door in the event anyone attempted to exit.

While awaiting the backup officers, Officer Hernandez was approached by Tom Minor, who said he lived in the upstairs flat directly across the street. He stated that he had heard the window breaking and had called the police. The backup officers, Sergeant Duke and Officer Pabon, arrived approximately 20 minutes after Officer Hernandez requested their presence. Sergeant Duke remained at the front with Officer Hernandez, and Officer Pabon took the same route as Officer Elmsford to meet him at the back door. During a search of the interior, the officers discovered that the cash register had been pried open but that no shelves appeared in disarray. After determining that the store was empty, they contacted the store owner, whose name and phone number were near the counter adjacent to the cash register. Officers Hernandez and Elmsford indicated to the dispatcher they would await the owner, David Days, who indicated he would arrive within no more than 20 minutes. Sgt. Duke and Officer Pabon departed to resume patrol.

**31.** According to the passage, which officer spoke with Tom Minor?
   **a.** Hernandez
   **b.** Elmsford
   **c.** Duke
   **d.** Pabon

**32.** Where did the burglary occur?
   **a.** a second-story flat
   **b.** a grocery store and gas station
   **c.** on Elmsford Street
   **d.** a small alley

**33.** Approximately what time did the backup officers arrive?
   **a.** 4:10 A.M.
   **b.** 4:20 A.M.
   **c.** 4:30 A.M.
   **d.** 4:40 A.M.

**34.** What was the immediate sign of forced entry?
   **a.** The front door was smashed.
   **b.** A front window to the right of the door was smashed.
   **c.** A front window to the left of the door was smashed.
   **d.** There was blood leading away from the front door.

**35.** How did the suspect(s) most likely exit the location?
   **a.** Through the front door.
   **b.** Through the smashed window.
   **c.** Through the back door.
   **d.** There is not enough information to determine.

*Answer questions 36–40 based on the following passage.*

Crime prevention through environmental design (CPTED) grew out of the concept of defensible space developed by an architect and urban planner. Sometimes referred to as designing out crime, it has become an important tool for police in assisting communities in crime prevention efforts. The theory is based on the belief that design of the physical environment can create opportunities for people to come together and at the same time can remove the opportunity for criminals to act freely. It does this by concentrating on a facility's design, landscaping, and security technology, including a combination of security and police personnel, to create a series of preventive measures that combine to reduce problems or disruptions to a facility. These same preventive measures are meant to provide a sense of confidence to the public that a location is secure.

CPTED is most cost-effective when included in original design plans because this saves the costs associated with renovating or moving existing facilities. An example of a CPTED-based renovation in a mall or a transit facility would be moving the payment area of a parking lot where crimes have occurred closer to where it can be seen by general users or by the facility's security officer. In this case, the placement of the payment area increases safety through the environmental decision of moving it into a safer area. The same example in a new facility would require someone with knowledge of CPTED principles considering the placement of the payment area during the design phase so as to prevent having to move it later.

**36.** According to the passage, police departments are most likely to use CPTED when
   **a.** helping communities develop crime prevention strategies.
   **b.** looking for car thieves on city streets.
   **c.** designing new police stations.
   **d.** all of the above.

**37.** The passage states that CPTED was developed by
   **a.** police community relations units.
   **b.** parking lot developers.
   **c.** an architect and urban planner.
   **d.** private security directors.

**38.** Based on the passage, CPTED would be least useful when
   **a.** renovating a suburban train station.
   **b.** renovating a shopping mall.
   **c.** renovating a private residence.
   **d.** renovating a public-access interior courtyard in a museum.

**39.** According to the passage, CPTED is most cost-effective
   **a.** in renovations.
   **b.** in new construction.
   **c.** when combined with other uniformed patrol tactics.
   **d.** when combined with plainclothes patrol tactics.

**40.** As a police officer, you would most likely be expected to have a knowledge of CPTED as a
   **a.** homicide detective.
   **b.** crime prevention officer.
   **c.** crime scene investigator.
   **d.** stationhouse sergeant.

*Answer questions 41–45 based on the following passage.*

On April 20, 2006, at 2:00 P.M., Officers Watts and Johnson were on patrol in a marked black and white police vehicle. Watts was driving the police vehicle westbound on First Street approaching Broadway when the officers observed Daniel Bardus driving a green Chevrolet northbound on Broadway. Both police officers noted that Bardus continued northbound through the intersection, failing to come to a complete stop for the posted stop sign.

Watts negotiated a right turn and began to follow Bardus. Watts activated the vehicle's emergency lights while Johnson radioed in Bardus's license number. Instead of stopping, Bardus accelerated to 60 mph. Johnson radioed the dispatch center, stating that the officers were in pursuit of Bardus. The dispatch center acknowledged the pursuit and informed Watts and Johnson that the car being driven by Bardus was stolen.

A few minutes into the pursuit, Watts and Johnson were joined by a second police vehicle driven by Sergeant Ducis. Shortly after Ducis joined the pursuit, Bardus attempted a left turn off of Broadway onto Platea Street, but Bardus was traveling too fast and his vehicle's tires lost traction, sending him into a violent spinout. Bardus's vehicle spun out of control and struck a light post approximately 150 feet west of Broadway. Bardus exited his vehicle and ran northbound between the houses.

The passenger officer in the police car was the first to begin chasing Bardus on foot between the houses and tackled him with the partner officer. The sergeant followed seconds behind. Officer Watts handcuffed Bardus and helped him to his feet. The last officer on the scene searched Bardus and found a small handgun in Bardus's left front pocket.

**41.** Why did the officers initially try to stop Bardus?
- **a.** He was driving a stolen car.
- **b.** He failed to stop for the officers.
- **c.** He violated a stop sign.
- **d.** He was carrying a gun.

**42.** What is the most likely address of Bardus's capture?
- **a.** 250 Platea Street
- **b.** 250 Broadway
- **c.** 100 Broadway
- **d.** 250 First Street

**43.** Which officer tackled Bardus?
- **a.** Watts
- **b.** Johnson
- **c.** Ducis
- **d.** unknown

**44.** Who found the handgun?
- **a.** Watts
- **b.** Johnson
- **c.** Ducis
- **d.** unknown

**45** According to the passage, how many total vehicles were involved in the pursuit?
- **a.** one
- **b.** two
- **c.** three
- **d.** four

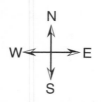

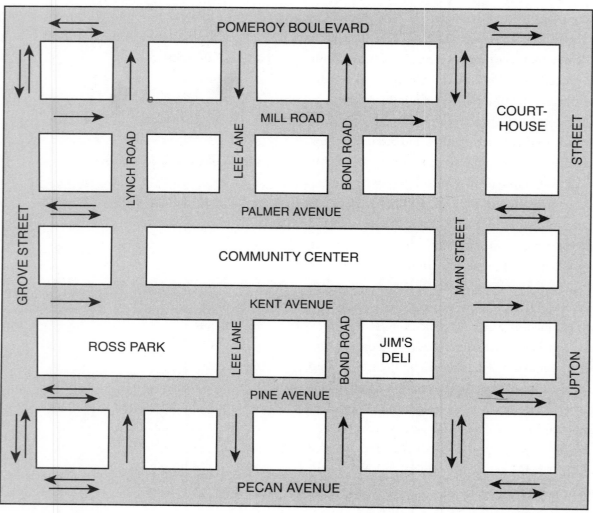

## Map Reading

*Answer questions 46–50 based on the map on the facing page. Review the directional arrows and the map key. You are not permitted to go the wrong way on a one-way street.*

**46.** While driving northbound on Main Street, Sergeant Nixey makes a left turn onto Palmer Avenue, then a right turn onto Lynch Road, and then a right turn onto Mill Road. What direction is he facing?
  **a.** east
  **b.** south
  **c.** west
  **d.** north

**47.** You are driving southbound on Main Street after having left the courthouse. After passing the Community Center and Jim's Deli, you make a left onto Pine Avenue, then a left onto Upton Street, then a right onto Palmer Avenue, and then a right onto Bond Road. What direction are you facing?
  **a.** west
  **b.** south
  **c.** north
  **d.** east

**48.** You and Officer Ali are in your patrol car facing east on Kent Avenue and Lee Lane when you are dispatched to a medical emergency at a residence located at the northeast corner of Lynch Road and Mill Road. After continuing east on Kent Avenue, what is your quickest route to reach the residence?
  **a.** North on Main Street to Mill Road, and then west on Mill Road to the northeast corner of Lynch Road and Mill Road.
  **b.** North on Main Street, then west on Pomeroy Boulevard, and then south on Lynch Road.
  **c.** South on Main Street, then west on Pine Avenue, then north on Grove Street, and then east on Mill Road to Lynch Road.
  **d.** North on Main Street, then west on Palmer Avenue, and then north on Lynch Road to Mill Road.

**49.** The number of roadways designated avenues that are two-way is
  **a.** one.
  **b.** two.
  **c.** three.
  **d.** four.

**50.** Officer Patel is parked at the northwest corner of Ross Park and wants to follow the most direct route to the Main Street and Palmer Avenue entrance to the courthouse. She should
  **a.** travel east on Kent Avenue and then north on Main Street to Palmer Avenue.
  **b.** travel east on Kent Avenue, then north on Lynch Road, and then east on Palmer Avenue.
  **c.** travel north on Grove Street, then east on Palmer Avenue to Main Street.
  **d.** travel north on Grove Street, then east on Mill Road, and then south on Main Street to Palmer Avenue.

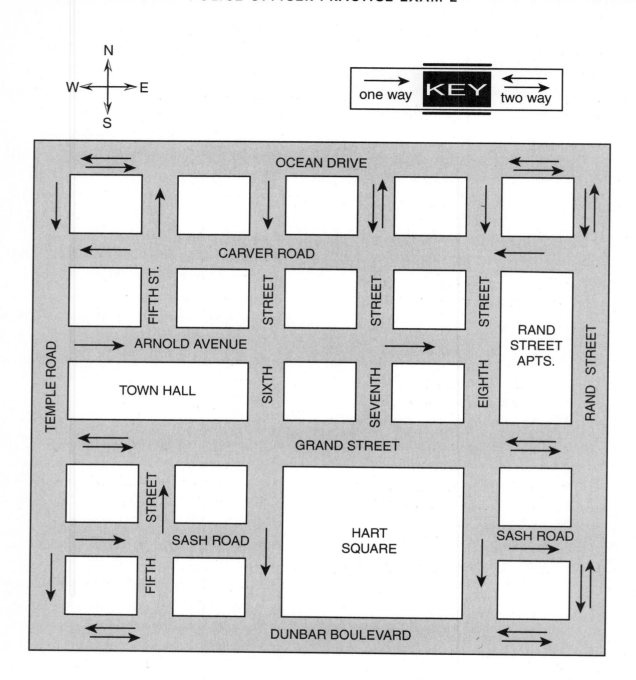

*Questions 51–55 are based on the map on the facing page. Review the directional arrows and the map key. You are not permitted to go the wrong way on a one-way street.*

**51.** You are driving eastbound on Dunbar Boulevard, when you arrive at Eighth Street you make a U-turn, and when you get to Fifth Street you make a right turn, and then a left turn onto Grand Street. What direction will you be facing on Grand Street?
   **a.** east
   **b.** west
   **c.** north
   **d.** south

**52.** Officers Chu and Kahn, patrolling together in a marked police vehicle, are driving on Eighth Street and are located facing southbound between Ocean Drive and Carver Road. Their dispatcher sends them to respond to a motorcycle accident that involved the operator losing control of his cycle and crashing into the northwest corner of Hart Square. The operator is not reporting any serious injuries, but the officers must take a report and ensure that no one else has been injured. After turning west onto Carver Road, what is their quickest route to Hart Square?
   **a.** South on Seventh Street, and then west on Grand Street to Sixth Street.
   **b.** South on Sixth Street to the corner of Grand Street.
   **c.** South on Temple Road and east on Grand Street.
   **d.** South on Temple Road, west on Arnold Avenue, and then south on Sixth Street.

**53.** The number of roadways (streets, drives, avenues, or boulevards) that are two-way is
   **a.** two.
   **b.** three.
   **c.** five.
   **d.** seven.

**54.** Officer Ryan has been dispatched to a burglar alarm call at a storefront on Sash Road and Rand Street. She is driving north on Fifth Street, having just passed Carver Road. After going north on Fifth Street, what is her quickest route to reach the call?
   **a.** West on Ocean Drive, south on Temple Road, east on Dunbar Boulevard, then north on Rand Street to Sash Road.
   **b.** East on Ocean Drive, south on Seventh Street, east on Grand Street, then north on Rand Street to Sash Road.
   **c.** East on Ocean Drive, then south on Rand Street to Sash Road.
   **d.** West on Ocean Drive, south on Temple Road, east on Arnold Avenue, south on Sixth Street, east on Dunbar Boulevard, then north on Rand Street to Sash Road.

**55.** The number of roadways that continue on two sides of landmarks is
   **a.** none.
   **b.** one.
   **c.** two.
   **d.** three.

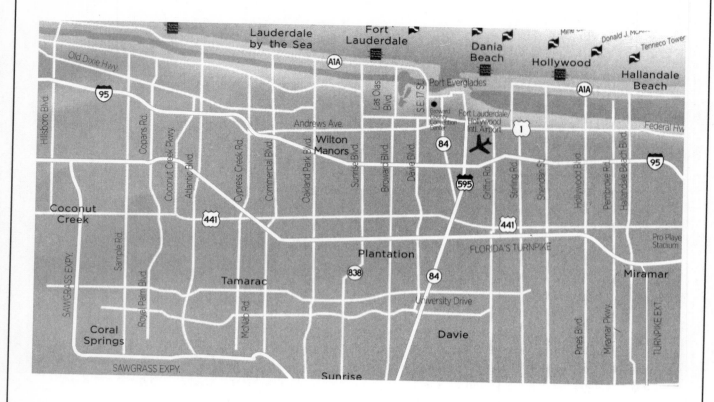

*Questions 56–60 are based on the map above. In this map of south Florida, Lauderdale by the Sea is the northern-most town on the coast; Hallendale Beach is the southernmost, and Sunrise is the westernmost.*

**56.** You have been dispatched to pick up the governor from the Fort Lauderdale/Hollywood International Airport and take him to the Broward County Convention Center. What direction will you be traveling in with the governor?
- **a.** northeast
- **b.** southwest
- **c.** southeast
- **d.** northwest

**57.** The Florida Turnpike runs roughly parallel to U.S. 441 between
- **a.** Coconut Creek Parkway and Pembroke Road.
- **b.** Oakland Park Boulevard and Hollywood Boulevard.
- **c.** Cypress Creek Road and Hollywood Boulevard.
- **d.** Oakland Park Boulevard and Pembroke Road.

**58.** Presuming that all the communities shown at the top of the map are directly on the Atlantic Ocean, which north/south roadway is not a direct route?
- **a.** Coconut Creek Parkway
- **b.** Oakland Park Boulevard
- **c.** Hollywood Boulevard
- **d.** Sheridan Street

**59.** To travel north from Miramar to Tamarac with a minimum of route changes, a Broward County sheriff's deputy taking the most direct route should travel on
  **a.** the Florida Turnpike.
  **b.** University Drive.
  **c.** Interstate 95.
  **d.** U.S. 441.

**60.** Wilton Manors is _____ of Coral Springs.
  **a.** northwest
  **b.** southwest
  **c.** southeast
  **d.** northeast

## Part Three: Judgment and Problem Solving

These questions ask you to use good judgment and common sense along with the information provided to answer each of the questions. Some information may be followed by more than one question pertaining to the same set of facts.

*Answer questions 61–63 based on the information provided in the following descriptive paragraph.*

Park Police Officer Gonzales was dispatched to the gift shop parking lot to take a report from Linda Opheimer, who reported that when she was placing a number of small items she had purchased into her vehicle's trunk, a young man reached into the trunk, grabbed a shopping bag that had already been in the trunk and fled toward the park's exit. She was unable to provide a description of the man, but provided the officer with a list of the contents of her shopping bag:

- 1 sweater valued at $260.00
- 3 gold-colored bracelets with charms attached, each valued at $365.00
- 1 computer game valued at $78.00
- 1 lizard-shaped pin with ruby eye valued at $130.00

**61.** What is the total value of the items reported stolen by Linda Opheimer?
  **a.** $833.00
  **b.** $1,485.00
  **c.** $1,563.00
  **d.** $1,653.00

**62.** What is the value of the jewelry items reported stolen by Linda Opheimer?
  **a.** $495.00
  **b.** $860.00
  **c.** $938.00
  **d.** $1,225.00

**63.** A day after the report, Linda Opheimer called Officer Gonzales and reported that the receipt for her sweater showed it was actually valued at $360.00 and that she had located the lizard-shaped pin in her jewelry box. The value of the stolen items should be recalculated to
  **a.** $1,426.00
  **b.** $1,462.00
  **c.** $1,592.00
  **d.** 1,952.00

1,533.⁰⁰

**64.** Campus Police Officer DeMarco is on patrol at about 3 A.M. on a Sunday morning. While checking the athletic field's parking lot, he discovers there are no cars in the lot but he observes a man laying face down on the pavement. He approaches the man and finds that he is breathing and moaning slightly. Officer DeMarco also notices a hypodermic needle on the pavement next to the man. He tries to wake the man but is unable to. The officer's best course of action is to

**a.** presume the man is sleeping, move him out of the way in case anyone drives through the parking lot, and continue his patrol.

**b.** arrest the man for possession of drug paraphernalia.

**c.** call for an ambulance and have the man transported to a medical facility.

**d.** call for a supervisor.

**65.** Your town is suffering from its second year of drought and the mayor has issued an edict forbidding restaurants from serving water to patrons unless they request it. You are dining with friends while off-duty, and your waiter serves water to the entire table of six although no one has requested it. Your best course of action is to

**a.** identify yourself to the restaurant manager and discretely remind her of the edict.

**b.** arrest the restaurant manager and call for a patrol car to transport you both to the stationhouse.

**c.** arrest the waiter and call for a patrol car to transport you both to the stationhouse.

**d.** issue summonses to both the restaurant manager and the waiter.

**66.** Your town is suffering from its second year of drought and the mayor has issued an edict forbidding residents from washing cars on Monday, Wednesday, and Friday and forbidding shopkeepers from washing down their sidewalks on Tuesday and Thursday. You are on foot patrol in the business district on Thursday afternoon and are dispatched to respond to Bill's Bike Shop, where for the second time this week you observe Bill hosing down the work area of his shop despite your having warned him of the edict on Tuesday. Your best course of action is to

**a.** arrest Bill and transport him to the stationhouse for processing.

**b.** issue a warning to Bill.

**c.** issue a summons to Bill.

**d.** quickly duck into a nearby store so that you may report to the dispatcher that you did not observe Bill violating the water edict.

*Answer questions 67 and 68 based on the information provided in the following descriptive paragraph.*

Police Officer Madigan, who was off duty and in civilian clothes, was driven home by two civilian friends after they all attended a wedding reception at which they had at least three or four cocktails each. As he exited his friend's car, he noticed what appeared to be a burglar exiting his front door and carrying his laptop computer. Officer Madigan used his cell phone to call his department's dispatcher.

**67.** Which part of the Officer Madigan's description would be most helpful to officers hoping to catch the burglar?

**a.** He was running with a pronounced limp.

**b.** He carried a laptop computer.

**c.** He wore a ski mask.

**d.** He wore a red bandana.

**68.** After calling the department's dispatcher, Officer Madigan's next action should be
   **a.** get back in his friend's car and have the friend try to pursue the burglar.
   **b.** aim his firearm at the sky and fire a warning shot in the hope of scaring the burglar into dropping the laptop.
   **c.** enter his residence and await the responding officers.
   **d.** aim his firearm at the fleeing burglar while yelling, "Stop, police!"

**69.** Officer Madeira has noticed that daytime residential burglaries in her district have increased during the past two months. Which of the following situations, occurring around 1:00 P.M., should the officer investigate?
   **a.** A teenaged boy dancing down the sidewalk, with an MP3 player in his right hand.
   **b.** A woman walking door to door pulling a small backpack on wheels.
   **c.** A man parked in the shade eating a sandwich and watching children at play.
   **d.** A man walking down the street carrying a medium-sized television set.

**70.** Officer Celer is on patrol by herself at about 4 A.M. She is driving down a residential street when she sees dark smoke coming out of a house. As she pulls to the curb, she observes a man carrying a gas can exit the house and run down the street. What is her best course of action?
   **a.** Call for backup before pursuing the man with a gas can.
   **b.** Notify dispatch of the fire, request backup, and pursue the man with the gas can.
   **c.** Notify dispatch of the fire and the man running from the scene, then use the garden hose at the front of the house to fight the fire.
   **d.** Notify dispatch about both the fire and the man running from the scene, then attempt to wake anyone in the house and render aid if it is safe to do so.

**71.** On a Sunday afternoon at about 2 P.M., Officer Dodrill is on routine patrol when he receives a radio call to respond to a silent burglary alarm in a commercial district. Dodrill knows that most of the businesses in that area are manufacturing firms that are generally closed on Sunday. Dodrill also knows that most silent burglary alarms are false activations. Which of the following is his best course of action?
   **a.** Because most of the calls are false, he should ignore it and request a dinner break from dispatch.
   **b.** Although most of the calls are false, the area is filled with closed manufacturing businesses, so he should activate his emergency lights and siren and proceed rapidly to the location.
   **c.** Although most of the calls are false, he should proceed directly to the location.
   **d.** Because most of the calls are false, he should continue to patrol his assigned area until he is nearer the location.

**72.** Officer Carmine was requested to transport two prisoners from the department holding facility to the county regional jail. After completing the transport, she checks the back seat of the police vehicle and notices two ten-dollar bills. What is her best course of action?

    **a.** Give the money to the regional jail personnel and tell them to give each prisoner ten dollars.

    **b.** Complete the appropriate department form explaining the circumstances and deposit the money with the department property or evidence officer.

    **c.** Take the money and send it to a local charity.

    **d.** Interview the prisoners and give the money to the one most likely to have misplaced it.

**73.** Transit Police Officer Harmon is informed by her sergeant that there has been a rash of auto-related crimes in the station parking lot, including four cars that have been broken into and six that were stolen from the lot. Of the situations she observes on her patrol, which is the one she should most likely investigate?

    **a.** A transient approaching people entering their cars at 6:30 P.M. and asking for a cigarette.

    **b.** Two young women sitting on the hood of a car parked closest to the train station.

    **c.** A young man walking from parked car to parked car looking in the driver's side window and pulling on door handles.

    **d.** A tow truck operator exiting his truck and attempting to open a car door for a middle-aged man standing nearby.

**74.** Officer Gomez is off-duty and driving in his personal vehicle. Gomez is on his way to work, so he has his badge, gun, and cell phone. He sees a traffic accident occur two blocks ahead of him at an intersection. As Gomez gets closer, he sees one of the drivers involved in the accident quickly exit his car and run away from the scene of the accident. What is Gomez's best course of action?

    **a.** Use his cell phone to report the accident, then stop and render aid.

    **b.** Use his cell phone to report the accident, then continue on to work.

    **c.** Report both the accident and the man running away, then use his personal vehicle to follow the man.

    **d.** Presume someone else will report the accident, and use his personal vehicle to pursue the man running from the accident.

**75.** Sergeant Janikowski is responsible for determining the vacation schedule for the coming year. According to the department vacation policy, choice of vacation is ranked according to seniority. Janikowski knows that Ducale is the least senior, James is more senior than Smyth, and Barton has less seniority than Smyth. Which officer should have first choice for his or her vacation?

    **a.** Ducale

    **b.** Smyth

    **c.** James

    **d.** Barton

**76.** In your state, a person is guilty of third degree robbery when he or she forcibly steals property. With only this information, which of the following is the least likely to be an example of third degree robbery?
   **a.** Thomas beats up a man on the street and steals his wallet and cell phone.
   **b.** Thomas pushes an elderly woman in the mall parking lot and runs away without taking anything after others start yelling at him.
   **c.** Thomas pushes a man off a bike and steals the bike.
   **d.** Thomas accosts a delivery worker and takes $4.00 in tips from him.

**77.** The Eastlake Police Department is taking requests from officers who are interested in joining the scooter patrol unit. Requests will be filled on the basis of seniority. Officer West has less seniority than Officer Church, but more than Officer Brody. Officer Rhodes has more seniority that Officer West, but less than Officer Church. Officer Church has withdrawn his request because he recently learned he will be promoted. Who will be the new scooter patrol officer?
   **a.** Rhodes
   **b.** Church
   **c.** West
   **d.** Brody

**78.** Officers Charles and Washington have been dispatched to 2104 Maple Avenue. Neighbors called 911 and said that they could hear Jeff threatening his wife Sara and that they were afraid he was about to beat her. Officer Charles notifies the dispatcher that they have arrived. He parks the car in front of 2102 Maple, and he and Officer Washington begin walking up the sidewalk to 2104 Maple Ave. What should the two officers do next?
   **a.** Knock on the front door and request entry.
   **b.** Listen at the door to see if they can tell what is going on inside.
   **c.** Talk to the neighbors who called before taking any action.
   **d.** Administer first aid to those who are injured.

**79.** Officer Wallace arrives at the scene of a domestic disturbance. After notifying the dispatcher of her arrival and parking her car a few houses away, Officer Wallace is at the house's front door. She listens for a few minutes and hears a woman sobbing. The house is dark and quiet except for the sounds of the woman crying. The next step Officer Wallace should take is to
   **a.** walk around to the rear of the house and listen at the back door.
   **b.** knock on the door and identify herself.
   **c.** call to the woman through the door to ask if she is injured.
   **d.** step to one side of the door before knocking.

**80.** Officers Stanley and DiMartino have just pulled up to the curb near 9000 Block Parkway on a domestic disturbance call. Neighbors are reporting sounds of breaking glass, yelling, and gunshots. What is the first thing the officers should do?
   **a.** Listen at the door to see if they can tell what is happening.
   **b.** Get the dispatcher to have a neighbor meet them outside to tell them what they heard.
   **c.** Radio in to the dispatcher when they arrive at the scene.
   **d.** Immediately run into the residence.

**81.** Officer Roberts is dispatched to a domestic disturbance at 3412 Runnymeade. When he arrives, he radios in to the dispatcher and parks at 3410 Runnymeade. As he approaches the house, the door flies open and a woman runs out. She is bleeding heavily from a cut on her arm and collapses at his feet, crying, "Help me, officer!" The next thing Officer Roberts should do is to
   **a.** apply first aid to the woman's wound.
   **b.** search the house for the suspect.
   **c.** separate the victim and the suspect.
   **d.** identify himself to the victim.

*Answer questions 82 and 83 based on the following information.*

Police Officer Wiggins is dispatched to a call concerning a two-vehicle accident. She obtains the following information:

| | |
|---|---|
| Time of accident: | 10 P.M. |
| Place of accident: | County Highway JJ |
| Injured party: | Thomas Jones |
| Nature of accident: | Injured party's motorcycle run off the road by a passenger vehicle |
| Driver of passenger vehicle: | Unknown female |
| Make and model of passenger vehicle: | Ford Fiesta, year unknown |

**82.** Officer Wiggins is writing up her report. Which of the following expresses the relevant information most clearly and accurately?
   **a.** Thomas Jones reported that at approximately 10 P.M. on County Highway JJ he was injured when his motorcycle was run off the road by a passenger vehicle driven by an unknown female.
   **b.** Thomas Jones reported that an unknown vehicle ran him and his motorcycle off the road at about 10 P.M. on County Highway JJ.
   **c.** Thomas Jones reported at 10 P.M. that an unknown Ford Fiesta forced his motorcycle off County Highway JJ.
   **d.** Thomas Jones reported that at sometime around 10 P.M. he was pushed off the road by an unknown driver of a Ford.

**83.** Which of the following is a correct assumption based solely on the material provided?
   **a.** The driver of the Ford Fiesta left the scene of the accident.
   **b.** The driver of the Ford Fiesta did not see Thomas Jones on his motorcycle.
   **c.** Thomas Jones was wearing a motorcycle helmet at the time of the accident.
   **d.** Thomas Jones is making up the whole story to cover up that he drove onto the shoulder of the road.

*Answer questions 84 and 85 based on the following information.*

Officer Jackson is collecting donations for a holiday party that officers are planning for 25 children enrolled in a pre-K program housed in a building across from the stationhouse. Fifteen officers, including Jackson, have each contributed $25 to the party. Three officers who are assigned to a different station but are the spouses of assigned officers have each contributed $15 toward the event. The three sergeants have contributed $30 each, the two lieutenants have contributed $40 each, and the captain has contributed $50.

**84.** The total amount of money that Officer Jackson has collected is
   **a.** $420.00
   **b.** $510.00
   **c.** $640.00
   **d.** $730.00

**85.** Officer Jackson has learned the amount of various party expenses, including

   $300.00 Sandwiches
   $100.00 Non-alcoholic beverages
   $80.00  Party favors

The remainder of the funds will be spent on small holiday gifts for the children. What is the amount of money that Officer Jackson will have left to spend on each child?
   **a.** $6.40
   **b.** $16.40
   **c.** $160
   **d.** none of the above

*Answer questions 86 and 87 based on the following information.*

The Kirkland Police Department requires that when a police officer believes a driver who has been stopped is driving under the under the influence of alcohol or narcotics, the officer should

1. have the driver get out of the vehicle
2. demonstrate each field sobriety test and request that the driver perform each of the requested tests
3. if the driver fails the tests, place the driver under arrest, making sure to explain to the driver why he or she is being arrested
4. call the dispatcher to request a vehicle to tow the driver's car to a holding facility

**86.** Officer Jiminez is working at a driving checkpoint where she is obligated to stop every third vehicle. Her third stop involves the ninth car that has travelled through the checkpoint. She informs the driver that he will have to perform a number of tests to prove his sobriety and immediately begins to demonstrate the first test. The driver exits the car, performs the first and subsequent tests satisfactorily, and is allowed by Officer Jiminez to return to his vehicle and continue on his journey. Under these circumstances, the actions taken by Officer Jiminez were

**a.** proper, because she did not arrest a driver who successfully performed the field sobriety tests.

**b.** improper, because she demonstrated the first test before having the driver exit his vehicle.

**c.** improper, because she did not stop every third car.

**d.** proper, because she did stop every third car.

**87.** Officer Marcos is on patrol when he sees a white Ford Thunderbird run a red light at the intersection of Maple and Walnut. The vehicle is weaving back and forth over the double yellow line in the center of the roadway. The driver pulls over to the side of the road for Officer Marcos five blocks later and gets out of his car. When Officer Marcos smells a strong odor of alcohol on the man's breath, he asks the driver to perform several sobriety tests. The driver says, "Okay," and immediately tries to stand on one leg, but cannot do so. Officer Marcos tells the driver he is under arrest for driving under the influence, and places him in the patrol car. He then calls for a tow truck to impound the Thunderbird. Under these circumstances, the actions taken by Officer Marcos were

**a.** improper, because he failed to demonstrate the sobriety tests for the driver.

**b.** proper, because it was obvious by the driver's actions that he would not pass a field sobriety test.

**c.** improper, because he did not tell the driver to get out of his car.

**d.** proper, because the driver could not stand on one leg.

POLICE OFFICER PRACTICE EXAM 2

*Answer questions 88–92 based on the following information.*

Police officers in the Overbrook Police Department have precise procedures on packaging evidence. The following steps are required to be carried out in the order listed:

1. Place each item in a separate container.
2. Seal each container to ensure that it cannot be opened without breaking the seal.
3. The officer who has collected the evidence should write his or her name and employee number on the seal.
4. The officer who has collected the evidence should place a tag on the container that identifies the case number, the date and time collected, where the item was found, a description of what the item is, who collected, it and what condition the item was in.
5. The officer should turn the evidence in personally to the Property Room without breaking the chain of custody by allowing anyone else to do this.

**88.** Officer Schwartz is the first officer to arrive at the scene of a burglar in Parkside Liquor Store. After making sure the scene is secure, she begins to collect evidence. The first item she finds is a screwdriver lying on the sidewalk in front of the glass doors leading into the store. The second item she sees is a small flashlight on the floor inside the building. Officer Schwartz places the screwdriver in a small plastic bag. What is the next thing she should do?
   a. Lock the screwdriver in the trunk of her patrol car.
   b. Seal the bag with evidence tape so that the bag cannot be opened.
   c. Write the case number and information about the evidence on the outside of the bag.
   d. Put the flashlight in the bag with the screwdriver.

**89.** Officer Thompson is dispatched to a vehicle collision that has resulted in a fatality to a pedestrian. The vehicle driver is suspected of having driven while intoxicated and has been placed under arrest by Officer Pica. Officer Jackson begins to search the vehicle and finds an empty glass beer bottle in the front seat along with a receipt from Eva's Quick Stop for a six-pack of beer. The first thing Officer Jackson should do with this evidence is to
   a. throw away the empty bottle and give the receipt to Officer Pica to attach to the suspect's arrest folder.
   b. attach a tag to the neck of the bottle, put the bottle and the receipt in a plastic bag and write the case number on the tag.
   c. place the bottle and the receipt in separate evidence bags.
   d. turn the bottle and the receipt in to the Property Room.

**90.** Two officers are dispatched to the scene of a past robbery. Officer Mack is assigned to collect all the physical evidence, while Officer Stein, the officer in charge, is responsible for interviewing the victim and the witnesses. Officer Stein is also responsible for keeping the crime scene from being entered or otherwise contaminated by onlookers. As Officer Mack is labeling the bag in which he has placed a knife that was possibly dropped by the robber, a witness points out to him a button lying on the sidewalk that the witness believes came from the robber's jacket. What should Officer Mack do next?

a. Seal the button in a container by itself, write his name on the seal, label the container, and give it to Officer Stein.

b. Let Officer Stein collect and package the button and label its container, since the information came from a witness that he was interviewing.

c. Let Officer Stein collect and package the knife and label its container, and then deliver it to the Property Room.

d. Place the button in a container, seal the container, write his name and information about the evidence on the label, and deliver it to the Property Room.

**91.** In reconsidering his actions, Officer Mack decided to ignore the button and concentrate on the knife. His action is

a. correct, because the witness could have been wrong that the button came from the robber's jacket.

b. incorrect, because he does not have enough information to determine whether the button might be an important piece of evidence.

c. incorrect, because since Officer Stein was responsible for the witnesses, Officer Mack should have ignored whatever the witness told him.

d. correct, because the witness might have actually been the robber and might have been trying to confuse the officers.

**92.** Officer Singh has collected evidence at a crime scene and placed it in a container. The first thing he should write on the evidence tag is

a. his name.

b. the case number.

c. his employee number.

d. the date.

*Answer questions 93–95 based on the following information.*

Police officers in the West Vonick Police Department must follow certain procedures when placing a person under arrest and transporting that person in a patrol car. The following steps are required to be carried out in the order listed:

1. Handcuff the prisoner securely.
2. Search the prisoner carefully for weapons and contraband.
3. Check the area where the prisoner will be seated in the patrol car for weapons or contraband.
4. Place the prisoner in the patrol car and engage the prisoner's seatbelt.
5. Transport the prisoner directly to the booking facility.
6. Upon arrival at the booking facility, check the seat and floorboard where the prisoner was seated for any weapons or contraband.

93. Officer Ling responded to a backup request by Officer Seamus. When Ling arrived at the scene, Officer Seamus had Michelle Bradley in custody for assault. Ling knew that Seamus is a 15-year veteran of the police department and very well respected by his peers, supervisors, and managers. Seamus asked Ling to transport Bradley to the station. Ling walked Bradley to his police car and began to search her. Seamus said to Ling, "I have already searched her." What is Ling's best course of action?
   a. Discontinue searching Bradley and transport her to the station.
   b. Discontinue searching Bradley, transport her out of Seamus's sight and re-search Bradley.
   c. Call a supervisor to the scene to make a decision about re-searching Bradley.
   d. Conduct a search of Bradley and tell Seamus that she would be more comfortable double-checking.

94. Officer Vitry is called to the scene of a traffic accident by Sergeant Medford. One of the drivers involved in the accident is an 82-year-old woman whose license expired three days ago. Medford tells Vitry to transport the woman to the station and stay with her until her son picks her up. Which of the following is Vitry's best course of action?
   a. Transport the woman after searching, handcuffing, and securing her seat belt.
   b. Search, seat belt, and transport the woman.
   c. Transport the woman.
   d. Transport the woman after securing her seat belt.

**95.** Officers Hogan and Romano responded to West Vonick High School on a call of a fight in progress which resulted in the arrest of Jeffrey Nichols for possession of a knife and a small amount of marijuana. The school principal asks Romano not to search Nichols so as not to embarrass him in front of other students. Officer Romano should
   **a.** briefly explain the department's policy to the principal and search the student.
   **b.** discontinue searching Nichols and transport him to the booking facility.
   **c.** call a supervisor to seek guidance.
   **d.** ignore the principal and search the student.

**96.** Officers Roberts and Reed are on bicycle patrol in the downtown area. Sergeant McElvey tells them that a white male has been committing robberies along the nearby bike path by stepping out of the bushes and threatening bicyclists with an iron pipe until they give him their bicycles. There have been three separate incidents, and the suspect descriptions are from three different victims.
   **Robbery #1:** Suspect is a white male, 20–25 years old, 5'9", 145 pounds, with a shaved head, wearing a skull earring in the left ear, floppy white T-shirt, worn light blue jeans, and black combat boots.
   **Robbery #2:** Suspect is a white male, 25–30 years old, dark brown hair in a military-style crew cut, 6'2", 200 pounds, wearing a white T-shirt with the words "Just Do It" on the back, blue surgical scrub pants, and black combat boots.
   **Robbery #3:** Suspect is a white male, 23 years old, 5'10", skinny build, no hair, wearing a tie-dyed T-shirt, blue baggy pants, dark shoes, and one earring.

Three days after Sergeant McElvey told the officers about the robberies, Officer Reed arrested a suspect for attempting to take a woman's mountain bike from her on the bicycle path.

The description of the suspect is as follows: **Robbery #4:** Suspect is a white male, 22 years old, 140 pounds, 5'10", with a shaved head and one pierced ear, wearing a plain white T-shirt two sizes too large for him, faded baggy blue jeans, and scuffed black combat boots.

After comparing the suspect description with those in the first three robberies, Officer Reed should consider the arrested man as a suspect in which of the other robberies?
   **a.** Robbery #1, Robbery #2, and Robbery #3
   **b.** Robbery #1, but not Robbery #2 or Robbery #3
   **c.** Robbery #1 and Robbery #3, but not Robbery #2
   **d.** Robbery #1 and Robbery #2, but not Robbery #3

**97.** Officer Troy arrives at the scene of a hit-and-run traffic accident. Ms. Chen tells him she was waiting for the light to change when a car struck her from behind. The driver backed up and left the scene. She saw his license plate as he left, as did three teenaged witnesses waiting for the school bus. The choices below list what each one reported. Which license plate number below is most likely the license plate of the hit-and-run vehicle?
   **a.** JXK 12L
   **b.** JYK 12L
   **c.** JXK 12I
   **d.** JXX I2L

**98.** Four eyewitnesses give descriptions of the get-away car used in a bank robbery. Which description is probably right?
   **a.** dark blue with a white roof
   **b.** dark green with a gray roof
   **c.** black with a gray roof
   **d.** dark green with a tan roof

Use the following information to answer questions 99–100.

The first officer to respond to the scene of a sexual assault has many responsibilities. The officer should take the following steps in the order listed:

1. Aid the victim if necessary by calling for an ambulance or administering first aid.
2. Try to calm and comfort the victim as much as possible.
3. If the attack is recent, get a suspect description from the victim and radio the dispatcher to put out a be-on-the-lookout broadcast.
4. Find out from the victim where the crime occurred.
5. Determine if there is any physical evidence on the victim that may need to be preserved, such as pieces of the suspect's skin or blood under the victim's fingernails.
6. If possible, have the victim change clothing, and then take the clothing he or she was wearing as evidence.
7. Convince the victim that he or she should undergo a medical exam for health and safety purposes, and so that evidence may be gathered.

**99.** At 2 A.M., Officer Maxwell is sent to the scene of a sexual assault at 1201 Roxy St. He arrives and finds the victim, Susan Jackson, sitting on the front porch crying. She tells him that a man crawled through her window and raped her. When the rapist ran out the front door, she called the police immediately. The next step Officer Maxwell should take is to
   **a.** take a look around the house to make sure the suspect is really gone.
   **b.** ask Jackson if she is injured and in need of medical attention.
   **c.** talk Jackson into going to the hospital for a medical exam.
   **d.** ask Jackson to describe her attacker.

**100.** Officer Augustine is at 2101 Reynolds Street talking to Betty Smith, the victim of a sexual assault. She is uninjured and is very calm. She gives Officer Augustine a detailed description of her attacker and says she thinks he may be headed for a nearby tavern. At this point, Officer Augustine should
   **a.** get into her patrol car and drive to the tavern.
   **b.** give the dispatcher the description of the suspect.
   **c.** take the victim straight to the hospital for a medical exam.
   **d.** have the victim change clothing.

# Answers

## Part One: Memorization and Visualization

**1. c.** Valeria Linda Guerra is the missing 15-year-old girl.

**2. d.** Lin Yang, also known as Linda Yang, is the 36-year-old female wanted for burglary.

**3. a.** Lin Yang is described as having last been seen in a casino in Grand Forks, ND; Luis Robert Hart is described as a known gambler and card-shark who frequents casinos in Atlantic City, NJ.

**4. d.** Although Tankle wears a patch over one eye, his only described permanent scar or mark is that his pinky finger is missing from knuckle to nail.

**5. b.** Luis Robert Hart is described as black but as light-skinned and often mistaken for Hispanic.

**6. a.** Caution was advised because Hart is known to carry knives and because Tankle is known to carry various tools that could be used as weapons.

**7. b.** The answer comes from the Remarks; the other choices are not mentioned in the information provided.

**8. c.** Refer to the Charges mentioned.

**9. b.** Refer to the Charges mentioned.

**10. d.** She is not wanted for a crime; she is missing.

**11. a.** Refer to the Identifying Scars or Marks.

**12. d.** Refer to the Remarks.

**13. a.** Refer to Remarks and Caution Advised.

**14. b.** See the Wanted By notation.

**15. c.** Finan is described as pictured with a beard and moustache; Hart is pictured with a moustache.

**16. b.** This is stated in the second paragraph of the reading.

**17. d.** All three elements are included in the definition of probable cause in the first paragraph of the reading.

**18. c.** See the second paragraph of the reading.

**19. c.** This is similar to the fact pattern in the case that resulted in the Terry decision. Choices **a**, **b**, and **d** are not in themselves suspicious.

**20. a.** See the first paragraph of the reading.

**21. c.** See the first paragraph of the reading.

**22. b.** See the third paragraph of the reading.

**23. b.** See the paragraph describing the facts of the case.

**24. b.** See the paragraph describing the facts of the case.

**25. d.** The decision to stop a suspect is made based on the individual's behavior and on the officer's training and experience; choice **d** presents an experienced officer working in a regular area, where the officer can be inferred to have both training and experience and to have awareness of a situation that appears out of the ordinary.

**26. b.** See the second paragraph of the reading.

**27. c.** Review the Supreme Court's ruling in the second paragraph of the reading. Choices **a**, **b**, and **d** present situations in which an experienced officer might determine a crime is about to be committed; choice **b** indicates the individual may be armed and dangerous.

**28. b.** A Terry stop permits an officer to search a person and to seize a weapon that may be found in the course of a search. None of the other choices pertain to the facts of the case or the information provided in the reading.

**29. c.** At the moment there is no urgency because it appears the suspects are waiting for the bank to close. Because you may be unable to handle two suspects alone, keeping the suspects under surveillance while awaiting backup is your best course of action.

**30. b.** The behavior is unusual, and appears out of place, and the individual is behaving in a way that the officer could believe a crime of theft has been committed. Choices **a**, **c**, and **d** are common occurrences that, without any additional behavior, should not arouse the suspicions of an experienced officer.

## Part Two: Reading Skills

**31. a.** The information is provided in the second paragraph.

**32. b.** The type of location is described in the second sentence.

**33. d.** The call was at 4:10 A.M.; the first officers arrived at 4:20 A.M. and called for backup, which arrived 20 minutes later, making it 4:40 A.M.

**34. b.** The information appears in the third sentence. Although further investigation of the direction of the glass and other clues could determine that this was actually the point of exit or was intended to mislead police, at this initial stage it would be acceptable to make this assumption.

**35. d.** No information about how the suspects might have exited is provided. Although you may initially infer they entered through the smashed window, at least until other evidence is obtained, there is nothing to indicate how they might have exited.

**36. a.** The second sentence explains the theory's use in developing crime prevention strategies.

**37. c.** This information appears in the first sentence of the passage.

**38. c.** The entire passage pertains to public spaces; a private residence is not a public space.

**39. b.** This information appears in the first sentence of the second paragraph.

**40. b.** The second sentence links CPTED to crime prevention efforts, so you should infer the correct answer. The knowledge might be helpful to others also, but not as directly as to crime prevention personnel.

**41. c.** The information appears in the last sentence of the first paragraph.

**42. a.** Platea Street is the only possible address; Bardus exited his vehicle on Platea, 150 feet west of Broadway, and ran between the buildings.

**43. b.** Jones was driving the police car; only Johnson could have been the passenger who gave chase.

**44. a.** Sergeant Ducis was the last officer on the scene; he performed the search that yielded the gun.

**45. c.** Watt's and Johnson's, Bardus's, and Ducis's vehicles were all involved in the pursuit.

**46. a.** When Sergeant Nixey makes the first left turn, he is facing west, when he turns right onto Lynch Road he is facing north, and when he turns right again onto Mill Road he is facing east.

**47. c.** Bond Road is a one-way northbound street, so if you turn right onto Bond Road, you will be facing north.

**48. d.** It is the only route that does not require any backtracking. Choice **a** requires going the wrong way on Mill Road; choice **b** puts the patrol the wrong way on Lynch Road, and choice **c** is too indirect because it places the patrol car moving away from the location of the call.

**49. c.** Four roadways are designated avenues. Of these, Pecan, Pine, and Palmer are two-way avenues; Kent is not.

**50. a.** This route requires the fewest turns. Choice **b** is a less direct route; choices **c** and **d** require going in the wrong direction on Kent Avenue to reach Grove Street since Kent Avenue is a one-way going eastbound.

51. **b.** When you make the U-turn, you will be traveling westbound; when you make the right turn at Fifth Street, you will be traveling northbound; and when you make the left turn at Grand Street, you will be traveling westbound.

52. **b.** This is the most direct route; the other choices involve extra turns and take the officers out of their way to reach the location.

53. **c.** Five roadways are two-way; Ocean Drive, Grand Street, Dunbar Boulevard, Rand Street, and Seventh Street.

54. **c.** It is the most direct route; choice **a** has Officer Ryan making a turn west on Fifth Street; choices **b** and **d** require too many turns to be efficient.

55. **c.** Fifth Street continues north and south of Town Hall and Sash Road continues west and east of Hart Square. If you selected choice **d** to include the Rand Street Apts., note that Arnold Avenue stops at the apartments and does not continue east of that landmark.

56. **d.** Based on the map, the convention center is slightly northwest of the airport.

57. **d.** This is the section of the Florida Turnpike that runs almost perfectly parallel to U.S. 441.

58. **a.** Coconut Creek Parkway ends at Old Dixie Highway; the other streets are shown on the map as going directly to the oceanfront communities.

59. **a.** Choice **b** is incorrect because University Drive does not start far enough south for a journey from Miramar; choices **c** and **d** are incorrect because they are farther north than the deputy needs to go to reach Tamarac.

60. **d.** Based on the coordinates, going towards the top of the map is going north and going from left to right is going east.

## Part Three: Judgment and Problem Solving

61. **c.** This is a problem in multiplication and addition. You must remember to multiply the value of the bracelets ($365 \times 3$) before adding it to the other figures.

62. **d.** This is also a problem in multiplication and addition. You must remember the number of bracelets and you must be sure to include only the jewelry (choice **c** also includes the computer game).

63. **b.** You must recalculate the figures by adding the additional value of the sweater ($100) and subtracting the value of the pin ($130), remembering not to transpose any numbers in your calculations.

64. **c.** Protecting the man takes precedence over making an arrest; calling a supervisor to a scene when the officer should be able to make the decision is never the best option.

65. **a.** These edict violations are not sufficient for you to take off-duty police action, which if taken at all should be reserved for serious crimes.

66. **c.** You have previously warned Bill, so issuing a summons is appropriate if you prefer not to warn him again because he failed to heed your warning earlier in the week.

67. **a.** The man's apparent limp is the least likely element of the description to change and therefore is the most helpful to pursuing officers.

68. **c.** Officer Madigan is off-duty, in civilian clothes, and has consumed alcohol; choices **a**, **b**, and **d** are dangerous to all involved; choices **b** and **d** are also likely to violate his department's procedures pertaining to discharging a firearm.

**69. d.** It is the most appropriate; people generally do not walk down the street carrying large appliances.

**70. d.** Human life always takes precedence over property. In any pursuit, an officer should weigh the risks associated with capturing the suspect against human life, particularly of ━━━ people.

**79. d.** Standing to one side of the door before knocking is the next step in the procedure after listening at the door.

**80. c.** The first step is for the officers to tell the dispatcher they have arrived at the scene.

**81. a.** The woman is bleeding and needs first aid. Choice **b** is not an option in the list of procedures. There aren't two people to separate as suggested in choice c. The woman knows he ━━━ need to iden-

87. **a.** Step 3 in the procedures instructs the officer to demonstrate each sobriety test, which Officer Marcos did not do.

88. **b.** Sealing the bag is step 2 on the list of procedures.

89. **c.** Putting each item of evidence in a separate container is step 1 on the list of procedures.

90. **d.** This choice includes all the procedures.

91. **b.** All evidence at a crime scene should be collect

96. **c.** The suspect described in Robbery #2 has a crew-cut, is at least five inches taller than the other suspects, and is about 60 pounds heavier. The other descriptions are more likely to be of the same person because they describe a similar build and mention one earring or a pierced ear.

97. **a.** The witnesses seem to agree that

# Scoring

A passing score for police exams in most cities is 70%. If the real exam consists of 100 questions, like the test you just took, each question would be worth one point. Thus, your score on this exam is the same as your percentage.

While a total score of at least 70 usually lands you on the eligibility list, in many cities, you need to do much better than just pass the exam to have a chance at a job. Many cities rank applicants according to their test scores, so that the higher you score on the exam, the better your chance of being called to go through the next steps in the selection process. In addition, veterans and/or residents of the city may have points added to their test scores, so that the best possible score is actually more than 100. If your city conducts this kind of ranking, your goal isn't just to score 70 and pass—you need the highest score you can possibly reach.

Use this practice exam as a way to analyze your performance. Pay attention to the areas where you miss the most questions. If most of your mistakes are in the reading comprehension questions, then you know you need to practice your reading skills. Or perhaps you had difficulty memorizing the wanted posters. Once you see where you need help, then you should study the chapters in this book on the relevant skills to develop your test-taking strategies.

To help you see where you should concentrate, break down your scores according to the three sections below:

Part One:      _____ questions correct
Part Two:      _____ questions correct
Part Three:    _____ questions correct

Write down the number of correct answers for each section and then add up all three numbers for your overall score. Each question is worth one point, and the total you arrive at after adding all the numbers is also the percentage of questions that you answered correctly on the test.

For now, forget about your total score; what's more important right now is your scores on the individual sections of the exam.

Below is a table that will show you which of the instructional chapters correspond to the three parts of the exam. Your best bet is to review all of the chapters carefully, but you will want to spend the most time on the chapters that correspond to the kind of question that you found most difficult.

| EXAM PART | CHAPTER |
|-----------|---------|
| One | 10 |
| Two | 9 and 10 |
| Three | 9 and 10 |

Depending on your score on the exam you just took, you might breeze through these instructional chapters, or really buckle down and study hard. Either way, the chapters give you what you need to score your best.

After you've read the relevant chapters, take the second exam of this type, in Chapter 12, to see how much you've improved.

CHAPTER

# 7 ▶ POLICE OFFICER PRACTICE EXAM 3

### *CHAPTER SUMMARY*

This is the third practice exam in this book based on the entry-level civil service exam that police departments around the country administer to prospective police officers. If the police department you're applying to uses an exam called the LECR (Law Enforcement Candidate Record), this is the exam for you.

This practice police exam has two parts. The first part has two sections: verbal comprehension and number and letter recall. In the verbal section, you are given ten minutes to answer questions on synonyms and antonyms. The number and letter recall section lasts only nine minutes and consists of 100 questions. You are asked to remember certain number-letter combinations from a given table. You will have the table in front of you as you complete these questions.

The second part of the exam consists of 185 questions about your personal background. This exam includes 20 sample personal background questions to help familiarize you with the format.

Incorrect answers count against you in the first part of the exam. It's better to leave questions blank than to close your eyes and point at an answer. A good rule of thumb is to guess only if you can definitely eliminate at least two of the four given answers.

When you finish the exam, check the answer key at the end of the test, and see how well you scored. Because there are no correct or incorrect answers on the personal background questions, no answer key is included for this section.

## Police Officer Practice Exam 3
## Verbal Section

1. ⓐ ⓑ ⓒ ⓓ
2. ⓐ ⓑ ⓒ ⓓ
3. ⓐ ⓑ ⓒ ⓓ
4. ⓐ ⓑ ⓒ ⓓ
5. ⓐ ⓑ ⓒ ⓓ
6. ⓐ ⓑ ⓒ ⓓ
7. ⓐ ⓑ ⓒ ⓓ
8. ⓐ ⓑ ⓒ ⓓ
9. ⓐ ⓑ ⓒ ⓓ
10. ⓐ ⓑ ⓒ ⓓ
11. ⓐ ⓑ ⓒ ⓓ
12. ⓐ ⓑ ⓒ ⓓ
13. ⓐ ⓑ ⓒ ⓓ
14. ⓐ ⓑ ⓒ ⓓ
15. ⓐ ⓑ ⓒ ⓓ
16. ⓐ ⓑ ⓒ ⓓ
17. ⓐ ⓑ ⓒ ⓓ
18. ⓐ ⓑ ⓒ ⓓ
19. ⓐ ⓑ ⓒ ⓓ
20. ⓐ ⓑ ⓒ ⓓ
21. ⓐ ⓑ ⓒ ⓓ
22. ⓐ ⓑ ⓒ ⓓ
23. ⓐ ⓑ ⓒ ⓓ
24. ⓐ ⓑ ⓒ ⓓ
25. ⓐ ⓑ ⓒ ⓓ
26. ⓐ ⓑ ⓒ ⓓ
27. ⓐ ⓑ ⓒ ⓓ
28. ⓐ ⓑ ⓒ ⓓ
29. ⓐ ⓑ ⓒ ⓓ
30. ⓐ ⓑ ⓒ ⓓ
31. ⓐ ⓑ ⓒ ⓓ
32. ⓐ ⓑ ⓒ ⓓ
33. ⓐ ⓑ ⓒ ⓓ
34. ⓐ ⓑ ⓒ ⓓ
35. ⓐ ⓑ ⓒ ⓓ
36. ⓐ ⓑ ⓒ ⓓ
37. ⓐ ⓑ ⓒ ⓓ
38. ⓐ ⓑ ⓒ ⓓ
39. ⓐ ⓑ ⓒ ⓓ
40. ⓐ ⓑ ⓒ ⓓ
41. ⓐ ⓑ ⓒ ⓓ
42. ⓐ ⓑ ⓒ ⓓ
43. ⓐ ⓑ ⓒ ⓓ
44. ⓐ ⓑ ⓒ ⓓ
45. ⓐ ⓑ ⓒ ⓓ
46. ⓐ ⓑ ⓒ ⓓ
47. ⓐ ⓑ ⓒ ⓓ
48. ⓐ ⓑ ⓒ ⓓ
49. ⓐ ⓑ ⓒ ⓓ
50. ⓐ ⓑ ⓒ ⓓ

## Number and Letter Recall Section

1-75. ⓐ ⓑ ⓒ ⓓ ⓔ

## Number and Letter Recall Section (continued)

76. ⓐ ⓑ ⓒ ⓓ ⓔ
77. ⓐ ⓑ ⓒ ⓓ ⓔ
78. ⓐ ⓑ ⓒ ⓓ ⓔ
79. ⓐ ⓑ ⓒ ⓓ ⓔ
80. ⓐ ⓑ ⓒ ⓓ ⓔ
81. ⓐ ⓑ ⓒ ⓓ ⓔ
82. ⓐ ⓑ ⓒ ⓓ ⓔ
83. ⓐ ⓑ ⓒ ⓓ ⓔ
84. ⓐ ⓑ ⓒ ⓓ ⓔ

85. ⓐ ⓑ ⓒ ⓓ ⓔ
86. ⓐ ⓑ ⓒ ⓓ ⓔ
87. ⓐ ⓑ ⓒ ⓓ ⓔ
88. ⓐ ⓑ ⓒ ⓓ ⓔ
89. ⓐ ⓑ ⓒ ⓓ ⓔ
90. ⓐ ⓑ ⓒ ⓓ ⓔ
91. ⓐ ⓑ ⓒ ⓓ ⓔ
92. ⓐ ⓑ ⓒ ⓓ ⓔ
93. ⓐ ⓑ ⓒ ⓓ ⓔ

94. ⓐ ⓑ ⓒ ⓓ ⓔ
95. ⓐ ⓑ ⓒ ⓓ ⓔ
96. ⓐ ⓑ ⓒ ⓓ ⓔ
97. ⓐ ⓑ ⓒ ⓓ ⓔ
98. ⓐ ⓑ ⓒ ⓓ ⓔ
99. ⓐ ⓑ ⓒ ⓓ ⓔ
100. ⓐ ⓑ ⓒ ⓓ ⓔ

## Personal Background Section

1. ⓐ ⓑ ⓒ ⓓ
2. ⓐ ⓑ ⓒ ⓓ ⓔ ⓕ
3. ⓐ ⓑ ⓒ ⓓ ⓔ ⓕ
4. ⓐ ⓑ ⓒ ⓓ
5. ⓐ ⓑ ⓒ ⓓ ⓔ ⓕ ⓖ ⓗ
6. ⓐ ⓑ ⓒ ⓓ ⓔ ⓕ
7. ⓐ ⓑ ⓒ ⓓ

8. ⓐ ⓑ ⓒ ⓓ ⓔ
9. ⓐ ⓑ ⓒ ⓓ ⓔ
10. ⓐ ⓑ ⓒ ⓓ
11. ⓐ ⓑ ⓒ ⓓ
12. ⓐ ⓑ ⓒ ⓓ ⓔ
13. ⓐ ⓑ ⓒ ⓓ ⓔ
14. ⓐ ⓑ ⓒ ⓓ ⓔ ⓕ

15. ⓐ ⓑ ⓒ ⓓ ⓔ
16. ⓐ ⓑ ⓒ ⓓ
17. ⓐ ⓑ ⓒ ⓓ
18. ⓐ ⓑ ⓒ ⓓ ⓔ ⓕ
19. ⓐ ⓑ ⓒ ⓓ
20. ⓐ ⓑ ⓒ ⓓ ⓔ ⓕ

# Police Officer Practice Exam 3

## Part One: Verbal Section

*You have ten minutes for this section. Choose the correct answer for each question.*

**1.** Which word means the *same* as COERCE?
   **a.** compel
   **b.** permit
   **c.** waste
   **d.** deny

**2.** Which word means the *same* as COLLABORATE?
   **a.** cooperate
   **b.** coordinate
   **c.** entice
   **d.** elaborate

**3.** Which word means the *opposite* of ABSTRACT?
   **a.** concentrated
   **b.** simple
   **c.** concrete
   **d.** understandable

**4.** Which word means the *opposite* of DESPONDENT?
   **a.** pessimistic
   **b.** dejected
   **c.** exultant
   **d.** miserable

**5.** Which word means the *same* as HEFTY?
   **a.** robust
   **b.** slight
   **c.** trivial
   **d.** unimportant

**6.** Which word means the *same* as NOCTURNAL?
   **a.** dawn
   **b.** night
   **c.** morning
   **d.** afternoon

**7.** Which word means the *opposite* of IMPARTIAL?
   **a.** complete
   **b.** prejudiced
   **c.** unbiased
   **d.** erudite

**8.** Which word means the *same* as IMPERATIVE?
   **a.** immaterial
   **b.** important
   **c.** insignificant
   **d.** irrelevant

**9.** Which word means the *opposite* of JUDICIOUS?
   **a.** partial
   **b.** litigious
   **c.** imprudent
   **d.** unrestrained

**10.** Which word means the *opposite* of TREPIDATION?
   **a.** apprehension
   **b.** anxiety
   **c.** concern
   **d.** confidence

**11.** Which word means the *same* as EGRESS?
   **a.** opening
   **b.** access
   **c.** exit
   **d.** entrance

**12.** Which word means the *same* as GARBLED?
   **a.** lucid
   **b.** unintelligible
   **c.** devoured
   **d.** outrageous

**13.** Which word means the *same* as COMPLIANCE?
   **a.** defiance
   **b.** destitute
   **c.** conformity
   **d.** combination

**14.** Which word means the *opposite* of PRESUMPTION?
   **a.** guess
   **b.** guidance
   **c.** certainty
   **d.** comportment

**15.** Which word means the *opposite* of AMBIGUOUS?
   **a.** apathetic
   **b.** certain
   **c.** equivocal
   **d.** indefinite

**16.** Which word means the *same* as EXPOSE?
   **a.** relate
   **b.** develop
   **c.** reveal
   **d.** pretend

**17.** Which word means the *opposite* of CHRONIC?
   **a.** fatal
   **b.** quick
   **c.** bucolic
   **d.** infrequent

**18.** Which word means the *same* as BOUNDARY?
   **a.** limit
   **b.** external
   **c.** internal
   **d.** litigation

**19.** Which word means the *opposite* of DETAIN?
   **a.** promote
   **b.** increase
   **c.** incur
   **d.** release

**20.** Which word means the *opposite* of AUDIBLE?
   **a.** mandatory
   **b.** planned
   **c.** optical
   **d.** silent

**21.** Which word means the *opposite* of REVERENCE?
   **a.** disrespect
   **b.** loyalty
   **c.** frustration
   **d.** prosperity

**22.** Which word means the *same* as ECSTATIC?
   **a.** inconsistent
   **b.** positive
   **c.** wild
   **d.** exhilarated

**23.** Which word means the *same* as APATHY?
   **a.** hostility
   **b.** depression
   **c.** indifference
   **d.** concern

**24.** Which word means the *opposite* of NEUTRAL?
   **a.** partisan
   **b.** adamant
   **c.** fertile
   **d.** aggravated

**25.** Which word means the *same* as COMPLY?
   **a.** subdue
   **b.** entertain
   **c.** flatter
   **d.** obey

**26.** Which word means the *same* as COURTESY?
   **a.** civility
   **b.** congruity
   **c.** conviviality
   **d.** rudeness

**27.** Which word means the *opposite* of CRITICAL?
   **a.** inimical
   **b.** judgmental
   **c.** trivial
   **d.** massive

**28.** Which word means the *opposite* of
   CREDIBILITY?
   **a.** harmony
   **b.** disharmony
   **c.** honesty
   **d.** dishonesty

**29.** Which word means the *opposite* of
   DETERRENT?
   **a.** encouragement
   **b.** obstacle
   **c.** proponent
   **d.** advantage

**30.** Which word means the *same* as DESPAIR?
   **a.** mourning
   **b.** disregard
   **c.** despondency
   **d.** pessimism

**31.** Which word means the *opposite* of
   HIERARCHICAL?
   **a.** monarchical
   **b.** egalitarian
   **c.** placid
   **d.** oligarchical

**32.** Which word means the *same* as CONTINUOUS?
   **a.** intermittent
   **b.** adjacent
   **c.** incessant
   **d.** contiguous

**33.** Which word means the *same* as EVOKE?
   **a.** summon
   **b.** satisfy
   **c.** emancipate
   **d.** eradicate

**34.** Which word means the *opposite* of EXPLICIT?
   **a.** modest
   **b.** innocent
   **c.** suggested
   **d.** embodied

**35.** Which word means the *opposite* of
   LABORIOUS?
   **a.** arduous
   **b.** easy
   **c.** complex
   **d.** specific

**36.** Which word means the *opposite* of FORTUNATE?
   **a.** excluded
   **b.** hapless
   **c.** hardworking
   **d.** lucky

**37.** Which word means the *same* as ANTERIOR?
   **a.** outside
   **b.** inside
   **c.** back
   **d.** front

**38.** Which word means the *same* as DISPARITY?
   **a.** imbalance
   **b.** insensitive
   **c.** incognito
   **d.** interpret

**39.** Which word means the *opposite* of INCOHERENT?
   **a.** comprehensible
   **b.** tentative
   **c.** disciplined
   **d.** muddled

**40.** Which word means the *same* as INTIMIDATE?
   **a.** condescend
   **b.** convince
   **c.** coerce
   **d.** cooperate

**41.** Which word means the *same* as RECOGNIZE?
   **a.** indemnity
   **b.** identify
   **c.** petition
   **d.** pardon

**42.** Which word means the *opposite* of INTENTIONAL?
   **a.** accidental
   **b.** calculated
   **c.** willful
   **d.** amicable

**43.** Which word means the *opposite* of ATTAIN?
   **a.** achieve
   **b.** answer
   **c.** futile
   **d.** fail

**44.** Which word means the *same* as INACCESSIBLE?
   **a.** reality
   **b.** rendezvous
   **c.** remote
   **d.** random

**45.** Which word means the *opposite* of IRRATIONAL?
   **a.** logical
   **b.** incorrect
   **c.** disregard
   **d.** damaged

**46.** Which word means the *opposite* of DECENCY?
   **a.** civility
   **b.** vulgarity
   **c.** wastefulness
   **d.** jagged

**47.** Which word means the *same* as ADJOINING?
   **a.** distance
   **b.** secluded
   **c.** rancorous
   **d.** adjacent

**48.** Which word means the *same* as CURSORY?
  **a.** careful
  **b.** hasty
  **c.** coordinated
  **d.** dissimilar

**49.** Which word means the *opposite* of MISCONSTRUE?
  **a.** understand
  **b.** injure
  **c.** massive
  **d.** minor

**50.** Which word means the *same* as REVISION?
  **a.** blond
  **b.** modification
  **c.** moderate
  **d.** repulse

## Recall Section

In this section, each set of 25 questions is preceded by a key that consists of letter sets and numbers. Each question consists of one of the letter sets followed by numbers. Use the key to pick the number that goes with each letter set, and then fill in the appropriate circle on the answer sheet. You have nine minutes for this section.

**KEY 1**

| NUB | FED | SRT | AXZ | JIK | DGB | IFA | CSB | LEW |
|-----|-----|-----|-----|-----|-----|-----|-----|-----|
| 12  | 92  | 44  | 24  | 16  | 55  | 36  | 99  | 26  |

| LGF | VGB | QOP | WQA | BCV | PLG | YTR | RCJ | MAZ |
|-----|-----|-----|-----|-----|-----|-----|-----|-----|
| 32  | 88  | 31  | 17  | 78  | 27  | 61  | 23  | 45  |

| GYH | KLV | PON | FAS | QLG | XEG | RIF | NDF | HUN |
|-----|-----|-----|-----|-----|-----|-----|-----|-----|
| 25  | 68  | 74  | 21  | 91  | 56  | 11  | 89  | 33  |

|     |     | a  | b  | c  | d  | e  |     |     |     | a  | b  | c  | d  | e  |
|-----|-----|----|----|----|----|----|-----|-----|-----|----|----|----|----|----|
| 1.  | LEW | 26 | 78 | 99 | 43 | 33 | 14. | HUN | 75 | 33 | 39 | 54 | 38 |
| 2.  | KLV | 18 | 44 | 68 | 89 | 25 | 15. | SRT | 19 | 44 | 91 | 13 | 31 |
| 3.  | WQA | 27 | 17 | 55 | 32 | 71 | 16. | DGB | 55 | 24 | 64 | 18 | 39 |
| 4.  | PON | 63 | 22 | 74 | 81 | 59 | 17. | YTR | 11 | 87 | 35 | 52 | 61 |
| 5.  | QLG | 19 | 34 | 25 | 72 | 91 | 18. | RCJ | 65 | 23 | 47 | 23 | 31 |
| 6.  | RIF | 21 | 11 | 53 | 39 | 70 | 19. | NDF | 63 | 41 | 81 | 78 | 89 |
| 7.  | MAZ | 15 | 73 | 93 | 45 | 31 | 20. | FAS | 96 | 18 | 32 | 21 | 11 |
| 8.  | QOP | 73 | 44 | 14 | 31 | 59 | 21. | FED | 71 | 36 | 41 | 92 | 38 |
| 9.  | NUB | 12 | 21 | 88 | 53 | 36 | 22. | GYH | 25 | 90 | 32 | 28 | 19 |
| 10. | BCV | 56 | 78 | 32 | 94 | 11 | 23. | AXZ | 78 | 24 | 74 | 91 | 26 |
| 11. | LGF | 57 | 19 | 55 | 32 | 78 | 24. | JIK | 16 | 27 | 39 | 42 | 63 |
| 12. | VGB | 23 | 21 | 59 | 49 | 88 | 25. | PLG | 43 | 27 | 54 | 41 | 59 |
| 13. | XEG | 63 | 41 | 56 | 39 | 92 |     |     |    |    |    |    |    |

## KEY 2

| OGF | EGO | JOK | DJA | OXE | KOG | OGI | IXJ | NAA |
|---|---|---|---|---|---|---|---|---|
| 23 | 88 | 24 | 45 | 68 | 35 | 14 | 32 | 41 |

| NFO | FED | HIG | AXA | JIV | DGO | IFA | XHO | OED |
|---|---|---|---|---|---|---|---|---|
| 43 | 93 | 47 | 36 | 75 | 11 | 25 | 73 | 55 |

| GOH | KOE | KON | FAH | JOG | XEG | IIF | NAF | HFN |
|---|---|---|---|---|---|---|---|---|
| 31 | 58 | 54 | 34 | 94 | 15 | 44 | 83 | 22 |

|  |  | a | b | c | d | e |
|---|---|---|---|---|---|---|
| 26. | OED | 35 | 45 | 11 | 23 | 55 |
| 27. | KOE | 68 | 47 | 54 | 83 | 58 |
| 28. | DJA | 35 | 58 | 33 | 45 | 92 |
| 29. | KON | 34 | 54 | 12 | 23 | 50 |
| 30. | JOG | 15 | 58 | 23 | 34 | 94 |
| 31. | IIF | 44 | 64 | 88 | 12 | 25 |
| 32. | NAA | 47 | 52 | 32 | 41 | 24 |
| 33. | JOK | 62 | 33 | 54 | 24 | 13 |
| 34. | NFO | 52 | 43 | 47 | 64 | 63 |
| 35. | OXE | 43 | 24 | 68 | 53 | 34 |
| 36. | OGF | 11 | 36 | 54 | 48 | 23 |
| 37. | EGO | 32 | 88 | 13 | 43 | 86 |
| 38. | XEG | 52 | 46 | 15 | 23 | 33 |

|  |  | a | b | c | d | e |
|---|---|---|---|---|---|---|
| 39. | HFN | 61 | 22 | 23 | 14 | 28 |
| 40. | HIG | 51 | 32 | 45 | 47 | 24 |
| 41. | DGO | 15 | 43 | 11 | 23 | 58 |
| 42. | OGI | 24 | 85 | 21 | 14 | 54 |
| 43. | IXJ | 32 | 47 | 34 | 62 | 24 |
| 44. | NAF | 52 | 94 | 84 | 47 | 83 |
| 45. | FAH | 35 | 48 | 23 | 34 | 41 |
| 46. | FED | 93 | 35 | 23 | 43 | 52 |
| 47. | GOH | 54 | 25 | 90 | 31 | 28 |
| 48. | AXA | 42 | 36 | 14 | 42 | 13 |
| 49. | JIV | 31 | 60 | 23 | 38 | 75 |
| 50. | KOG | 98 | 35 | 54 | 64 | 37 |

**KEY 3**

| | | | | | | | | |
|---|---|---|---|---|---|---|---|---|
| NAM 51 | KAE 58 | YAD 54 | FBM 94 | JAN 74 | XEN 15 | IYD 44 | DBF 85 | MFD 22 |
| ANF 27 | ENA 88 | LAK 24 | DJB 95 | AXY 18 | KAN 59 | ANI 14 | IXJ 52 | DBB 41 |
| DFA 45 | FEQ 75 | MIN 43 | BXY 56 | XIV 35 | DNA 11 | IFB 25 | XMA 35 | AED 55 |

| | | a | b | c | d | e | | | a | b | c | d | e |
|---|---|---|---|---|---|---|---|---|---|---|---|---|---|
| 51. | AED | 55 | 45 | 11 | 25 | 99 | 64. | MFD | 61 | 82 | 22 | 14 | 28 |
| 52. | KAE | 68 | 43 | 54 | 85 | 58 | 65. | MIN | 51 | 12 | 43 | 48 | 24 |
| 53. | DJB | 55 | 58 | 19 | 95 | 72 | 66. | DNA | 15 | 11 | 85 | 25 | 58 |
| 54. | KAN | 58 | 74 | 12 | 25 | 59 | 67. | ANF | 27 | 85 | 21 | 14 | 54 |
| 55. | JAN | 15 | 58 | 25 | 51 | 74 | 68. | IXJ | 52 | 43 | 54 | 62 | 24 |
| 56. | IYD | 44 | 64 | 88 | 12 | 25 | 69. | DBF | 92 | 74 | 84 | 43 | 85 |
| 57. | DBF | 43 | 85 | 52 | 41 | 24 | 70. | FBM | 15 | 48 | 25 | 94 | 41 |
| 58. | LAK | 62 | 17 | 54 | 24 | 15 | 71. | FEQ | 75 | 65 | 25 | 45 | 52 |
| 59. | DFA | 52 | 45 | 43 | 69 | 65 | 72. | NAM | 54 | 25 | 70 | 51 | 28 |
| 60. | AXY | 45 | 24 | 18 | 59 | 54 | 73. | BXY | 42 | 56 | 14 | 59 | 15 |
| 61. | ANF | 11 | 96 | 94 | 48 | 27 | 74. | XIV | 51 | 60 | 25 | 58 | 35 |
| 62. | ENA | 52 | 88 | 15 | 42 | 86 | 75. | KAN | 78 | 45 | 59 | 64 | 56 |
| 63. | XEN | 52 | 46 | 15 | 25 | 99 | | | | | | | |

## KEY 4

| | | | | | | | | |
|---|---|---|---|---|---|---|---|---|
| LFA | FRQ | MAT | BLY | LAV | DTA | AFB | LMA | ARD |
| 45 | 75 | 43 | 56 | 35 | 11 | 25 | 35 | 55 |
| TAK | CAR | YAR | KMB | JAT | LRT | AKD | RBF | MRD |
| 51 | 58 | 54 | 94 | 74 | 15 | 44 | 85 | 22 |
| ATF | RTA | LAC | DJB | ALY | CAK | ATB | ALJ | DBK |
| 27 | 88 | 24 | 95 | 18 | 59 | 14 | 52 | 41 |

| | | a | b | c | d | e | | | a | b | c | d | e |
|---|---|---|---|---|---|---|---|---|---|---|---|---|---|
| 76. | ARD | 43 | 85 | 55 | 41 | 24 | 89. | MRD | 61 | 82 | 22 | 14 | 28 |
| 77. | CAR | 58 | 45 | 43 | 69 | 65 | 90. | MAT | 51 | 12 | 43 | 48 | 24 |
| 78. | DJB | 45 | 24 | 18 | 59 | 95 | 91. | LFA | 78 | 45 | 59 | 64 | 56 |
| 79. | CAK | 58 | 74 | 12 | 25 | 59 | 92. | ATF | 52 | 43 | 54 | 62 | 27 |
| 80. | JAT | 68 | 43 | 74 | 85 | 58 | 93. | ALJ | 27 | 85 | 21 | 14 | 52 |
| 81. | AKD | 62 | 17 | 54 | 44 | 15 | 94. | RBF | 92 | 74 | 85 | 43 | 84 |
| 82. | DBK | 41 | 64 | 88 | 12 | 25 | 95. | YAR | 15 | 54 | 25 | 94 | 41 |
| 83. | LAC | 55 | 45 | 11 | 24 | 99 | 96. | FRQ | 54 | 75 | 70 | 51 | 28 |
| 84. | DTA | 11 | 96 | 94 | 48 | 27 | 97. | TAK | 51 | 60 | 25 | 58 | 35 |
| 85. | ALJ | 55 | 52 | 19 | 95 | 72 | 98. | BLY | 42 | 56 | 14 | 42 | 15 |
| 86. | ATF | 15 | 11 | 85 | 27 | 58 | 99. | LAC | 75 | 65 | 25 | 24 | 52 |
| 87. | RTA | 52 | 86 | 15 | 42 | 88 | 100. | CAK | 15 | 59 | 25 | 51 | 74 |
| 88. | LRT | 52 | 46 | 15 | 25 | 99 | | | | | | | |

## Part Two:
## Personal Background Section

*Answer each question honestly. Mark only one answer unless the question directs you otherwise. There is no time limit for this section.*

1. If I were to witness a coworker involved in employee theft, my initial reaction would be to
   a. report the person to my superiors.
   b. reprimand the person myself.
   c. ignore the person's actions.
   d. document the person's actions.

2. As a job applicant, my most important goal in an employment interview is to
   a. impress the interviewer.
   b. learn about the position.
   c. learn about salary and benefits.
   d. demonstrate my positive characteristics.
   e. demonstrate my commitment and professionalism.
   f. demonstrate my sense of humor.

3. My favorite type of movie is
   a. action/adventure.
   b. suspense.
   c. romance.
   d. comedy.
   e. drama.
   f. other

4. I feel the primary role of a parent is to
   a. educate.
   b. discipline.
   c. protect.
   d. provide.

5. On a typical weekend afternoon, I am likely to (Mark all that apply)
   a. catch up on work.
   b. go to a movie.
   c. go to a cultural event.
   d. go to a sporting event.
   e. spend quiet time alone.
   f. spend time with family or friends.
   g. engage in physical activity.
   h. do chores around the house.

6. If a close family member were in a local nursing home, I would prefer to visit
   a. several times a week.
   b. once a week.
   c. once or twice a month.
   d. irregularly.
   e. on holidays and special occasions.
   f. not at all.

7. If I come across a difficult word while reading or working, I am most likely to
   a. try to determine its meaning based on context.
   b. look it up in the dictionary.
   c. jot it down and ask someone about its meaning.
   d. skip over it on the assumption that I can understand what I am reading without knowing the word.

8. I believe my most productive work period is during
   a. the morning.
   b. the afternoon.
   c. the evening.
   d. the late night.
   e. any time period.

9. The word that best describes my driving style is
   a. patient.
   b. impatient.
   c. observant.
   d. aggressive.
   e. cautious.

10. If I observe a vehicle broken down along a busy highway, I am most likely to
    a. stop and offer assistance.
    b. call the police to report what I saw.
    c. continue driving, assuming someone else will help out.
    d. respond if I am not in a hurry.

11. In school, I generally completed assignments
    a. ahead of time.
    b. just in time.
    c. on time sometimes and late sometimes.
    d. most often late.

12. Other than gaining an education, my main priority in school was
    a. making friends.
    b. participating in sports.
    c. determining a career path.
    d. participating in extracurricular activities.
    e. having a good time.

13. If I disagreed with the methods of a teacher, I would
    a. approach him or her directly.
    b. write him or her a note.
    c. approach his or her supervisor.
    d. not do anything about it.
    e. drop the class.

14. In school, I demonstrated the most enthusiasm for
    a. math classes.
    b. science classes.
    c. social science/social studies classes.
    d. liberal arts classes.
    e. physical education classes.
    f. industrial arts classes.

15. When I complete a major project at work, I am most likely to
    a. begin focusing immediately on another project.
    b. expect immediate feedback from colleagues.
    c. expect feedback from supervisors.
    d. appreciate the sense of accomplishment.
    e. desire some time off.

16. I feel that becoming romantically involved with a coworker is
    a. wrong.
    b. sometimes unwise but unavoidable.
    c. acceptable under most circumstances.
    d. acceptable if kept discreet.

17. When I am given a rush assignment at work, I am most likely to feel
    a. challenged.
    b. that I am being treated unfairly.
    c. flustered or overwhelmed.
    d. energized.

**18.** If a coworker asks for a loan, I will
  **a.** provide it without hesitation.
  **b.** say yes if it is a small amount.
  **c.** say no.
  **d.** provide it, but set up a specific repayment date.
  **e.** base my decision on my evaluation of the particular coworker's trustworthiness.
  **f.** base my decision on the closeness of my relationship with this coworker.

**19.** In a small-class setting at school, I would
  **a.** speak up often.
  **b.** prefer that the teacher did not call on me.
  **c.** respond only if asked to.
  **d.** feel self-conscious about expressing myself.

**20.** If someone I know tells me he or she is considering dropping out of high school, my first reaction would be to
  **a.** express my disappointment.
  **b.** describe how the person's life might be with and without an education.
  **c.** try hard to convince him or her to remain in school.
  **d.** list his or her options and let the person decide for himself or herself.
  **e.** refer him or her to someone else.
  **f.** tell him or her dropping out is not an option.

# Answers

## Verbal

1. a.
2. a.
3. c.
4. c.
5. a.
6. b.
7. b.
8. b.
9. c.
10. d.
11. c.
12. b.
13. c.
14. c.
15. b.
16. c.
17. d.
18. a.
19. d.
20. d.
21. a.
22. d.
23. d.
24. a.
25. d.
26. a.
27. c.
28. d.
29. a.
30. c.
31. b.
32. c.
33. a.
34. c.
35. b.
36. b.
37. d.

38. a.
39. a.
40. c.
41. b.
42. a.
43. d.
44. c.
45. a.
46. b.
47. d.
48. b.
49. a.
50. b.

## Recall

1. a.
2. c.
3. b.
4. c.
5. e.
6. b.
7. d.
8. d.
9. a.
10. b.
11. d.
12. e.
13. c.
14. b.
15. b.
16. a.
17. e.
18. b. or D
19. e.
20. d.
21. d.
22. a.
23. b.
24. a.

25. b.
26. e.
27. e.
28. d.
29. b.
30. e.
31. a.
32. d.
33. d.
34. b.
35. c.
36. e.
37. b.
38. c.
39. b.
40. d.
41. c.
42. d.
43. a.
44. e.
45. d.
46. a.
47. d.
48. b.
49. e.
50. b.
51. a.
52. e.
53. d.
54. e.
55. e.
56. a.
57. b.
58. d.
59. b.
60. c.
61. e.
62. b.

63. c.
64. c.
65. c.
66. b.
67. a.
68. a.
69. e.
70. d.
71. a.
72. d.
73. b.
74. e.
75. c.
76. c.
77. a.
78. e.
79. e.
80. c.
81. d.
82. a.
83. d.
84. a.
85. b.
86. d.
87. e.
88. c.
89. c.
90. c.
91. b.
92. e.
93. e.
94. c.
95. b.
96. b.
97. a.
98. b.
99. d.
100. b.

# Scoring

The passing score for the exam is computed using formulas that subtract for incorrect answers and take into consideration the personal background section. Scoring on the personal background section varies, so focus on the first section in determining your score.

## Verbal Score

First, count the questions you answered correctly. Then, count the number of questions you answered incorrectly and divide by four. Subtract the results of the division from the number you got correct for your raw score. Questions you didn't answer have no effect on your score.

1. Number of correct questions: _____
2. Number of incorrect questions: _____
3. Divide number 2 by 4: _____
4. Subtract number 3 from number 1: _____

The result of number 4 is your raw score on the verbal section.

## Recall Score

Count the recall questions you answered correctly. Then, count the number of questions you answered incorrectly and divide by five. Subtract the results of the division from the number you got correct, and that's your score. Questions you didn't answer don't count.

1. Number of correct questions: _____
2. Number of incorrect questions: _____
3. Divide number 2 by 5: _____
4. Subtract number 3 from number 1: _____

The result of number 4 above is your raw score on the recall section.

## What the Scores Mean

Generally, if you scored at least 70% on each section—that's 35 on verbal and 70 on recall—you can figure that you would probably pass the first part of the test if you took it today. But then, your goal isn't just to pass. Because your rank on the eligibility list may be based on your written exam score among other factors, you want to score as high as you can. Unless you scored nearly 100%, you will want to spend some time in study and practice.

Your score isn't the main point of taking this practice exam. Analyzing your performance is much more important. Use this analysis to focus your study and practice between now and exam day.

- **Did you find that you didn't know many of the words in the verbal section?** Then you should plan to spend a lot of time on the vocabulary section of Chapter 8.
- **Did you have trouble with the recall section?** Then you need to study and practice the number recall section in Chapter 10.
- **Did you feel that you would have been able to get the correct answers if only you'd had enough time?** You might want to review the time management tips in Chapter 3, The LearningExpress Test Preparation System.
- **Did you do pretty well overall but feel you could use an extra edge?** That's the point of this whole book. Stick with it, and you will do well on exam day.

Whether you feel you performed well or poorly on this practice exam, your next step is to work with Chapters 9 and 10, which cover the three kinds of questions on the exam. You can decide whether to spend a lot of time or just a little on the individual chapters based on how you did on the practice exam.

After you've read the relevant chapters, take the second exam of this type, in Chapter 13, to see how much you've improved.

# GRAMMAR, VOCABULARY, AND SPELLING

### *CHAPTER SUMMARY*

A police officer's job involves far more writing than most candidates realize. It is for this reason that so many multiple-choice questions concentrate on testing for grammar, vocabulary, and spelling to gauge your grasp of the English language. This chapter reviews the types of skills tested on the exams and provides examples of the types of questions you should expect to see on sentence structure, capitalization, punctuation, subject-verb agreement, verb tenses, pronouns, vocabulary, and spelling.

**W**hen you take a police test, you are not expected to be familiar yet with police procedures or legal issues. For those types of questions, all the information you need to answer the questions correctly will be provided in the test booklet. You are, though, expected to have knowledge of grammar, vocabulary, and spelling. Testing for knowledge in these areas helps a department determine whether your language and comprehension skills are sufficient for you to master the material that all police officers are expected to learn in the academy and throughout their careers.

   This chapter reviews some key grammar areas and provides you with sample questions to give you a better understanding of what will be tested and how the questions will be presented. If you know you are weak in these areas, try to read more—reading helps you internalize the rules discussed in this chapter. Also, try to speak correctly, even in casual conversation, to improve your ear as well as your eye for correct usage. If you are not a native English speaker, or if you feel unsure of your abilities in this area, purchase a college-level grammar text or one of the books listed at the end of the chapter.

# Sentence Structure

The basis of everything you read and everything you will be asked to write is a complete sentence. A paragraph is a collection of complete sentences. Although many portions of police reports require you only to fill in or check boxes, almost all reports require some narrative. *Narrative* means you will be asked to write about what happened, what others did or said, and what action(s) you took. All this information must be in standard, proper English, with no slang or jargon (police-talk that others will not understand), and in complete sentences. Poorly written reports will most likely be sent back to you by a supervisor for you to rewrite. If you concentrate on what you want to say and then on how you want to say it, you are less likely to make the kinds of grammar and spelling errors that will cost you points on the exam and that will later cause you to have rewrite your work.

## *Sentence Fragments*

You probably recall from high school or college English classes that the basis of a sentence is a *subject* and a *verb* that join together with other words to form one complete idea. A *sentence fragment* generally lacks a subject or a verb and does not contain a complete idea. Look at the following pairs of word groups. The first in each pair is a sentence fragment; the second is a complete sentence.

| FRAGMENT | COMPLETE SENTENCE |
|---|---|
| The officer on foot patrol. | The officer was on foot patrol. |
| Exploding from the barrel of the gun. | The bullet exploded from the barrel of the gun. |

Many exams test your grasp of sentences by giving you four examples from which you will have to select the proper, complete sentence. To get you in the mindset for these questions, look at the word group pairs below and select the ones that are complete sentences.

- **a.** We saw the squad car approaching.
- **b.** When we saw the squad car approaching.

- **a.** Before the prison was built in 1972.
- **b.** The prison was built in 1972.

- **a.** Because we were on duty in the morning.
- **b.** We were on duty in the morning.

If you chose **1. a, 2. b, 3. b**, you were correct. You might have noticed that the groups of words are the same, but the fragments have an extra word at the beginning. These words are called *subordinating conjuctions*. If a group of words that would normally be a complete sentence is preceded by a subordinating conjunction, something more is needed to complete the thought.

In the following three sentences, the thoughts have been completed.

- When we saw the squad car approaching, we flagged it down.
- Before the prison was built in 1972, the old jail-house was demolished.
- Because we were on duty in the morning, we went to bed early.

Here is a list of words that are frequently used as subordinating conjunctions. Use each in a sentence to get a better idea of the rule. Be careful, though. Sometimes a group of words that begin with a subordinating conjunction can still be a complete sentence. You must read the entire sentence before deciding if it is correct or incorrect.

| | |
|---|---|
| after | that |
| although | though |
| as | unless |
| because | until |
| before | when |
| if | whenever |
| once | where |
| since | wherever |
| than | while |

## Run-On Sentences

A *run-on sentence* is a sentence that contains more than one idea (usually meaning it has more than one subject and more than one verb) and lacks proper punctuation. To recognize a run-on sentence, look for two or more ideas run together (hence the phrase *run-on*) that are not separated by a comma or a semicolon. If a sentence is a true run-on, you should be able to find a place in the word grouping where you could add a period to make two correct sentences. If you can tell when a group of words is not a sentence, you can probably tell when two or more sentences have been run together. The types of questions that ask you to find a run-on sentence will be identical to those that ask you to find fragments. You will be given four choices—one will be a complete sentence and the others will be run-ons. You will be asked to indicate which one is correct. To get you in mindset for these questions, look at the word group pairs below and select the ones that are complete sentences.

a. We went to the academy we had a good time.
b. We went to the academy, where we had a good time.

a. The rookies were all young and were male and female and some kept sloppy bunks.
b. The rookies, both young men and women, kept sloppy bunks.

a. Studying grammar is hard and more difficult than I thought and it reminds me too much of grade school.
b. Studying grammar is hard; it is difficult and it reminds me too much of grade school.

You should have selected choice **b** in all three sets. In each case, choice **a** put too many ideas into one sentence and do not use any punctuation to separate those ideas. Remember, a good way to find run-on sentences is to look for a place where you can put a period to separate one part of the long string of words. If both halves of the original sentence can stand alone with a subject and verb and each conveys a complete idea, you have probably located a run-on sentence. Some run-on sentences can be fixed with a comma separating the two ideas; others require a semicolon.

## Fragment and Run-On Sample Questions

These six questions provide examples of how fragment and run-on questions will appear on many police officer exams. Note that they may be phrased slightly differently; some may ask you to find the complete sentence, others may ask you to find the fragment or the run-on.

1. Which of the following groups of words is a complete sentence?
   a. The contraband buried beneath the floorboards beside the fireplace.
   b. After we spent considerable time considering all the possibilities before making our decision.
   c. After considering all the evidence, the detective made a decision on who might have committed the crime.
   d. In addition to the methods the detective used to solve the crime.

**2.** Which of the following groups of words is a complete sentence?

   **a.** Because he was a cop.

   **b.** This was fun to do.

   **c.** Whether we learned.

   **d.** If we ever see them again.

**3.** Select the group of words that are NOT a complete sentence.

   **a.** The historical account of the incident bore the most resemblance to fact.

   **b.** The historical account was factual.

   **c.** When the historical account became known.

   **d.** The historical account shocked the professor.

**4.** Which of the following groups of words is a run-on sentence?

   **a.** Jack and Jill went up a hill and Jack fell down and Jill picked him up and then Jack and Jill went home.

   **b.** Jack and Jill went up a hill to fetch a pail of water.

   **c.** Jack and Jill went up a hill to fetch a pail of water but got lost along the way.

   **d.** Jack and Jill went up a hill to fetch a pail of water the day before yesterday.

**5.** Which of the following group of word is NOT a run-on sentence?

   **a.** Whenever I put on my uniform, I am filled with a sense of pride.

   **b.** The special services unit completed its work and made a report and before going home asked the chief whether she wanted to read it.

   **c.** We slept soundly, and we never heard the alarm and we missed breakfast.

   **d.** Whenever I put on my uniform I am filled with a sense of pride and then I wonder what I would have done if I had not become a police officer and I don't have any idea.

**6.** Which of the following group of words is NOT a run-on sentence?

   **a.** I went home and went to sleep and Jimmy woke me up and came over and then we did homework.

   **b.** I went home, went to sleep, woke up, and then did homework.

   **c.** I went home and then I went to sleep and then Jimmy woke me up and then he came over and then we did homework.

   **d.** ALL are run-on sentences.

## Answers

**1. c.** Despite starting with the subordinate conjunction *after*, choice **c** contains a subject, verb, and complete thought. None of the other choices express complete thoughts.

**2. b.** Choice **b** is the only group of words that contains a complete thought. If you read the others carefully, you should have asked yourself *what*, because something was missing. *What* was supposed to happen because he was a good cop; *what* would happen whether we learned; *what* happened if we ever see them again?

**3. c.** Choice **c** is the only group of words that does not contain a complete thought. If you read it carefully, you would have asked yourself: *What* happened when the historical account became known? Once that question came into your mind, you should have recognized that the group of words did not contain a complete thought. Note also that this question did not ask *which is*; it asked *which is not*. You must read the question carefully to make sure that you know what you are being asked to look for.

**4. a.** Choice **a** can be separated into difference sentences wherever the word *and* appears or by using commas to replace some of the *ands*. The other choices express single thoughts or are properly constructed to convey more than one idea.

**5. a.** Choice **a** is the only one that is comprised of one complete thought with proper punctuation between the subordinate clause and the rest of the sentence.

**6. b.** Although choice **b** includes a number of verbs, there is only one subject and there is continuous action by only one person.

## Capitalization

You may encounter questions that test your ability to capitalize correctly. Here is a quick review of the most common capitalization rules.

- Capitalize the first word of a sentence. If the first word is a number, write it as a word.
- Capitalize the pronoun *I*.
- Capitalize the first word of a quotation: I said, "What's the name of your dog?" Do not capitalize the first word of a partial quotation: He called me "the most diligent officer" he had ever seen.
- Capitalize proper nouns and proper adjectives. See the table on the next page for more about proper nouns and adjectives.

The following passage contains no capitalized words. Circle those letters that should be capitalized.

when I first saw the black hills on january 2, 2010, i was shocked by their beauty. we had just spent new year's day in sioux falls, south dakota and had headed west toward our home in denver, colorado. as we traveled along interstate 90, i could see the black hills rising slightly in the distance. president calvin coolidge had called them "a wondrous sight to behold." i understood why. after driving through the badlands and stopping at wall drug in wall, south dakota, we liked the way the evergreen-covered hills broke the barren monotony of the landscape. my oldest daughter said, "dad, look! there's something that's not all white." we could see why the lakota regarded the black hills as a holy ground. we saw mount rushmore and custer state park, the home of the largest herd of buffalo in north america. we also drove the treacherous spearfish canyon road. fortunately, our jeep cherokee had no trouble with the ice and snow on the winding road.

| CAPITALIZATION | |
|---|---|
| CATEGORY | EXAMPLE (PROPER NOUNS) |
| days of the week, months of the year | Friday, Saturday; January, February |
| holidays, special events | Christmas, Halloween; Two Rivers Festival, Dilly Days |
| names of individuals | John Jay, Rudy Giuliani, George Billeck |
| names of structures, buildings | Lincoln Memorial, Principal Building |
| names of trains, ships, aircraft | Queen Elizabeth, Chicago El |
| product names | Corn King hams, Ford Mustang |
| cities and states | Des Moines, Iowa; Juneau, Alaska |
| streets, highways, roads | Grand Avenue, Interstate 29, Deadwood Road |
| landmarks, public areas | Continental Divide, Grand Canyon, Glacier National Park |
| bodies of water | Atlantic Ocean, Mississippi River |
| ethnic groups, languages, nationalities | Asian-American, English, Arab |
| official titles | Mayor Daley, President Johnson |
| institutions, organizations, businesses | Dartmouth College, Lions Club, General Motors Corporation |
| proper adjectives | English muffin, Polish sausage |

Check your circled version against the corrected version of the passage that follows.

When I first saw the Black Hills on January 2, 2010, I was shocked by their beauty. We had just spent New Year's Day in Sioux Falls, South Dakota and had headed west toward our home in Denver, Colorado. As we traveled along Interstate 90, I could see the Black Hills rising slightly in the distance. President Calvin Coolidge had called them "a wondrous sight to behold." I understood why. After driving through the Badlands and stopping at Wall Drug in Wall, South Dakota, we liked the way the evergreen-covered hills broke the barren monotony of the landscape. My oldest daughter said, "Dad, look! There's something that's not all white." We could see why the Lakota regarded the Black Hills as a holy ground. We saw Mount Rushmore and Custer State Park, the home of the largest herd of buffalo in North America. We also drove the treacherous Spearfish Canyon Road. Fortunately, our Jeep Cherokee had no trouble with the ice and snow on the winding road.

## Practice

Now try these sample questions. Choose the option that is capitalized correctly.

**4. a.** This year we will celebrate christmas on Tuesday, December 25 in Manchester, Ohio.
   **b.** This year we will celebrate Christmas on Tuesday, December 25 in manchester, Ohio.
   **c.** This year we will celebrate Christmas on Tuesday, December 25 in Manchester, Ohio.
   **d.** This year we will celebrate christmas on Tuesday, December 25 in manchester, Ohio.

**5. a.** Abraham Adams made an appointment with Mayor Burns to discuss the building plans.
   **b.** Abraham Adams made an appointment with Mayor Burns to discuss the Building Plans.
   **c.** Abraham Adams made an appointment with mayor Burns to discuss the building plans.
   **d.** Abraham Adams made an appointment with mayor Burns to discuss the Building Plans.

**6. a.** Abigail Dornburg, MD, was named head of the review board for Physicians Mutual.
   **b.** Abigail Dornburg, MD, was named Head of the Review Board for Physicians Mutual.
   **c.** Abigail Dornburg, MD Was named head of the review board for Physicians mutual.
   **d.** Abigail dornburg, MD, was named head of the review board for Physicians Mutual.

## Answers

  **4. c.**
  **5. a.**
  **6. a.**

# Punctuation

A section on the written exam may test your punctuation skills. Make sure you know how to use periods, commas, and apostrophes correctly.

## Periods

Here is a quick review of the rules regarding the use of a period.

- Use a period at the end of a sentence that is not a question or an exclamation.
- Use a period after an initial in a name: Millard K. Furham.
- Use a period after an abbreviation, unless the abbreviation is an acronym.
  Abbreviations: Mr., Ms., Dr., A.M., General Motors Corp., Allied Inc.
  Acronyms: NASA, AIDS, MTV
- If a sentence ends with an abbreviation, use only one period: We brought food, tents, sleeping bags, etc.

To prepare you for questions involving proper use of a period, look at the pairs of sentences and select the ones that are correct.

**a.** General Motors Corp. makes Chevrolet cars.
**b.** Mr Darcy reported his Chevrolet stolen.

**a.** Jan. 1 falls on a Monday next year.
**b.** January. 1 falls on a Monday next year.

**a.** Our team is the best!
**b.** Our team is the worst!.

You should have selected choice **a** in all three sets. In the first pair, the abbreviation Mr. requires a period. In the second pair, January does not require a period when it is spelled out rather than abbreviated. In the third pair, there is no need for two forms of punctuation at the end of the sentence.

## Commas

Using commas correctly can make the difference between presenting information clearly and distorting the facts. The following chart demonstrates the necessity of commas in written language. How many people are listed in the sentence?

| COMMAS AND MEANING | |
|---|---|
| Number undetermined | My sister Diane John Carey Melissa and I went to the fair. |
| Four people | My sister Diane, John Carey, Melissa, and I went to the fair. |
| Five people | My sister, Diane, John Carey, Melissa, and I went to the fair. |
| Six people | My sister, Diane, John, Carey, Melissa, and I went to the fair. |

Here is a quick review of the most basic rules regarding the use of commas.

- Use a comma before *and, but, so, or, for, nor,* and *yet* when they separate two groups of words that could be complete sentences.
  **Example:** The S.W.A.T. leader laid out the attack plan, and the team executed it to perfection.
- Use a comma to separate items in a series.
  **Example:** The student driver stopped, looked, and listened when she got to the railroad tracks.

- Use a comma to separate two or more adjectives modifying the same noun.
  **Example:** The hot, black, rich coffee tasted great after an hour in below-zero weather. (Notice that there is no comma between *rich* [an adjective] and *coffee* [the noun *rich* describes]).
- Use a comma after introductory words, phrases, or clauses in a sentence.
  **Examples:** *Usually,* the class begins with a short writing assignment. [introductory word]
  *Racing down the street,* the yellow car ran a stoplight. [introductory phrase]
  *After we responded to the call,* we returned to our normal patrol. [introductory clause]
- Use a comma after a name followed by Jr., Sr., or some other abbreviation.
  **Example:** The class was inspired by the speeches of Martin Luther King, Jr.
- Use a comma to separate items in an address.
  **Example:** The car stopped at 1433 West G Avenue, Orlando, Florida, 36890.
- Use a comma to separate a day and a year, as well as after the year.
  **Example:** I was born on July 21, 1954, during a thunderstorm.
- Use a comma after the greeting of a friendly letter and after the closing of any letter.
  **Example:** Dear Uncle Jon,
  Sincerely yours,
- Use a comma to separate contrasting elements in a sentence.
  **Example:** Your essay needs strong arguments, not strong opinions, to convince me.
- Use commas to set off appositives (words or phrases that explain or identify a noun).
  **Example:** My partner, a rookie, is named Ron.

The following passage contains no commas or periods. Add commas and periods as needed.

Dr Newton Brown Jr a renowned chemist has held research positions for OPEC Phillips Petroleum Inc Edward L Smith Chemical Designs and R J Reynolds Co His thorough exhaustive research is recognized in academic circles as well as in the business community as the most well-designed reliable data available Unfortunately on July 6 2000 he retired after a brief but serious illness He lives in a secluded retirement community at 2401 Beach Sarasota Springs Florida

Check your version against the following corrected version.

Dr. Newton Brown, Jr., a renowned chemist, has held research positions for OPEC, Phillips Petroleum Inc., Edward L. Smith Chemical Designs, and R.J.Reynolds Co. His thorough, exhaustive research is recognized in academic circles, as well as in the business community, as the most well-designed, reliable data available. Unfortunately, on July 6, 2000, he retired after a brief but serious illness. He lives in a secluded retirement community at 2401 Beach, Sarasota Springs, Florida.

Look at the pairs of sentences involving proper use of a period, and select the ones that are correct.

**a.** Our team works well together, but so does the team from the other stationhouse.
**b.** Our team did well on the test yet we were beaten by the team from the other stationhouse.

**a.** The crime was reported by John Smith, Jr.
**b.** John Smith Jr. reported the crime.

**a.** My partner lives at 1234 West Grove Street, New Haven Connecticut.
**b.** My partner lives at 1234 West Grove Street, New Haven, Connecticut.

You should have selected choice **a** in all three sets. In the first pair, the comma was omitted before "yet." In the second pair, the comma was omitted before "Smith." In the third pair, a comma should separate the name of the city from the state in which it is located.

## Apostrophes

Apostrophes communicate important information in written language. Here is a quick review of the two most important rules regarding the use of apostrophes.

■ Use an apostrophe to show that letters have been omitted from a word to form a contraction.
**Examples:** do not = don't; national = nat'l; I will = I'll; it is = it's
■ Use an apostrophe to show possession. See the table below for more examples.
**Examples:** Juan's dog; Nikia's house

| APOSTROPHES TO SHOW POSSESSION | | |
|---|---|---|
| SINGULAR NOUNS (ADD 'S) | PLURAL NOUNS ENDING IN S (ADD ') | PLURAL NOUNS NOT ENDING IN S |
| boy's | boys' | men's |
| child's | kids' | children's |
| lady's | ladies' | women's |

To get you in the mindset for questions involving proper use of an apostrophe, look at each pair of sentences and select the version that is correct.

**a.** Juan's dog chewed its bone.
**b.** Juan's dog chewed it's bone.

**a.** The men's locker room was always messier than the women's locker room.
**b.** The mens' locker rooms were always messier than the women's locker rooms.

**a.** Don't fingerprint a prisoner without first safeguarding you're weapon.
**b.** Don't fingerprint a prisoner without first safeguarding your weapon.

In the first pair, you should have selected choice **a.** In choice **b,** "it's" is not the possessive, but is the contraction "it is." In the second pair, the correct choice is **a** because there is no need to add an *s* to the word *men,* which already indicates plural. *Women's* should follow the same format as *men's.* In the third pair, you should have selected choice **b** because "you're" is not possessive, but is the contraction for "you are."

# Verbs

Verbs are the action words of sentences. They tell the reader what the subject of the sentence (generally a noun) is doing, did, or will do. For instance, in the simple sentence *Suzzane likes Tom,* "Suzanne" is the subject (the doer of the action), "likes" is the verb (the action), and "Tom" is the object (the recipient of the action). As sentences get longer and the ideas they express become more complex, so do issues surrounding how the verb is used and which formed a verb you need to use. The following sections on verbs provide a refresher in basic verb usage.

## Subject-Verb Agreement

In written language, a subject must agree with its verb in number. In other words, if a subject is singular, the verb must be singular. If the subject is plural, the verb must be plural. If you are unsure whether a verb is singular or plural, apply this simple test. Fill in the blanks in the two sentences below with the matching form of the verb. The verb form that best completes the first sentence is singular. The verb form that best completes the second sentence is plural.

One person _____. [Singular]
Two people _____. [Plural]

Look at these examples using the verbs *speak* and *do.* Try it yourself with any verb that confuses you.

One person *speaks.*    One person *does.*
Two people *speak.*    Two people *do.*

### Pronoun Subjects

Few people have trouble matching noun subjects and verbs, but pronouns are sometimes difficult for even the most sophisticated writers. Some pronouns are always singular, others are always plural, and still others can be either singular or plural, depending on the usage.

These pronouns are always singular:

| | |
|---|---|
| each | everyone |
| either | no one |
| neither | nobody |
| anybody | one |
| anyone | somebody |
| everybody | someone |

The indefinite pronouns *each, either,* and *neither* are most often misused. You can avoid a mismatch by mentally adding the word *one* after the pronoun and removing the other words between the pronoun and the verb. Look at the following examples.

Each **of the officers** wants his own squad car.
Each **one** wants his own squad car.

Either **of the suspects** knows where the stolen merchandise is located.
Either **one** knows where the stolen merchandise is located.

These sentences may sound awkward because many speakers misuse these pronouns, and you are probably used to hearing them used incorrectly. Despite that, the substitution trick (inserting *one* for the words following the pronoun) will help you avoid this mistake.

Some pronouns are always plural and require a plural verb:

| | |
|---|---|
| both | many |
| few | several |

Other pronouns can be either singular or plural:

| | |
|---|---|
| all | none |
| any | some |
| most | |

The words or prepositional phrases following these pronouns determine whether they are singular or plural. If what follows the pronoun is plural, the verb must be plural. If what follows is singular, the verb must be singular.

**All** of the **work is** finished.
**All** of the **jobs are** finished.
**Is any** of the **pizza** left?
**Are any** of the **pieces** of pizza left?

**None** of the **time was** wasted.
**None** of the **minutes were** wasted.

## Subjects Joined by *and*

If two nouns or pronouns are joined by *and*, they require a plural verb.

He **and** she want to buy a new house.
Jack **and** Jill want to buy a new house.

## Subjects Joined by *or* or *nor*

If two nouns or pronouns are joined by *or* or *nor*, they require a singular verb. Think of them as two separate sentences and you'll never make a mistake in agreement.

He **or** she wants to buy a new house.
He wants to buy a new house.
She wants to buy a new house.

Neither Jack **nor** Jill is good at basketball.
Jack is not good at basketball.
Jill is not good at basketball.

### *Practice*

Circle the correct verb in each of the following sentences.

1. Every other day either Bert or Ed (takes, take) out the trash.
2. The woman in question (works, work) at the Civic Center box office.
3. A good knowledge of the rules (helps, help) you understand the game.
4. Each of these factors (causes, cause) the crime rate to increase.
5. (Have, Has) either of them ever arrived on time?

### Answers

1. takes
2. works
3. helps
4. causes
5. Has

## Verb Tense

The tense of a verb tells a reader when the action occurs. Present tense verbs tell the reader to imagine the action happening as it is being read, while past tense verbs tell the reader that the action has already happened. Read the following two paragraphs. The first one is written in the present tense, the second in the past tense. Notice the difference in the verbs. They are highlighted to make them easier to locate.

As Officer Horace **opens** the door, he **glances** around cautiously. He **sees** signs of danger everywhere. The centerpiece and placemats from the dining room table **are scattered** on the floor next to the table. An end table in the living room **is lying** on its side. He **sees** the curtains flapping and **notices** glass on the carpet in front of the window.

As Officer Horace **opened** the door, he **glanced** around cautiously. He **saw** signs of danger everywhere. The centerpiece and placemats from the dining room table **were scattered** on the floor next to the table. An end table in the living room **was lying** on its side. He **saw** the curtains flapping and **noticed** glass on the carpet in front of the window.

You can distinguish present tense from past tense by simply fitting the verb into a sentence.

| VERB TENSE | |
|---|---|
| PRESENT TENSE (TODAY, I ___ . . .) | PAST TENSE (YESTERDAY, I ___ . . .) |
| drive | drove |
| think | thought |
| rise | rose |
| catch | caught |

The important thing to remember about verb tense is to keep it consistent. If a passage begins in the present tense, keep it in the present tense unless there is a specific reason to change—to indicate that some action occurred in the past, for instance. If a passage begins in the past tense, it should remain in the past tense. Verb tense should never shift as it does in the following sentence.

**Wrong:** Officer Terry **opens** the door and **saw** the unruly crowd.

**Correct:** Officer Terry **opens** the door and **sees** the unruly crowd.
Officer Terry **opened** the door and **saw** the unruly crowd.

However, sometimes it is necessary to use a different verb tense in order to clarify when an action occurred. Read the following sentences and the explanations following them.

The sergeant **sees** the criminal that you **caught**. [The verb *sees* is in the present tense, indicating that the action is occurring in the present. However, the verb *caught* is in the past tense, indicating that the criminal was caught at some earlier time.]

The prison that **was built** over a century ago **sits** on top of the hill. [The verb phrase *was built* is in the past tense, indicating that the prison was built in the past. However, the verb *sits* is in the present tense, indicating that the action is still occurring.]

## Practice

*Choose the option that uses the verb tense correctly.*

**6. a.** When I work hard, I always get what I want.
   **b.** When I works hard, I always gets what I want.
   **c.** When I work hard, I always got what I wanted.
   **d.** When I worked hard, I always get what I wanted.

**7. a.** It all started after I came home and am in my room studying for the police exam.
   **b.** It all started after I came home and was in my room studying for the police exam.
   **c.** It all starts after I come home and was in my room studying for the police exam.
   **d.** It all will start after I came home and are in my room studying for the police exam.

**8. a.** The suspect became nervous and dashes into the house and slams the door.
   **b.** The suspect becomes nervous and dashed into the home and slammed the door.
   **c.** The suspect becomes nervous and will dash into the home and will slam the door.
   **d.** The suspect became nervous and dashed into the house and slammed the door.

**9.** Sergeant Phillips _____ promoted to lieutenant next year.
   **a.** has been
   **b.** was
   **c.** will be
   **d.** be

## Answers

**6. a.** Choice **a** is the only one in which the tenses agree and the subject and verb (first person singular) also agree.
**7. b.** Choice **b** is the only sentence in which the two past tenses match.

**8. d.** Choice **d** is the only one in which all three verbs became, dashed, and slammed) are in the same tense and agree with the subject of the sentence.
**9. c.** *Next year* tells you that the future tense is required.

# Pronouns

## Pronoun Case

Most of the time, a single pronoun in a sentence is easy to use correctly. In fact, most English speakers would readily identify the mistakes in the following sentences.

**Me** went to the prison with **he**.
My partner gave **she** a ride to work.

Most people know that *Me* in the first sentence should be *I* and that *he* should be *him*. They would also know that *she* in the second sentence should be *her*. Such errors are easy to spot when the pronouns are used alone in a sentence. The problem occurs when a pronoun is used with a noun or another pronoun. See if you can spot the errors in the following sentences.

The rookie rode with Jerry and **I**.
Belle and **him** are going to the courthouse.

The errors in these sentences are not as easy to spot as those in the sentences with a single pronoun. The easiest way to attack this problem is to turn the sentence with two pronouns into two separate sentences. Then the error once again becomes very obvious.

The rookie rode with Jerry.
The rookie rode with **me** (not I).

Belle **is** going to the courthouse. [Notice the singular verb *is* in place of *are*.]
**He** (not *him*) is going to the courthouse.

## Pronoun Agreement

Another common error in using pronouns involves singular and plural pronouns. Like subjects and verbs, pronouns must match the number of the nouns they represent. If the noun a pronoun represents is singular, the pronoun must be singular. On the other hand, if the noun a pronoun represents is plural, the pronoun must be plural. Sometimes a pronoun represents another pronoun. If so, either both pronouns must be singular or both pronouns must be plural. Consult the list of singular and plural pronouns you saw earlier in this chapter.

> The **officer** must take a break when **she** (or **he**) is tired. [singular]
> **Officers** must take breaks when **they** are tired. [plural]

> **One** of the rookies misplaced **her** file. [singular]
> **All** of the rookies misplaced **their** files. [Plural]

If two or more singular nouns or pronouns are joined by *and,* use a plural pronoun to represent them.

> **Buddha and Muhammad** built religions around **their** philosophies.
> If **he and the sergeant** want to know where I was, **they** should ask me.

If two or more singular nouns or pronouns are joined by *or,* use a singular pronoun. If a singular and a plural noun or pronoun are joined by *or,* the pronoun should agree with the closest noun or pronoun it represents.

> **Matthew or Jacob** will loan you **his** extra radio.
> **The elephant or the moose** will furiously protect **its** young.

> Neither **the officers** nor **the sergeant** was sure of **his** location.
> Neither **the sergeant** nor **the officers** was sure of **their** location.

## Practice

*Circle the correct pronoun in the following sentences.*

**10.** Andy or Arvin will bring (his, their) camera so (he, they) can take pictures of the party.

**11.** One of the file folders isn't in (its, their) drawer.

**12.** The uniform store sent Bob and Ray the shirts (he, they) had ordered.

**13.** Benny and (he, him) went to the courthouse with Bonnie and (I, me).

**14.** Neither my cousins nor my uncle knows what (he, they) will do tomorrow.

## Answers

**10.** his, he
**11.** its
**12.** they
**13.** he, me
**14.** he

# Easily Confused Words Pairs

The following word pairs are often misused in written language. By reading the following explanations and looking at the examples, you can learn to use these words correctly every time.

As you take the portion of the test that assesses your writing skills, apply what you know about the rules of grammar:

- Look for complete sentences.
- Check for periods, commas, and apostrophes.
- Look for subject-verb agreement and consistency in verb tense.
- Check the pronouns to make sure the correct form is used and that the number (singular or plural) is correct.
- Check those easily confused pairs of words.
- When determining which answer is correct to any one question, don't go back and review answer choices that you have already eliminated as being wrong.
- Always read all of the answer choices before selecting one. You may find an even better answer if you keep looking.

### Its/It's

*Its* is a possessive pronoun that means "belonging to it." *It's* is a contraction for *it is* or *it has*. The only time you will ever use *it's* is when you can also substitute the words *it is* or *it has*.

### Who/That

*Who* refers to people. *That* refers to things.

> There is the officer **who** helped me recover my car.
> The woman **who** invented the copper-bottomed kettle died in 1995.
> This is the house **that** was burglarized.
> The bullets **that** I needed were no longer in stock.

### There/Their/They're

*Their* is a possessive pronoun that shows ownership. *There* is an adverb that tells where an action or item is located. *They're* is a contraction for the words *they are*. Here is an easy way to remember these words.

- *Their* means belonging to them. Of the three words, *their* can be most easily transformed into the word *them*. Extend the *r* on the right side and connect the *i* and the *r* to turn *their* into *them*. This clue will help you remember that *their* means "belonging to them."

- If you examine the word *there*, you can see that it contains the word *here*. Whenever you use *there*, you should be able to substitute *here*. The sentence should still make sense.
- Imagine that the apostrophe in *they're* is actually a very small letter *a*. Use *they're* in a sentence only when you can substitute *they are*.

### Your/You're

*Your* is a possessive pronoun that means "belonging to you." *You're* is a contraction for the words *you are*. The only time you should use *you're* is when you can substitute the words *you are*.

### To/Too/Two

*To* is a preposition or an infinitive.

- As a preposition: *to* the jail, *to* the bottom, *to* my church, *to* our garage, *to* his school, *to* his hideout, *to* our disadvantage, *to* an open room, *to* a ballad, *to* the precinct
- As an infinitive (*to* followed by a verb, sometimes separated by adverbs): *to* walk, *to* leap, *to* see badly, *to* find, *to* advance, *to* read, *to* build, *to* sorely want, *to* badly misinterpret, *to* carefully peruse

*Too* means also. Whenever you use the word *too*, substitute the word *also*. The sentence should still make sense.

*Two* is a number, as in *one, two*. If you memorize this, you will never misuse this form.

### Practice

The key is to think consciously about these words when you see them in written language. Circle the correct form of these easily confused words in the following sentences.

**15.** (Its, It's) (to, too, two) late (to, too, two) remedy the problem now.
**16.** This is the officer (who, that) gave me the directions I needed.
**17.** (There, Their, They're) going (to, too, two) begin construction as soon as the plans are finished.
**18.** We left (there, their, they're) house after the storm subsided.
**19.** I think (your, you're) going (to, too, two) get at least (to, too, two) extra shifts.
**20.** The crime syndicate moved (its, it's) home base of operations.

### Answers

**15.** It's, too, to
**16.** who
**17.** They're, to
**18.** their
**19.** you're, to, two
**20.** its

## Vocabulary

Having a good vocabulary is important when reading, writing, or speaking. While all police officers and police officer applicants are encouraged to use a dictionary to look up the meaning of words they are unfamiliar with, it is not good use of their time to have to run to a dictionary to check every third word they see. Police officers must understand complex laws, regulations, and procedures. While you cannot be expected to be familiar with many of these terms as well as the specialized words you will be introduced to, you will need to be able to use the English language efficiently.

If your written exam has a section that tests vocabulary, which is very likely, the questions are most likely to cover synonyms, antonyms, context, and/or homophones.

### Synonyms and Antonyms

*Synonyms* are words that share the same or nearly the same meaning as other words.
*Antonyms* are words that are opposite or nearly opposite the meaning of other words.

The most common question type that tests for your understanding of words that are similar to or different from one another will give you a short sentence or phrase with a word underlined and provide four choices from which you are to select either the synonym or the antonym. Root words can sometimes help you answer these questions, but you must be careful to avoid so-called "false friends," or words that look or sound alike and seem to have similar meanings but may not.

Make sure to read the brief instructions prior to the series of questions carefully so that you know which choice you are looking for; a tricky question may provide both a synonym and an antonym as one of the choices to catch whether you read the question closely.

## Synonym and Antonym Sample Questions

*Choose the synonym of the underlined word in questions 21–23*

**21.** The defendant's attorney was eager to <u>expedite</u> the trial process.
   **a.** reverse
   **b.** appeal
   **c.** accelerate
   **d.** explain

**22.** The new lieutenant had trouble learning how to <u>delegate</u> authority.
   **a.** understand
   **b.** accept
   **c.** assign
   **d.** feign

**23.** The Oak Hill Police Department is housed in an <u>obsolete</u> building.
   **a.** spacious
   **b.** out-of-date
   **c.** modern
   **d.** costly

*Choose the antonym of the underlined word in questions 24–26.*

**24.** The citizens of Rock Hill were <u>unanimous</u> in the view that the police department should hire at least five new police officers.
   **a.** unsure
   **b.** divided
   **c.** uniform
   **d.** out-spoken

**25.** Which word means the opposite of <u>refute</u>?
   **a.** verify
   **b.** inform
   **c.** unite
   **d.** argue

**26.** Officer Tomas went about his duties very <u>purposefully</u>.
   **a.** casually
   **b.** carefully
   **c.** seriously
   **d.** earnestly

## Answers

**21. c.**

**22. c.**

**23. b.**

**24. b.** *Unanimous* means uniform or in agreement; the opposite is *divided*.

**25. a.** *Refute* means to disprove or show to be false; the opposite is to *verify*, or to show to be accurate or true. Note that this question is arranged somewhat differently than the previous ones, but is still testing your vocabulary skills. This question style may be more difficult than the sentence format because you have no context to help you determine the meaning.

**26. a.** *Purposefully* means with purpose, or seriously; the opposite is *casually*. Note that in this question, the root word *purpose* would have helped you in figuring out the answer.

## Context

*Context* refers to the text surrounding a word from which you develop its meaning. You may be unaware that you use context whenever you come across a word you are unfamiliar with when you try to figure out its meaning through the rest of the words in the sentence or phrase. Context questions are similar to synonyms and antonyms but may seem easier because they give you a full sentence to help you figure out which of the choices is the best. You are able to put the words into the context of the sentence. However, the sentence may be phrased in such a way that more than one of the choices initially appears correct. You must still read carefully even if you rely on the process of elimination more than you are able to with other questions.

## Context Sample Questions

*For questions 27–32, select the word that means the same or almost the same as the underlined word.*

**27.** The members of the jury were <u>appalled</u> by the wild and uncontrolled behavior of the witness
   **a.** horrified
   **b.** amused
   **c.** surprised
   **d.** dismayed

**28.** Despite the fact that he appeared to have financial resources, the defendant claimed to be <u>destitute.</u>
   **a.** wealthy
   **b.** ambitious
   **c.** solvent
   **d.** impoverished

**29.** Though she was <u>distraught</u> over the disappearance of her child, the woman was calm enough to give Officer Chu her daughter's description.
   **a.** punished
   **b.** distracted
   **c.** composed
   **d.** anguished

**30.** The unrepentant criminal expressed no <u>remorse</u> for his actions.
   **a.** sympathy
   **b.** regret
   **c.** reward
   **d.** complacency

**31.** Professor Washington was a very _____ woman known for her reputation as a scholar.
   **a.** stubborn
   **b.** erudite
   **c.** illiterate
   **d.** disciplined

**32.** His _____ was demonstrated by his willingness to donate large amounts of money to worthy causes.
   **a.** honesty
   **b.** loyalty
   **c.** selfishness
   **d.** altruism

## Answers

**27. a.** Choice **a** is more appropriate than choice **d** because it indicates a stronger emotion that more closely matches *appalled*. Choices **b** and **c** do have the same meaning.
**28. d.** The phrase *Despite the fact* alerts you to look for the opposite of *financial resources*.
**29. d.** The words *though* and *disappearance of her child* alert you to look for the opposite of *calm*.

**30. b.** Remorse means *regret for one's actions.* If you know that *repentant* comes from the root *repent*, someone who is *unrepentant* would be someone not repenting, or not *regretting* or being *sorry about.*

**31. b.** The key words are *professor* and *scholar.* Even if you are unfamiliar with the word *erudite*, the other choices, with the possible exception of **d**, *disciplined*, do not fit the description of a scholar. Note that the format of this and the next question are slightly different from the first four; here, rather than have an underlined word to start from, you are expected to fill in a blank directly from the context of the sentence. Do not fall into a trap of trying to select the word based on the size of the space; in other words, a short space does not mean you should select the shortest word in the list of choices, nor does a long space mean you should select the longest word.

**32. d.** The phrase *large amounts of money to worthy causes* is the key to the definition you are looking for. Even if you are unfamiliar with the word *altruism*, the other choices do not describe generosity, a word you may be more familiar than altruism.

## Homophones

Don't be fooled by words that sound alike but have entirely different meanings. The best way to identify these easily confused words is by studying them and quizzing yourself until you have the meanings and spellings memorized. A list of homophones that are often found on written exams follows this section. Review the list carefully and consult your dictionary to determine the meanings of any words that you are unsure of.

## Homophone Sample Questions

*Questions 33–38 each provide two choices of words that are homophones. Select the word that makes sense in each sentence.*

**33.** Officer Markus slammed on his _____ to avoid hitting a car that had stalled in the intersection.
   **a.** break
   **b.** brake

**34.** Our sergeant asked us to _____ him before responding to the parade.
   **a.** meet
   **b.** meat

**35.** The mayor told the police commission to _____ six new police officers; I hope I will be one of them.
   **a.** hire
   **b.** higher

**36.** We learned in the police academy to keep unauthorized persons away from a crime _____.
   **a.** seen
   **b.** scene

**37.** Lieutenant Bashari did not know _____ he was on the promotion list.
   **a.** weather
   **b.** whether

**38.** I was thrilled to learn I had _____ the defensive driving course.
   **a.** passed
   **b.** past

## Homophones

| | | |
|---|---|---|
| ad, add | hear, here | rap, wrap |
| affect, effect | heard, herd | right, write |
| allowed, aloud | higher, hire | road, rode |
| bare, bear | hoarse, horse | roll, role |
| bored, board | hole, whole | sale, sail |
| boulder, bolder | hours, ours | scene, seen |
| brake, break | incite, insight | see, sea |
| bred, bread | knew, new | soar, sore |
| build, billed | know, no | stair, stare |
| cent, scent | lead, led | steel, steal |
| cereal, serial | leased, least | sun, son |
| cite, sight, site | lesson, lessen | sweet, suite |
| counsel, council | made, maid | tents, tense |
| course, coarse | marshal, martial | their, there, they're |
| days, daze | meat, meet | threw, through |
| died, dyed | morning, mourning | throne, thrown |
| due, do, dew | one, won | tide, tied |
| facts, fax | pact, packed | to, too, two |
| fair, fare | pail, pale | trooper, trouper |
| feat, feet | passed, past | vary, very |
| find, fined | patience, patients | wade, weighed |
| flour, flower | pause, paws | ware, wear, where |
| for, fore, four | peace, piece | weight, wait |
| great, grate | plain, plane | weather, whether |
| groan, grown | poor, pour | wood, would |
| guessed, guest | rain, reign | your, you're |
| heal, he'll | raise, rays | |

### Answers

**33. b.** *Brake* is the word for a stopping device; *break* means to damage something.

**34. a.** *Meet* means get together; *meat* is something you eat.

**35. a.** *Hire* means to employ; *higher* is a comparative based on the word *high*.

**36. b.** *Scene* is a place of occurrence; *seen* is the past participle of *see*.

**37. b.** *Whether* indicates an alternative; *weather* pertains to temperature, moisture, wind, velocity, and atmospheric conditions.

**38. a.** *Passed* indicates to undergo a trial or test with favorable results; *past* indicates no longer current.

# Ways to Improve Your Vocabulary

- Learn groups of synonyms for words.
- Learn new words in context.
- Memorize common word roots, prefixes, and suffixes.
- Create and use flashcards regularly.

# Spelling

Most spelling questions will be presented to you in a multiple-choice format. You are most likely to be given four choices to select from; one, obviously, is the correct spelling of a word and the other three are incorrect. For a small number of questions, you might be given the option to select "none of the above." If this is an available choice, do not make the assumption that it is always the correct one. It is possible that a crafty question designer has presented this choice even if one of the three other choices is correct. While questions are generally not meant to trick you, there might be a few that are designed to make sure you are reading carefully and not just marking off answers in a pre-arranged pattern.

By presenting you with choices, the questions give you the opportunity to separate correct from incorrect spelling. This can be helpful because the word might look familiar enough for you to guess even if you are not sure, but if your knowledge of spelling rules is vague, the incorrect spelling may look as good to you as the correct one. There are far too many words in the English language with irregular spelling for you to memorize every word that does not follow a general rule, but a few general rules can be helpful. As you read them you will probably recall having heard them many years ago, probably as early as grade school. For instance:

- *i* before *e*, except after *c*, or when *ei* sounds like *a* as in n*ei*ghbor or w*ei*gh. Other examples: p*ie*ce [of cake] but rec*ei*ve.

- *gh* can replace *f* or be silent. (examples: *enough*, *night*, *tough*)
- drop the *e* when adding *-ing*. Examples: *hope* becomes *hoping*, *cope* becomes *coping*, *license* becomes *licensing*, a related rule has to do with a final *y*, which sometimes changes to an *i* (example: *study*, *studying*, but *studied*)

One of the best ways to study spelling is similar to the techniques for homophones. After reviewing the rules and a grammar text, make lists of words that seem to give you particular problems. Flash cards can also be helpful and are easy to study from if you use public transportation on your way to school or work or if you have small stretches of free time such as a work break or meal period.

## Using Spelling Lists

Some test makers will give you a list of words to study before you take the test. If you have a list to work with, here are some suggestions.

- Divide the list into groups of three, five, or seven words to study. Consider making flash cards of the words you don't know.
- Highlight or circle the tricky elements in each word.
- Cross out or discard any words that you already know for certain. Don't let them get in the way of the ones you need to study.
- Say the words as you read them. Spell them out loud or in your mind so you can hear the spelling.

Here's a sample spelling list. These words are typical of the words that appear on exams. If you are not given a list by the agency that's testing you, study this one.

| | | |
|---|---|---|
| achievement | doubtful | ninety |
| allege | eligible | noticeable |
| anxiety | enough | occasionally |
| appreciate | enthusiasm | occurred |
| asthma | equipped | offense |
| arraignment | exception | official |
| autonomous | fascinate | pamphlet |
| auxiliary | fatigue | parallel |
| brief | forfeit | personnel |
| ballistics | gauge | physician |
| barricade | grieve | politics |
| beauty | guilt | possess |
| beige | guarantee | privilege |
| business | harass | psychology |
| bureau | hazard | recommend |
| calm | height | referral |
| cashier | incident | recidivism |
| capacity | indict | salary |
| cancel | initial | schedule |
| circuit | innocent | seize |
| colonel | irreverent | separate |
| comparatively | jeopardy | specific |
| courteous | knowledge | statute |
| criticism | leisure | surveillance |
| custody | license | suspicious |
| cyclical | lieutenant | tentative |
| debt | maintenance | thorough |
| definitely | mathematics | transferred |
| descend | mortgage | warrant |

## How to Answer Spelling Questions

- Sound out the word in your mind. Remember that long vowels inside words usually are followed by single consonants: *sofa, total, crime*. Short vowels inside words usually are followed by double consonants: *dribble, scissors, toddler*.
- Give yourself auditory (listening) clues when you learn words. Say *Wed-nes-day* or *lis-ten* or *bus-i-ness* to yourself so that you remember to add the letters you do not hear.
- Look at each part of a word. See if there is a root, prefix, or suffix that will always be spelled the same way. For example, in *uninhabitable*, *un-*, *in-*, and *-able* are always spelled the same. What's left is *habit*, a self-contained root word that's pretty easy to spell.

## Spelling Sample Questions

*To answer questions 39–44, choose the correct spelling of the word that fits in the blank.*

**39.** Office Solis purchased a new car and learned that her _____ is more expensive than for her old car.
- **a.** insurance
- **b.** assurance
- **c.** insurence
- **d.** insurrence

**40.** We will _____ go to the movies tonight.
- **a.** probly
- **b.** probebly
- **c.** probably
- **d.** none of the above

**41.** After returning from leave, Sergeant Abu said he felt _____.
  **a.** terriffic
  **b.** teriffic
  **c.** terrific
  **d.** tarrific

**42.** We sharpshooters had the greatest number of _____ target shots.
  **a.** accurate
  **b.** acurate
  **c.** accuret
  **d.** accurit

**43.** Because we work in a large city, we must learn how to _____ park our vehicles.
  **a.** parrellel
  **b.** parellel
  **c.** paralel
  **d.** parallel

**44.** Our academy instructors warned us not to use _____ force.
  **a.** exessive
  **b.** eksessive
  **c.** excessive
  **d.** exccessive

## Answers
**39. a.**
**40. c.**
**41. c.**
**42. a.**
**43. d.**
**44. c.**

# CHAPTER

# 9

# READING COMPREHENSION AND JUDGMENT

### CHAPTER SUMMARY

Two of the most important skills a police officer must have are the ability to read and the ability to exercise good judgment. Like the previous chapter, this chapter reviews the skills tested on the exams and provides examples of the types of questions you should expect to see. These questions on the police officer exam measure your ability to read and understand text and to exercise good judgment based on short situations that the questions present to you.

## Reading Comprehension

Reading comprehension is an important skill for understanding the material taught during the police academy. Information presented to you will include a large number of legal principles and court decisions; detailed reports, procedures, and forms; suspect descriptions; and many other documents that you will refer to regularly in the course of your work. To make sure that you are able to understand the material that will be presented to you in the academy and throughout your career, the reading comprehension portion of the written test is designed to measure how well you understand what you read.

These tests are most often multiple-choice; you will be given brief passages to read and then you will be asked a series of questions based on each. They are very similar to exams you have probably taken in high school and college. Along with sample questions, this chapter provides you with advice and strategies for maximizing your test score.

In addition to spending time with this chapter, consider adding more reading to your daily schedule of activities. Just as you can become a better baseball pitcher by practicing your pitches, you can become a better—and more thorough—reader by practicing reading. After you read something, think about what you read. Did you understand it? Were there words or phrases you should look up in the dictionary? Were issues presented that were unfamiliar to you? Ask yourself these and other questions to be sure that you not only *read* the words themselves, but that you *understood* what you read.

After studying the sample questions later on in the chapter, make up similar questions for yourself for passages you read on your own. Do not be intimidated; the passages you will be given on your written exam are no more difficult than a newspaper article or a high school or college textbook. Practicing, though, will raise your current level of reading comprehension and will benefit you not only on the exam, but in all aspects of your career.

## Types of Reading Comprehension Questions

You have probably encountered reading comprehension questions before, where you are given a passage to read and then have to answer multiple-choice questions about it. This kind of question has two advantages for you as a test taker:

1. Any information you need to know is right in front of you.
2. You're being tested only on the information provided in the passage.

The disadvantage, however, is that you have to know where and how to find information quickly in an unfamiliar text. This makes it easy to fall for one of the incorrect answer choices, especially since they're designed to mislead you.

The best way to excel on this passage/question format is to be very familiar with the kinds of questions that are typically asked on the test. Questions most frequently fall into one of the following four categories:

1. fact or detail
2. main idea or title
3. inference or interpretation
4. vocabulary definition

In order to succeed on a reading comprehension test, you need to thoroughly understand each of these four types of questions.

### Fact or Detail

Facts and details are the specific pieces of information that support the passage's main idea. Generally speaking, facts and details are indisputable—things that don't need to be proven, like statistics (18 million people) or descriptions (a green overcoat). While you may need to decipher paraphrases of facts or details, you should be able to find the answer to a fact or detail question directly in the passage. This is usually the simplest kind of question; however, you must be able to separate important information from less important information. The main challenge in answering this type of question is that the answer choices can be confusing because they are often very similar to each other. You should read each answer choice carefully before selecting one.

### Main Idea or Title

The main idea of a passage is the thought, opinion, or attitude that governs the whole passage. It may be clearly stated, or only implied. Think of the main idea as an umbrella that is general enough to cover all of the specific ideas and details in the passage. Sometimes, the questions found after a passage will ask you about the main idea, while others use the term *title*. Don't be misled; main idea and title questions are the same. They both require you to know what the passage is mostly about. Often, the incorrect answers to a main idea or title question are too detailed to be correct. Remember that the main idea of a passage or the best title for a passage is general, not specific.

If you are lucky, the main idea will be clearly stated in the first or last sentence of the passage. At other times, the main idea is not stated in a topic sentence but is implied in the overall passage, and you will need to determine the main idea by inference. Because there may be a lot of information in the passage, the trick is to understand what all that information adds up to—what it is that the author wants you to know. Often, some of the wrong answers to main idea questions are specific facts or details from the passage. A good way to test yourself is to ask, "Can this answer serve as a net to hold the whole passage together?" If not, chances are you have chosen a fact or detail, not a main idea.

## Inference or Interpretation

Inference or interpretation questions ask you what the passage means or implies, not just what it actually says. They are often the most difficult reading comprehension question because they require you to draw meaning from the text that might not be directly stated. When you draw inference, you are like a detective looking for clues, because inferences are conclusions that you draw based on the clues the writer has given you. The clues might come from word choice or from specific details that suggest a conclusion or point of view. When you speak with someone, the person's tone of voice is a clue. So is a facial expression or body language such as a shrug or a nod. But when you read something, these important clues are not available to

you—only the words and their arrangement can help you draw inferences. In a sense, you are reading between the lines to make a judgment about what the author is saying. In this way, inference or interpretation questions are really judgment questions.

A good way to test whether you have drawn a correct inference is to ask yourself: What evidence do I have for this inference? If the answer is none, you probably have reached an improper conclusion. You need to be sure that your inference is based on something that is suggested or implied in the passage itself, not on your own ideas about the subject matter. Like the good detective that you might someday become, you need to base your conclusions on evidence—the information you are given –not on random hunches or guesses.

## Improving Your Ability to Make Inferences

What are the most important ways to improve your ability to make inferences? Two were already given to you; the first is to read more and quiz yourself on what you have read, and the second is to improve your vocabulary. The wider your knowledge of the English language, the better the chances that you will be familiar with all the words in a reading passage and won't have to guess at what the subject matter is about. A third tip is to read slowly and carefully, trying not to skip over words that you do not think are important. In today's multitasking world, where people are often doing so many things at one time, it is easy to forget that the more things we do at once, the more likely we are to make mistakes.

By reading carefully, you will learn to beware of absolutes. Questions that contain the words *always*, *only*, *never*, and similar words should be answered carefully against what the passage said. The passage might have said *sometimes*, *frequently*, or *almost never*, which means that an answer with absolutes will almost always be wrong. To get you in the mindset for these

## Tips for Improving Your Reading Comprehension Score

**Before the test:**

- Practice, practice, practice!
- Working with a friend or family member, select paragraphs from an article in the newspaper and have your partner create questions to ask you about it.
- Read short passages from articles or books and make up questions for yourself.

**During the test:**

- Read the questions first, before you read the passage, so you will know what words and ideas to look out for.
- Focus your attention; don't let your mind wander during the reading of the test passages.
- If one part of a passage confuses you, just read on until you are finished. Then go back and look at the confusing part again.
- Look at each one of the multiple-choice answers, then compare each with the paragraph to see which ones can be eliminated.
- Focus on the main idea of the text. What is the passage mostly about?
- Don't skip any sentences when reading the passage.
- Don't let your own knowledge of the subject matter interfere with your answer selection. Stick with the information that is given in the passage.
- Read the passage actively, asking yourself questions about the main idea and jotting down notes in the margin.

---

questions, try to treat the reading passage samples as seriously as you would an actual exam. Read the directions, read each passage carefully, and check your answers before going on to the next passage.

### Reading Passage Sample Questions

Read each passage carefully and then answer the questions based on it. Read carefully the first time; if you are unsure of an answer, return to the passage to locate the material the question asks you about.

### Practice Passage 1

In the last two decades, community policing has been frequently touted as the best way to reform urban law enforcement. The idea of putting more officers on foot patrol in high crime areas where relations between the police and residents have often been strained was initiated in Houston in 1983 under the leadership of then-Chief Lee Brown. He argued that officers should be accessible to the community at the street level and believed, as others in law enforcement began to see, that officers assigned to the same area over a period of time had a better chance to build a network of trust with neighborhood residents. The trust would translate into merchants and residents in the area letting police officers know about criminal activity in the neighborhood and would support police intervention. Once out of their police cars, Brown and others believed, the officers would also be more involved in community activities that could prevent crime. Since then, many large cities have initiated Community Oriented Policing (COP), but the results have been mixed. Some cities found that the police and the residents were grateful for the opportunity to work together.

Others have found that unrealistic expectations by citizens and resistance from officers who were not pleased with this style of policing worked to prevent COP from being effective. It seems possible, therefore, that even a good idea may need improvement before it can be truly called a reform—and that what may work in one city may not work as well in others.

1. Community policing was introduced in Houston
   a. in the late 1970s.
   b. in the early 1980s.
   c. when Carter was president.
   d. when Lee Brown left to join another department.

2. The phrase a *network of trust* in this passage suggests that
   a. police officers can rely only on each for support.
   b. community members rely on the police to protect them.
   c. police and community members rely on each other.
   d. community members trust only each other.

3. Lee Brown was
   a. the only police chief who believed in community policing.
   b. the mayor at the time community policing was introduced.
   c. the last police chief to consider community policing in Houston.
   d. none of the above

4. The best title for this passage would be
   a. Community Policing and Lee Brown's Career.
   b. Community Problem: The Solution to Drug Problems.
   c. Communities and Cops: Partners for Peace.
   d. Community Policing: An Uncertain Future.

5. The word *touted* in the first sentence of the passage most nearly means
   a. praised.
   b. denied.
   c. exposed.
   d. criticized.

## Answers

1. **b.** Choice **b** comes most directly from the passage, which provides you with the year 1983 and which falls within the definition of the early 1980s. Choice **a** is not supported by the passage. Choice **c** is not related to information in the passage. Choice **d** may have tricked you if you knew that Lee Brown left Houston to become the police commissioner in New York City. Choice **d** makes an important point: Do not let knowledge that is not part of the passage influence your choice of answers.

2. **c.** The passage is very specific as to who or what the network of trust referred to. Notice that choices **a** and **d** use the word *only*, one of the absolutes you were reminded earlier to give careful consideration to when answering questions.

3. **d.** Choice **a** is incorrect because the passage states that *Brown and others believed*; choice **b** again presents outside information that may confuse you (Brown became the mayor of Houston many years after he instituted community policing); choice **c** is not discussed in the passage.

4. **d.** A good title should express the main idea of the passage. In this passage, the main idea comes at the end. You should read first sentences and last sentences very carefully because they often summarize the main idea of the passage, on which the title will often be based. While this is not always true, it is smart reading to check these sentences first whenever a question asks you to indicate the main idea or a suggested title.

5. **a.** Even if you do not know the definition of the word *touted*, since the paragraph speaks positively about community policing, the other words do not fit the passage.

## Practice Passage 2

Over the years there has been some evidence that crime rates are linked to social trends such as demographic and socioeconomic changes. Crime statistics showed a decline in the post-World War II era of the 1940s and 1950s. Following the Vietnam War in the 1970s, however, reported crime was on the rise, only to be followed by lower numbers of reported crimes in the 1980s. One of the reasons for these fluctuations appears to be age. When the population is younger, as it was in the 1960s when the baby boomers came of age, there seems to be a greater incidence of crime throughout the nation. A second cause for this rise and fall of crime rates appears to be economic. Rising crime rates seem to follow falling economies. A third reason cited as a reason that crime rates seem cyclical is the ebb and flow of public policy decisions. These decisions sometimes protect personal freedoms at the expense of government control but at other times seem to swing in the opposite direction. A youthful, economically disadvantaged population that is not secured by social controls of family or community or by government authority is likely to correlate with an upswing in reported crime.

7. Crime statistics seem to rise when populations are
   **a.** younger.
   **b.** older.
   **c.** immigrants.
   **d.** veterans.

8. The main idea of the passage is that
   **a.** times of prosperity show lower levels of reported crime.
   **b.** when the economy slows, crime rates rise.
   **c.** the incidence of reported crime is related to several social and economic variables.
   **d.** secure families are less likely to be involved in crime.

9. The passage describes police as
   a. having no role in crime prevention.
   b. having no influence on crime statistics.
   c. influencing crime statistics by the number of police they arrest.
   d. none of the above

10. The best title for this passage would be
    a. Wars and Crime Statistics.
    b. Why Crime Rates Rise and Fall.
    c. Youth and Crime Rates.
    d. Poverty and Crime Statistics.

11. Crime statistics can be used to argue that crime is
    a. random.
    b. cyclical.
    c. demographic.
    d. social.

## Answers

7. **a.** The word *young* appears in relation to the baby boomers; the other choices present descriptions that do not appear in the passage.

8. **c.** Choice **c** is the only one that summarizes what the entire passage is about; the other choices pull small details from the passage but do not provide an overview.

9. **d.** The passage does not mention police at all; while you might infer from this that choices **a** and **b** are correct, the question asks you what *the passage describes*.

10. **b.** It is the only one that expresses the sum of the details that each of the other answers give a small piece of.

11. **b.** The passage mentions the *cyclical nature of crime statistics*.

## Practice Passage 3

In recent years, issues of public and personal safety have become a major concern to many Americas. Violent incidents in fast food restaurants, libraries, hospitals, schools and colleges, offices, and shopping malls have led many to seek greater security inside their homes and in many public buildings and areas. Sales of burglar alarms, motion detectors, and closed circuit television systems (CCTV) have skyrocketed since the 1990s. Convenience stores, gas stations, jewelry stores, and even the United States Postal Service have barricaded their staffs behind safety glass enclosures and focus cameras on many work stations that involve handling money. Communities employ private security forces and encourage homeowners to install alarm systems and other security devices. While some people sympathize with the reasons behind these efforts, others have voiced concern that these measures, are helping to create a siege mentality. There is fear that such a mentality will lead to a general distrust of others among people that could foster a dangerous isolationism within neighborhoods and among neighbors.

12. The passage suggests which of the following about community security?
    a. Communities are more dangerous today than they were before the 1990s.
    b. Too much concern for security could destroy trust among neighbors.
    c. Poor security has led to an increase in public violence.
    d. Isolated neighborhoods are unsafe neighborhoods.

13. The word *foster* in the last sentence most nearly means
    a. adopt.
    b. encourage.
    c. prevent.
    d. secure.

**14.** The author believes that
   **a.** more security is needed to make neighborhoods safer.
   **b.** people should spend more on home security.
   **c.** people such not ignore the problems created by excessive safety concerns.
   **d.** security devices are the best protection against violent crime.

**15.** The violent incidents described in the passage include
   **a.** school shootings.
   **b.** parking lot crime.
   **c.** employees shooting their co-workers.
   **d.** none of the above.

**16.** In the last sentence, the phrase *siege mentality* means
   **a.** hostility.
   **b.** defensiveness.
   **c.** fear.
   **d.** corruption.

## Answers

**12.** **b.** The key word is *distrust*, which implies that neighbors will become suspicious of one another if they are worried about safety.

**13.** **b.** *Foster* means nurture or help to grow. Even if you are unfamiliar with this word, the phrases *general distrust* and *dangerous isolationism* should indicate to you that the two are interconnected in the way that *foster* tells you.

**14.** **c.** The phrase *dangerous isolationism* should convey the author's disapproval of the move toward more reliance on security devices. The other choices imply approval of the trend.

**15.** **d.** Although the passage mentions locations where each of the types of crimes listed in the other choices might occur, the passage never mentions any actual crimes; it speaks only of public concerns over personal safety.

**16.** **b.** A *siege mentality* is felt by those who believe they are under attack; such people want to *defend* themselves, the root of the word *defensive*.

## Practice Passage 4

At 2:20 A.M., while on regular patrol in their marked police car, Police Officers Turner and Thompson were told by their dispatcher to respond to a call from Tom's All Night Wash and Dry at 69 Coleville Street. They arrived at 2:30 A.M. and found two paramedics trying to revive 70-year-old Jonathan Jones, who was semi-conscious on the tiled floor. The manager of the Wash and Dry, Tim Thomas (a brother of the owner, Tom) and a patron, Joe Murphy, told the officers that two young men they had never seen before rushed into the laundry, grabbed a few items from one of the dryers, and on their way out brushed by Mr. Jones, who fell and hit his head. Another patron, Suzanne Solaro, disagreed that the young men were not regular patrons of the laundry. She said she regularly did her wash after midnight and saw them often; she volunteered to the officers that the young men's names were Manny and Jack. While the patrons were speaking with the officers, Mr. Jones seemed to regain more of his senses and resisted the paramedics' attempts to place him on a stretcher and take him to Victory Hospital. The officers convinced Mr. Jones that he should go to the hospital; the ambulance left Tom's Wash and Dry at 2:54 A.M. Although Ms. Solaro provided the officers with descriptions of Manny and Jack, no arrests were made. An investigation is pending.

**17.** Which of the following persons most likely called police to Tom's Wash and Dry?
  **a.** Tim Thomas
  **b.** Joe Murphy
  **c.** Suzanne Solaro
  **d.** Tom Thomas

**18.** The main reason Manny and Jack were said to have entered the laundry was
  **a.** to commit a robbery.
  **b.** to pick up their laundry.
  **c.** to attack Jonathan Jones.
  **d.** none of the above

**19.** What was the main reason Manny and Jack were removed from the laundry?
  **a.** They were arrested for assault.
  **b.** They were injured when they slipped on the tile floor.
  **c.** They were identified by the offices as wanted for questioning in a past crime.
  **d.** none of the above

**20.** According to the passage, which of the following statements is accurate?
  **a.** Tim's All Night Wash and Dry is located at 69 Coleville Street.
  **b.** Police Officers Turner and Thompson were dispatched to a call at the laundry.
  **c.** Jonathan Jones died at the scene.
  **d.** Manny and Jack are regular patrons at the laundry.

**21.** It would be correct to infer that
  **a.** Manny and Jack know Jonathan Jones from the laundry.
  **b.** Joe Murphy and Suzanne Solaro are dating.
  **c.** there were no other patrons in the laundry.
  **d.** none of the above

## Answers

**17. a.** The manager of the establishment, particularly since he is the brother of the owner, would have been the most likely to be concerned about the victim being injured on the premises. While choices **b** and **c** are logical, they are not as good an inference as choice **a**. Choice **d** is incorrect; there is no indication that Tom Thomas was on the premises at the time of the incident.

**18. d.** The officers do not have sufficient information to draw a conclusion. Based only on the statements of the manager and the male patron, it might appear that choice **a** was correct, but if the female patron recognized the men as regulars, they might not have chosen to commit a robbery where they were known, even though it stretches the imagination that the laundry they grabbed was their own (choice **b**). Based on the information, choice **c** is also unlikely, but not impossible if the officers assume the men were better at masking their intentions than they probably were. Based on what the officers know, it is impossible to answer the question.

**19. d.** Manny and Jack were not removed from the laundry; according to the witnesses, they left on their own.

**20. b.** Choice **b** is the only one that does not contain inaccuracies; choice **a** provides an incorrect name of the laundry; choice **c** is contrary to Jones speaking with the paramedics and the police officers; choice **d** may or may not be accurate based on different accounts of the witnesses.

**21. d.** There are not facts to support any of the other choices; police officers must take care when reporting on incidents to which they responded to provide only the facts they know to be true.

## If English Isn't Your First Language

When nonnative speakers of English have trouble with reading comprehension tests, it's often because they lack the cultural, linguistic, and historical frame of reference that native speakers enjoy. People who have not lived in or been educated in the United States often don't have the background information that comes from reading American newspapers, magazines, and textbooks.

A second problem for nonnative English speakers is the difficulty in recognizing vocabulary and idioms (expressions like *chewing the fat*) that assist comprehension. In order to read with good understanding, it's important to have an immediate grasp of as many words as possible in the text. Test takers need to be able to recognize vocabulary and idioms immediately so that the ideas those words express are clear.

### The Long View

Read newspapers, magazines, and other periodicals that deal with current events and matters of local, state, and national importance. Pay special attention to articles that are related to law enforcement.

Be alert to new or unfamiliar vocabulary or terms that occur frequently in the popular press. Use a highlighter pen to mark new or unfamiliar words as you read. Keep a list of those words and their definitions. Review them for 15 minutes each day. Though at first you may find yourself looking up a lot of words, don't be frustrated—you will look up fewer and fewer words as your vocabulary expands.

### During the Test

When you are taking your written exam, make a picture in your mind of the situation being described in the passage. Ask yourself, "What did the writer mostly want me to think about this subject?"

Locate and underline the topic sentence that carries the main idea of the passage. Remember that the topic sentence—if there is one—may not always be the first sentence. If there doesn't seem to be one, try to determine what idea summarizes the whole passage.

---

As you probably noticed, the last sample reading passage was different from the first four. The intention was to show you that your ability to read, understand, and draw inferences from passages is applicable to many different types of reading exercises. Depending on the test you take, you might be asked questions about a number of different types of passages. Your plan of action, though, should always be the same. Read the passage carefully and take a moment to think about it before going on to the questions. Then read the questions carefully, looking for key words or phrases. Try to answer the questions in the order they are presented, but if one question confuses you and you cannot find the answer by glancing back at the passage, go on to the next one. Sometimes questions are interrelated, and the one that seemed confusing may become clear as you read through the additional questions.

If you approached the practice passages under conditions similar to the actual written test, you might want to give yourself a short break before going on to the judgment section of this chapter. While it is true that during the actual test you are unlikely to get any break between test parts, since you are still in practice mode it would be good to stretch your legs and think about why you did well—or did not do well—on the reading passages.

# Judgment

What is judgment? A dictionary definition will say something like the ability to see and distinguish relationships or alternatives. Another definition might talk about the ability to think critically and make reasonable decisions based on existing information. Some people equate judgment to common sense.

Police officers must make many decisions in the course of their patrol duties. Despite the existence of procedure manuals and directives, these could never cover every event and the way that event might unfold. If a police department tried to put every situation that could occur into its manual, that manual would be literally too heavy to pick up.

Since it would be impossible for police departments to put applicants into real-world situations to observe their decision-making capabilities, they rely on different types of testing to do this for them. Most written exams will have a section where judgment is tested through multiple-choice questions. You will read a brief passage, usually one describing a police-related situation, and you will be given choices about what action you should take. To answer correctly, you will need to use your common sense, good judgment, and, of course, good reading skills because if you misunderstand the situation presented to you, you are likely to apply the wrong solution.

Some tests achieve the same results by showing the candidates brief videos and asking them to verbally answer questions similar to those they would otherwise have read. The video presentations are less common; they add expense to the testing and run the risk of technical difficulties that prevent all candidates from having the same chance to see the situation clearly. They may also be more difficult for the candidate because unless there are provisions for the videos to be replayed, you do not have the opportunity to reconsider your answer as you do with a question you read in a test booklet.

Whichever mechanism is used in your test—reading the questions from a booklet or viewing the situations on video—judgment questions fall into two general categories: situational judgment and application of rules and procedures. This section looks at each category and provides samples to help you analyze your abilities in this area.

## Situational Judgment

Situational judgment questions ask you to think like a police officer. Do not be concerned that you do not know the laws, rules, or procedures that you are being asked to apply. The questions (or the videos) will tell you everything you need to know. You will be given a situation and you will be asked how you would have handled it if you were the police officer who responded to that event. To help you focus, you are given choices. As is traditional in multiple-choice questions you might be given four choices, or you might be given three specific actions with a fourth choice of "**d.** none of the above." These questions are not meant to trick you; there will always be only one best answer. As with any reading comprehension question, make sure you understand the situation that is presented to you. Look for key words; look for context; consider the definitions of any words you do not know; and look for names, locations, and facts that could play a role in your decision-making.

Some judgment questions, like the reading comprehension questions, may give you one passage and ask for a series of decision based on it. In those cases, the later questions may be based on the first one, taking a format similar to "what would you do next?" Other questions will have only one question based on each situation. Do not allow yourself to fall into a pattern; the test might start with requiring you to answer only one question based on a situation and then move into a more complex situation with more than one question based on it. To get you in the mindset for judgment questions, here are samples of a one-question situation and of a situation with multiple parts.

## Judgment Sample Questions

**22.** You are a school resource officer assigned to Millburn Middle School. The school principal calls you to his office to report that 12-year-old Thomas has written obscene graffiti on the gym wall and has threatened 11-year-old Mark with a beating if he told anyone. Mark told his teacher, who in turn told the principal, who now wants you to arrest Thomas. The principal tells you that he has also grabbed Thomas by the arm, marched him back to the gym and forced him to erase what he wrote under threat of being expelled. Your best course of action is to

**a.** Take Thomas into custody for criminal mischief and making threats, handcuff him, and call your dispatcher to request a police car to transport you and Thomas to your district station for processing.

**b.** Take the principal into custody for simple assault and making threats, handcuff him, and call your dispatcher to request a police car to transport you and the principal to your district station for processing.

**c.** Speak with the principal out of range of either Thomas or Mark and suggest that the situation be handled as other than a police matter.

**d.** Call a supervisor to respond to the scene.

**23.** Campus Police Officer Skoronski is directing traffic at the entrance to the college's athletic arena after the end of a homecoming basketball game. A small, compact car stalls and the driver is unable to restart his engine. He is blocking one of the two lanes leading out of the arena area. There is a shoulder on only the right-side lane; the roadway is flat. What should Skoronski do?

**a.** Call for a tow truck to move the vehicle.

**b.** Push the car onto the shoulder of the road so that other traffic may proceed.

**c.** Tell the driver to keep trying to start the car and hope he will be successful.

**d.** Direct traffic around the stalled vehicle by having the cars drive on the shoulder of the road.

**24.** While patrolling a suburban light rail station platform at about 10 P.M., Transit Police Officer Lynch is stopped by a middle-aged woman who is crying and holding a piece of ice from a soda cup to a bruise on the side of her face. She tells Officer Lynch that her boyfriend, who is standing off to the side near parked vehicles, hit her twice after an argument about when the train was arriving. Office Lynch should

**a.** arrest the woman on suspicion of prostitution.

**b.** ask the women from whom she obtained the soda and ice.

**c.** take a statement from the man identified as the boyfriend.

**d.** take the woman's statement and detain the boyfriend for questioning.

**25.** Police officers are trained to call for another officer to provide backup when a situation seems to require additional personnel. In which of the following situations would it be most necessary for you, responding as a single-office patrol unit on the 4 P.M. to midnight shift, to request backup assistance?

**a.** Two women who appear to be neighbors are shouting at one another from their front lawns.

**b.** Two women are threatening each other with bottles in the shopping mall parking lot.

**c.** An intoxicated man is staggering on the sidewalk adjacent to police headquarters.

**d.** Teenagers are making noise in a local park's playground.

*Answer questions 26 and 27 based on the following situation.*

You have been assigned to traffic duty at a busy intersection and two situations occur during your patrol; one involves a car with out-of-state license plates, and the other involves a motorcycle with in-state plates driven by someone exceeding the speeding limit by about 10 miles per hour.

**26.** The car bearing out-of-state plates is about to turn into a one-way street going the wrong way. You should

**a.** pull the vehicle over and issue a summons to the driver.

**b.** ignore the driver since the street he is trying to enter runs for only a block before becoming a two-way street.

**c.** advise the driver to get a copy of the city's traffic regulations if he intends to keep driving locally.

**d.** advise the driver of his error and permit him to continue on his way without entering the one-way street.

**27.** The person you pulled over on the speeding motorcycle identifies himself as a sergeant from a neighboring department who is off-duty and on his way to pick up his wife from work. You should

**a.** give the police officer either a summons or a warning on the same basis as you would any other motorist.

**b.** apologize for not recognizing a local-area police supervisor and permit him to proceed.

**c.** not issue a summons but report the situation to your supervisor.

**d.** not issue a summons but report the sergeant to a higher-ranking member of his department.

### Answers

**22.** **c.** In this situation, only choice **c** is the best possible answer. Arresting either the student or the principal are overreactions, particularly since they are both fully identified and can be located in the future if the arrest of either is necessary. While it is correct that it is an officer's obligation to arrest under certain circumstances, neither the principal nor the student have committed a crime so serious that you are required to take police action at the scene. Choice **d** is one you might have to resort to if the principal is unwilling to consider your suggestion to handle the matter without an arrest, but in all but the most dire situations, calling a supervisor should not be your first course of action.

**23.** **b.** As in the question above, each of the options is possible but only one is the best choice. While you might not think the officer should engage in the manual labor of pushing someone else's vehicle, this is the most direct option for getting traffic flowing. Remember also that the situation indicated the car was a small, compact model, diminishing the possibility it would be too heavy for the officer to push, particularly if the driver or any others in the immediate area assist. Choices **a** and **c** would not resolve the immediate problem of getting traffic moving. Choice **d** increases the possibility of accidents or another vehicle becoming disabled on the shoulder.

**24.** **d.** Probable cause has been established for a charge of at least simple assault by the women's statement and the boyfriend should be detained and most likely arrested.

**25.** **b.** Only choice **b** presents a situation that is potentially life-threatening to the participants or to the officer. Choice **d** may at some point require assistance if you approach the teenagers and their subsequent actions indicate a possibility of danger, but as described here, the situation has not risen to that level.

**26.** **d.** Although going the wrong way on a one-way street creates a dangerous situation, in this instance the driver was stopped by you before committing any violation; while not ticketing the driver, you should warn him and possibly alert him to how one-way streets are marked in your jurisdiction if you believe he was confused.

**27.** **a.** Another police officer who is pulled over for a traffic violation should be treated just as any other motorist would be; you have the authority to exercise discretion as to whether or not to issue a summons to any motorist in this situation.

## Tips for Answering Situational Judgment Questions

- Read carefully, but don't read anything into the situation that isn't there.
- Think like a cop: Safety first. Use the least possible force.
- Use your common sense.

## Application of Laws and Procedures

The exam will very likely include judgment questions that ask you to apply rules, laws, police, or procedures to particular situations. These questions actually combine reading comprehension and judgment because you must first be sure you understand the set-up to the question before selecting an answer. These questions try to put you in the shoes of police officers by forcing you to apply the knowledge provided in the question. This simulates having to apply your knowledge of the laws of your city or state, or department procedures, and then use that knowledge to decide what to do in a given situation.

Although the principles of answering the questions are the same, to help you get into the mindset of these types of questions the first three samples pertain to application of laws and the second three pertain to application of police procedures. If you are familiar with laws or police procedures, be guided only by what you are told in the question and do not read into it material that is not there.

## Application of Laws and Procedures Sample Questions

28. Shoplifting is defined as the theft of goods from a store, shop, or place of business during business hours where the suspect takes the good(s) past the last point of opportunity to pay for the merchandise without attempting to offer payment. Based on this definition, which of the following is the best example of shoplifting?

   a. Terry enters the Bag and Save grocery store and gets a piece of candy. After going to the counter, he finds he has no money. The store clerk tells him to take the candy and he leaves the store eating it.

   b. Terry enters T & T Electronics to purchase batteries. He puts a package of batteries into his coat pocket while looking at new laptop computers and then turns to leave the store. In the store's doorway, Terry remembers the batteries and returns to the check-out line to pay for them.

   c. Terry enters Phil's Pharmacy to pick up a prescription. After paying, he walks over to the cologne counter, places a bottle in his left front pocket, and walks out of the pharmacy.

   d. Terry and his mother enter Healthy Foods grocery. Terry picks up a candy bar, eats it, hands his mother the wrapper, and then walks out of the store while his mother stands in the checkout line. His mother places the empty wrapper on the counter along with the other groceries, and the clerk scans the price of the candy along with the other items.

*Answer questions 29 and 30 based on the definition of criminal mischief.*

Criminal mischief occurs when a person intends to do damage to the property of another, and without any legal right to do so, damages that person's property. If the property is worth more than $250, it is a felony and constitutes criminal mischief in the first degree. If the property is worth $250 or less, it is criminal mischief in the second degree, which is a misdemeanor.

**29.** According to the definition given, which situation is the best example of criminal mischief in the first degree?
   **a.** The Barker twins, Joe and Tony, celebrating their high school graduation, place a cherry bomb next to their neighbor's lawn chairs, destroying $90 worth of outdoor furniture.
   **b.** The Barker twins' noisy graduation party is annoying their next door neighbor, who is trying to read a book. The neighbor scratches the door of a car belonging to one of the guests, doing about $190 worth of damage.
   **c.** At the Barker twins' graduation party, Victoria is admiring Joe's BB gun. She fires the weapon, shattering the Barkers' living room picture window and causing about $800 worth of damage.
   **d.** Leaving the Barker twins' graduation party, Carlos, who is driving his mother's car without her permission, mistakenly hits the gas pedal instead of the brake while backing up and collides with another guest's car, doing about $1,000 worth of damage.

**30.** Mr. Barker has an ongoing feud with his neighbor, Mr. Marks. He is annoyed when he discovers that his wife lent the Markses a lawn mower that he had purchased only a week prior. In attempting to take the mower from the Markses garage, he damages it sufficiently to make it worthless. According to the definition of criminal mischief, Mr. Barker could be charged with
   **a.** felony criminal mischief.
   **b.** misdemeanor criminal mischief.
   **c.** felony or misdemeanor criminal mischief based on the value of the mower.
   **d.** none of the above.

*Answer questions 31 and 32 based on the procedure described.*

Police officers are prohibited from firing warning shots under any and all circumstances. Police officers are also prohibited from firing at moving vehicles unless their vehicle is being shot at or the other vehicle is being used in the commission of a crime that is likely to cause death to the victim, the offender, or the police officer.

**31.** Based on the information above, which interpretation is most accurate?
   **a.** When their lives are threatened, police officers may fire warning shots.
   **b.** When their lives are threatened, police officers may fire at a moving vehicle.
   **c.** Police officers may fire warning shots from their police car.
   **d.** Police officers may never fire either warning shots or from their police car.

**32.** Campus Police Officer Urbana is pursuing a driver who has sped through the parking lot payment gate without paying the $7 parking fee and is leaving campus. Based on her department's policies, she should

   **a.** open fire on the suspect by trying to shoot through the driver's rear window.

   **b.** open fire and try to shoot out one of the suspect's rear tires.

   **c.** put on her lights and siren to attempt to overtake the driver before he leaves campus.

   **d.** try to copy down the driver's license plate number and check it against the college's parking records.

**33.** Eastville Police Department has a procedure that officers must follow when handling found property, which is defined as property that was discovered by anyone, including a police officer, but is not evidence from a crime scene. In such instances, officers should:

   **1.** Write and turn in before the end of their shift a report stating who found the property, what the property is comprised of; where it was found, and where it was located.

   **2.** Complete a property tag that contains the report number, the officer's name, badge number, and the date and time the property was turned in, and attach the tag to the property.

   **3.** Turn the property in to the Property Room before the end of the shift on which the property was turned in.

While on patrol in a marked police car, Office Lee was flagged down by a pedestrian, Carl Warren, who wanted to turn in a gold-colored watch that he found on the sidewalk in front of 200 Elm Street. The watch's wristband was broken; Warren told the officer he thought it might have fallen off as someone walked up the street. He handed the watch to Officer Lee without providing any additional information other than his name and that he lived in town. Officer Lee wrote the property report using the information provided by Warren and placed a tag on the property that contained the report number, his name, his badge number, and the date and time the watch came into his possession. Before resuming patrol, he placed the watch in the glove box of his patrol car, and he turned the report in an hour after preparing it. The next morning, he turned the watch in to the Property Room. Based on his department's procedure, Officer Lee acted

   **a.** improperly because he should have obtained more information from Warren.

   **b.** properly because he turned his report in before the end of his shift.

   **c.** improperly because he did not turn the property in to the Property Room before the end of his shift.

   **d.** improperly because he made no attempt to locate the property's owner.

### Answers

**28. c.** Choice **c** is the only one that fits the definition of shoplifting because an item left the store without authorization and the individual did not attempt to pay for it. In choice **a** a person with authority permitted the customer to leave without paying; in choice **b** the customer returned to pay before leaving the store, and in choice **d** the item was paid for even if it had already been eaten.

**29. c.** Choice **c** is the only one that combines the intent and dollar value to match the definition of criminal mischief in the first degree. In choices **a** and **b**, the dollar value was below $250 and in choice **d** there was no intent to do damage.

**30. d.** The definition specifies that the property must *belong to another*, but Mr. Barker damaged only his own property.

**31. b.** Choice **b** is the only one that correctly interprets the directive. Choice **a** is incorrect because police officers may never fire warning shots; if their lives are threatened, they should not be firing merely to warn. Choice **c** is incorrect because police officers may never fire warning shots; this choice confuses warning shots with firing from a vehicle. Choice **d** is incorrect because police officers may sometimes fire from their cars.

**32. d.** This question is an example of combining judgment with application of policies. Choices **a** and **b** are incorrect based on the shooting policy; choice **c** is not covered directly but gets at your judgment as to the value of undertaking what could turn into a dangerous car chase over $7.

**33. c.** The procedure calls for turning in property to the Property Room before the end of the shift during which it is located.

## Tips for Answering Application Questions

- Read what's there, not what you think should have been there.
- Read through all the choices before you pick an answer.
- Find the exact spot in the law or the procedure that supports your answer.

## Improving Your Judgment Skills

After having tested yourself on these judgment questions, you should have some ideas about how to improve your skills for this section of your exam. These types of questions ask you to see yourself as the officer you hope to become. You are asked to consider your safety and the safety of others, to be guided by the principle of using the least force necessary to resolve a situation, and how to read carefully and interpret laws and procedures to particular situations.

To improve your judgment skills, you should read, read, and read. After you read something, think about what you read and quiz yourself on the content. Learn to use a dictionary to learn the meanings of words you do not recognize. Before going to the dictionary, see if you can figure out the word's meaning from the context of what you read. This will enhance your vocabulary, which will help you not only on the written test but in all areas of your life. It will also help your self-confidence, which will benefit you on all areas of the exam, particularly on the judgment questions.

Self-confidence gives you the sense that you are able to understand and solve problems rather than read something and immediately believe that it is too complex or too technical for you to master. Self-confidence will also help you to focus on what you know rather

# 10 ▶ MATH, MAPS, AND MEMORY AND OBSERVATION

### *CHAPTER SUMMARY*

Many police exams will test your ability to solve basic math problems and other number-based questions and to read maps. As a police officer, you will be expected to calculate the value of items and to estimate distances traveled or distances from a particular point to another. Map reading tests whether you will be able to navigate streets and roadways of your jurisdiction and whether you can follow simple directions. Memory-based and observation questions test your ability to look at pictures or scenes and recall important details of what you have observed. As in the other review chapters, there are tips for improving your abilities in these crucial areas.

## Math for Police Officers

Questions in the math section of a police applicant exam are generally straightforward. Most will entail arithmetic operations (addition, subtraction, multiplication, division); some will require you to combine these operations to determine your answer. Each question will provide you with all the information you need to answer it. You may be given scratch paper or you may be told that you may write on the test booklet to perform your calculations. If the test itself or the proctor do not make clear where you can do your calculations, do not be afraid to ask for instructions. If you will be permitted to use a calculator, you should have received this information along with other test-day instructions. If nothing was mentioned, you might consider bringing a small calculator on the test date, but do not remove it from your bag without first learning whether it is permissible to do so.

# Glossary of Terms

| | |
|---|---|
| **Denominator** | The bottom number in a fraction. **Example:** 2 is the denominator in $\frac{1}{2}$. |
| **Difference** | Subtract. The difference of two numbers means subtract one number from the other. |
| **Divisible by** | A number is divisible by a second number if that second number divides *evenly* into the original number. **Example:** 10 is divisible by 5 ($10 \div 5 = 2$, with no remainder). However, 10 is not divisible by 3. (See *multiple of*) |
| **Even integer** | Integers that are divisible by 2, like . . . $-4, -2, 0, 2, 4$. . . . (See *integer*) |
| **Integer** | Numbers along the number line, like . . . $-3, -2, -1, 0, 1, 2, 3$. . . . Integers include the whole numbers and their opposites. (See *whole number*) |
| **Multiple of** | A number is a multiple of a second number if that second number can be multiplied by an integer to get the original number. **Example:** 10 is a multiple of 5 ($10 = 5 \times 2$); however, 10 is not a multiple of 3. (See *divisible by*) |
| **Negative number** | A number that is less than zero, like $-1, -18.6, -\frac{3}{4}$. |
| **Numerator** | The top part of a fraction. **Example:** 1 is the numerator of $\frac{1}{2}$. |
| **Odd integer** | Integers that aren't divisible by 2, like . . . $-5, -3, -1, 1, 3$. . . . |
| **Positive number** | A number that is greater than zero, like $2, 42, \frac{1}{2}, 4.63$. |
| **Prime number** | Integers that are divisible only by 1 and themselves, like $2, 3, 5, 7, 11$. . . . All prime numbers are odd, except for 2. The number 1 is not considered prime. |
| **Product** | Multiply. The product of 2 numbers means the numbers are multiplied together. |
| **Quotient** | The answer you get when you divide. **Example:** 10 divided by 5 is 2; the quotient is 2. |
| **Real number** | All the numbers you can think of, like $17, -5, \frac{1}{2}, -23.6, 3.4329, 0$. Real numbers include integers, fractions, and decimals. (See *integer*) |
| **Remainder** | The number left over after division. **Example:** 11 divided by 2 is 5, with a remainder of 1. |
| **Sum** | Add. The sum of two numbers means the numbers are added together. |
| **Whole number** | Numbers you can count on your fingers, like $1, 2, 3$. . . . All whole numbers are positive. |

With or without a calculator, the first step in answering the math questions, as with all questions, is to read the question carefully to determine what you are being asked to calculate and what facts you are being given to assist you. If you do not understand what you are being asked to do, you will be unable to do it. The vast majority of the calculations will have to do with distances traveled, items reported missing or stolen, travel expense vouchers, or other situations that a police officer on patrol could be expected to encounter.

## Solving Math Problems

Just as with the verbal and reading skills sections of the entry exam, some of the math questions you will be presented with will be based on police situations and others will have nothing to do with policing. Some math problems will be presented within stories or situations where you have to pick out the math; others may be presented without any context attached. This is similar to the vocabulary questions, where, you may recall, some provided you with sentences and asked you to provide a synonym or antonym for an underlined word, while others provided you with just the word and no sentence to help you develop context. To some test takers, the math without a story will be easier because there is nothing to do except math, while to others this will be intimidating for the identical reason. To get you accustomed to answering math questions that do not come with a story attached, calculate the answers to the following questions.

## Math-Only Sample Questions

**1.** $(13 \times 9) + 14 =$
   **a.** 117
   **b.** 131
   **c.** 119
   **d.** 139

**2.** $(67 - 9) + 80 =$
   **a.** 138
   **b.** 183
   **c.** 85
   **d.** 58

**3.** $(80 + 20) \div 10 =$
   **a.** 100
   **b.** 120
   **c.** 50
   **d.** none of the above

**4.** $25 \times (2 + 10) =$
   **a.** 50
   **b.** 250
   **c.** 300
   **d.** none of the above

**5.** $\frac{1}{4} + \frac{1}{3} =$
   **a.** 12
   **b.** $\frac{7}{12}$
   **c.** 9
   **d.** none of the above

**6.** $\frac{4}{9} - \frac{2}{9} =$
   **a.** $\frac{1}{9}$
   **b.** $\frac{2}{9}$
   **c.** $\frac{3}{9}$
   **d.** 2

## Answers

**1.c.** Perform the operations in the parentheses first: $13 \times 9 = 117$; then add 14 to get the answer of 131.

**2.a.** Perform the operations in the parentheses first: $67 - 9 = 58$; then add 80 to get the answer of 138. Notice that the incorrect choices contain errors you might readily make. Choice **b** transposes two numbers from the correct answer; choice **c** transposes the numbers of an incorrect answer; choice **d** is the correct answer for the calculation within the parentheses but does not include the $+ 80$.

**3.d.** Perform the operations in the parentheses first: $80 + 20 = 100$. Then divide by 10 to get the answer of 10.

**4.c.** In this problem, the parentheses surrounds the second group of numbers, so you must do that calculation first: $2 + 10 = 12$, then multiply by 25 to get the answer of 300.

**5.b.** Adding fractions can be confusing. If the fractions have the same bottom numbers, just add the top numbers and write the total over the bottom. If the fractions have different bottom numbers, you must find the *least common denominator*, which means finding the same bottom number for each. It is always the smallest number that all the bottom numbers can be evenly divided into. In this problem, $\frac{1}{4} = \frac{3}{12}$ and $\frac{1}{3} = \frac{4}{12}$, for a sum of $\frac{7}{12}$. If you have no recollection of this from high school or college, you should purchase a math review book along with your other test study aids.

**6.b.** In subtracting fractions, if the fractions have the same bottom numbers, just subtract the top numbers and write the difference over the bottom number. If they do not have the same bottom numbers, you will have to follow the rules for determining the least common denominator, which was not necessary in this question.

# Math Strategies

Now that you have gotten back into the rhythm of working with numbers, review the strategies presented. You probably relied on many of them without even realizing it, but seeing them listed will help you remember how you derived your answers.

- **Do not work solely in your head; use the test booklet or scratch paper.** Remember to use paper and pencil to take notes, draw pictures, or calculate. You might think it is quicker to answer the problems in your head, but it will lead to errors and prevent you from double-checking your answers.
- **Read the question in chunks, preferably a sentence at a time.** Just as with other sections of the exam, read slowly and carefully to make sure you know what the question says and what type of calculations you are being asked to perform.
- **Circle the question.** This will help you before and after doing the calculations. First, after reading the set-up situation, circle the actual question so you know what you are being asked about. Second, after solving the problem and developing an answer, reread the circled question to double-check that you did what the problem asked you to do.
- **Make a plan.** Before you begin to write anything down, especially numbers, consider how you will solve the problem based on what you are looking for.
- **Check your work after doing the math.** It is possible to get a false sense of security after doing the calculations and discovering that your answer matches one of the multiple-choice answers provided. This is the major reason that you should consider looking at the choices provided only *after* you do your own calculation and check your work.

To check your work:
- Ask yourself whether your answer makes sense or is a reasonable answer to the situation provided.
- Re-read the question and fill your answer in to assure that it makes sense in the context of the numbers.
- If it is a problem that can be answered by involving more than one set of calculations, use the alternate format to see if you derive the same answer.

- **Approximate or round off when appropriate.** This may help you initially or as a way to check your answers. For example:

  $5.98 = $8.97 is a little less than $14. (Add: $6 + $9)
  .9876 $\times$ 5.0342 is close to 5. (Multiply: 1 $\times$ 5)
- **Glance at the answer choices for clues.** The answer choices may provide you with an indication of what the question is looking for, particularly if the answers contain fractions or decimals. Remember, though, not to rely on the answer choices so completely that you fail to perform the actual calculations to arrive at an answer. If you are not penalized on your exam for incorrect answers, when you have completed the math section, you might consider using the answers provided to guess, but, again, do not use the answer choices as a way to avoid doing the math.

- **If a question stumps you, move on and come back to it later.** But this strategy should only be followed for a question that does not contain multiple parts. If there is only one calculation for the question and you are completely stumped, leave it and move to the next question. If the question that has you confused is part of a series of questions based on the same set of facts and numbers, consider carefully whether you will have time to come back to more than one question or whether you should try to puzzle it out before moving on.

With these strategies in mind, you can practice combining numbers with math problems that are given to you in words. In some ways, these might be easier because there is a short story you can follow to lead you to the calculations, but you must read carefully or you will miss the formula you need to make the proper calculations. It is likely that the majority of the questions on your exam will be word problems. With this knowledge, review the sample questions to make sure you read each one carefully and use the words to help you determine what calculations you need to make.

## Word Problems

Many of the math problems on tests are word problems. A word problem can include any kind of math, including simple arithmetic, fractions, decimals, percentages, and even algebra and geometry.

The hardest part of any word problem is translating English into math. When you read a problem, you can frequently translate it word for word from English statements into mathematical statements. At other times, however, a key word in the word problem hints at the mathematical operation to be performed. Here are the translation rules:

**EQUALS**  **key words: is, are, has**

| English | Math |
| --- | --- |
| The rookie **is** 20 years old. | $R = 20$ |
| There **are** 7 hats. | $H = 7$ |
| Officer Judi **has** commendations. | $J = 5$ |

**ADDITION**  **key words: sum; more, greater, or older than; total; all together**

| English | Math |
| --- | --- |
| The **sum** of two numbers is 10. | $X + Y = 10$ |
| Karen has $5 **more than** Sam. | $K = 5 + S$ |
| The base is 3″ **greater than** the height. | $B = 3 + H$ |
| Judi is 2 years **older than** Tony. | $J = 2 + T$ |
| The **total** of three numbers is 25. | $A + B + C = 25$ |
| How much do Joan and Tom have **all together**? | $J + T = ?$ |

**SUBTRACTION**    key words: difference, less or younger than, fewer, remain, left over

| English | Math |
| --- | --- |
| The **difference** between two numbers is 17. | $X - Y = 17$ |
| Mike has 5 **fewer** cats **than** twice the number Jan has. | $M = 2J - 5$ |
| Jay is 2 years **younger than** Brett. | $J = B - 2$ |
| After Carol ate 3 apples, $R$ apples **remained**. | $R = A - 3$ |

**MULTIPLICATION**    key words: of, product, times

| English | Math |
| --- | --- |
| 20% **of** the stolen radios | $.20 \times R$ |
| Half **of** the recruits | $\frac{1}{2} \times R$ |
| The **product** of two numbers is 12. | $A \times B = 12$ |

**DIVISION**    key word: per

| English | Math |
| --- | --- |
| 15 drops **per** teaspoon | $\frac{15 \text{ drops}}{\text{teaspoon}}$ |
| 22 miles **per** gallon | $\frac{22 \text{ miles}}{\text{gallon}}$ |

## Distance Formula: Distance = Rate × Time

The key words are movement words like *plane, train, boat, car, walk, run, climb, travel,* and *swim*.

- How far did the **plane travel** in 4 hours if it averaged 300 miles per hour?

  $D = 300 \times 4$

  $D = 1,200$ miles

- Ben **walked** 20 miles in 4 hours. What was his average speed?

  $20 = r \times 4$

  5 miles per hour $= r$

## Solving a Word Problem Using the Translation Table

Remember the problem at the beginning of this chapter about the jelly beans?

Juan ate $\frac{1}{3}$ of the jelly beans. Maria then ate $\frac{3}{4}$ of the remaining jelly beans, which left 10 jelly beans. How many jelly beans were there to begin with?

**a.** 60    **b.** 80    **c.** 90    **d.** 120    **e.** 140

We solved it by *working backward*. Now let's solve it using our translation rules.

Assume Juan started with $J$ jelly beans. Eating $\frac{1}{3}$ **of** them means eating $\frac{1}{3} \times J$ jelly beans. Maria ate a fraction of the **remaining** jelly beans, which means we must **subtract** to find out how many are left: $J - \frac{1}{3} \times J = \frac{2}{3} \times J$. Maria then ate $\frac{3}{4}$, leaving $\frac{1}{4}$ **of** the $\frac{2}{3} \times J$ jelly beans, or $\frac{1}{4} \times \frac{2}{3} \times J$ jelly beans. Multiplying out $\frac{1}{4} \times \frac{2}{3} \times J$ gives $\frac{1}{6}J$ as the number of jelly beans left. The problem states that there were **10 jelly beans left**, meaning that we set $\frac{1}{6} \times J$ **equal** to 10:

$$\frac{1}{6} \times J = 10$$

Solving this equation for $J$ gives $J = 60$. Thus, the correct answer is choice **a** (the same answer we got when we *worked backward*). As you can see, both methods—working backward and translating from English to math—work. You should use whichever method is more comfortable for you.

## Math Word Problems Sample Questions

**7.** Officer Miller pledged $3.00 for every mile his son walked in the Police Athletic League Walkathon. If his son walks nine miles, how much will Officer Miller owe?
   **a.** $3.00
   **b.** $12.00
   **c.** $18.00
   **d.** $27.00

**8.** Officer Beque has been writing six speeding tickets every week. At this rate, how long will it take for her to write 27 tickets?
   **a.** 3 weeks
   **b.** 3.5 weeks
   **c.** 4 weeks
   **d.** 4.5 weeks

**9.** The chief's administrative aide is able to type 85 words per minute. How many minutes will it take him to type a report containing 1,020 words?
   **a.** 11
   **b.** $11\frac{1}{2}$
   **c.** 12
   **d.** $12\frac{1}{2}$

**10.** Chief Wallace is writing a budget request to upgrade the office computer. The request includes the purchase of 4 GB of RAM, which will cost $100, two new software programs at $350 each, an external hard drive that costs $249, and printer ink for $49. What is the total amount the budget request should be written for?
   **a.** $998.00
   **b.** $1,098.00
   **c.** $1,349.00

**d.** $1, 398.00

*Answer questions 11 and 12 based on the following information.*

Mrs. O'Leary called a transit police detective to report that her overnight bag was stolen when she dozed off while waiting for the train departing New York City en route to Philadelphia. The overnight bag was worth approximately $150. The bag contained the following items:

- 1 change of clothing, including dress, shoes, and underclothing valued at $200
- 1 makeup case valued at $50
- 2 bottles of perfume that were gifts for her granddaughters valued at $60 each
- 1 pair of gold earrings valued at $200
- 2 silver rings valued at $100 each
- $300 in cash

11. You are the detective who received this report. Based on the items listed, what should you write on your report as the value of the stolen money and property?
    **a.** $770.00
    **b.** $1,070.00
    **c.** $1,100.00
    **d.** $1,220.00

12. Two days later, after returning home, Mrs. O'Leary called to say that she had made some errors in her initial report. She discovered she had not taken the gold earrings on the trip nor had she taken one of the two silver rings. Your amended report should now indicate which figure as the value of the stolen money and property?
    **a.** $570.00
    **b.** $770.00
    **c.** $920.00
    **d.** $1,020.00

13. Joan is preparing for the police applicant physical by getting into better shape. Last weekend she walked 25 miles in 4.5 hours. What was her average speed?
    **a.** 4.5 miles per hour
    **b.** 5 miles per hour
    **c.** 5.5 miles per hour
    **d.** 6 miles per hour

14. If a patrol car is driven at the speed of 60 miles per hour for 45 minutes, how far will it have traveled?
    **a.** 40 miles
    **b.** 45 miles

**c.** 50 miles

**d.** none of the above

## Answers

**7. d.** This is a simple multiplication calculation: $3 \times 9 = 27$.

**8. d.** Divide the total number of tickets by the number Officer Beque writes weekly ($27 \div 6$) to obtain the answer.

**9. c.** The calculation is similar to Question 3. Divide the total number of words in the report by the speed at which the administrative aide types ($1,020 \div 85$) to obtain the answer. In Question 3 the answers were presented to you in decimals; in this question you are given fractions, but your use of division is the same.

**10. b.** This is an addition problem, but you must make sure that you read how many of each item at each cost to be sure you add up the proper numbers. Choice **a** omits one of the items; choices **c** and **d** could come from assuming 4 GB of RAM was $400 rather than $100 for that portion of the purchase.

**11. d.** There are two ways to reach the total; you can add each item separately or you can multiply to obtain the total for perfume and rings (of which there were more than one) and then add the sums. If you made an error, you may have simply made an error in multiplication or addition or you may have forgotten to include all the items. If you did not answer this question correctly, go back and determine whether your errors were in the math or the reading of the question.

**12. c.** If you totaled the items correctly in Question 5, you now have to subtract the value of the earrings ($200) and the value of one ring ($100), add these to total $300, and subtract that from the correct total. There are important lessons to be learned from these two questions. The most important one is to read and do your calculations carefully on these multi-part questions; if you get the first part wrong, you are likely to also get the second part wrong. In many cases, the question developer predicts the errors you might make and provides choices to the second question that seem logical even if incorrect. Knowing this, you must read the question carefully. If you are permitted to write in your test booklet, consider placing a circle around all the items you will have to calculate and then underlining the numbers of each item so you remember whether there are two pairs of earrings or one ring or similar combinations of items.

**13. c.** In this problem, you must divide the number of miles walked by the time it took ($25 \div 4.5$) to obtain the answer.

**14. b.** Convert the 45 minutes to 0.75 hour, which is the time, then multiply: 60 mph $\times$ 0.75 = 45 miles.

Notice that question 14 presumes that you know that 45 minutes is $\frac{3}{4}$ or .75 of an hour. If you have forgotten how to convert fractions to decimals or generally feel uncomfortable with fractions, decimals, percents, or other math terms and functions, you should purchase one of the many math guides and workbooks that are available. There are also a number of internet sites that can provide you with math assistance. Reviewing a guidebook or an internet study site may help you overcome what has been called *math anxiety*—the fear many people have that they are unable to do even the simplest math problems.

Since most of the material you will be tested on does not require advanced math knowledge, do not permit yourself to tense up over these sections of the exam. Whether you are permitted to bring a calculator to the test or are expected to figure out the problems the old-fashioned way on paper, just relax and answer the questions.

Before explaining the non-math number questions you are likely to see on your exam, here are some extra sample math questions.

## Bonus Math Sample Questions

**15.** Officers Cubera and Stubbs have been assigned to transport two prisoners from the stationhouse to the county jail. The total trip is $54\frac{1}{2}$ miles. If they have completed $23\frac{1}{5}$ miles, how many miles do they still have to go?
   **a.** $31\frac{7}{15}$
   **b.** $31\frac{13}{15}$
   **c.** $21\frac{4}{15}$
   **d.** $31\frac{4}{15}$

**16.** Officers Kiergaard and Spuno made an arrest for possession of 28 ounces of marijuana, which was separated into $3\frac{1}{2}$-ounce bags. How many packages of marijuana did they find in the suspect's possession?
   **a.** 4
   **b.** 6
   **c.** 8
   **d.** 10

**17.** $(500 \div 5) + 3 \times 24 =$
   **a.** 100
   **b.** 172
   **c.** 2,472
   **d.** none of the above

**18.** The Mission City Police Department has a higher than average percentage of women on its staff. If 20% of the staff in this department of 200 are women, how many women officers does Mission City employ?
   **a.** 10
   **b.** 20
   **c.** 30
   **d.** 40

**19.** Of the 760 crimes committed in Copperville last month, 76 involved grand larceny. What percentage of the crimes involved grand larceny?
   **a.** .01%
   **b.** .76%
   **c.** 1%
   **d.** 10%

**20.** The number of traffic summons issued by members of the Sun City traffic squad for the last six months was 127, 130, 135, 142, and 160. What was the average number of summonses per month?
   **a.** 127
   **b.** 135
   **c.** 139
   **d.** 142

## Answers

**15. a.** Because the fractions do not have the same bottom number, you have to work with the least common denominator.

**16. c.** Divide the number of ounces by the number of bags ($28 \div 3\frac{1}{2}$) to obtain the answer.

**17. b.** You must solve the division first: $500 \div 5 = 100$. The equation now become $100 + 3 \times 24$. An acronym you can use to remember this is PEMDAS, which stands for *parenthesis, exponents, multiplication, division, addition, subtraction*. If you follow PEMDAS, after doing the math within the parenthesis, you do the multiplication: $3 \times 24 = 72$, which provides a much easier equation to work with, $100 + 72 = 172$.

**18. d.** To multiply the size of the department by the percentage of women, add a decimal point to arrive at .20 and multiply by the number of employees in the department: $.20 \times 200 = 40$. You might know that 10% can be derived in your head by dropping the last 0, which in this instance would be 20 women. Since 20% is double 10%, you can now double the number of women to the correct answer of 40.

**19. d.** This is a typical percent problem that involves finding what percent one number is of another number. It is a simple one because, if you remember from the previous question that the figure 10% will always involve dropping the last number, the figures 760 and 76 provide an immediate clue.

**20. c.** To calculate an average, add up each item being averaged and divide by the total number of items. In this question, you must add: $127 + 130 + 135 + 142 + 160 = 694$ and then divide by $5 = 138.8$, a total which permits you to round it off to the next highest full number, 139.

## Other Number-Based Questions

Police officers work with numbers that have nothing to do with solving math problems. You might be given an address, you might be given cross streets, or you might receive a notification from the dispatcher to be on the lookout for a certain license plate number or a particular make and model of a motor vehicle. Each of these will require you to have recall of letter and number combinations. The questions in this area, like so many others, actually test for two skills—your visual perception and your short-term memory. Letter and number recall can be tested for in two ways; one involves giving you a grid (similar to Practice Exam 3) and another provides multiple-choice questions that ask you to select the choice that matches a letter-and-number combination at the start of the question.

## Number Recall Questions

When you encountered the recall questions in Practice Exam 3 of this book, you probably thought, "What in the world does this have to do with law enforcement work? This looks like a test for clerical workers!" On the face of it, being able to match number combinations to letter combinations doesn't look like something police officers have to do every day—and it isn't. But this portion of the exam is testing two important skills: your visual perception and your short-term memory. Indirectly, the recall portion also tests your ability to keep your cool under pressure. You have a short amount of time to answer a lot of questions. If you can keep your head and work methodically through the task, you demonstrate your capacity to maintain composure under fire—a vital ability for any police officer.

You can't really study for this portion of the exam. What you can do is familiarize yourself with the recall question format and practice with it. If you know what to expect, you will have an edge over candidates who arrive on test day unfamiliar with this unusual type of question.

Some of the tests that use the grid style of question place a time limit on your answers. In these situations, you will be shown the grid (either in your test booklet or on video) and then given a certain amount of time to answer questions about it. In others, you will be permitted to check the grid to answer the questions just as you are able to with other question types. Here is a brief example of a grid, although the ones on your test might be larger and more complicated:

**KEY**

| SWO | BDT | MUB | LIH | R I Z |
|-----|-----|-----|-----|-------|
| 84  | 28  | 42  | 48  | 24    |

|      |     | a  | b  | c  | d  | e  |
|------|-----|----|----|----|----|----|
| **1.** | MUB | 28 | 48 | 24 | 42 | 84 |
| **2.** | SWO | 48 | 24 | 84 | 28 | 42 |
| **3.** | RIZ | 24 | 84 | 42 | 48 | 28 |
| **4.** | BDT | 42 | 28 | 48 | 84 | 24 |

In this grid, the question numbers are 1 through 4; they appear in bold type on the left-hand side. The answer choices are the lower-case letters in bold type (**a** through **e**) directly under the key. You might have five choices, as shown here (reflected in choice **a** through choice **e**) or you might have the more traditional four-choice option. A typical question would be to ask you which of the number combinations goes with MUB. The answer is 42, so you would fill in the **d** circle on your answer sheet. Similarly, the number that goes with SWO in question 2 is 84, so you would select choice **c**. The answer for question 3 is choice **a**, and for question 4 it is choice **b**.

With the grid in front of you, this seems quite easy, although there is a possibility of getting confused over the question number and the grid number. This exercise becomes more complicated if the letter/number combinations are removed and you must recall them from memory. Some agencies that rely on a grid pattern memory test expect you to answer 100 questions in 9 minutes, which averages out to 5.4 seconds per answer. If you are wondering if the only reason for this exercise is to confuse you and give you grid-phobia to add to your math anxiety, the answer is no. Agencies that use grid patterns believe they provide indications of good perceptual skills, reliable short-term memory, the ability to work quickly without sacrificing accuracy, and the ability to work well under pressure.

## Number Pattern Recall Questions

Another type of number-related question on applicant exams is designed to test your ability to recognize patterns or to recall and repeat a series of numbers. These most often will present you with a series of numbers and letters that resemble license plates or driver's license numbers and ask you to select which choice repeats the numbers and letters correctly. Some questions may disregard sequence and ask you merely to select the choice that contains all letters or numbers that are provided to you at the top of the question.

- Focus and stay calm.
- Work methodically on one question at a time.
- Say the letter and number combinations to yourself silently as you look for them.
- Skip any questions you find difficult.
- Don't expect to finish all the questions.

Here are examples of each type of sequence question:

**21.** Find the choice that contains numbers and letters in the same order in which they appear in this question.

**4 G 8 9 L W 78 26 X**

a. 9, 7, 8, X
b. 4, W, 78, X
c. LW, 78, 26, G
d. none of the above

**22.** Find the choice that contains numbers and letters in the same order in which they appear in this question.

**7 RAN 9 DOM 4 Q R 2 S**

a. 9 D O 4 M
b. R A 9 M 8 S
c. 9 DOM 4 Q
d. 79 4Q 2 D

**23.** Find the choice that contains numbers and letters in the same order in which they appear in this question.

**D S N 2 4 6 1 0 0**

a. N, 4, 6, 1
b. O, 0, N, 7
c. D, T, 2, 6
d. none of the above

**24.** Find the choice that contains only numbers and letters that appear in this question.

**46 GT 89 L W 68 26 X**

a. 89, L, 68, W
b. 26, W, 78, X
c. LW, 4, 6, 26
d. none of the above

**25.** Find the choice that contains only numbers and letters that appear in this question.

**N 7 O P 4 X 2 Y 2**

a. 7, X, Y, Z
b. O, 4, 3, 2
c. P, X, 2, Z
d. none of the above

**26.** Find the choice that contains only numbers and letters that appear in this question.

**GO PACK GB 4**

a. PACK GB 10
b. GB 4 PUG
c. 4 GO TB 4
d. GB PACK 4

## Answers

21. **b.** All the numbers and letters in choice **b** appear in the order in which they appear in the sequence.

22. **c.** All the numbers and letters in choice **b** appear in the order in which they appear in the sequence.

23. **d.** None of the choices contains letters and numbers in the same order in which they appear in the question.

24. **a.** All the numbers and letters in choice **a** appear somewhere in the question, although not necessarily in the same order as in the correct choice.

25. **d.** None of the choices contains only letters and numbers that appear in the sequence.

26. **d.** All the numbers and letters in choice **d** appear somewhere in the question, although not necessarily in the same order as in the correct choice.

Go to the end of this chapter for even more practice with recall questions.

## Map Reading

Map reading is a learned skill. It is related to math in that it often involves understanding directions and being able to calculate distance and time. If you have ever been lost, you know that it can be frustrating and at times even frightening. For a police officer, the ability to know where you are, gauge direction and distance, and figure out how to get from one place to another can mean the difference between the saving the life of a caller, a colleague, or even, under extreme conditions, yourself.

Depending on the size and type of the jurisdiction of your department, finding your way around can be fairly easy once you understand the town's grid pattern and become familiar with its outlying areas. But in some instances, particularly if you work in a special jurisdiction agency, you may travel through numerous towns and villages or may be expected to patrol areas that are often unmarked and that do not adhere to a logical grid pattern. You will be expected to copy down the address given to you by the dispatcher, locate it quickly on you map, and proceed to the call for assistance. Once you get there, you may require assistance from others; this means you must also be able to describe your location sufficiently for backup officers, supervisors, fire, or emergency medical personnel to also respond to the scene.

Like so many other skills, map reading involves practice. While some individuals may have better innate senses of direction than others, practice is the only way to become good at map reading. Map questions test whether you have the ability to follow spatial and directional information and also to convey it to others. Is it possible to study for map questions? Yes, it is. The easiest way to study is to read maps. Just like you can improve your vocabulary and English usage by reading more you can improve your map reading skills by studying maps. Most maps use a commonly-established set of symbols; learn what they are and train yourself to look for them as soon as you open a map. Also look immediately for the directional information (north, south, east, or west) to help you orient yourself.

The maps on police exams are often in a simple grid pattern. The north-south-east-west directions will be clearly marked and there will be a key explaining any symbols that are not self-explanatory. There will be instructions on which questions should be answered based on each map; there will usually be more than one question per map. If your jurisdiction includes map questions on its exam, there is very likely to be more than one set of these questions.

As with all questions, you must read the map questions carefully. Before answering any of the map questions, be sure you are looking at the correct map for the series of questions you will be answering. Then begin by studying the map carefully, looking for the directional arrows and any large, obvious locations. Do not be concerned about moving the map around during the test. If you feel you can get a better sense of the map's directional qualities by holding it up or turning it around, do so. Since your answer sheet will be separate from the question book, the proctor of the exam should not prevent you from doing this. If you are concerned, raise your hand and ask the proctor whether this is permissible.

The directional arrows will help you prepare yourself for questions that may be based solely on directions or getting from one point on the map to another. But there are other features that will help you. If a hospital is prominently displayed on the map, there is likely to be at least one question asking you how you would arrive there or proceed from there to someplace else. The same is true if a library, police station, or cemetery is a prominent feature of the map. The buildings or locations that are prominently featured also act as landmarks, just as they do when you actually are on the road. How many times have you instructed someone coming to your home to turn left at the municipal hospital, or right at the fire station? It is likely your test questions will be similar.

Try to understand immediately what the map depicts; a map may be of highways, city streets and avenues, or bus routes or railroad tracks. Unless you are taking the test for a handful of very large municipal agencies, it is likely that your test will be used by more than one police department. This means that the maps may not be specific to the agency you are testing for. If you are taking the exam for a municipal police department, you may be startled to find that the map may be based on highways and rural routes rather than city streets. If you are taking the test for a transporta-

tion agency or parks and recreation department, you may not see a single map that depicts the jurisdiction you will actually police.

The key to success on answering the map questions is to take your time and to study the map carefully before turning to the questions. If you jump directly to the questions and then try to look at the map only to find the answer to the specific question, you may miss important information. In your haste to see only what you think the question pertains to, you may also misread the question and the answer choices. Consider that the test developer, while not specifically trying to trick you, may have written answer choices that provide similar names of streets, avenues, or other key map features.

## Finding the Shortest Route and Finding the Direction

The two most common types of map questions involve finding the shortest route from one location on the map to another and identifying the directional relationship between two or more locations on the map.

For questions involving finding the shortest route, first study the map to see where you are and to get your bearings just as you would in your own vehicle. Read the question, remembering to turn the map in any direction if this helps you get a better sense of place. Now figure out the best route without first looking at the answer choices, which may prejudice your judgment. Once you have done this, look at each answer choice and trace the suggested route with your finger or the point of your pencil. Do this with each choice. If none of the choices are the one you mapped out, and if none of the choices are "**d.** none of the above," take another look at your route to see if you missed something the question presented. If you missed a crucial piece of information or misread the map, start over and reconsider each of the choices presented by the question.

Finding the direction questions may take two forms; sometimes they are based on a map, but some-

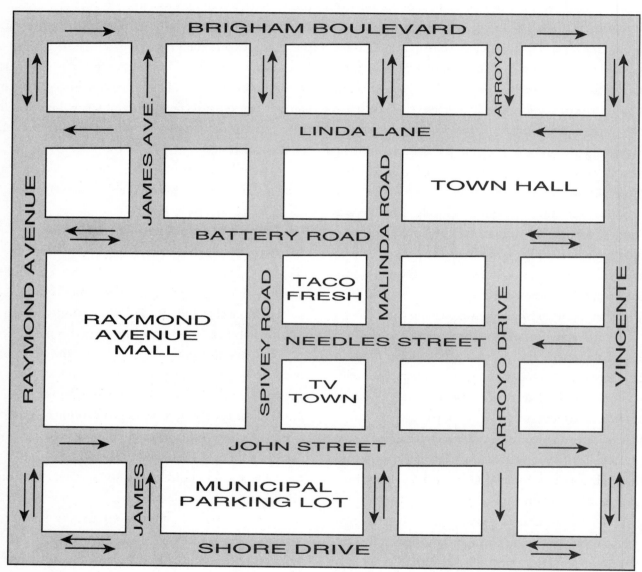

times the information will be in words only. If there is a map, follow the same method, tracing your path after reading the question and then comparing your route to each of the answer choices and selecting the choice that matches your route. If the question is in words only, read carefully to make sure you understand where the question places you and where it wants you to go. Consider drawing a very rough map based on the words to help you follow the path of the question.

For practice thinking through map questions, study the map provided and then answer the questions based on it.

## Map Reading Sample Questions

*Answer questions 27–32 based on the map. Review the directional arrows and the map key. You are not permitted to go the wrong way on a one-way street.*

**27.** Officers Singh and Bean have just completed a call at the southeast corner of the Raymond Avenue Mall. They are notified of a silent alarm going off at a residence located at the northwest corner of Arroyo Drive and Linda Lane. What is the quickest route for the officers to take to reach the residence?

   **a.** Turn north on Spivey Road, then east on Linda Lane, and then north on Arroyo Drive.

   **b.** Turn east on John Street, then north on Vincente, then west on Linda Lane, then north on Malinda Road, and then east on Brigham Boulevard to Arroyo Drive.

   **c.** Turn north on Spivey Road, then east on Brigham Boulevard, and then south on Arroyo Drive.

   **d.** Turn north on Spivey Road, then east on Battery Road, then north on Malinda Road, and then east on Brigham Boulevard.

**28.** Officers Mayweather and Schultz have just crossed Needle Street while driving southbound on Arroyo Drive. They are dispatched to a call of an altercation between a bus driver and a passenger at a bus stop located at Raymond Avenue and Battery Road. What is the quickest route for the officers to take to the bus stop?

   **a.** Continue south on Arroyo Drive, then west on John Street, then north on Malinda Road, then west on Needle Street, then north on Spivey Road, and then west on Battery Road to Raymond Avenue.

   **b.** Continue south on Arroyo Drive, then west on Shore Drive, and then north on Raymond Avenue to Battery Road.

   **c.** Make a U-turn on Arroyo Drive and then go west on Battery Road to Raymond Avenue.

   **d.** Continue south on Arroyo Drive, then east on Shore Drive, then north on Vincente, and then west on Battery Road to Raymond Avenue.

**29.** Officer Riccadelli is driving west on Battery Road. She makes a right turn onto James Avenue, then a left turn onto Linda Lane, then a right turn onto Raymond Avenue, and then a right turn onto Brigham Road. What direction is she facing?

   **a.** east

   **b.** south

   **c.** west

   **d.** north

- Read carefully and follow all directions.
- Feel free to move the map around during the test to face the direction you find comfortable.
- Find your starting point.
- Find your ending point.
- Use a small object as your police car and find the shortest route, paying special attention to the traffic signals.

**30.** What is the number of two-way roadways (whether streets, avenues, or drives) depicted on the map?
   **a.** two
   **b.** four
   **c.** six
   **d.** eight

**31.** What is the number of roadways (whether streets, avenues, or drives) that intersect with Spivey Road?
   **a.** one
   **b.** three
   **c.** five
   **d.** seven

**32.** You have been assigned to escort the mayor from the northwest corner of the Raymond Avenue Mall and John Street to the entrance to Town Hall, which is located a few feet to the left of the northeast corner of the building. Following the most direct route, how many turns will you have to make?
   **a.** one
   **b.** two
   **c.** three
   **d.** four

## Answers

**27. c.** This is the simplest way around the one-way streets and Town Hall. Since Linda Lane is one-way, some backtracking is required. However, since the residence is only one block off Brigham Boulevard, turning eastbound on Brigham requires the least amount of back-tracking. Choice **a** directs the officers to turn the wrong way down a one-way street; choice **b** requires too much backtracking, and choice **d** leaves the officers on Brigham Boulevard rather than on Linda Lane.

**28. b.** This route is the most direct because it requires the fewest turns. Choice **a** requires the officers to go the wrong way on John Street; choice **c** disregards that Arroyo Drive is one-way south, and choice **d** takes the officers too far east.

**29. a.** If Officer Riccadelli turns right onto James Avenue, she will be facing north. A left turn onto Linda Lane turns her west again, and a right turn onto Raymond Avenue turns her north. The final right turn onto Brigham Boulevard turns her east.

**30. c.** Battery Road and Shore Drive are the east-west two-way roadways and Raymond Avenue, Spivey Road, Malinda Road, and Vincente are the north-south two-way roadways.

**31. c.** The roadways are Brigham Boulevard, Linda Lane, Battery Road, Needle Street, and John Street.

**32. c.** You must make a right onto Battery Road, a left onto Vincente, and a left onto Linda Lane. Choice **a** would have required you to enter Linda Lane the wrong way; choice **b** does not take into account that the entrance is to the left of the northeast corner of the building; and choice **d** takes you out of your way.

## Words-Only Directional Sample Questions

Now that you have mastered finding your route with maps, here are six words-only directional questions to give you a sense of how the two types of question differ.

**33.** Officer Johan is driving south on Columbus Avenue. After making a U-turn and turning left, in what direction will he now be driving?
   **a.** north
   **b.** south
   **c.** east
   **d.** west

**34.** Officers of the Hot Springs Police Department are staking out a paint factory. Officer Walther is north of Officer Smith. Officer Grant is north of Officer Walther. Officer Balbo is located south of Officer Grant. Based on these assignments, which of the following is definitely true?
   **a.** Officer Walther is the farthest north of the four officers.
   **b.** Officer Balbo is the farthest south of the four officers.
   **c.** Officer Smith is south of Officer Grant.
   **d.** Officer Balbo is south of Officer Walther.

**35.** A sergeant who is responding to a police officer's request for a non-emergency meeting is driving north on Kettle Road. At the intersection of Kettle Road and Keely Street, the sergeant turns west on Keely and yields to an ambulance crossing Keely and entering the intersection from the right. The ambulance is heading in what direction?
   **a.** north
   **b.** south
   **c.** east
   **d.** west

*Answer questions 36–38 based on the following paragraph.*

While driving on a two-way north-south road, Officer Silvio is directed by the dispatcher to respond to East Village, which he knows is west of the Bald Mountain, which is east of Officer Silvio's present location. Officer Silvio also knows that the road he is currently on is east of East Village.

**36.** If Officer Silvio is driving south and reaches an east-west road that leads to East Village, he should
a. keep going straight.
b. turn right.
c. turn left.
d. make a U-turn and travel north.

**37.** If Officer Silvio is driving north and reaches a two-way east-west road that leads to East Village, he should
a. keep going straight.
b. turn right.
c. turn left.
d. make a U-turn and travel south.

**38.** If Officer Silvio is located south of East Village and Bald Mountain and is driving south when he receives the call, he should
a. keep going straight.
b. turn right at the next intersection.
c. turn left at the next intersection.
d. make a U-turn and travel north.

## Answers

**33. d.** When Officer Johan completes the U-turn, he will be heading north; when he makes a left-hand turn, he will be heading west.

**34. c.** Officer Smith is south of Officer Grant. Officer Walther cannot be farthest north because Grant is north of Walther. Balbo is south of Grant but may or may not be south of Walther; therefore, Balbo may not be farthest south, nor south of Walther.

**35. b.** The sergeant was traveling west, so the ambulance to the right is traveling south.

**36. b.** Turning right would be turning west, and East Village is west of the road. Choice **a** is incorrect because continuing south would not bring him west; choice **c** is incorrect because turning left would be heading east; choice **d** is incorrect because traveling north would not bring him west.

**37. c.** Turning left is turning west, and East Village is west of the road. Choice **a** is incorrect because continuing north would not bring him west; choice **b** is incorrect because turning right would be heading east; choice **d** is incorrect because traveling south would not bring him west.

**38. d.** He must travel north to the east-west road prior to turning west. Choice **a** is incorrect because continuing south would not bring him west; choice **b** is incorrect because he would be south of East Village; choice c is incorrect because turning left would be turning east.

# Memory and Observation

Memory and observation questions may be based on photos or drawings (similar to maps) or on reading passages followed by questions to determine whether you remember or understood what you read. Since a number of other portions of this book provide sample reading passages, this section will focus on memory and observation questions based on photos or drawings. As you prepare for these questions, keep in mind that people remember much more than they think they do. We are all quick to say we do not remember something when we are really just having trouble bringing it to our immediate recall. Your mind is like a computer: Although information may be stored there, your recall system may not be operating at top efficiency. Rather than panic that you do not remember anything, relax and draw on the mental connections you made using the tips provided for each type of question. By studying these chapters and taking the practice exams, you are also at an advantage because you know to expect these types of questions.

## Memorizing Wanted Poster Information

Quite often, the drawings you will be asked about in memory questions center on wanted posters. Although other questions that involve photos or drawings may sometimes permit you to look back at the artwork to answer the questions, memory questions invovling the wanted posters almost never permit you to look back at either the drawings or the information accompanying them.

Generally you will be given four or five drawings of the wanted individuals along with pedigree information (age, sex, race), descriptions (height, weight, hair and eye color, and distinguishing scars or marks), and why and by whom they are wanted. Some agencies send you this material to study in advance of the actual exam but advise you not to bring the material to the exam site. If this is not done, the material will be presented to you either as a handout or on video for a period of time (generally 15 minutes) and then removed when you answer the questions. These kinds of questions can be found in Practice Exams 2 and 5.

There are a number of memory aids you can use for wanted poster questions.

- **Remember details about the individuals.** What are their names; do their names have ethnic associations that match their photos to help keep them separate in your mind. Do they have aliases that could form the basis of questions? Are the aliases logical and reflected in other information? For example: Does someone with an alias of Hawkeye have a tattoo of a hawk? Is this person's family name Hawk or Hawke? Names, aliases, and tattoos are often closely related, as are aliases related to one's work or whether one is described as belonging to a gang, or other group.

- **Group the individuals logically.** How many are men; how many are women; how many are juveniles? Are they all wanted for crimes or are some missing persons? How many have scars or tattoos or are described as possibly armed? While this may seem to contradict remembering details about the individuals, it complements it because you will be able to quickly answer questions that draw on comparisons among the individuals. For example: How many of the individuals have tattoos; how many are believed to be armed?

- **Look at the names and types of agencies seeking the individuals.** You might be asked how many are wanted by a local police department, or by a federal agency.

- **Create associations.** It might be helpful to associate some of the individuals with names or facts that are familiar to you, but this strategy works best when you are given the material prior to the test. If you view the photos for the first time at the test site with only 15 minutes, you might spend too much time making associations and not have time to look closely at the details of each poster.

To get you in the mindset to answer wanted poster questions, study the two wanted posters and accompanying information and answer the five questions that follow. Remember that in the actual test you will be given four or five posters, which means that there is more to remember and the questions will cover more information. For now, though, two will give you a sense of how to prepare for these types of questions.

## *WANTED*
### Thomas Torellini

**ALIASES:** Tommy the Turtle

**WANTED BY:** New York State Police

**CHARGES:** Robbery, Motor Vehicle Theft

**DESCRIPTION:**

    **Age:** 55

    **Race:** Caucasian

    **Height:** 6'1"

    **Weight:** 195 lbs.

    **Hair:** Brown

    **Eyes:** Brown

**IDENTIFYING SCARS OR MARKS:** Missing right eye is generally covered by a patch; tattoo of turtle on left bicep; sometimes shaves head.

**REMARKS:** Hitchhikes on interstate highways; robs those in vehicle at knifepoint and on two occasions fled in the vehicles, leaving the driver on the side of the road.

**CAUTION:** Known to carry a knife; has a record of violent crime and is a parole violator.

## WANTED
### Marvin Romano Mackey

**ALIASES:** Mack the Knife
**WANTED BY:** Minneapolis, MN, Police Department
**CHARGES:** Burglary
**DESCRIPTION:**

> **Age:** 29
> **Race:** Caucasian
> **Height:** 5'7"
> **Weight:** 165
> **Hair:** Black
> **Eyes:** Brown

**IDENTIFYING SCARS OR MARKS:** Scar on left cheek from a knife-fight, tattoo of Italian flag on right calf.
**REMARKS:** Positively identified from surveillance cameras as having committed three burglaries in the Mall of America, suspected of at least two additional burglaries; has relatives in St. Paul and is believed to ride a Honda 750 cc motorcycle.

**39.** Who is/are described as armed?
  **a.** Thomas Torellini
  **b.** Marvin Romano Mackey
  **c.** Thomas Torellini and Marvin Romano Mackey
  **d.** none of the above

**40.** Who is/are described as having a tattoo?
  **a.** Thomas Torellini
  **b.** Marvin Romano Mackey
  **c.** Thomas Torellini and Marvin Romano Mackey
  **d.** neither of the above

**41.** Who is/are wanted by a state police department?
  **a.** Marvin Romano Mackey
  **b.** Thomas Torellini
  **c.** Marvin Romano Mackey and Thomas Torellini
  **d.** neither of the above

**42.** Which wanted individual is the older of the two?
  **a.** Marvin Romano Mackey
  **b.** Thomas Torellini
  **c.** They are the same age.
  **d.** The information is not provided.

**43.** Of the identifying scars or marks provided for Thomas Torellini, which is likely to be the most useful in identifying him without conducting a search?
  **a.** a missing right eye
  **b.** a shaved head
  **c.** a tattoo on his left bicep
  **d.** a scar on his left cheek

## Answers

**39.** **a.** A caution is provided only for Thomas Torellini; despite the fact that Mackey's alias is Mack the Knife, there is no indication he is armed.

**40.** **c.** See the identifying scars or marks section for both men.

**41.** **b.** Review the wanted by notations for each man.

**42.** **a.** Review the ages listed: Torellini is 55, Mackey is 29.

**43.** **a.** Choice **b** can be changed easily by growing hair, wearing a hat or a wig; choice **c** requires Torellini to be wearing a short-sleeved or sleeveless shirt when stopped; choice **d** is part of the description of Mackey.

These questions relied on fairly simple recall because there were only two individuals. Imagine similar questions with four names or combinations for each question, and you will have a better idea of why it is important to review the memory tips and develop a system for processing the data.

## Street or Crime Scene Memorization and/or Observation

Another type of question based on a photo or drawing might be of a crime scene or street scene, or a photo of items taken from an arrested person. In some instances, the photo or drawing will be quite realistic; in others it will be a rough sketch. Do not focus on the quality of the image; rather, use the allotted time to remember as much as you can about the scene or the items. These questions may be presented as memory questions or as observation questions. If they are memorization questions, you will not be permitted to look back at the material, which will be presented to you in an identical fashion to the wanted posters. If they are observation questions, you will be permitted to keep the artwork in front of you. Even if you are permitted to keep the material available while answering the questions, you may find that time does not allow you to look back frequently, so if you do not remember large portions of what you saw, you might be unable to answer the questions fully.

The photo that appears on p. 240 is less complex than some you might be asked to review but it will provide you with a good idea of how observation questions are set up.

*Use the photo to answers questions 44–46.*

**44.** From the photo, it is most logical to presume that the Broadway Station intersects with
　　**a.** Highway D 18.
　　**b.** Downing Thruway.
　　**c.** Highway I-25.
　　**d.** Union Station.

**45.** The number of destinations other than Broadway Station that are shown in the photo is
　　**a.** one.
　　**b.** two.
　　**c.** three.
　　**d.** none.

**46.** Information that could be useful to passengers is located in the photo
　　**a.** towards the top.
　　**b.** towards the bottom.
　　**c.** on the viewer's left.
　　**d.** There is no information useful to passengers.

## Answers

**44. c.** I-25 is prominent in the station name and is designated in the style common for the Interstate Highway System.

**45. c.** Three other station names are shown: 18th and California, 30th and Downing, and Union Station.

**46. a.** Station and interchange information appears overhead, at the top of the photo; choices **b** and **c** are incorrect because no information is provided in those areas; choice **d** is incorrect because it contradicts the correct choice **a**.

- Use a methodical approach to memorization.
- Find ways to create links between your long-term memory and short-term memory.
- For questions based on pictures, "read" the picture from top to bottom or left to right.
- For questions based on materials you receive in advance, study the materials for a few minutes every day before the test.
- Visualize as you read passages, forming the words into a moving picture in your mind.
- Read the questions carefully; make sure you're answering the question that's being asked.
- Practice your memory and observation skills in your daily routine.

## Extra Practice with Recall Questions

There's no way you can really study for the recall section of the test, but you can practice. So here's an extra bonus section: a complete recall section of 100 questions so you can practice. There's an answer sheet on the opposite page—tear it out of the book so you can use it with the test. If you do not own this book, use a piece of scrap paper.

To review: You'll be given a key; in this case, each key has 27 letter-number combinations. The questions consist of one of the three-letter combinations from the key, followed by five two-digit numbers. Your job is to find the number combination that goes with the given three-letter combination and mark the corresponding circle on the answer sheet.

Remember, time is of the essence. Before you do this practice section, review the strategy tips in this chapter. Then get prepared: Tear out the answer sheet or get a piece of scrap paper, get a couple of pencils, and situate yourself at a table or desk where you can work undisturbed. Then set a timer for nine minutes, which is the amount of time you'll be allowed for this section on the real test. And then begin. Remember the key to success: Focus and stay calm.

When you've finished this practice section, check your answers against the answer key that follows. You'll probably find you did better than in the practice exam in Chapter 7. And you'll have another chance to improve your recall skills when you take the second practice exam of this type in Chapter 13.

## Number and Letter Recall Section

| | | | | | | | | | | | | | | | | |
|---|---|---|---|---|---|---|---|---|---|---|---|---|---|---|---|---|
| 1. | ⓐ ⓑ ⓒ ⓓ | 36. | ⓐ ⓑ ⓒ ⓓ | 71. | ⓐ ⓑ ⓒ ⓓ |
| 2. | ⓐ ⓑ ⓒ ⓓ | 37. | ⓐ ⓑ ⓒ ⓓ | 72. | ⓐ ⓑ ⓒ ⓓ |
| 3. | ⓐ ⓑ ⓒ ⓓ | 38. | ⓐ ⓑ ⓒ ⓓ | 73. | ⓐ ⓑ ⓒ ⓓ |
| 4. | ⓐ ⓑ ⓒ ⓓ | 39. | ⓐ ⓑ ⓒ ⓓ | 74. | ⓐ ⓑ ⓒ ⓓ |
| 5. | ⓐ ⓑ ⓒ ⓓ | 40. | ⓐ ⓑ ⓒ ⓓ | 75. | ⓐ ⓑ ⓒ ⓓ |
| 6. | ⓐ ⓑ ⓒ ⓓ | 41. | ⓐ ⓑ ⓒ ⓓ | 76. | ⓐ ⓑ ⓒ ⓓ |
| 7. | ⓐ ⓑ ⓒ ⓓ | 42. | ⓐ ⓑ ⓒ ⓓ | 77. | ⓐ ⓑ ⓒ ⓓ |
| 8. | ⓐ ⓑ ⓒ ⓓ | 43. | ⓐ ⓑ ⓒ ⓓ | 78. | ⓐ ⓑ ⓒ ⓓ |
| 9. | ⓐ ⓑ ⓒ ⓓ | 44. | ⓐ ⓑ ⓒ ⓓ | 79. | ⓐ ⓑ ⓒ ⓓ |
| 10. | ⓐ ⓑ ⓒ ⓓ | 45. | ⓐ ⓑ ⓒ ⓓ | 80. | ⓐ ⓑ ⓒ ⓓ |
| 11. | ⓐ ⓑ ⓒ ⓓ | 46. | ⓐ ⓑ ⓒ ⓓ | 81. | ⓐ ⓑ ⓒ ⓓ |
| 12. | ⓐ ⓑ ⓒ ⓓ | 47. | ⓐ ⓑ ⓒ ⓓ | 82. | ⓐ ⓑ ⓒ ⓓ |
| 13. | ⓐ ⓑ ⓒ ⓓ | 48. | ⓐ ⓑ ⓒ ⓓ | 83. | ⓐ ⓑ ⓒ ⓓ |
| 14. | ⓐ ⓑ ⓒ ⓓ | 49. | ⓐ ⓑ ⓒ ⓓ | 84. | ⓐ ⓑ ⓒ ⓓ |
| 15. | ⓐ ⓑ ⓒ ⓓ | 50. | ⓐ ⓑ ⓒ ⓓ | 85. | ⓐ ⓑ ⓒ ⓓ |
| 16. | ⓐ ⓑ ⓒ ⓓ | 51. | ⓐ ⓑ ⓒ ⓓ | 86. | ⓐ ⓑ ⓒ ⓓ |
| 17. | ⓐ ⓑ ⓒ ⓓ | 52. | ⓐ ⓑ ⓒ ⓓ | 87. | ⓐ ⓑ ⓒ ⓓ |
| 18. | ⓐ ⓑ ⓒ ⓓ | 53. | ⓐ ⓑ ⓒ ⓓ | 88. | ⓐ ⓑ ⓒ ⓓ |
| 19. | ⓐ ⓑ ⓒ ⓓ | 54. | ⓐ ⓑ ⓒ ⓓ | 89. | ⓐ ⓑ ⓒ ⓓ |
| 20. | ⓐ ⓑ ⓒ ⓓ | 55. | ⓐ ⓑ ⓒ ⓓ | 90. | ⓐ ⓑ ⓒ ⓓ |
| 21. | ⓐ ⓑ ⓒ ⓓ | 56. | ⓐ ⓑ ⓒ ⓓ | 91. | ⓐ ⓑ ⓒ ⓓ |
| 22. | ⓐ ⓑ ⓒ ⓓ | 57. | ⓐ ⓑ ⓒ ⓓ | 92. | ⓐ ⓑ ⓒ ⓓ |
| 23. | ⓐ ⓑ ⓒ ⓓ | 58. | ⓐ ⓑ ⓒ ⓓ | 93. | ⓐ ⓑ ⓒ ⓓ |
| 24. | ⓐ ⓑ ⓒ ⓓ | 59. | ⓐ ⓑ ⓒ ⓓ | 94. | ⓐ ⓑ ⓒ ⓓ |
| 25. | ⓐ ⓑ ⓒ ⓓ | 60. | ⓐ ⓑ ⓒ ⓓ | 95. | ⓐ ⓑ ⓒ ⓓ |
| 26. | ⓐ ⓑ ⓒ ⓓ | 61. | ⓐ ⓑ ⓒ ⓓ | 96. | ⓐ ⓑ ⓒ ⓓ |
| 27. | ⓐ ⓑ ⓒ ⓓ | 62. | ⓐ ⓑ ⓒ ⓓ | 97. | ⓐ ⓑ ⓒ ⓓ |
| 28. | ⓐ ⓑ ⓒ ⓓ | 63. | ⓐ ⓑ ⓒ ⓓ | 98. | ⓐ ⓑ ⓒ ⓓ |
| 29. | ⓐ ⓑ ⓒ ⓓ | 64. | ⓐ ⓑ ⓒ ⓓ | 99. | ⓐ ⓑ ⓒ ⓓ |
| 30. | ⓐ ⓑ ⓒ ⓓ | 65. | ⓐ ⓑ ⓒ ⓓ | 100. | ⓐ ⓑ ⓒ ⓓ |
| 31. | ⓐ ⓑ ⓒ ⓓ | 66. | ⓐ ⓑ ⓒ ⓓ | | |
| 32. | ⓐ ⓑ ⓒ ⓓ | 67. | ⓐ ⓑ ⓒ ⓓ | | |
| 33. | ⓐ ⓑ ⓒ ⓓ | 68. | ⓐ ⓑ ⓒ ⓓ | | |
| 34. | ⓐ ⓑ ⓒ ⓓ | 69. | ⓐ ⓑ ⓒ ⓓ | | |
| 35. | ⓐ ⓑ ⓒ ⓓ | 70. | ⓐ ⓑ ⓒ ⓓ | | |

## KEY 1

| BNB | FDE | RST | XAZ | JKI | DEB | FIV | ABS | QBN |
|-----|-----|-----|-----|-----|-----|-----|-----|-----|
| 21 | 29 | 44 | 42 | 61 | 55 | 63 | 99 | 62 |

| GFL | BVG | POQ | GAQ | BXC | WGL | YIR | RJC | BAZ |
|-----|-----|-----|-----|-----|-----|-----|-----|-----|
| 23 | 88 | 13 | 71 | 87 | 72 | 16 | 32 | 54 |

| MHY | KVT | NOP | SEF | LQG | GEX | HIK | DTE | MUQ |
|-----|-----|-----|-----|-----|-----|-----|-----|-----|
| 42 | 86 | 47 | 12 | 19 | 65 | 11 | 98 | 33 |

| | | a | b | c | d | e | | | a | b | c | d | e |
|----|-----|----|----|----|----|----|-----|-----|----|----|----|----|----|
| 1. | MHY | 62 | 78 | 99 | 42 | 33 | 14. | GFL | 75 | 23 | 93 | 45 | 83 |
| 2. | FIV | 81 | 44 | 47 | 98 | 63 | 15. | RST | 91 | 44 | 19 | 31 | 13 |
| 3. | WGL | 72 | 71 | 55 | 23 | 17 | 16. | JKI | 55 | 42 | 46 | 61 | 93 |
| 4. | POQ | 36 | 22 | 47 | 13 | 95 | 17. | DTE | 11 | 98 | 53 | 25 | 16 |
| 5. | LQG | 91 | 43 | 52 | 27 | 19 | 18. | KVT | 65 | 32 | 86 | 23 | 13 |
| 6. | NOP | 12 | 11 | 35 | 47 | 70 | 19. | BXC | 36 | 87 | 18 | 14 | 98 |
| 7. | SEF | 51 | 37 | 39 | 54 | 12 | 20. | BAZ | 54 | 81 | 23 | 12 | 11 |
| 8. | GEX | 37 | 44 | 41 | 65 | 95 | 21. | GAQ | 17 | 63 | 71 | 29 | 30 |
| 9. | FDE | 29 | 12 | 88 | 35 | 63 | 22. | DEB | 55 | 29 | 23 | 82 | 91 |
| 10. | BVG | 65 | 88 | 23 | 49 | 11 | 23. | BNB | 87 | 21 | 47 | 19 | 62 |
| 11. | MUQ | 75 | 91 | 55 | 33 | 87 | 24. | RJC | 61 | 32 | 93 | 24 | 36 |
| 12. | HIK | 32 | 11 | 95 | 94 | 88 | 25. | QBN | 34 | 72 | 45 | 62 | 95 |
| 13. | HIK | 63 | 14 | 65 | 93 | 42 | | | | | | | |

## KEY 2

| | | | | | | | | |
|---|---|---|---|---|---|---|---|---|
| GOF | EOG | JKO | DAJ | XOE | KGO | OIG | JIX | ANA |
| 32 | 88 | 42 | 54 | 86 | 53 | 41 | 23 | 14 |
| | | | | | | | | |
| FNO | FDE | IHG | ASA | BVI | GDO | IAF | OXW | LDO |
| 34 | 39 | 74 | 63 | 57 | 11 | 52 | 37 | 55 |
| | | | | | | | | |
| GYH | MAE | TGN | AFH | JTG | XEH | IQF | PAH | QFA |
| 13 | 85 | 45 | 43 | 49 | 51 | 44 | 38 | 20 |

| | | a | b | c | d | e | | | a | b | c | d | e |
|---|---|---|---|---|---|---|---|---|---|---|---|---|---|
| 26. | JTG | 35 | 49 | 11 | 23 | 55 | 39. | AFH | 61 | 22 | 43 | 14 | 28 |
| 27. | KGO | 68 | 47 | 53 | 83 | 35 | 40. | QFA | 51 | 32 | 45 | 20 | 24 |
| 28. | GOF | 35 | 58 | 33 | 45 | 32 | 41. | XEH | 51 | 43 | 11 | 23 | 58 |
| 29. | JKO | 42 | 54 | 12 | 23 | 50 | 42. | XOE | 24 | 86 | 21 | 14 | 54 |
| 30. | EOG | 15 | 88 | 23 | 34 | 94 | 43. | PAH | 32 | 47 | 38 | 62 | 24 |
| 31. | ASA | 44 | 63 | 88 | 12 | 25 | 44. | IQF | 52 | 44 | 84 | 47 | 83 |
| 32. | GYH | 47 | 52 | 13 | 41 | 24 | 45. | ANA | 35 | 48 | 23 | 34 | 14 |
| 33. | OXW | 62 | 33 | 54 | 24 | 37 | 46. | GDO | 93 | 11 | 23 | 43 | 52 |
| 34. | FDE | 52 | 43 | 47 | 39 | 63 | 47. | IAF | 52 | 25 | 90 | 31 | 28 |
| 35. | DAJ | 43 | 24 | 68 | 53 | 54 | 48. | IHG | 42 | 36 | 74 | 42 | 13 |
| 36. | TGN | 11 | 36 | 45 | 48 | 23 | 49. | BVI | 31 | 57 | 23 | 38 | 75 |
| 37. | FNO | 34 | 88 | 13 | 43 | 86 | 50. | LDO | 98 | 35 | 55 | 64 | 37 |
| 38. | MAE | 52 | 46 | 85 | 23 | 33 | | | | | | | |

## KEY 3

| KAM | LAE | YAN | MFD | JAD | XYD | IEN | DBF | MFB |
|-----|-----|-----|-----|-----|-----|-----|-----|-----|
| 15  | 85  | 45  | 49  | 47  | 51  | 44  | 58  | 22  |

| ABK | ENA | LNF | DPB | ATR | KXJ | ANI | IDB | BGN |
|-----|-----|-----|-----|-----|-----|-----|-----|-----|
| 72  | 88  | 42  | 59  | 81  | 19  | 41  | 25  | 14  |

| DAF | QEF | MNI | BYX | XIC | DNH | IYU | LMQ | JFD |
|-----|-----|-----|-----|-----|-----|-----|-----|-----|
| 54  | 16  | 34  | 51  | 53  | 11  | 52  | 53  | 55  |

|     |     | a  | b  | c  | d  | e  |     |     | a  | b  | c  | d  | e  |
|-----|-----|----|----|----|----|----|-----|-----|----|----|----|----|----|
| 51. | LAE | 68 | 34 | 45 | 85 | 58 | 64. | MNI | 11 | 96 | 94 | 48 | 34 |
| 52. | MFB | 58 | 74 | 12 | 22 | 59 | 65. | YAN | 51 | 45 | 43 | 48 | 24 |
| 53. | DPB | 55 | 58 | 19 | 95 | 59 | 66. | KAM | 42 | 56 | 15 | 42 | 17 |
| 54. | BGN | 55 | 54 | 14 | 52 | 99 | 67. | JFD | 27 | 55 | 21 | 94 | 54 |
| 55. | ABK | 15 | 58 | 25 | 51 | 72 | 68. | ATR | 81 | 34 | 45 | 83 | 24 |
| 56. | QEF | 62 | 16 | 54 | 24 | 15 | 69. | IYU | 29 | 47 | 84 | 52 | 58 |
| 57. | KXJ | 52 | 45 | 43 | 69 | 19 | 70. | IEN | 15 | 84 | 52 | 49 | 44 |
| 58. | JAD | 44 | 64 | 88 | 47 | 25 | 71. | DAF | 75 | 65 | 25 | 54 | 52 |
| 59. | DNH | 43 | 85 | 25 | 11 | 24 | 72. | IDB | 25 | 52 | 70 | 15 | 82 |
| 60. | BYX | 45 | 24 | 18 | 51 | 45 | 73. | XYD | 61 | 82 | 51 | 14 | 28 |
| 61. | LNF | 42 | 11 | 58 | 25 | 58 | 74. | DBF | 51 | 60 | 25 | 58 | 35 |
| 62. | ENA | 52 | 88 | 51 | 42 | 86 | 75. | XIC | 53 | 46 | 15 | 25 | 99 |
| 63. | MFD | 78 | 49 | 95 | 46 | 56 |     |     |    |    |    |    |    |

## KEY 4

| GHT | JAV | DRT | SLV | HMZ | DTA | AGB | PDL | GRX |
|-----|-----|-----|-----|-----|-----|-----|-----|-----|
| 45 | 75 | 43 | 56 | 35 | 11 | 25 | 35 | 55 |

| HGF | RTS | LQC | DZB | ALW | CWK | PTF | MKS | WER |
|-----|-----|-----|-----|-----|-----|-----|-----|-----|
| 51 | 58 | 54 | 94 | 74 | 15 | 44 | 85 | 22 |

| VAF | CXR | YEG | KUB | JMT | SQN | ZKD | RTF | ZOT |
|-----|-----|-----|-----|-----|-----|-----|-----|-----|
| 27 | 88 | 24 | 95 | 18 | 59 | 14 | 52 | 41 |

|  |  | a | b | c | d | e |
|--|--|---|---|---|---|---|
| 76. | DZB | 26 | 78 | 94 | 42 | 33 |
| 77. | KUB | 95 | 44 | 74 | 98 | 63 |
| 78. | SLV | 72 | 71 | 56 | 23 | 17 |
| 79. | CXR | 36 | 22 | 88 | 13 | 95 |
| 80. | HGF | 51 | 73 | 39 | 45 | 12 |
| 81. | DTA | 12 | 11 | 35 | 47 | 70 |
| 82. | VAF | 19 | 43 | 25 | 27 | 19 |
| 83. | DRT | 37 | 43 | 41 | 65 | 95 |
| 84. | ZOT | 29 | 41 | 88 | 53 | 36 |
| 85. | HMZ | 35 | 88 | 23 | 49 | 11 |
| 86. | WER | 75 | 91 | 55 | 22 | 78 |
| 87. | JAV | 32 | 11 | 75 | 49 | 88 |
| 88. | LQC | 63 | 14 | 54 | 93 | 42 |

|  |  | a | b | c | d | e |
|--|--|---|---|---|---|---|
| 89. | YEG | 75 | 24 | 93 | 45 | 83 |
| 90. | CWK | 15 | 44 | 91 | 31 | 13 |
| 91. | ALW | 75 | 42 | 46 | 61 | 93 |
| 92. | ZKD | 11 | 98 | 53 | 14 | 16 |
| 93. | JMT | 65 | 32 | 80 | 23 | 18 |
| 94. | RTF | 36 | 52 | 18 | 14 | 89 |
| 95. | PDL | 54 | 81 | 35 | 12 | 11 |
| 96. | GHT | 71 | 36 | 45 | 92 | 30 |
| 97. | PTF | 44 | 92 | 23 | 28 | 19 |
| 98. | GRX | 87 | 12 | 47 | 55 | 26 |
| 99. | AGB | 16 | 25 | 39 | 24 | 63 |
| 100. | SQN | 34 | 27 | 54 | 26 | 59 |

## *Answers*

| | | | |
|---|---|---|---|
| 1. d. | 26. b. | 51. d. | 76. c. |
| 2. e. | 27. c. | 52. d. | 77. a. |
| 3. a. | 28. e. | 53. e. | 78. c. |
| 4. d. | 29. a. | 54. c. | 79. c. |
| 5. e. | 30. b. | 55. e. | 80. a. |
| 6. d. | 31. b. | 56. b. | 81. b. |
| 7. e. | 32. c. | 57. e. | 82. d. |
| 8. d. | 33. e. | 58. d. | 83. b. |
| 9. a. | 34. d. | 59. d. | 84. b. |
| 10. b. | 35. e. | 60. d. | 85. a. |
| 11. d. | 36. c. | 61. a. | 86. d. |
| 12. b. | 37. a. | 62. b. | 87. c. |
| 13. d. | 38. c. | 63. b. | 88. c. |
| 14. b. | 39. c. | 64. e. | 89. b. |
| 15. b. | 40. d. | 65. b. | 90. a. |
| 16. d. | 41. a. | 66. c. | 91. a. |
| 17. b. | 42. b. | 67. b. | 92. d. |
| 18. c. | 43. c. | 68. a. | 93. e. |
| 19. b. | 44. b. | 69. d. | 94. b. |
| 20. a. | 45. e. | 70. e. | 95. c. |
| 21. c. | 46. b. | 71. d. | 96. c. |
| 22. a. | 47. a. | 72. a. | 97. a. |
| 23. b. | 48. c. | 73. c. | 98. d. |
| 24. b. | 49. b. | 74. d. | 99. b. |
| 25. d. | 50. c. | 75. a. | 100. e. |

# 11 ▶ POLICE OFFICER PRACTICE EXAM 4

C H A P T E R

### *CHAPTER SUMMARY*

Practice Exam 4 tests your basic reading and writing skills. Compare your performance with earlier practice exams. If you have read the review chapters carefully, you should have a better idea of how to analyze the questions to arrive at the best answers.

L
ike Practice Exam 1 (Chapter 5), this practice exam is an example of a basic reading and writing skills exam like those used by many agencies around the country. This exam also contains 100 questions, and is divided into two parts, although Part Two is somewhat different from the earlier practice exams.

Part One: 60 clarity of expression (grammar), vocabulary, spelling and reading comprehension questions.

Part Two: 40 questions that require you to fill in the missing words in a two-paragraph passage. This portion of the exam is different from fill-in exams you may be familiar with. Read the instructions carefully before filling in any blank spaces.

The directions for each type of question are included in the test. Since you are now experienced at taking the practice exams, decide before you begin whether you will take your time and analyze along the way how you are doing, or whether you will create conditions similar to the actual test and time yourself closely. Since the amount of time you will be given for the actual test may be different for different departments, rather than setting a hard time limit, see how long it takes you to complete the test and then try to find out what the time limits are for the departments you plan to test for.

When you turn the page, you will find the answer sheet for Part One, followed by the answer sheet for Part Two, the test itself, and, finally, the answers and explanations.

## Police Officer Practice Exam Part One

| | | | | | | | | | | | | | |
|---|---|---|---|---|---|---|---|---|---|---|---|---|---|
| 1. | ⓐ | ⓑ | ⓒ | ⓓ | 26. | ⓐ | ⓑ | ⓒ | ⓓ | 51. | ⓐ | ⓑ | ⓒ | ⓓ |
| 2. | ⓐ | ⓑ | ⓒ | ⓓ | 27. | ⓐ | ⓑ | ⓒ | ⓓ | 52. | ⓐ | ⓑ | ⓒ | ⓓ |
| 3. | ⓐ | ⓑ | ⓒ | ⓓ | 28. | ⓐ | ⓑ | ⓒ | ⓓ | 53. | ⓐ | ⓑ | ⓒ | ⓓ |
| 4. | ⓐ | ⓑ | ⓒ | ⓓ | 29. | ⓐ | ⓑ | ⓒ | ⓓ | 54. | ⓐ | ⓑ | ⓒ | ⓓ |
| 5. | ⓐ | ⓑ | ⓒ | ⓓ | 30. | ⓐ | ⓑ | ⓒ | ⓓ | 55. | ⓐ | ⓑ | ⓒ | ⓓ |
| 6. | ⓐ | ⓑ | ⓒ | ⓓ | 31. | ⓐ | ⓑ | ⓒ | ⓓ | 56. | ⓐ | ⓑ | ⓒ | ⓓ |
| 7. | ⓐ | ⓑ | ⓒ | ⓓ | 32. | ⓐ | ⓑ | ⓒ | ⓓ | 57. | ⓐ | ⓑ | ⓒ | ⓓ |
| 8. | ⓐ | ⓑ | ⓒ | ⓓ | 33. | ⓐ | ⓑ | ⓒ | ⓓ | 58. | ⓐ | ⓑ | ⓒ | ⓓ |
| 9. | ⓐ | ⓑ | ⓒ | ⓓ | 34. | ⓐ | ⓑ | ⓒ | ⓓ | 59. | ⓐ | ⓑ | ⓒ | ⓓ |
| 10. | ⓐ | ⓑ | ⓒ | ⓓ | 35. | ⓐ | ⓑ | ⓒ | ⓓ | 60. | ⓐ | ⓑ | ⓒ | ⓓ |
| 11. | ⓐ | ⓑ | ⓒ | ⓓ | 36. | ⓐ | ⓑ | ⓒ | ⓓ | | | | | |
| 12. | ⓐ | ⓑ | ⓒ | ⓓ | 37. | ⓐ | ⓑ | ⓒ | ⓓ | | | | | |
| 13. | ⓐ | ⓑ | ⓒ | ⓓ | 38. | ⓐ | ⓑ | ⓒ | ⓓ | | | | | |
| 14. | ⓐ | ⓑ | ⓒ | ⓓ | 39. | ⓐ | ⓑ | ⓒ | ⓓ | | | | | |
| 15. | ⓐ | ⓑ | ⓒ | ⓓ | 40. | ⓐ | ⓑ | ⓒ | ⓓ | | | | | |
| 16. | ⓐ | ⓑ | ⓒ | ⓓ | 41. | ⓐ | ⓑ | ⓒ | ⓓ | | | | | |
| 17. | ⓐ | ⓑ | ⓒ | ⓓ | 42. | ⓐ | ⓑ | ⓒ | ⓓ | | | | | |
| 18. | ⓐ | ⓑ | ⓒ | ⓓ | 43. | ⓐ | ⓑ | ⓒ | ⓓ | | | | | |
| 19. | ⓐ | ⓑ | ⓒ | ⓓ | 44. | ⓐ | ⓑ | ⓒ | ⓓ | | | | | |
| 20. | ⓐ | ⓑ | ⓒ | ⓓ | 45. | ⓐ | ⓑ | ⓒ | ⓓ | | | | | |
| 21. | ⓐ | ⓑ | ⓒ | ⓓ | 46. | ⓐ | ⓑ | ⓒ | ⓓ | | | | | |
| 22. | ⓐ | ⓑ | ⓒ | ⓓ | 47. | ⓐ | ⓑ | ⓒ | ⓓ | | | | | |
| 23. | ⓐ | ⓑ | ⓒ | ⓓ | 48. | ⓐ | ⓑ | ⓒ | ⓓ | | | | | |
| 24. | ⓐ | ⓑ | ⓒ | ⓓ | 49. | ⓐ | ⓑ | ⓒ | ⓓ | | | | | |
| 25. | ⓐ | ⓑ | ⓒ | ⓓ | 50. | ⓐ | ⓑ | ⓒ | ⓓ | | | | | |

## *Police Officer Practice Exam Part Two*

WRITE 1ST LETTER OF WORD HERE

CODE LETTERS HERE

| 1 | 2 | 3 | 4 | 5 | 6 | 7 | 8 | 9 | 10 |
|---|---|---|---|---|---|---|---|---|---|

A B C D E F G H I J K L M N O P Q R S T U V W X Y Z

| 11 | 12 | 13 | 14 | 15 | 16 | 17 | 18 | 19 | 20 |
|---|---|---|---|---|---|---|---|---|---|

A B C D E F G H I J K L M N O P Q R S T U V W X Y Z

| 21 | 22 | 23 | 24 | 25 | 26 | 27 | 28 | 29 | 30 |
|---|---|---|---|---|---|---|---|---|---|

A B C D E F G H I J K L M N O P Q R S T U V W X Y Z

| 31 | 32 | 33 | 34 | 35 | 36 | 37 | 38 | 39 | 40 |
|---|---|---|---|---|---|---|---|---|---|

A B C D E F G H I J K L M N O P Q R S T U V W X Y Z

# Practice Exam 4: Part One

## *Section One: Clarity*
*In each of the following sets of sentences, select the one that is most clearly written.*

**1. a.** The words *Equal Justice under Law* is carved above the main entrance to the Supreme Court.
   **b.** The words *Equal Justice under Law* has been carved above the main entrance to the Supreme Court.
   **c.** The words *Equal Justice under Law* carved above the main entrance to the Supreme Court.
   **d.** The words *Equal Justice under Law* are carved above the main entrance to the Supreme Court.

**2. a.** I asked the witness to hand over the suspect's jacket found at the scene to Officer Smith and I.
   **b.** To Officer Smith and I, I asked the witness to hand over the suspect's jacket found at the scene.
   **c.** I asked the witness to hand over the suspect's jacket found at the scene to Officer Smith and me.
   **d.** I asked the witness that she hand over the suspects' jacket found at the scene to me and to Officer Smith.

**3. a.** Both the weather and the time of year influences the crime rate in New York City.
   **b.** Both the weather and the time of year influence the crime rate in New York City.
   **c.** Either the weather and the time of year influences the crime rate in New York City.
   **d.** Both the weather and the time of year influencing the crime rate in New York City.

**4. a.** Neither Jim Green nor Carla McKenzie was granted parole.
   **b.** Neither Jim Green or Carla McKenzie were granted parole.
   **c.** Neither Jim Green nor Carla McKenzie were granted parole.
   **d.** Neither Jim Green or Carla McKenzie was granted parole.

**5. a.** Officer Williams arrived on the scene first, moreover Officer Jenkins arrived 15 minutes later.
   **b.** Officer Williams arrived on the scene first, Officer Jenkins arrived 15 minutes later.
   **c.** Officer Williams arrived on the scene first, and Officer Jenkins arrived 15 minutes later.
   **d.** Officer Williams arrived on the scene first, next officer Jenkins arrived 15 minutes later.

**6. a.** For a variety of many reasons, more people applied to the police academy this year than ever before.
   **b.** More people, for various different reasons, applied to the police academy this year than ever before.
   **c.** For a number of reasons, more people applied to the police academy this year than ever before.
   **d.** For a wide variety of different reasons, more and more people applied to the police academy this year than ever before.

**7. a.** The firefighters sold less raffle tickets than they sold last year.
  **b.** The firefighters sold fewer raffle tickets than they sold last year.
  **c.** The firefighters sold fewer raffle tickets than they sell last year.
  **d.** The firefighters sell less raffle tickets than they sold last year.

**8. a.** When the police arrived, they saw the gun laid on the bed.
  **b.** When the police arrived, they saw the gun lieing on the bed.
  **c.** When the police arrived, they saw the gun lying on the bed.
  **d.** When the police arrived, they saw the gun laying on the bed.

**9. a.** Sandra Day O'Connor, the first woman to serve on the Supreme Court, she appointed by President Ronald Reagan in 1981.
  **b.** Sandra Day O'Connor, the first woman to serve on the Supreme Court, and appointed by President Ronald Reagan in 1981.
  **c.** Sandra Day O'Connor, the first woman to serve on the Supreme Court, then appointed by President Ronald Reagan in 1981.
  **d.** Sandra Day O'Connor, the first woman to serve on the Supreme Court, was appointed by President Ronald Reagan in 1981.

**10. a.** Patrol effectiveness is often measured in response time.
  **b.** Patrol effectiveness are often measured in response time.
  **c.** Patrols effectiveness is often measured in response time.
  **d.** Patrol's effectiveness are often measured in response time.

**11. a.** A police officer cannot risk their job by getting in trouble.
  **b.** Police officer cannot risk they job by getting in trouble.
  **c.** A police officer cannot risk her job by getting in trouble.
  **d.** Police officers cannot risk his/her jobs by getting in trouble.

**12. a.** Getting beat up should not be part of a police officer's job.
  **b.** Getting beaten up should not be part of a police officer's job.
  **c.** Getting beaten up should not be apart of a police officer's job.
  **d.** Getting beat up should not be part of a police officers job.

**13. a.** Sergeant Jones and me responded to a call.
  **b.** Me and Sergeant Jones responded to a call.
  **c.** Sergeant Jones and I responded to a call.
  **d.** Myself and Sergeant Jones responded to a call.

**14. a.** Of the two horses in the mounted unit, Jonsie is the most bravest.
  **b.** Of the two horses in the mounted unit, Jonsie is the braver.
  **c.** Of the two horses in the mounted unit, Jonsie is the more brave.
  **d.** Of the two horses in the mounted unit, Jonsie is the least bravest.

**15. a.** It's a long way from Albany to New York City.
  **b.** Its a long way from Albany to New York City.
  **c.** Its' a long way from Albany to New York City.
  **d.** Its's a long way from Albany to New York City.

## Section Two: Vocabulary

*In each of the following sentences, select the work or phrase that most nearly means the same as the underlined word.*

**16.** The sergeant emphasized the use-of-force <u>continuum.</u>
   **a.** collection
   **b.** scale
   **c.** prohibition
   **d.** training

**17.** Under the agency's arrest policy, police officers have more <u>discretion</u> with infractions and some misdemeanors than with more serious offenses.
   **a.** choice
   **b.** limits
   **c.** responsibility
   **d.** aptitude

**18.** The evidence kit was running low on <u>disposable</u> gloves.
   **a.** irreplaceable
   **b.** authorized
   **c.** synthetic
   **d.** throwaway

**19.** He based his conclusion on what he <u>inferred</u> from the evidence, not on what he actually observed.
   **a.** intuited
   **b.** imagined
   **c.** surmised
   **d.** implied

**20.** The police officer used the <u>pretext</u> of a traffic violation to investigate the gang activity.
   **a.** example
   **b.** idea
   **c.** literature
   **d.** excuse

**21.** For health reasons, the evidence lab is required to <u>sanitize</u> the work area after each analysis.
   **a.** photograph
   **b.** inventory
   **c.** purify
   **d.** contaminate

**22.** Officer Green was thought to be one of the most <u>astute</u> officers on the force.
   **a.** perceptive
   **b.** inattentive
   **c.** stubborn
   **d.** studious

**23.** The judge ruled that the evidence was <u>immaterial</u>, which angered the defense team.
   **a.** appropriate
   **b.** germane
   **c.** considerable
   **d.** irrelevant

**24.** The matter reached its conclusion only after <u>diplomatic</u> efforts by both sides.
   **a.** tactful
   **b.** delaying
   **c.** elaborate
   **d.** combative

**25.** The suspect refused to show remorse for his <u>flagrant</u> disregard for the law.
   **a.** immoral
   **b.** malicious
   **c.** callous
   **d.** outright

**26.** Lieutenant Thomas does not like people to make their own decisions; he tends to <u>stifle</u> creativity.
a. encourage
b. discourage
c. foster
d. enjoy

**27.** Generally, when crimes receive media attention, the police are <u>inundated</u> with calls from people who claim to have witnessed the crime.
a. provided
b. fooled
c. flooded
d. annoyed

**28.** In police agencies that follow civil service law, it is generally a <u>prerequisite</u> to serve as a police officer prior to being promoted to higher rank.
a. required
b. optional
c. preferable
d. useful

**29.** It is <u>essential</u> to pass the written police exam before moving ahead in the hiring process.
a. required
b. optional
c. unnecessary
d. likely

**30.** Captain Perry <u>espoused</u> a high-level of esprit de corps.
a. criticized
b. ridiculed
c. undermined
d. supported

## Section Three: Spelling

*In each of the following sentences, select the correct spelling of the missing word.*

**31.** Bodily _____ are often the best source of DNA evidence at crime scenes.
a. flueds
b. fluids
c. fluedes
d. fluides

**32.** It is my _____ that the police officers in this county do a fine job.
a. beleif
b. bilief
c. belief
d. beleaf

**33.** An officer must be _____ to the distress of a crime victim.
a. sinsitive
b. sensitive
c. sensative
d. sinsative

**34.** Most local police officers work for a _____ police department.
a. municipal
b. municiple
c. municepal
d. municeple

**35.** The District Attorney announced his intention to _____ the suspected drug smugglers.
a. prosecute
b. prossecute
c. prosacute
d. prosecuute

**36.** Officer Brady found herself in a very dangerous _____.

   **a.** sittuation

   **b.** situation

   **c.** situachun

   **d.** situacion

**37.** An _____ donor contributed $10,000 to the police officers' fundraiser for the children's hospital.

   **a.** annonimous

   **b.** anonimous

   **c.** annonymous

   **d.** anonymous

**38.** The deputy gave his _____ that the report would be completed on time.

   **a.** asurrance

   **b.** assurance

   **c.** assurence

   **d.** assureance

**39.** To maintain peak physical condition, a police officer must eat well and get plenty of _____.

   **a.** excercise

   **b.** exercise

   **c.** exersize

   **d.** exercize

**40.** Officer Forster immediately reported the problem to her _____.

   **a.** superviser

   **b.** supervizer

   **c.** supervizor

   **d.** supervisor

**41.** Our physical training instructor _____ the importance of continuing to work out after we complete the academy.

   **a.** emphasized

   **b.** empasized

   **c.** amphsized

   **d.** emphazed

**42.** During the lecture on questioning witnesses, the instructor said it was important to _____ those you wanted to question so everyone did not give the same answer.

   **a.** seperate

   **b.** separate

   **c.** sepperate

   **d.** separtate

**43.** To save time during an interview, a police officer should not ask questions that are _____.

   **a.** irrevalent

   **b.** irrevelent

   **c.** irrelevant

   **d.** irravalent

**44.** Sergeant Smart has been studying every night for the promotion exam to _____.

   **a.** lieutenant

   **b.** lutenant

   **c.** lieutenont

   **d.** lieutenent

**45.** One of the roles of a forensic specialist is to _____ evidence.

   **a.** analysis

   **b.** analyze

   **c.** analise

   **d.** annalize

## Section Four: Reading Comprehension

*For each of the reading passages, answer the questions based on what is stated or implied in the passage.*

*Answer questions 46–50 based on the following passage.*

Criminology researchers who take a normative view on crime define crime as a behavior that deviates from established norms, culture, and values. In this view, what is criminal is that which is not normally engaged in or sanctified by society at large. The laws regarding the use of marijuana provide a good lens with which to understand the normative view. Prior to the twentieth century, it was not illegal to use or possess marijuana. In 1915, Utah passed the first law against marijuana use, and through the years the laws became more widespread and serious. In the 1950s, the Boggs Act and the Narcotics Control Act set mandatory sentences for drug crimes, including marijuana, which had a first offense penalty of two to ten years in prison and a $20,000 fine. However, by the early 1970s, views on the use of marijuana were beginning to change. Many researchers attribute the change in views not to an increase in the medical or scientific understanding of the drug, but to the increased use of the drug for recreational and medicinal purposes by a larger segment of society. During this time, many states began to significantly decriminalize their marijuana laws, and by the late 1980s, individual states began to legalize the use of marijuana for certain medical conditions.

**46.** In what year did Utah pass a law against marijuana?
 a. 1970
 b. 1915
 c. 1956
 d. 1941

**47.** According to the passage, the view that crime is a behavior that deviates from established norms, culture, and values is the
 a. police view.
 b. criminology view.
 c. normative view.
 d. Boggs view.

**48.** Based on the passage, which of the following phrases best sums up the normative view's reason for the recent decriminalization of marijuana?
 a. societal acceptance
 b. moral depravity
 c. prison overcrowding
 d. gang violence

**49.** Based on the passage, which of the following is NOT correct?
 a. Societal views on marijuana began to change in the 1970s.
 b. It is now legal to possess marijuana for medical conditions in some states.
 c. It is now legal to possess marijuana for recreational use in some states.
 d. Based on changes in attitudes toward drugs, the federal government has decriminalized use of marijuana.

**50.** Based on the passage, which of the following is correct?
 a. The Boggs Act set mandatory sentences for the possession of marijuana.
 b. The Narcotics Control Act decriminalized marijuana use in the 1980s.
 c. Doctors may prescribe marijuana for medical use anywhere in the nation.
 d. Marijuana use ebbs and flows depending on cultural changes.

*Answer questions 51–55 based on the following passage.*

When it began its 20th season in Fall 2009, "Law & Order" tied "Gunsmoke" as longest-running prime-time drama on United States television. Many countries also have popular police dramas. In Germany, a police procedural called "Tatort" has been seen for almost four decades. "Tatort" translates into English as "crime scene." The show predates the unification of eastern and western Germany in 1990, and reflects a more local influence than in United States television. For instance, "Law & Order" focuses on the same pair of detectives and only the crime changes each week, but "Tatort" has local versions with various detectives working in different cities. There are actually 15 distinct versions that are produced locally.

It is interesting that in a nation with very few homicides, murders dominate on the shows regardless of what city is featured. The focus on homicides is similar to "Law & Order." In comparison to the United States, in 2007 Germany had 862 homicides in a country of 84 million people, compared to the U.S. where there were 20 times as many homicides but only four times as many people. Possibly reflecting that there is less violent crime in Germany than in the U.S., the program tends to show less violence and to concentrate more on developing the character of the detectives and showing how they go about solving the crimes that they investigate. In this way, it may actually combine some elements of other U.S. shows that concentrate on so-called special victims or on forensic investigations, and where, as on "Tatort," a number of the featured detectives are women.

**51.** When did "Tatort" begin broadcasting?
   **a.** 1989
   **b.** 1990
   **c.** about 40 years ago
   **d.** none of the above

**52.** One way that "Tatort" differs from "Law & Order" is
   **a.** many pairs of detectives are featured.
   **b.** all the detectives are all male.
   **c.** the episodes all feature sex-related crimes.
   **d.** the detectives rarely make an arrest.

**53.** One way in which "Tatort" and "Law & Order" are similar is
   **a.** there are regional versions.
   **b.** the crimes featured are mostly homicides.
   **c.** the detectives work in many different cities.
   **d.** the detectives are all male.

**54.** Using the information provided in the passage, the closest estimate of the number of homicides in the U.S. in 2007 is
   **a.** 1,680
   **b.** 3,448
   **c.** 17,240
   **d.** 68,860

**55.** According to the passage, "Tatort" is similar to U.S. police forensic shows because
   **a.** its focus is on how detective go about solving cases.
   **b.** its detectives are male and female pairs.
   **c.** its focus is on sex crimes.
   **d.** the passage does not raise any similarities.

*Answer questions 56-60 based on the following passage.*

At 9:30 P.M., while parked at 916 Woodward Avenue, Officers Whitebear and Morgan were asked to respond to an anonymous complaint of a disturbance at 826 Rosemary Lane. When they arrived, they found the back door open and the jamb splintered. They drew their weapons, identified themselves, and entered the dwelling, where they found Mr. Darrell Hensley, of 1917 Roosevelt Avenue, sitting on the couch. Mr. Hensley calmly stated he was waiting for his wife. At that point, two children emerged from a hallway: Dustin Hensley, age 7, who lives in the dwelling, and Kirstin Jackson, age 14, Dustin's babysitter, who lives at 916 Ambrose Street. Kirstin stated she and Dustin had been sitting at the kitchen table when the back door was kicked in and Mr. Hensley entered, shouting obscenities and calling for Karen Hensley, Dustin's mother. Kirstin then hid with Dustin in a hallway storage closet. The officers contacted Mrs. Hensley at her place of employment at O'Reilley's Restaurant at 415 Ralston. At 9:55, she returned home and showed an Order of Protection stating Mr. Hensley was not to have contact with his wife or child. Mr. Hensley was placed under arrest and taken in handcuffs to the station house.

**56.** Based on Darrell Hensley's behavior when he first arrived at his wife's house, what was his most likely motivation for being there?
   **a.** to see his child for a scheduled visitation
   **b.** to provoke a confrontation with his wife
   **c.** to have a place to stay that night
   **d.** to reconcile peacefully with his family

**57.** Who called the police to investigate the disturbance described in the passage?
   **a.** the babysitter
   **b.** the arrestee's wife
   **c.** a neighbor
   **d.** an unknown person

**58.** Based on the information in the passage, what is the most likely reason the officers drew their weapons before entering the Hensley home?
   **a.** There were signs of forced entry into the house.
   **b.** There was an Order of Protection against Mr. Hensley.
   **c.** Children were in danger inside the premises.
   **d.** They knew Mr. Hensley to be a violent man.

**59.** Based on the information in the passage, what was Mr. Hensley's demeanor when the police first spoke to him?
   **a.** He was enraged.
   **b.** He was remorseful.
   **c.** He was matter-of-fact.
   **d.** He was confused.

**60.** Based on information in the passage, Mr. Hensley
   **a.** lives in the house at 826 Rosemary Lane.
   **b.** does not live in the house at 826 Rosemary Lane.
   **c.** is a welcome visitor at the house at 826 Rosemary Lane.
   **d.** none of the above

# Practice Exam 4: Part Two

This is a test of your reading ability. In the following passages, words have been omitted. Each numbered set of dashed blank lines indicates where a word is left out; each dash represents one letter of the missing word. The correct word should not only make sense in the sentence but also have the number of letters indicated by the dashes.

Read through the whole passage, and then begin filling in the missing words. Fill in as many missing words as possible. If you aren't sure of the answer, take a guess.

Then mark your answers on the answer sheet on page 254 as follows: Write the **first letter** of the word you have chosen in the square under the number of the word. Then blacken the circle of that letter of the alphabet under the square.

**Only the blackened alphabet circles will be scored.** The words you write on this page and the letters you write at the top of the column on the answer sheet **will not be scored.** Make sure that you blacken the appropriate circle in each column.

Many people become angry when they hear that prison inmates have the opportunity to study for their **1)** _ _ _ _ school equivalency diplomas, take college courses, and even earn **2)** _ _ _ _ _ _ _ degrees while they are serving **3)** _ _ _ _. Such educational services are often provided at **4)** _ _ charge to the inmates, which means that the **5)** _ _ _ _ _ are borne by taxpayers. Many people see these **6)** _ _ _ _ educational services as coddling criminals, and providing rewards for lawbreakers. Higher education is **7)** _ _ _ _ _ _ _ _ _ and it is frustrating to many people to see convicted criminals **8)** _ _ _ for free what working people have to struggle so hard to **9)** _ _ _ _ _ _ _ for their children. On the other hand, those **10)** _ _ _ support educational services for inmates argue that it is in society's **11)** _ _ _ _ interest to provide such services. Rather **12)** _ _ _ _ being seen as a reward for **13)** _ _ _ _ _ _ _ _ _, education should be viewed as an investment in social order. A decent **14)** _ _ _ _ _ _ _ _ _ will make the ex-offender **15)** _ _ _ _ employable, and that, in turn, should remove one **16)** _ _ _ _ _ _ for repeat offenses—the inability to earn a living in a socially acceptable **17)** _ _ _. We should not **18)** _ _ _ _ educational opportunities to those in **19)** _ _ _ _ _ _ if we expect them to become useful citizens when **20)** _ _ _ _ leave.

Members for high-risk occupations like law enforcement and firefighting form tightly knit groups. The dangers they share naturally **21)** _ _ _ _ _ them close, as does the knowledge that their **22)** _ _ _ _ _ are sometimes in one another's hands. The bonds of loyalty and trust help police **23)** _ _ _ _ _ _ _ _ work more effectively. However, the sense **24)** _ _ loyalty can be taken to **25)** _ _ _ _ _ _ _ _. Sometimes officers believe that they always must defend their comrades' actions. What happens though, **26)** _ _ _ _ those actions are wrong? Frank Serpico found a disturbing **27)** _ _ _ _ _ _ to that question. Serpico **28)** _ _ _ _ _ _ the New York City Police Department assuming **29)** _ _ _ _ high moral standards were typical of his fellow officers. When he **30)** _ _ _ _ _ out otherwise, he was faced with a dilemma: **31)** _ _ _ _ _ _ he violate the trust of his fellow officers by exposing the corruption, **32)** _ _ should he close his **33)** _ _ _ _ because loyalty to his **34)** _ _ _ _ _ _ officers outweighed all other moral (and legal) considerations? Serpico made his **35)** _ _ _ _ _ _. Public attention was focused on police **36)** _ _ _ _ _ _ _ _ _ and the NYPD was improved as a **37)** _ _ _ _ _ _, but those improvements came at a tremendous personal **38)** _ _ _ _ to Serpico. Ostracized and reviled by other officers, who felt **39)** _ _ _ _ _ _ _ _, Serpico eventually left the **40)** _ _ _ _ _.

# Answer Key: Part One

## Section One: Clarity

1. **d.** This is the only choice that is a complete sentence and has subject-verb agreement. In choices **a** and **b**, the subject *words* is plural and does not agree with the singular verb. Choice **c** is a sentence fragment.

2. **c.** In choices **a** and **b** the pronoun *I* is incorrect. Choice **d** is an awkward construction and misuses the possessive to indicate more than one suspect but only one jacket.

3. **b.** Choice **a** is wrong because the plural subject does not agree with the singular verb. Choice **c** is poorly written; the sentence should read, *Either the weather or the time of year…* Choice **d** is a sentence fragment.

4. **a.** When using *neither . . . nor*, also use a singular verb. Choice **c** is incorrect because it uses a plural verb. Choice **d** is incorrect because *neither* is always used with *nor*. In choice **b**, both the use of *neither* with *or* and the plural verb are incorrect.

5. **c.** The other choices are comma splices or run-on sentences.

6. **c.** This is the only choice that avoids wordiness or redundancies. In choice **a**, the phrase *variety of many* is redundant. In choice **b**, *various different* is redundant. In choice **d**, *variety of different reasons, more and more* is both wordy and redundant.

7. **b.** Choices **a** and **d** are incorrect because *less* is used with quantities that cannot be counted, e.g. *less* power, *less* risk. Use *fewer* with nouns that can be counted, e.g., *fewer* cars, *fewer* raffle tickets. In choice **c**, *fewer* is correct, but there is an unnecessary shift in verb tense—from past to present.

8. **d.** The simplest rule to remember is that things *lay* and people *lie*. If the sentence involved a person, it would be *they saw Thelma lying on the bed*.

9. **d.** This is the only choice that does not contain faulty subordination.

10. **a.** Choices **b** and **d** are not correct because they lack subject-verb agreement. Choice **c** is incorrect because *patrol* requires an apostrophe.

11. **c.** The subject, modifier and noun are all singular.

12. **b.** This is the only choice that uses the correct verb form and correct possessive.

13. **c.** The sentence requires the first person pronoun *I*.

14. **b.** Since there are only two horses, the comparative is correct.

15. **a.** Although contractions should be avoided in formal writing, choice **a** is the only correct form of the contraction for *it is*.

## Section Two: Vocabulary

16. **b.** *Continuum* is a succession along a line; in this use, along a scale is the closest in meaning.

17. **a.** To exercise *discretion* means to make a decision on your own based on choices, making choice **a** the closest in meaning.

18. **d.** *Disposable* means replaceable; in this context, it refers to items that are meant to be disposed of after use.

19. **c.** *Inferred* most closely means surmised; both mean to understand something from its context or use.

20. **d.** *Pretext* implies to do something as an excuse to do something else.

21. **c.** To *sanitize* means to clean, make sanitary, or, as choice **c**, to purify.

22. **a.** *Astute* means crafty or sharp, making choice **a** the closest in meaning.

23. **d.** *Immaterial* means not relevant; choice **d** is the closest in meaning.
24. **a.** To handle a situation in a *diplomatic* way means to exercise tact, sensitivity, or discretion, making choice **a** the closest in meaning.
25. **d.** *Flagrant* means deliberately conspicuous; choice **d** is the closest in meaning.
26. **b.** *Stifle* means to discourage.
27. **c.** Flooded most nearly means *inundated*.
28. **a.** A *prerequisite* is a requirement.
29. **a.** *Essential* means basic or indispensable; choice **a** is the closest in meaning.
30. **d.** *Espoused* means supported or adopted a position or cause.

## Section Three: Spelling
31. **b.**
32. **c.**
33. **b.**
34. **a.**
35. **a.**
36. **b.**
37. **d.**
38. **b.**
39. **b.**
40. **d.**
41. **a.**
42. **b.**
44. **a.**
45. **b.**

## Section Four: Reading Comprehension
50. **a.** The passage states *that the Boggs Act and the Narcotics Control Act set mandatory sentences for drug crimes, including marijuana.*
51. **a.** The third sentence tells you that the show has been seen for almost four decades; a decade is 10 years, so 40 years is the best answer.

52. **a.** The last sentence of the first paragraph contains this information.
53. **b.** The second sentence of the second paragraph contains this information.
54. **c.** The passage provides the number of homicides in Germany (862) and tells you that the U.S. figure was 20 times higher; you must multiply 862 × 20 to derive the answer.
55. **a.** The last two sentences of the second paragraph present this comparison.
56. **b.** Mr. Hensley has forced open the door and has told police he is waiting for his wife. Choice **a** is incorrect; Mr. Hensley's child hid from him in a closet, and he evidently didn't try to get the child to come out. Choice **c** is incorrect, because Mr. Hensley has a residence of his own at 1917 Roosevelt. Mr. Hensley evidently didn't intend peaceful reconciliation (choice **d**), since he kicked the door in.
57. **d.** The first sentence of the passage states that the complaint was anonymous.
58. **a.** The door had been kicked in. The officers didn't know any of the other facts until after they were inside the house.
59. **c.** Mr. Hensley spoke to the police *calmly*, and he made a seemingly matter-of-fact statement. There is no indication in the passage that Mr. Hensley was enraged at police or that he was remorseful or confused.
60. **b.** Based on the information that Mrs. Hensley has an Order of Protection stating that Mr. Hensley is not to have contact with her or his child, it can be inferred that he does not currently live at the house at 826 Rosemary Lane.

## Answer Key: Part Two

1. high
2. college
3. time
4. no
5. costs
6. free
7. expensive
8. get
9. provide
10. who
11. best
12. than
13. lawbreakers
14. education

15. more
16. reason
17. way
18. deny
19. prison
20. they
21. bring
22. lives
23. officers
24. of
25. extremes
26. when
27. answer
28. joined

29. that
30. found
31. should
32. or
33. eyes
34. fellow
35. choice
36. corruption
37. result
38. cost
39. betrayed
40. force

## Scoring

Scoring this exam is identical to Practice Exam 1. Since each correct answer was worth one point, your total number of correct answers gives you your percentage. Since most police departments require a score of at least 70 percent, you will need to answer at least 70 questions correctly in a 100 question exam. If you did not improve your score from the earlier practice exams, try to analyze where your errors are occurring. Closely review the review chapters in this book that discuss the areas you are having the most difficulty. Once you have completed your review, consider retaking a practice exam you have already completed before going on to a new one. Taking the same exam more than once, particularly if you separate your test-taking by a few days or even a week, may provide you with a deeper understanding of where your difficulties are arising.

In addition to studying, give some thought to whether your nerves are preventing you from doing well on the practice exams. If that is the case, try to give yourself positive motivation so that you do not undermine the benefits of study by allowing yourself to become too jittery or tense before taking the practice exams. To boost your own confidence, remind yourself that the practice exams will help you prepare for your actual test—and give you a strong advantage over those who come into the test site unprepared.

# 12 ▶ POLICE OFFICER PRACTICE EXAM 5

### CHAPTER SUMMARY

Practice Exam 5 tests map reading, memory, judgment, common sense, reading, and math. It is similar in structure to Practice Exam 2. Compare your performance specifically with Practice Exam 2, but also with the other practice exams you have completed.

**T**his practice exam is an example of a test that focuses on job-related skills. Even if the exam you take does not look exactly like this one, many police exams test for the same skills, so taking the exam will provide you with important practice and with an opportunity to analyze your test-taking abilities.

In addition to the pencils you will need to fill in the answer sheet, try to take this exam using an alarm clock or stopwatch. Set the timer for 15 minutes to study the memory materials that come directly after the answer sheet. Then reset your timer for $2\frac{1}{2}$ hours, which is about the amount of time you can expect on an actual test to answer 100 questions. To do this properly, you should set aside at least $3\frac{1}{2}$ hours, including the 15-minute study time, the time for the test, and time after the test to review your answers and see where you need to continue studying. As in the other practice exam chapters, the study material, answer sheet, and test questions are followed by an explanation of the correct answers and information on how to score your exam.

## Police Officer Practice Exam 5

| | | | | | | | | | | | | | | |
|---|---|---|---|---|---|---|---|---|---|---|---|---|---|---|
| 1. | ⓐ | ⓑ | ⓒ | ⓓ | 36. | ⓐ | ⓑ | ⓒ | ⓓ | 71. | ⓐ | ⓑ | ⓒ | ⓓ |
| 2. | ⓐ | ⓑ | ⓒ | ⓓ | 37. | ⓐ | ⓑ | ⓒ | ⓓ | 72. | ⓐ | ⓑ | ⓒ | ⓓ |
| 3. | ⓐ | ⓑ | ⓒ | ⓓ | 38. | ⓐ | ⓑ | ⓒ | ⓓ | 73. | ⓐ | ⓑ | ⓒ | ⓓ |
| 4. | ⓐ | ⓑ | ⓒ | ⓓ | 39. | ⓐ | ⓑ | ⓒ | ⓓ | 74. | ⓐ | ⓑ | ⓒ | ⓓ |
| 5. | ⓐ | ⓑ | ⓒ | ⓓ | 40. | ⓐ | ⓑ | ⓒ | ⓓ | 75. | ⓐ | ⓑ | ⓒ | ⓓ |
| 6. | ⓐ | ⓑ | ⓒ | ⓓ | 41. | ⓐ | ⓑ | ⓒ | ⓓ | 76. | ⓐ | ⓑ | ⓒ | ⓓ |
| 7. | ⓐ | ⓑ | ⓒ | ⓓ | 42. | ⓐ | ⓑ | ⓒ | ⓓ | 77. | ⓐ | ⓑ | ⓒ | ⓓ |
| 8. | ⓐ | ⓑ | ⓒ | ⓓ | 43. | ⓐ | ⓑ | ⓒ | ⓓ | 78. | ⓐ | ⓑ | ⓒ | ⓓ |
| 9. | ⓐ | ⓑ | ⓒ | ⓓ | 44. | ⓐ | ⓑ | ⓒ | ⓓ | 79. | ⓐ | ⓑ | ⓒ | ⓓ |
| 10. | ⓐ | ⓑ | ⓒ | ⓓ | 45. | ⓐ | ⓑ | ⓒ | ⓓ | 80. | ⓐ | ⓑ | ⓒ | ⓓ |
| 11. | ⓐ | ⓑ | ⓒ | ⓓ | 46. | ⓐ | ⓑ | ⓒ | ⓓ | 81. | ⓐ | ⓑ | ⓒ | ⓓ |
| 12. | ⓐ | ⓑ | ⓒ | ⓓ | 47. | ⓐ | ⓑ | ⓒ | ⓓ | 82. | ⓐ | ⓑ | ⓒ | ⓓ |
| 13. | ⓐ | ⓑ | ⓒ | ⓓ | 48. | ⓐ | ⓑ | ⓒ | ⓓ | 83. | ⓐ | ⓑ | ⓒ | ⓓ |
| 14. | ⓐ | ⓑ | ⓒ | ⓓ | 49. | ⓐ | ⓑ | ⓒ | ⓓ | 84. | ⓐ | ⓑ | ⓒ | ⓓ |
| 15. | ⓐ | ⓑ | ⓒ | ⓓ | 50. | ⓐ | ⓑ | ⓒ | ⓓ | 85. | ⓐ | ⓑ | ⓒ | ⓓ |
| 16. | ⓐ | ⓑ | ⓒ | ⓓ | 51. | ⓐ | ⓑ | ⓒ | ⓓ | 86. | ⓐ | ⓑ | ⓒ | ⓓ |
| 17. | ⓐ | ⓑ | ⓒ | ⓓ | 52. | ⓐ | ⓑ | ⓒ | ⓓ | 87. | ⓐ | ⓑ | ⓒ | ⓓ |
| 18. | ⓐ | ⓑ | ⓒ | ⓓ | 53. | ⓐ | ⓑ | ⓒ | ⓓ | 88. | ⓐ | ⓑ | ⓒ | ⓓ |
| 19. | ⓐ | ⓑ | ⓒ | ⓓ | 54. | ⓐ | ⓑ | ⓒ | ⓓ | 89. | ⓐ | ⓑ | ⓒ | ⓓ |
| 20. | ⓐ | ⓑ | ⓒ | ⓓ | 55. | ⓐ | ⓑ | ⓒ | ⓓ | 90. | ⓐ | ⓑ | ⓒ | ⓓ |
| 21. | ⓐ | ⓑ | ⓒ | ⓓ | 56. | ⓐ | ⓑ | ⓒ | ⓓ | 91. | ⓐ | ⓑ | ⓒ | ⓓ |
| 22. | ⓐ | ⓑ | ⓒ | ⓓ | 57. | ⓐ | ⓑ | ⓒ | ⓓ | 92. | ⓐ | ⓑ | ⓒ | ⓓ |
| 23. | ⓐ | ⓑ | ⓒ | ⓓ | 58. | ⓐ | ⓑ | ⓒ | ⓓ | 93. | ⓐ | ⓑ | ⓒ | ⓓ |
| 24. | ⓐ | ⓑ | ⓒ | ⓓ | 59. | ⓐ | ⓑ | ⓒ | ⓓ | 94. | ⓐ | ⓑ | ⓒ | ⓓ |
| 25. | ⓐ | ⓑ | ⓒ | ⓓ | 60. | ⓐ | ⓑ | ⓒ | ⓓ | 95. | ⓐ | ⓑ | ⓒ | ⓓ |
| 26. | ⓐ | ⓑ | ⓒ | ⓓ | 61. | ⓐ | ⓑ | ⓒ | ⓓ | 96. | ⓐ | ⓑ | ⓒ | ⓓ |
| 27. | ⓐ | ⓑ | ⓒ | ⓓ | 62. | ⓐ | ⓑ | ⓒ | ⓓ | 97. | ⓐ | ⓑ | ⓒ | ⓓ |
| 28. | ⓐ | ⓑ | ⓒ | ⓓ | 63. | ⓐ | ⓑ | ⓒ | ⓓ | 98. | ⓐ | ⓑ | ⓒ | ⓓ |
| 29. | ⓐ | ⓑ | ⓒ | ⓓ | 64. | ⓐ | ⓑ | ⓒ | ⓓ | 99. | ⓐ | ⓑ | ⓒ | ⓓ |
| 30. | ⓐ | ⓑ | ⓒ | ⓓ | 65. | ⓐ | ⓑ | ⓒ | ⓓ | 100. | ⓐ | ⓑ | ⓒ | ⓓ |
| 31. | ⓐ | ⓑ | ⓒ | ⓓ | 66. | ⓐ | ⓑ | ⓒ | ⓓ | | | | | |
| 32. | ⓐ | ⓑ | ⓒ | ⓓ | 67. | ⓐ | ⓑ | ⓒ | ⓓ | | | | | |
| 33. | ⓐ | ⓑ | ⓒ | ⓓ | 68. | ⓐ | ⓑ | ⓒ | ⓓ | | | | | |
| 34. | ⓐ | ⓑ | ⓒ | ⓓ | 69. | ⓐ | ⓑ | ⓒ | ⓓ | | | | | |
| 35. | ⓐ | ⓑ | ⓒ | ⓓ | 70. | ⓐ | ⓑ | ⓒ | ⓓ | | | | | |

# Police Officer Practice Exam 5

## Part One: Memorization and Visualization

You have 15 minutes to study the memory material at the beginning of the exam before starting the practice test, which begins with questions about what you have memorized.

The memory questions are divided into two distinct forms of memorization. The first part contains wanted posters and the second part is an article on law enforcement concerns about the dangers of text mes-saging while driving. After reviewing the posters and reading the article for a total of 15 minutes for both sections, turn the page and answer the test questions about the material. To create the same conditions as the actual test, **do not refer back to the study booklet to answer the questions**.

You have two options when you complete Part One. If you want to continue to create actual test con-ditions, go on directly to the rest of the test. If you are curious about how well you answered these questions, review the answers for this portion before continuing with the rest of the exam.

### WANTED
### Thomas Alberto Velez

**ALIASES:** Bert Velez

**WANTED BY:** King County, WA, Sheriff's Department

**CHARGES:** Robbery

**DESCRIPTION:**

    **Age:** 55

    **Race:** Hispanic

    **Height:** 5'9"

    **Weight:** 200 lbs.

    **Hair:** Bald

    **Eyes:** Brown

**IDENTIFYING SCARS OR MARKS:** Tattoo on left wrist of a bear with the words "el oso" in the animal's body.

**REMARKS:** Wanted for robbing three gas stations along Route 5 between the hours of 9 P.M. and 1 A.M.; generally claims to be a motorist in need of gas who needs to change large bills.

**CAUTION:** Subject is known to carry a .357 caliber Ruger.

## *WANTED*
### Patrick P. O'Brien

**ALIASES:** Patty O'Brien, Paddy O'Brien

**WANTED BY:** Charleston, WV, Police Department

**CHARGES:** Burglary, Solicitation

**DESCRIPTION:**

    **Age:** 25

    **Race:** White

    **Height:** 5'4"

    **Weight:** 125 lbs.

    **Hair:** Blond

    **Eyes:** Hazel

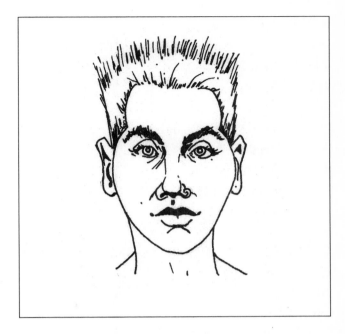

**IDENTIFYING SCARS AND MARKS:** Six-inch surgical scar on left shoulder blade; needle tracks on inner right forearm.

**REMARKS:** Known prostitute, transsexual, and drug addict. Often solicits in Shady Grove area and has been identified as breaking into at least two retail stores in that immediate area. Was last seen dressing as a female with short, orange-tinted hair. Has family in Virginia and may be traveling there by bus.

**CAUTION:** Has been known to carry a switchblade knife and to fight police.

## WANTED
### Ali Mohammad

**ALIASES:** The Sheik, Ali Baba

**WANTED BY:** Dearborn, MI, Police Department

**CHARGES:** Attempted Murder

**DESCRIPTION:**

    **Age:** 27

    **Race:** Middle Eastern

    **Height:** 5'8"

    **Weight:** 190 lbs.

    **Hair:** Black

    **Eyes:** Black

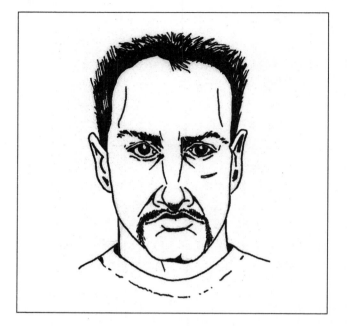

**IDENTIFYING SCARS OR MARKS:** Thin scar on cheek under left eye.

**REMARKS:** Fired at employer Mohammad Arizi after altercation in Arizi's gas station. Frequents riverboat casinos. Often wears a full beard. Speaks with an obvious Middle Eastern accent.

**CAUTION:** Known to carry a .38 caliber revolver, make unknown.

## WANTED
### Michael Adam Rosen

**ALIASES:** Adam Rose, Michael Rose

**WANTED BY:** Vancouver, WA, Police Department

**CHARGES:** Assault with a deadly weapon

**DESCRIPTION:**

> **Age:** 27
> **Race:** White
> **Height:** 6'1"
> **Weight:** 210 lbs.
> **Hair:** Black
> **Eyes:** Brown

**IDENTIFYING SCARS OR MARKS:** Tattoo of a tear drop at the base of left eye, BC Lions logo tattooed on upper right shoulder.

**REMARKS:** Stabbed fellow Devil's Disciple gang member in right upper chest after fight over a female gang member. Left leg is shorter than right leg due to a motorcycle accident; walks with a visible limp. Native of Vancouver, British Columbia, Canada, known to cross the U.S.-Canada border frequently; speaks with an obvious Canadian accent.

# *MISSING*
## Rosa Seranno

**ALIASES:** Rosita Seranno, Little Rosie

**DESCRIPTION:**

    **Age:** 48

    **Race:** Hispanic

    **Height:** 5'4"

    **Weight:** 190 lbs.

    **Hair:** Black

    **Eyes:** Brown

**IDENTIFYING SCARS OR MARKS:** Birthmark under left eye.

**REMARKS:** Wandered away from the Happy Valley home for the developmentally disabled; last seen at Happy Valley train station at 4 P.M. on Monday, September 14. Has run away in the past and been found panhandling at the train station. Understands simple questions and commands but has the mental age of a 9-year-old child; will often answer questions asked in English with a reply in Spanish.

**IF LOCATED:** Call the Happy Valley, FL, Police Department at 305-237-4444 or the Twin County, FL, Transit Police at 305-372-1212.

## Reading Passage

Across the United States, many people in the criminal justice system are turning their attention away from those who are driving while intoxicated to those who are sending text messages while driving.

The nation's toughest law to crack down on text messaging (commonly referred to as texting) behind the wheel was passed in Utah in May 2009, after two scientists were killed by a young man whose truck crossed over the yellow line while he was involved in sending and receiving text messages with his girlfriend. The young man's car clipped the scientists' pickup truck, causing it to spin across the road and turn over, killing both occupants. After an intense investigation by a local police officer to prove that texting caused the accident, state officials passed the new law which calls for up to 15 years in prison when a driver who is texting causes a fatality. This is the same penalty that drunken drivers who kill someone face. Under the law, texting is no longer viewed as an accident but is considered reckless behavior.

Another state that has criminalized distracted driving is Alaska, which passed a law in 2007 that made it a crime punishable by 20 years in prison if a driver causes a fatal accident when a television, video monitor or computer is on inside the vehicle and in the driver's field of vision. That law also covers texting, but does not cover using a phone to make a call. Although not as specific as Utah's law, the Alaska law also stemmed from an accident in which a driver killed two motorists. In that case, the driver was watching a movie on a video monitor mounted on the dashboard of his vehicle.

The U.S. Department of Transportation has been studying what has been called distracted driving rather than drunken driving. The definition includes talking on a cell phone while driving, sending or receiving text messages while driving, or participating in other multitasking activities that take the driver's eyes or attention off the road. Concerns have been rising; the National Highway Traffic Safety Administration estimated that in 2002, one quarter-million accidents and almost 1,000 deaths were could be attributed to drivers' use of cell phones, whether texting or talking.

But changing the law raises complex legal questions. Drunken drivers can be identified by using a Breathalyzer and setting a specific limit to define intoxication (generally a blood alcohol level of .08), but it is more difficult to define being distracted or to prove that someone was so distracted that he or she caused an accident. Although telephone records can be used to prove whether text messages were being sent and received, laws pertaining to search and seizure and privacy can make these records difficult for police to obtain.

Not all people agree on what creates a distraction. While most agree that texting or watching television would be a distraction, what about simply making a cell phone call or talking on a cell phone? This may seem less distracting than hitting keys for sending a text message, but how many people may forget they are driving and start to make gestures or move around in the driver's seat while arguing on the phone or telling a funny story? Another issue with just talking rather than texting is that many states allow drivers to talk on the phone while driving as long as they are using earpieces or wireless headsets, so it is not enough for a police officer to merely observe a driver holding a phone.

Until these issues are resolved, many government agencies have issued rules to employees forbidding them from texting while in their official vehicles. A few have even banned answering or making a cell phone call. At least one U.S. senator and one member of the House of Representatives, both from New York, have called for a federal ban on sending text messages while driving. One auto maker, the Ford Motor Company, has endorsed the suggested legislation. The federal law would make nationwide the text-message bans that by 2009 had been enacted in 14 states and the District of

Columbia. Although a number of groups previously were not in favor of such bans because they would be too difficult to enforce, safety experts and government officials have spoken out in support of the legislation. In polls, members of the public seem to be in over-whelmingly in favor of the texting ban for all drivers.

One group that is not in favor of the law is truck drivers, many of whom receive updated information about deliveries via texts or laptop computer in their truck cabs. A representative of the American Trucking Association has voiced concern that the proposed legis-lation will cost truckers millions of dollars in wasted time if they must pull over to the side of the road to receive information rather than receive it while they are driving. While they do not condone texting while driv-ing, many truckers say that the small computers they have come to rely on require less concentration than using phones while driving. A study by a transportation institute in Virginia disputed this, concluding that truck-ers who used on-board computers had 10 times greater a risk of crashing, nearly crashing, or wandering out of their lane than truckers who did not use them.

Whatever the end result will be, distracted driv-ing is an example of how laws change as technology and gadgets become more readily available and alter what behavior our society deems acceptable.

## Part One: Memorization and Visualization

*Answer questions 1-15 based on the wanted posters you have just studied. Do not refer back to the study material to answer these questions.*

1. Which individuals were involved in incidents that took place in gas stations?
   a. Thomas Alberto Velez and Ali Mohammad
   b. Thomas Alberto Velez and Patrick O'Brien
   c. Ali Mohammad and Michael Adam Rosen
   d. Michael Adam Rosen and Rosa Seranno

2. Which individuals were described as speaking with accents?
   a. Ali Mohammad and Rosa Seranno
   b. Michael Adam Rosen and Thomas Alberto Velez
   c. Ali Mohammad and Michael Adam Rosen
   d. none of the above

3. Which individual was described as possibly answering questions in a language other than English?
   a. Ali Mohammad
   b. Rosa Seranno
   c. Thomas Alberto Velez
   d. Michael Adam Rosen

4. How many individuals were described as having scars on the left sides of their faces?
   a. one
   b. two
   c. three
   d. four

5. How many individuals were described as having tattoos?
   a. one
   b. two
   c. three
   d. four

6. Which individuals are being sought by agencies located in the state of Washington?
   a. Thomas Alberto Velez and Patrick P. O'Brien
   b. Patrick P. O'Brien and Ali Mohammad
   c. Ali Mohammad and Michael Adam Rosen
   d. Michael Adam Rosen and Thomas Alberto Velez

**7.** Which individual is being sought by more than one police department?
   **a.** Michael Adam Rosen
   **b.** Rosa Seranno
   **c.** Patrick P. O'Brien
   **d.** Ali Mohammad

**8.** Which individuals were described as having tattoos of animals?
   **a.** Thomas Alberto Velez and Patrick P. O'Brien
   **b.** Patrick P. O'Brien and Ali Mohammad
   **c.** Ali Mohammad and Michael Adam Rosen
   **d.** Michael Adam Rosen and Thomas Alberto Velez

**9.** How many individuals were described as possibly being armed?
   **a.** one
   **b.** two
   **c.** three
   **d.** four

**10.** Which individuals were described as possibly armed with handguns?
   **a.** Thomas Alberto Velez and Patrick P. O'Brien
   **b.** Thomas Alberto Velez and Ali Mohammad
   **c.** Ali Mohammad and Michael Adam Rosen
   **d.** Michael Adam Rosen and Patrick P. O'Brien

**11.** Which individuals are the most likely to be dressed in women's clothing?
   **a.** Rosa Seranno and Patrick P. O'Brien
   **b.** Rosa Seranno and Michael Adam Rosen
   **c.** Rosa Seranno and Ali Mohammad
   **d.** Rosa Seranno and Thomas Alberto Velez

**12.** Which of the individuals is not being sought for a criminal matter?
   **a.** Thomas Alberto Velez
   **b.** Patrick P. O'Brien
   **c.** Ali Mohammad
   **d.** Rosa Seranno

**13.** Which individual was described as carrying a knife?
   **a.** Thomas Alberto Velez
   **b.** Patrick P. O'Brien
   **c.** Ali Mohammad
   **d.** Rosa Seranno

**14.** Which individual was described as a drug addict?
   **a.** Thomas Alberto Velez
   **b.** Patrick P. O'Brien
   **c.** Ali Mohammad
   **d.** Michael Adam Rosen

**15.** The remarks on which two individuals made mention of public transportation?
   **a.** Rosa Seranno and Thomas Alberto Velez
   **b.** Ali Mohammad and Patrick P. O'Brien
   **c.** Rosa Seranno and Patrick P. O'Brien
   **d.** Rosa Seranno and Michael Adam Rosen

*Answer questions 16–30 based on the reading passage. Do not refer back to the study material to answer these questions.*

**16.** A good title for the reading passage is
   **a.** Issues Surrounding Driving While Intoxicated.
   **b.** Issues Surrounding Driving While Texting.
   **c.** Utah Passes a Law Against Texting.
   **d.** Alaska Passes a Law Against TVs in Automobiles.

**17.** The law that made texting while driving a felony
was based on the principle that texting is
   **a.** unnecessary.
   **b.** the same as being drunk.
   **c.** reckless behavior.
   **d.** foolish behavior.

**18.** The state that has made driving while text messaging a felony is
   **a.** Utah.
   **b.** New York.
   **c.** Alaska.
   **d.** Virginia.

**19.** The state that has made it a felony to cause a fatal
accident when a television, video monitor or
computer is on inside the car and in the driver's
field of vision is
   **a.** Utah.
   **b.** New York.
   **c.** Alaska.
   **d.** Virginia.

**20.** At least one U.S. senator and one member of the
House of Representatives have called for a federal
ban on text messaging while driving. Both are
from which state?
   **a.** Utah
   **b.** New York
   **c.** Alaska
   **d.** Virginia.

**21.** Driving while text messaging has been compared
to what other crime?
   **a.** homicide
   **b.** motor vehicle theft
   **c.** driving while intoxicated
   **d.** none of the above

**22.** The cause of the accident in which the driver
killed two scientists was discovered by
   **a.** intense police investigation.
   **b.** a confession by the driver.
   **c.** a confession by the person the driver was text
   messaging.
   **d.** statements by the defendant's mother.

**23.** Information cited in the passage about the number of deaths and accidents caused by distracted
drivers was compiled by the
   **a.** Department of Justice.
   **b.** Department of Motor Vehicles.
   **c.** National Highway Traffic Safety
   Administration.
   **d.** United States Congress.

**24.** The number of accidents recorded in 2002 that
were attributed to drivers' use of cell phones was
   **a.** 100.
   **b.** 1,000.
   **c.** 250,000.
   **d.** 500,000.

**25.** According to the passage, the number of deaths
in 2002 that were attributed to drivers' use of cell
phones was about
   **a.** 100.
   **b.** 1,000.
   **c.** 250,000.
   **d.** 500,000.

**26.** The passage states that concerns about texting
have led some government agencies forbid their
employees from
   **a.** taking their official cars home.
   **b.** texting while driving.
   **c.** taking passengers in their vehicles.
   **d.** all of the above

**27.** By 2009, text messaging bans had been enacted by
   **a.** Utah and Alaska.
   **b.** Utah, Alaska, and New York.
   **c.** 14 states and the District of Columbia.
   **d.** the U.S. Congress.

**28.** What group is mentioned as having voiced displeasure over increased oversight of communications in moving vehicles?
   **a.** the auto industry
   **b.** the association representing truckers
   **c.** the auto industry with the exception of the Ford Motor Company
   **d.** the telecommunications industry

**29.** The polls cited in the passage indicate that members of the public
   **a.** are against a ban on texting in moving vehicles.
   **b.** are undecided on a ban on texting in moving vehicles.
   **c.** are of different opinions based on age and income.
   **d.** are in favor of a ban on texting in moving vehicles.

**30.** According to the passage, what area of law could make enforcing laws on texting or using phone in vehicles difficult to enforce?
   **a.** Laws involving driving while intoxicated.
   **b.** Laws surrounding search and seizure.
   **c.** Laws surrounding stop and frisk.
   **d.** none of the above

## Part Two: Reading Skills
### Map 1

Answer questions 31–35 based on Map 1. Review the directional arrows and the map key. You are not permitted to go the wrong way on a one-way street.

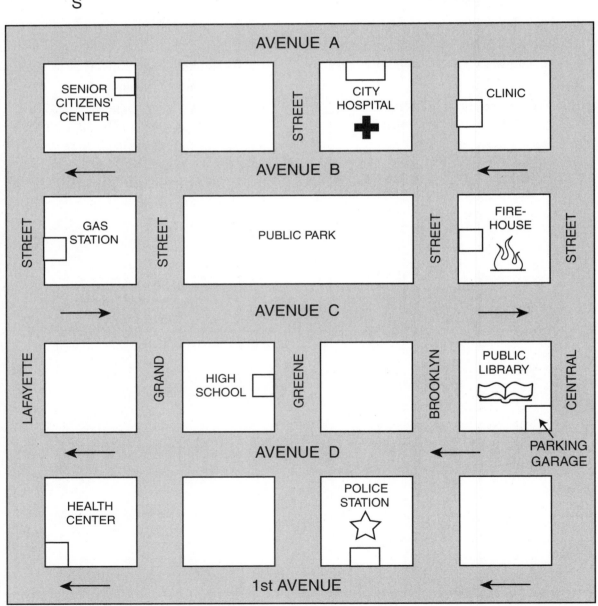

**31.** A library patron has decided to purchase gas before heading home. She exits the library garage directly onto Avenue D. Without disobeying any traffic regulations, her quickest route to the gas station is
   **a.** north on Central Street to Avenue C, then west on Avenue C to the gas station.
   **b.** west on Brooklyn Street to Avenue B, then north on Avenue B to the gas station.
   **c.** west on Avenue D to Grand Street, then north on Grand Street to the gas station.
   **d.** west on Avenue D to Lafayette Street, then north on Lafayette Street to the gas station.

**32.** You are on foot patrol in front of the Brooklyn Street entrance to the firehouse when an elderly man stops you and asks you for directions to the senior citizens' center. You should tell him to
   **a.** walk across the street to the senior citizens' center.
   **b.** walk north on Brooklyn Street, then west on Avenue B, then north on Grand Street.
   **c.** walk south on Brooklyn Street, then west on Avenue C, then north on Grand Street.
   **d.** walk north on Brooklyn Street, then west on Avenue B, the north on Lafayette Street, then east on Avenue A, and the south on Grand Street.

**33.** Dr. Raji works at the health center and frequently sees patients at the city hospital. He prefers to avoid traffic around the high school and pubic park as much as possible. To do this, his best legal route from the health center to the hospital is
   **a.** west on 1st Avenue, north on Lafayette Street, then east on Avenue A.
   **b.** west on 1st Avenue, north on Lafayette Street, east on Avenue C, north on Brooklyn Street, and then west on Avenue A.

   **c.** east on 1st Avenue, north on Central Street, then west on Avenue A.
   **d.** west on 1st Avenue, north on Lafayette Street, east on Avenue B, north on Greene Street, and then east on Avenue A.

**34.** Your brother-in-law is a paramedic at the city hospital who goes to the library every Monday night to study for his nursing degree. His shortest legal route from the hospital to the library is
   **a.** west on Avenue A, south on Lafayette Street, east on Avenue C, and then south on Central Street to the library entrance.
   **b.** east on Avenue B and south on Central Street to the library entrance.
   **c.** west on Avenue A, south on Lafayette Street, and then east on Avenue D to the library entrance.
   **d.** east on Avenue A, then south on Central Street to the library entrance.

**35.** You and your partner are dispatched from the police station to a fight at the northwest corner of the public park. The most direct legal route to drive there is
   **a.** east to Central Street, north on Central Street to Avenue B, and west on Avenue B to Grand Street.
   **b.** west to Grand Street, then north on Grand Street to Avenue B.
   **c.** east to Brooklyn Street, north on Brooklyn Street to Avenue B, and west on Avenue B to Grand Street.
   **d.** west to Greene Street, north on Green Street to Avenue C, and east on Avenue C to Brooklyn Street.

## Map 2

*Answer questions 36–40 based on Map 2. Review the directional arrows and the map key. You are not permitted to go the wrong way on a one-way street.*

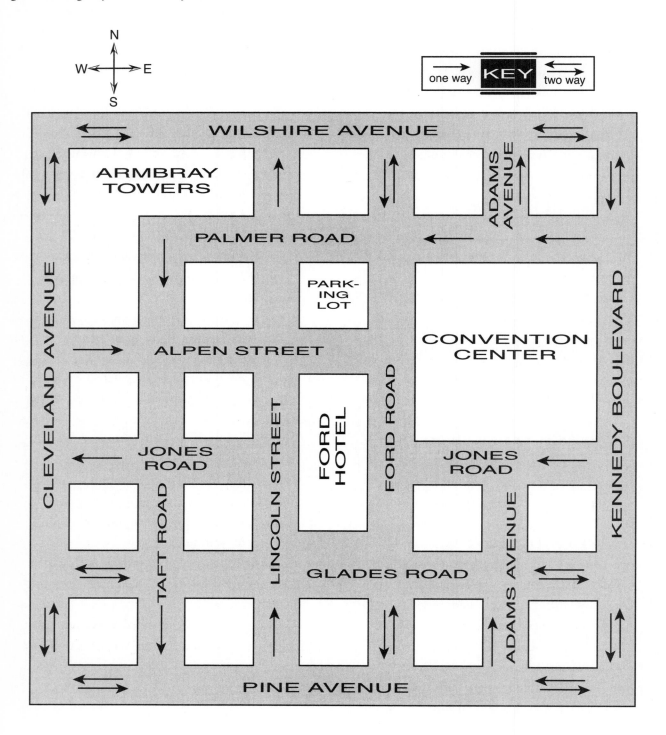

**36.** Officers Adamo and DelBello are parked facing north on Lincoln Street just past Alpen Street when they are notified by the dispatcher to respond to an accident involving a car and a motorcycle that occurred at the intersection of Adams Avenue and Pine Avenue. Obeying all traffic regulations, their most direct route to the accident is to

 **a.** continue north on Lincoln Street, then east on Wilshire Avenue, then south on Ford Road, then east on Glade Road, and then south on Adams Avenue to the accident scene.

 **b.** continue north on Lincoln Street, then west on Palmer Road, then south on Taft Road, and then east on Pine Avenue to the accident scene.

 **c.** make a U-turn on Lincoln Street, then south on Lincoln Street, and then east on Pine Avenue to the accident scene.

 **d.** continue north on Lincoln Street, then east on Wilshire Avenue, then south on Kennedy Boulevard, and then west on Pine Avenue to the accident scene.

**37.** Officer Romuldo is driving southbound on Kennedy Boulevard when he makes a right turn onto Glade Road, then a left onto Taft Road, a right onto Pine Avenue, another right onto Cleveland Avenue, and, finally, a right onto Wilshire Avenue. In which direction is Officer Romuldo now facing?

 **a.** north

 **b.** south

 **c.** east

 **d.** west

**38.** The number of roadways designated avenues that are two-way is

 **a.** one.

 **b.** two.

 **c.** three.

 **d.** four.

**39.** The number of roadways (whether streets, avenues, roads, or boulevards) designated one-way is

 **a.** two.

 **b.** four.

 **c.** six.

 **d.** eight.

**40.** Officers Touhy and Castro are on foot patrol in front of Ambray Towers walking south on Cleveland Avenue when they are dispatched to the entrance of the Ford Hotel on Ford Road between Glades Road and Alpen Street. To reach this entrance with a minimum number of turns, their best route is to

 **a.** continue south on Cleveland Avenue, turn east at Alpen Street, and then south at Ford Road.

 **b.** continue south on Cleveland Avenue, turn east at Jones Road, north at Lincoln Street, east at Alpen Street, and then south at Ford Road.

 **c.** turn around to head north on Cleveland Avenue, turn east on Wilshire Avenue, then south at Ford Road.

 **d.** turn around to head north on Cleveland Avenue, turn east on Wilshire Avenue, south on Lincoln Street, east on Alpen Street, and south at Ford Road.

## Map 3

*Answer questions 41–45 based on Map 3. Note that the directional arrow can be found within the section of the map designated Park Savannah.*

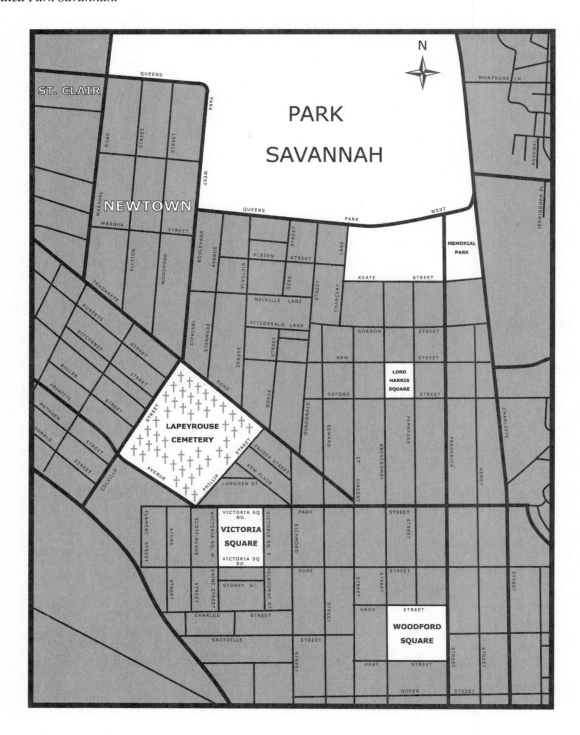

**41.** The St. Clair section is located in what direction from the Newtown section?
   **a.** southwest
   **b.** southeast
   **c.** northeast
   **d.** northwest

**42.** The streets that pass Memorial Park on the west and east are
   **a.** Queens Park West and Keate Street.
   **b.** Queens Park West and Gordon Street.
   **c.** Frederick Street and Charlotte Street.
   **d.** Frederick Street and Henry Street.

**43.** The streets that provide direct routes from Park Savannah to Lapeyrouse Cemetery are
   **a.** Victoria Avenue and Cipriani Boulevard.
   **b.** Victoria Avenue, Stanmore Avenue, and Cipriani Boulevard.
   **c.** Dundonald Street and Stanmore Avenue.
   **d.** Borde Street, Victoria Avenue, and Stanmore Avenue.

**44.** You are on foot patrol at the northeast corner of Woodford Square and have been dispatched to a report of a sick person at the closest corner of Victoria Square. Your most direct path to reach the ill individual would be to walk
   **a.** north to Duke Street and west to the intersection of Victoria Square South and Victoria Square East.
   **b.** south to Sackville Street and east to Victoria Square.
   **c.** north to Park Street and west to the intersection of Victoria Square North and Victoria Square East.
   **d.** north to Park Street and east to the intersection of Victoria Square North and Park Street.

**45.** You are on foot patrol at the northeast corner of Victoria Square and have been dispatched to a report of a fight at the southwest corner of Lord Harris Square. Your most direct path to reach the location would be to walk
   **a.** east on Park Street and north on Abercromby Street to the intersection with Oxford Street.
   **b.** east on Park Street and north on Pembroke Street to the intersection with Oxford Street.
   **c.** east on Park Street, north on Vincent Street, and east on Oxford Street to Abercromby Street.
   **d.** east on Park Street and north on Pembroke Street to the intersection with New Street.

## Reading Passage 1

*Answer questions 46-50 based on the following passage.*

Many police departments have begun to use a new method of photo lineups. The new technique is called sequential blind photo lineups because instead of showing a witness four or six suspects' photos at the same time, the witnesses are shown the photos one after another—in sequence instead of all together.

Among the largest police departments using this system are Dallas, Boston, Minneapolis, and Denver. Their goal is to limit the number of situations in which witnesses make mistakes trying to identify suspects, but most departments nationwide still continue to use the traditional six-pack of photos that are shown to witnesses in one group, even though the misidentification rate for the old method is higher than for the new one.

As another protection against misidentification, in the sequential system, detectives do not know who the suspect is. This prevents them from giving intentional or unintentional hints to a witness to look at one of the photos more carefully or longer than at the others. An unintentional clue by a detective might be holding his or her breath when a witness points at one photo amongst the group or smiling slightly to show pleasure if the witness seems to linger over the photo the detective knows is the suspect.

Many police departments also want to improve their identification rates when they conduct lineups. One way they do this is by assuring witnesses that they will continue to investigate a case even if a positive identification is not made. Police have found that this reduces the pressure on the witness to choose one of the suspects in the lineup out of fear that without an indentification, the case would no longer be investigated.

A nationally known expert on police identification methods praised the changes, citing an analysis of 26 studies that showed that presenting mug shots sequentially resulted in fewer identifications, but that these identifications were more accurate. Lowering the percentage of misidentifications is very important to the police and to the criminal justice system so that innocent people are not convicted based on a witness's incorrect identification. According to the Innocence Project, a New York legal center specializing in overturning wrongful convictions, more than 75% of those who have been released from prison after DNA analysis indicated they could not have committed the crime, but were sent to prison based on witness misidentification.

**46.** A good title for this passage would be
   **a.** New Approaches to Identifying Suspects.
   **b.** Wrongful Convictions.
   **c.** Criticizing the Police.
   **d.** Changes in the Dallas Police Department.

**47.** The new photo lineup system shows witnesses the photos of suspects
   **a.** all at the same time.
   **b.** in groups of four.
   **c.** in groups of six.
   **d.** one at a time.

**48.** One major reason given for the new system is that it
   **a.** takes longer so the detective makes more overtime.
   **b.** results in fewer misidentifications.
   **c.** takes less time because the photos are shown for only a few seconds.
   **d.** No reason for the change is explained in the passage.

**49.** The passage states that the detectives who are showing the photos do not know which photo shows the suspect in order to ensure that
   **a.** the suspect goes free.
   **b.** the witness is less likely to be frightened of the suspects.
   **c.** the detective does not intentionally or unintentionally influence the witness.
   **d.** No reason is explained in the passage.

**50.** According to the passage, lowering the percentages of misidentifications is important so that
   **a.** detectives' time is not wasted on cases that cannot be fully investigated.
   **b.** witnesses' time is not wasted looking at photos of people who could not possible have committed the crime.
   **c.** witnesses are not intimidated by the suspects whose photos they view.
   **d.** people are not convicted of crimes they did not commit.

## Reading Passage 2

*Answer questions 51–55 based on the following passage.*

A 2009 study conducted on the use of body armor by law enforcement agencies found that almost all the agencies surveyed provided body armor to officers, but that only 59% of the agencies required the officer to wear the armor—and even then, the requirement applied only some of the time. The study was conducted by the Police Executive Research Forum (PERF) in partnership with the Department of Justice's Bureau of Justice Administration and was based on a nationally representative sample of law enforcement agencies. Of those who received the survey, 80%, or 782 agencies, responded.

Fully 99% of the agencies ensured that body armor was available to officers either by purchasing it for them or by providing a cash allowance for them to purchase it on their own. This is a large increase over past surveys: In 1987, only 28% of agencies surveyed did this; by 1993, the percentage had climbed to 82%; and by 2000 it was over 90%.

Although 59% of the responding agencies mandate that body armor be worn at least some of the time, fewer than half of these have a written policy, making enforcement difficult. Also, only 29% provide trauma plates for added protection to an officer's torso. Many agencies also did not have fit or maintenance policies; 12% said officers were not fitted for body armor other than receiving a size that approximates their body size, and that 90% of the agencies did not conduct inspections to ensure that the armor fits well or is properly maintained. Lastly, about 25% of the agencies had no policy concerning replacement of old or worn body armor, nor was there information on how often they actually replace the officers' body armor.

Among the improvements that agencies can make in their polices and practices, PERF suggested that agencies provide controls on fitting armor to individual officers, create policies on maintenance of the equipment, and also undertake periodic inspections to assure that the body armor is in good condition.

**51.** A good title for this passage would be
   **a.** What To Do With Worn Body Armor.
   **b.** Improving Police Body Armor.
   **c.** Why Police Don't Wear Their Body Armor.
   **d.** Providing Body Armor to Police Officers.

**52.** Approximately what percentage of police departments have policies requiring officers to wear their body armor at least some of the time?
- **a.** 25%
- **b.** 60%
- **c.** 75%
- **d.** 100%

**53.** About what percentage of police departments have replacement policies pertaining to body armor?
- **a.** 25%
- **b.** 59%
- **c.** 90%
- **d.** 99%

**54.** From the passage, you can infer that those who undertook the study would like to see
- **a.** officers have more freedom to decide when to wear their body armor.
- **b.** stronger policies within police departments mandating that officers wear their body armor.
- **c.** less emphasis placed on body armor and the dangers of policing.
- **d.** Since this was a study, it is improper to infer anything.

**55.** Since 1987, the percentages of departments that ensure that body armor is available to officers has
- **a.** increased.
- **b.** decreased.
- **c.** stayed the same.
- **d.** been influenced by the economy.

## Reading Passage 3

*Answer questions 56–60 based on the following passage.*

Identify theft comes in many forms. It is the act of stealing someone's unique, personal identifying information to commit crimes such as stealing funds out of bank or financial accounts, or to completely assume someone else's identity to run up debts while fraudulently using that victim's name. The effects on these victims may not be only financial; they often extend deeper into victims' reputations and personal lives.

One of the newer and more notorious forms of identity theft is known as phishing. To commit this crime, identity thieves create e-mails and websites that mimic those of well-known organizations such as banks, corporations, and government agencies to trick users into believing they are disclosing their personal information for legitimate purposes.

There is no one law enforcement agency responsible for investigating identity theft crimes, and because identity theft is constantly evolving and is still considered by many to be a nontraditional crime, the lack of proper training and knowledge of the subject have created serious obstacles to law enforcement agencies in fighting identity theft and prosecuting its perpetrators.

**56.** Which of the following is identified by the passage as a challenge for law enforcement officials?
- **a.** Identify theft perpetrators are extremely difficult to apprehend.
- **b.** Many law enforcement agencies lack training in identity theft crimes.
- **c.** Many identity theft victims fail to come forward.
- **d.** Businesses tend to cover up identity theft crimes.

**57.** Based on the passage, which of the following is something an identity thief would NOT be interested in?
  **a.** bank account number
  **b.** full name
  **c.** Social Security number
  **d.** credit card number

**58.** According to details from the passage, which of the following would be an example of identity theft?
  **a.** taking out a loan in another person's name
  **b.** stealing a wallet that contains another person's personal identification
  **c.** using an alias
  **d.** any nontraditional crime

**59.** According to the passage, which of the following is NOT true?
  **a.** There is not one specific law enforcement agency responsible for investigating identity theft.
  **b.** Phishers use information for criminal purposes, such as identity theft and fraud.
  **c.** Phishing is the most common form of identity theft.
  **d.** Identity theft is still considered a nontraditional crime.

**60.** What would be the best title for this passage?
  **a.** Identity Theft: A Modern Crime
  **b.** Phishers and Fraud
  **c.** Identity Theft: Causes and Prevention
  **d.** Information Super-Highway Fraud

## Part Three: Judgment and Problem Solving

These questions ask you to use good judgment and common sense, along with the information provided, to answer each of the questions. Some passages may be followed by more than one question pertaining to the same set of facts.

*Use the following information to answer questions 61–62.*

Officer Velez is on foot patrol a block away from a nursing home when he receives a radio dispatch concerning a resident who has wandered away from the home. Based on information he receives, he is able to locate the resident and return her to the home. His scratch sheet on this case reads as follows:

| | |
|---|---|
| Date of occurrence: | October 3, 2009 |
| Time of occurrence: | Approximately 5:30 P.M. |
| Place of occurrence: | Rock Creek Nursing Home |
| Reporting person: | Suzanne Hannon |
| Resident: | Bertie Jones |
| Disposition: | Ms. Jones located at Rock Creek Railroad Station and returned to the nursing home. |

**61.** Officer Velez is writing up his aided case report. Which of the following expresses the above information most clearly and accurately?

    **a.** A resident, Suzanne Hannon, was found at Rock Creek Railroad Station at approximately 5:30 P.M. after wandering away from the Rock Creek Nursing Home; I brought her back to the home.

    **b.** On October 3, 2009, at approximately 5:30 P.M., Suzanne Hannon reported resident Bertie Jones missing from the Rock Creek Nursing Home. The resident was located at the Rock Creek Railroad Station by me and was returned to the nursing home.

    **c.** Bertie Jones was found at Rock Creed Railroad Station and taken to the Rock Creek Nursing Home at about 5:30 P.M. on October 3, 2009.

    **d.** On October 3, 2009, at approximately 5:30 P.M. Bertie Jones reported resident Suzanne Hannon missing from the Rock Creek Nursing Home. The resident was located at the Rock Creek Railroad Station by me and was returned to the nursing home.

**62.** Of the following assumptions you might make based on the fact pattern, which is the most likely to be accurate based on the material provided?

    **a.** Bertie Jones suffers from dementia.

    **b.** Suzanne Hannon works at the nursing home.

    **c.** Bertie Jones runs away from the nursing home regularly.

    **d.** Suzanne Hannon is Bertie Jones' private duty nurse.

The use of warnings may sometimes provide a satisfactory solution to a problem and may enhance the public perception of the department. Normally, the use of a warning occurs in traffic offenses, but warnings may occasionally be applied to misdemeanor criminal offenses. In determining whether a warning should be issued, the officer should consider:

1. the seriousness of the offense
2. the likelihood that the violator will heed the warning
3. the reputation of the violator, (i.e., known repeat offender, has received previous warnings, etc.)

**63.** Which of the following is the best example of a situation in which a police officer might issue a warning?

    **a.** a city councilperson who has been stopped for drunk driving

    **b.** a known heroin addict who is trespassing in an abandoned building

    **c.** a group of 14-year-old boys who are throwing rocks at each other

    **d.** a 35-year-old woman on probation for shoplifting who has been detained for stealing $2 from a local store

**64.** Which of the following is a situation where a police officer could NOT issue a warning?

    **a.** a minor traffic violation

    **b.** a ten-year-old who shoplifted a candy bar

    **c.** a felony assault

    **d.** a city councilperson accused of trespassing

**65.** Which of the following is the best situation for a police officer to issue a warning?
   **a.** a foreign tourist accused of stealing $500
   **b.** a 22-year-old soldier, home on leave, who is drunk in public
   **c.** an offender who has a warrant for failing to appear in court
   **d.** a 35-year-old man with an out-of-state driver's license who is accused of fraud

**66.** Last month, Officer Meadows had more arrests than Officer Ash. Officer Ash had more arrests than Officer Westerman, but fewer than Officer Governale. Which officer had the fewest arrests?
   **a.** Officer Ash
   **b.** Officer Governale
   **c.** Officer Meadows
   **d.** Officer Westerman

*Answer questions 67–71 based on the following passage.*

At approximately 8:15 A.M. on a sunny morning, Helen Moreno of 1523 Morton Avenue called her local police department to report a vehicle accident on Morton Avenue near Farley Street. She said she had just arrived home when she heard a collision from her living room. When Officer Rayburn arrived on the scene at 8:20 A.M. he observed three vehicles, including an armored truck, that all appeared to have been involved in the collision. He also observed that the driver of a green sedan that appeared to have been involved in the collision appeared to be unconscious. He checked the injured driver, who was not bleeding, and covered him with a blanket provided by Mrs. Moreno while notifying the dispatcher to send an ambulance and additional backup officers to the scene. Martin Wilcox of 1526 Morton Avenue, a passenger in the green sedan, identified the driver as Henry Woolf, his brother-in-law, who also resided at 1526 Morton Avenue. Mrs. Moreno identified the third vehicle involved in the accident, a blue convertible, as her car.

The ambulance arrived at 8:24 A.M. One minute later, four additional officers arrived, including Lieutenant Watts, who became the senior officer at the scene. She assigned Officers Rayburn and Stein to block off both streets and control local traffic, Officer Washington to securing the armored truck, and Officer Parisi to examine the skid marks on Farley Street. Wilcox told Watts that Woolf had stopped at the "T" intersection and then turned left onto Morton Avenue. Wilcox further explained that the driver's side of the vehicle in which he was a passenger was almost immediately struck by the truck, which was skidding down Morton. The impact caused the Woolf vehicle to strike Moreno's convertible. Frank Burroughs, the armored truck's driver, told Washington that he had been due at Security Bank at 8:10 A.M. and that his brakes had failed. He stated that he had not been speeding. After checking with the lieutenant and with Parisi, Washington issued Burroughs citations for speeding, for failing to obey a stop sign, and for giving false information in a traffic investigation.

**67.** Which of the following can be concluded about the Morton Avenue-Farley Street intersection?
   **a.** There were at least two stop signs there.
   **b.** Farley Street is a one-way street.
   **c.** Morton Avenue runs north and south.
   **d.** No cars were parked near the intersection.

**68.** Which scenario best represents the order in which the accident occurred?
  **a.** The Woolf vehicle struck the Moreno convertible, which struck the armored truck.
  **b.** The armored truck struck the Woolf vehicle, which struck the Moreno convertible.
  **c.** The Moreno vehicle struck, the armored truck, which struck the Woolf vehicle.
  **d.** The armored truck struck the Moreno convertible, which struck the Woolf vehicle.

**69.** Who examined evidence relating to Frank Burroughs's claim that his brakes failed?
  **a.** Officer Rayburn
  **b.** Officer Stein
  **c.** Officer Washington
  **d.** Officer Parisi

**70.** Which vehicle had been traveling on Farley Street?
  **a.** the green sedan
  **b.** the blue convertible
  **c.** the armored truck
  **d.** the ambulance

**71.** Which of the following can be concluded about Helen Moreno's convertible?
  **a.** It was parked on a steep incline.
  **b.** It was parked across the street from the Moreno residence.
  **c.** It was struck by the armored truck.
  **d.** It was unoccupied at the time of the accident.

**72.** Officer Greene has completed a radar assignment in the school zone near West High School. Before he starts his motorcycle, his foot slips on the kickstand, and the motorcycle falls over onto its left side. Officer Greene sees that both tires are on the ground, so he places both hands on the handle bars. What should the officer do now?
  **a.** Turn the ignition switch to off.
  **b.** Rock the bike on its engine guards.
  **c.** Position the bike so that the tires are touching the ground.
  **d.** Stand the bike upright.

**73.** The streets are slick following a brief rain. Officer Woodrow rolls her motorcycle to a stop at a red light. Her right foot slips, and she drops the motorcycle onto its right side. She turns the engine off at the ignition switch. What should she do next?
  **a.** Put the kickstand down so the bike can rest on it.
  **b.** Rock the bike on its engine guards to build momentum.
  **c.** Place both hands on the handlebars.
  **d.** Position the bike so that both tires are touching the ground.

**74.** Officer Wilson is on a motorcycle in pursuit of a vehicle that has refused to pull over for him. As the suspect and Officer Wilson reach Anderson Lane, the suspect makes a sharp left turn. Officer Wilson makes the turn too fast, and the motorcycle slides out from under him. He runs to the bike. What should he do next?
  **a.** Quickly stand the motorcycle upright and continue the pursuit.
  **b.** Turn off the ignition.
  **c.** Radio a description of the suspect vehicle, and then rock the bike on the engine guards.
  **d.** Put the kickstand down so that the bike will have something to rest on when he stands it up.

**75.** Officer North has been a police officer for 15 years, which is six years fewer than Officer Wilson but seven more than Officer Trainor. Officer Sanchez has been a police officer for five years more than Officer Trainor. How many years has Officer Sanchez been a police officer?
   **a.** 15
   **b.** 13
   **c.** 9
   **d.** 5

*Answer questions 76 and 77 based on the following definition.*

Reckless endangerment occurs when a person engages in conduct which creates a substantial risk of serious physical injury to another person, and when that person is aware of this risk of the conduct but continues anyway.

**76.** Which situation is the best example of reckless endangerment?
   **a.** Tom, an electrical worker on a bridge, walks on a narrow beam a hundred feet above a river, even though if he falls he is likely to die. He has been previously warned of this danger by his supervisor.
   **b.** Jeanette, a warehouse security guard, fires her weapon at an armed robber who is firing at her, missing the robber but almost hitting a woman who is walking past the warehouse.
   **c.** Peter stands adjacent to commuter railroad tracks and throws rocks at a moving train, trying to break as many windows as he can hit, even though he was previously warned by railroad police officers that this could cause serious injury and he would be arrested if observed doing so again.
   **d.** Suzanne accepts a dare to wade into the ocean on a day that a storm is believed to be brewing.

**77.** Based on the definition, two required elements of reckless endangerment are
   **a.** knowledge and conduct.
   **b.** knowledge and having been previously warned.
   **c.** conduct and ignorance.
   **d.** none of the above.

**78.** Fred is a business owner downtown who makes it well known that he hates the police and thinks they are all corrupt. Fred runs a red light downtown, almost causing a van to hit him, and then pulls over in front of his store, cursing loudly about the other driver's driving skills. Officer Martinez was standing on the corner and watched Fred run the light. What should he do?
   **a.** Write Fred a citation for running a red light.
   **b.** Warn Fred not to run red lights and hope this improves Fred's opinion of police.
   **c.** Suggest to Fred that he take defensive driving classes.
   **d.** Look into having someone check the timing of the lights in the downtown area.

**79.** Extortion is a less serious crime than burglary. Breaking and entering is more serious than extortion, but less serious than assault. Assault is more serious than burglary. Which crime is the most serious?
   **a.** burglary
   **b.** breaking and entering
   **c.** assault
   **d.** extortion

*Use the following information to answer questions 80–82.*

After arresting a suspect, officers should conduct a search for weapons and contraband by doing the following:

1. Make sure the prisoner's hands are handcuffed securely behind his or her back.
2. Check the waistband and area within reach of the prisoner's handcuffed hands.
3. Check the prisoner's cap or hat.
4. Check the neck area and both arms.
5. Check the prisoner's front pockets.
6. Check the inseam of the pants and crotch area.
7. Check the legs and ankles.
8. Check the prisoner's shoes.

**80.** Officer Linder arrests a man wearing a baseball cap, a T-shirt, blue jeans, and lace-up work boots. She checks to make sure the handcuffs are secure. She notices a bulge in his cap. What should Officer Linder do next?
   **a.** Check his front pockets.
   **b.** Check the cap for weapons.
   **c.** Check the prisoner's waistband.
   **d.** Check the area near his neck.

**81.** Officer Petrochowsky arrests a man for public intoxication. The man is wearing a cowboy hat, a long-sleeved shirt, dress slacks, and cowboy boots. The officer checks the prisoner's handcuffs and checks to make sure the waistband and back pocket area are clear of weapons. Suddenly, the prisoner sits down on the curb and refuses to stand up. Two other officers help get the prisoner to his feet. What should Officer Petrochowsky do next?
   **a.** Check the prisoner's cowboy hat.
   **b.** Check the prisoner's boots.
   **c.** Check the prisoner's waistband and back pocket area.
   **d.** Take the prisoner straight to jail before he tries to sit back down.

**82.** Officer Chastaine has a woman under arrest for possession of cocaine. She is wearing a scarf, a long dress, stockings, and high heels. He checks to make sure the handcuffs are secure on the woman. What should he do next?
   **a.** Check the suspect's scarf.
   **b.** Check the waistline of the suspect's dress and any pockets near her hands.
   **c.** Check the suspect's neck area.
   **d.** Check the suspect's shoes, which are partially hidden by her skirt.

*Use the information below to answer questions 83 and 84.*

Police Officers James and Chu were dispatched to investigate a report of attempted murder. They obtained the following information:

Date:           February 4, 2010
Victims:        Doctors James and Hildy Chew
Suspect:        Dana Williams, the victims' cook
Disposition:    Suspect arrested

83. Officer James is writing up the crime report. Which of the following expresses the information most clearly and accurately?
   a. Poisoning his employers, Doctors James and Hildy Chew, Dan Williams, their cook, was arrested on February 4, 2010, on suspicion of attempted murder.
   b. On January 4, 2010, cook Dan Williams was arrested on suspicion of attempted murder after giving poison to his employers, Doctors James and Hildy Chew.
   c. His employers, Doctors James and Hildy Chu, were almost murdered by Dan Williams, their cook, who tried to get them to eat poison.
   d. Dan Williams, a cook employed by Doctors James and Hildy Chew, was arrested on February 4, 2010 on suspicion of attempted murder. They were almost poisoned.

84. Which of the following is an incorrect assumption based on the material provided?
   a. Doctors James and Hildy Chew are married to one another.
   b. Doctors James and Hildy Chew employed a cook.
   c. Dan Williams was arrested.
   d. The doctors survived the attempted poisoning.

85. Winslow Elementary School is having a criminal mischief problem: Windows are being broken at the school between 7:00 P.M. and 6:00 A.M. Officer Link has talked to the school principal and is keeping a closer eye on the school. Which of the following situations should he investigate?
   a. At 1:00 A.M., Officer Link watches a man carrying a grocery sack cut through the schoolyard and come out on the other side of the school grounds. The officer can see a loaf of bread protruding out of the sack.
   b. At 11:00 P.M., a car pulls up in the school parking lot. Officer Link sees the driver turn on the cabin light and unfold a map.
   c. Around 11:30 P.M., Officer Link passes the school and sees two figures come out from behind one of the classroom buildings. They stop when they see him and then start walking, each in a different direction.
   d. At 9:00 P.M., several teenagers skateboard into the parking lot, set up a small wooden ramp, and practice skateboarding tricks.

86. In the K-9 Corps, Officer Thomas is partnered with Ranger, Officer Cain is partnered with Scout, Officer Stern is partnered with Laddie, and Officer Walker is partnered with Astro. If Officer Thomas switches partners with Officer Stern and Officer Stern then switches with Officer Cain, who is Officer Stern's new partner?
   a. Ranger
   b. Scout
   c. Laddie
   d. Astro

**87.** Officers aren't always required to make a custody arrest the very moment a law has been broken. A warrant can always be issued at a later date for the suspect if the person can be identified. Which of the following situations best illustrates this point?

**a.** Jeremy is well-known in his community for his appearance at political demonstrations. Police are called to the scene of a massive riot where Jeremy has incited over 100 college students to throw rocks and attack the outnumbered police force.

**b.** Melody is walking along the street when a man jumps out from the shadows, grabs her purse, and takes off running. Officer Bentley catches him one block later.

**c.** Antonio tells Officer DiAngelo that his cousin has been threatening to burn his house down. While Antonio is telling this story, a gasoline can comes crashing through the living room window.

**d.** Rachel, dragging a teenager by the jacket, walks up to Officer Xavier. She tells the officer that she caught the young man putting his hand into her coat pocket when she was waiting at the bus stop.

**88.** Four people saw Ramirez snatch a woman's purse. Which description of Ramirez is probably correct?

**a.** He wore blue pants and an orange sweatshirt.
**b.** He wore blue pants and a red sweatshirt.
**c.** He wore black pants and an orange sweatshirt.
**d.** He wore blue pants and an orange jacket.

*Use the following information to answer questions 89–91.*

Police officers are required to give out physical descriptions of suspects over police radios for other officers to assist in locating the person. A description should be given out in the following order:

1. race and sex
2. weapons the suspect may be carrying
3. approximate height and weight
4. color and length of hair
5. baseball cap or other headgear
6. coat, jacket, or shirt
7. long or short pants
8. footwear

**89.** Officer Lundy was on patrol when she saw a man on a sidewalk waving wildly at her. The man told her he'd been robbed about one block away by a white male carrying a lock-blade knife. The suspect has on white tennis shoes, olive drab fatigue pants, a black turtleneck, and a black baseball cap. He's about 6 feet tall and weighs about 180 pounds. What is the first thing Officer Lundy should put out over the radio when she begins describing the suspect?

**a.** a description of the suspect's knife
**b.** a description of the suspect's race and sex
**c.** a description of the suspect's pants
**d.** a description of the suspect's speaking voice

**90.** While investigating a possible burglary in progress, Officer Risher sees the burglar dart out the back door of the house and run through the backyard. Other officers are en route to help. He picks up his radio to put out a description of the suspect. He couldn't tell the race or sex of the suspect, but guessed the height to be 5′8″ and the weight about 140 pounds. He also couldn't tell if the suspect carried a weapon. He did see black pants, white high-top tennis shoes, a dark windbreaker, and a red baseball cap. What is the first thing Officer Risher should put out on the radio when he begins to give the description?
   **a.** a description of the suspect's race and sex
   **b.** a description of the suspect's pants
   **c.** a description of the suspect's shoes
   **d.** a description of the suspect's height and weight

**91.** Officer Scott is taking a report of a purse snatching at the mall. The victim says the thief was 5'10" tall, weighed about 160 pounds, had short red hair, and was wearing a New York Yankees baseball cap with gray warm-up pants and a gray sweatshirt. He was wearing black jogging shoes, was a white male, and appeared to be without weapons. Officer Scott begins her description with the race and sex of the suspect, but is interrupted by the victim. When she resumes her description, Officer Scott should begin with the
   **a.** suspect's footwear.
   **b.** suspect's headgear.
   **c.** suspect's height and weight.
   **d.** suspect's weapon.

*Answer questions 92-94 based on the following information.*

Criminal trespassing occurs when a person knowingly enters or remains unlawfully in a building. Burglary occurs when a person knowingly enters or remains unlawfully in a building or a dwelling with the intent to commit a crime therein. A dwelling is defined as a building where someone usually lodges overnight.

**92.** Which is the most accurate statement describing the crime of burglary?
   **a.** A person must have unlawful intent for the crime of burglary to be committed.
   **b.** A person can commit the crime of burglary only in a dwelling.
   **c.** Real property must be stolen for the crime of burglary to occur.
   **d.** A dwelling is anyplace where someone sleeps overnight.

**93.** Dalia and Larry missed their 1 A.M. train and hid behind some benches in the station's main waiting room until after the last train left the station, which was now closed to the public. When they were found by station police officers, they were warned by the officers but not arrested. Based on the information, Dalia and Larry
   **a.** committed burglary, since they remained unlawfully in a building.
   **b.** committed no crime, since they had no criminal intent.
   **c.** committed criminal trespass, even though they had no unlawful intent.
   **d.** committed no crime, because they had not read the sign that the station closed at 2 A.M.

**94.** A major difference between criminal trespass and burglary is

   **a.** the intent to commit a crime.

   **b.** the size of the building entered.

   **c.** the time of day that the building is entered.

   **d.** knowledge that the building has been entered.

**95.** The police department is staking out a warehouse. Officer Walters is stationed north of Officer Smits. Officer Foster is stationed north of Officer Walters. Officer Balboa is stationed south of Officer Foster. Given these facts, which of the following statements is definitely true?

   **a.** Officer Walters is the farthest north of all the officers.

   **b.** Officer Balboa is the farthest south of all the officers.

   **c.** Officer Smits is stationed south of Officer Foster.

   **d.** Officer Balboa is stationed south of Officer Walters.

Use the following information to answer question 96.

In many smaller police departments, the first officer to arrive at the scene of a homicide is often the same officer who will be responsible for taking photographs to preserve the scene. That officer should take the following steps in the order listed:

1. Make sure the crime scene is secure and assign another officer to be responsible for monitoring who comes in and out of the area.

2. Leave the crime scene as it is, not moving any objects or specific items of evidence until photos can be taken of the scene as it first appears to the officer.

3. Take a picture of the overall crime scene area, then take a more specific photo of the area where the body is, and then take photos of specific pieces of evidence.

4. After the first set of photographs is taken, shoot another set and put in an object such as a ruler that will give the pictures a sense of perspective.

5. Place the film in a container and write on the container the case number, the photographer's name and employee number, the date, and the location where the photographs were taken.

6. Take the film to the department photo lab to be developed.

**96.** Officer Scales received a call at 8:00 A.M. about a headless body found in a trash bin in an alley behind 4501 West Thompson Street. He arrives on scene and secures the area by having everyone step away from the trash bin and by assigning backup Officer Angel to keep onlookers away from the scene. He reaches inside the trash bin and moves a cardboard box so that he can see the body better. He steps back, takes an overall shot of the scene, then moves in closer and takes specific shots of the body and then of all items that appear to be potential evidence. He takes a second set of photographs of the scene using a ruler for a marker. He then places the film in an evidence container and writes his case number, name and employee number, the date, and the location of where the photos were taken. He takes the film to the department photo lab. Based on the information in the passage, Officer Scales's actions were

   **a.** improper, because he needed a flash unit given that the inside of the trash bin is dark.

   **b.** improper, because he didn't witness the development of the film himself to protect the chain of evidence.

   **c.** improper, because he moved the cardboard box before taking photographs of the scene as it first appeared.

   **d.** proper, because he fulfilled all the duties as outlined in the procedures.

**97.** The police department files information on crimes by date committed. Baker robbed a bank before Mitchell assaulted a police officer, but after Nelson stole a car. Edgar burgled a warehouse before Nelson committed his crime. In what order do these files appear at the police department?
- **a.** Nelson, Baker, Mitchell, Edgar
- **b.** Edgar, Nelson, Baker, Mitchell
- **c.** Baker, Mitchell, Edgar, Nelson
- **d.** Edgar, Mitchell, Nelson, Baker

Use the following information to answer question 98.

When called upon to work a collision scene, a police officer should do the following:

1. Have all drivers move all vehicles not in need of a tow truck out of the roadway.
2. Position the patrol car behind disabled vehicles to keep other traffic from becoming involved.
3. Turn on emergency lights so other traffic is warned of the problem.
4. Call tow trucks if needed.
5. Put on a reflective traffic vest if traffic direction becomes necessary.
6. Have the drivers, passengers, and witnesses step out of the roadway.
7. Collect information from drivers, passengers, and witnesses.

**98.** Officer Gofort has been dispatched to a four-car collision at Maple and Walnut. When he arrives, he notices that all four cars are in the same lane of traffic and have apparently run into the backs of each other. What is the first thing he should do?
- **a.** Call for four tow trucks to come to his location.
- **b.** Have the drivers move all driveable cars into a nearby parking lot.
- **c.** Put on his reflective vest.
- **d.** Collect information from all drivers, passengers, and witnesses.

**99.** Officer Littmar is driving by a mall when she is flagged down by four men at a bus stop. They tell her that they just watched a man jump out of a yellow taxicab and force a woman at gunpoint to get inside the cab with him. They drove away northbound on Exeter Street. All four witnesses say they saw the number painted on the side of the cab and give Officer Littmar the numbers. Which of the numbers below is most likely to be the true number painted on the side of the taxi?
- **a.** 9266
- **b.** 9336
- **c.** 9268
- **d.** 8266

**100.** Officer Manley is called to the scene of a theft of auto parts at Lucky Lube Auto Parts. The store manager, Alfonso, tells the officer that while he was waiting on another customer, a woman came inside the store, picked up a pen-shaped tire gauge, and ran out of the store without paying. He shouted at her to stop, but she kept running. Alfonso says he thinks this is the same woman who has been shoplifting up and down the strip mall for the past two weeks. Alfonso describes the woman as white, 5'2", 105 pounds, with light brown hair touching the tops of her shoulders, dark navy-blue wire rimmed glasses, and a pale blue dress. Officer Manley looks at four other reports to see if the same woman fits as a suspect in the other four thefts.

**Suspect in Theft #1:** Female, white, 5'2", 105 lbs., shoulder-length brownish hair, glasses, white sandals, stained pale-colored dress.

**Suspect in Theft #2:** Female, white, 5'3", 110 lbs., shoulder-length brown hair and wire-rimmed glasses, wearing a green dress.

**Suspect in Theft #3:** Female, white, 5'5", 125 lbs., dyed light blond hair, blue dress, bare feet.

**Suspect in Theft #4:** Female, white, 5'2", 112 lbs., light hair worn slightly below the shoulder, thin-framed metal glasses, light colored sandals, black dress.

Which of the suspects is the most likely culprit?
a. 2, 3, 4
b. 1, 2, 4
c. 1, 2, 3
d. 1, 3, 4

# Answer Key

## Part One: Memorization and Visualization

1. **a.** The remarks under the posters of Thomas Alberto Velez and Ali Mohammad mention gas stations.

2. **c.** The remarks under the posters of Ali Mohammad and Michael Adam Rosen describe them as having obvious accents. Rosa Seranno was describing as possibly answering questions in Spanish, but nothing was said about her speaking accented English.

3. **b.** Refer to the remarks.

4. **a.** Only the identifing scars or marks of Ali Mohammad mention a scar on the left side of the face.

5. **b.** Thomas Alberto Velez and Michael Adam Rosen are described as having tattoos.

6. **d.** Michael Adam Rosen is being sought by the Vancouver, *WA*, Police Department; Thomas Alberto Velez is being sought by the King County, *WA*, Sheriff's Department.

7. **b.** Refer to the information on whom to contact if Rosa Serrano is located.

8. **d.** Thomas Alberto Velez and Michael Adam Rosen are described as having tattoos; Velez's was of a bear, Rosen's of a lion.

9. **c.** Caution warnings are included for Thomas Alberto Velez, Patrick P. O'Brien, and Ali Mohammad.

10. **b.** Caution warnings that mention handguns are included for Thomas Alberto Velez and Ali Mohammad.

11. **a.** Rosa Seranno is the only female; Patrick P. O'Brien is described as a transsexual last seen dressing as a female.

12. **d.** Rosa Seranno is missing; the others are being sought for criminal matters.

13. **b.** The caution on Patrick P. O'Brien indicates he is known to carry a switchblade knife.

14. **b.** The remarks on Patrick P. O'Brien describe him as a drug addict and the identifying scars and marks reinforce this by mention of his having needle tracks on his forearm.

15. **c.** Rosa Seranno was last seen at a train station; Patrick P. O'Brien was described as possibly traveling out of state by bus.

16. **b.** Choice **a** does not address the overall theme of the passage, which mentions driving while intoxicated only in comparison to driving while text messaging; choices **c** and **d** recall specific facts from the passage but do not address its overall theme.

17. **c.** This information is contained in the last sentence of the second paragraph.

18. **a.** This information is contained in the first sentence of the second paragraph.

19. **c.** This information is contained in the third paragraph.

20. **b.** This information is contained in the seventh paragraph.

21. **c.** This comparison is made in the first, fourth, and fifth paragraphs.

22. **a.** See the comment in the second paragraph of the passage.

23. **c.** This information is contained in the fourth paragraph.

24. **c.** This information is contained in the fourth paragraph; you need to know that a quarter-million is the same as 250,000.

25. **b.** This information is contained in the fourth paragraph.

26. **b.** This information is contained in the seventh paragraph. This is also the most logical answer, since the passage as a whole is about texting while driving.

27. **c.** This information is contained in the seventh paragraph.
28. **b.** This information is contained in the eighth paragraph.
29. **d.** This information is contained in the seventh paragraph.
30. **b.** This information is contained in the fifth paragraph.

## Part Two: Reading Skills

31. **d.** Choice **a** requires going the wrong way on Avenue C; choice **b** is based on the wrong directions for the streets since Brooklyn Street runs north-south and Avenue B runs east-west; choice **c** leaves the driver one block east of the gas station.
32. **b.** Choice **a** will put the pedestrian in the park; choice **c** takes him out of his way; choice **d** is the least direct route.
33. **a.** Choice **b** is a longer route and goes by the high school; choice **c** requires going the wrong way on 1st Avenue; choice **d** is the least direct route.
34. **d.** Choice **a** is less direct; choice **b** does not start from the hospital and also involves going the wrong way on Avenue B; choice **c** is also indirect and involves going the wrong way on Avenue **d.**
35. **b.** Choices **a** and **c** require you to drive the wrong way on 1st Avenue; choice **d** will bring you to the southeast rather than the northwest corner of the park.
36. **b.** Choice **a** involves making unnecessary turns and puts the officers the wrong way on Adams Avenue; choice **b** is incorrect because Lincoln Street is one-way going north; choice **d** takes the officers out of their way and is the least direct route.

37. **c.** The turn onto Glade Road has Officer Romuldo going west; the left onto Taft Road turns him south; the right onto Pine Avenue turns him west again; the right onto Cleveland Avenue turns him back north; and the right onto Wilshire Avenue turns him east.
38. **c.** The two-way avenues are Cleveland, Pine, and Wilshire.
39. **c.** The one-way roadways are Palmer Road, Jones Road, Taft Road, Alpen Street, Lincoln Street, and Adams Avenue.
40. **a.** Since the officers are on foot, the traffic directional arrows are not relevant to their path. Choices **b**, **c**, and **d** all involve unnecessary turns onto less direct routes from Cleveland Avenue to Ford Road.
41. **d.** Based on the directional coordinates given to you, St. Clair is northwest of Newtown.
42. **c.** Choices **a** and **b** are incorrect because despite the word *west* in its name, Queens Park West is the northern boundary of Memorial Park; choice **d** is incorrect because Henry Street stops before reaching Memorial Park.
43. **b.** These are the only three streets that provide direct access from the park to the cemetery.
44. **a.** This is the most direct route from the northwest corner of Woodford Square to the southeast corner of Victoria Square.
45. **a.** Choice **b** takes you to the southeast corner, choice **c** gets you to the correct location but is less direct than choice **a**; choice **d** takes you to the northeast corner.
46. **a.** A title generally provides a summary of the topic; choices **b** and **d** are mentioned in the reading but are not its main themes; choice **c** does not at all capture what the reading is about.
47. **d.** This information is contained in the first paragraph of the passage.

**48. b.** This information is contained in the second paragraph of the passage; choices **a** and **c** are not discussed in the passage; choice **d** is incorrect because reasons for the change are discussed.

**49. c.** This information is contained in the third paragraph of the passage.

**50. d.** This information is contained in the last paragraph of the passage.

**51. d.** It is best to look at the first paragraph for a sense of an overall theme of a reading. While choices **a**, **b**, and **c** are mentioned briefly in the passage, none summarize the overall theme of the material.

**52. b.** The first paragraph states that 59% of the agencies required the officer to wear the armor at least some of the time, making choice **b** the closest available figure.

**53. c.** The passage states the 25% of agencies have no policy, meaning 75% of agencies have some sort of policy.

**54. b.** The suggestions from PERF are termed *improvements* and all pertain to strengthening polices rather than weakening them.

**55. a.** This information is contained in the second paragraph of the passage.

**56. b.** Do not be fooled by choice **a**: This may be true in many cases, but the passage explicitly states that *prosecuting its perpetrators* is more of a problem.

**57. b.** The first sentence of the passage states that identity theft *is the act of stealing someone's unique, personal identifying information.* Choices **a**, **c**, and **d** all meet that criteria. You may feel like your full name is unique, but is not uncommon for many people to have the same name. It is the combination of the name and other information that is unique.

**58. a.** The crux of identity theft is the misuse of personal information for financial gain.

**59. d.** Nowhere in the passage is it stated that phishing is the most common form of identity theft.

**60. a.** A question that asks for a title usually deals with a main idea. The title that best sums up what this passage is about is choice **a**.

## Part Three: Judgment and Problem Solving

**61. b.** This is the only choice that contains all the information in chronological order. Choices **a** and **d** misidentify the person reporting the incident as the person who was missing; choice **c** omits major portions of what occurred and provides only the conclusion of the event.

**62. b.** Any of the other answers may in fact be true, but the report does not provide sufficient detail for you to make these assumptions.

**63. c.** Choice **a** is not a strong choice because a person's reputation has more to do with criminal history, or lack thereof, than his or her standing in the community. Moreover, if the city councilperson were warned about drunk driving, there is nothing to indicate that he or she would not continue the behavior. Both the known heroin addict and the woman on probation have reputations, like a criminal history, that run counter to giving warnings.

**64. c.** Of all the situations, only the case of the felony crime clearly prohibits the issuance of a warning.

**65. b.** Generally, stealing over $500 (choice **a**) and most frauds (choice **d**) are felony crimes. Beyond that, the two offenders lack direct ties to the community that would indicate that a warning would be sufficient. Finally, a person with a warrant is generally not a good candidate for a warning because he or she has already failed to appear in court on a previous charge.

66. **d.** From most arrests to fewest, either Meadows or Governale had the highest number of arrests, followed by Ash and then Westerman, who had the fewest.

67. **a.** The Woolf vehicle had stopped at the "T" intersection before turning onto Morton, so there must have been a stop sign on Farley; Burroughs was cited for failing to obey a stop sign on Morton.

68. **b.** Wilcox told Lieutenant Watts that the armored truck struck the car in which he was a passenger, driven by Mr. Woolf, and that the Woolf vehicle subsequently struck Mrs. Moreno's convertible.

69. **d.** Officer Parisi examined the skid marks, which showed that the armored truck was braking.

70. **a.** The green sedan, with Mr. Woolf driving, had been driving down Farley Street before turning onto Morton at the "T" intersection.

71. **d.** Mrs. Moreno was in the house at the time of the accident.

72. **b.** The ignition is off because the bike has not been started. The officer has placed both hands on the handlebars and has seen that both tires are already positioned on the ground. Thus, the next thing he should do is to perform step 4 in the procedure, rock the bike on its engine guards.

73. **c.** The officer should place both hands on the handlebars after she has turned off the ignition. The other choices are correct steps but are out of order for this scenario.

74. **b.** The first step is always to turn the engine off. In the heat of the moment, it may seem reasonable to do what is listed in the other choices, but this would not be correct according to the procedures list.

75. **b.** Start with what is known: North has been a police officer for 15 years, which is six years fewer than Wilson, who therefore has 21 years. North's 15 years are seven more than Trainor's, so North has been an officer for eight years. If Sanchez has been a police officer for five more years than Trainor, then Sanchez has 13 years on the police force.

76. **c.** Peter has been warned that his actions are dangerous and could result in his arrest. In choice **a**, Tom has also been warned, but the danger is to himself, not to others.

77. **a.** The definition includes the phrases *engages in conduct* and *is aware of the risk*.

78. **a.** Fred's opinion of police has nothing to do with the situation. Officer Martinez should write the ticket because the situation was dangerous, and that is what he would do under normal circumstances. A warning is not appropriate because a collision was narrowly averted.

79. **c.** Assault is the most serious crime, followed, in descending order, by burglary, breaking and entering, and extortion.

80. **c.** The officer has already performed step 1 by making sure the handcuffs are secure. Checking the suspect's waistband and back pocket area is step 2, which she should perform next. She should not be distracted by the bulge in the cap, so choice **b** is not correct.

81. **a.** The officer should check the arrestee's hat because that is the next step after checking the waistband and back pocket area. The officer should not be distracted from the proper procedures because the intoxicated man is difficult to control. The other officers are there to assist, and he should be able to safely conduct his search.

**82. b.** The officer should check the waistband area and the area near the arrestee's hands, because that is the next step on the list of procedures. That the arrestee is a woman and is wearing a dress should not distract the officer from following procedure, since dresses may have pockets and waistbands.

**83. b.** Choice **a** implies that Williams was arrested in the act of poisoning. In choice **c** it is not clear that anyone was arrested; the doctors' surname is also misspelled. Choice **d** does not make clear who was poisoned, even though it would appear the pronoun *they* indicates the two doctors.

**84. a.** The doctors could be siblings, could have a parent/child or other family relationship, or could coincidentally have the same last name. Choices **b**, **c**, and **d** are correct assumptions because they are based on information provided in the question.

**85. c.** The odd behavior and the location of the two figures should cause the officer to investigate, given the problems the school has been having.

**86. b.** After all the switches were made, Officer Stern's partner was Scout. Officer Thomas's partner was Laddie, Officer Cain's was Ranger, and Officer Walker's was Astro.

**87. a.** Outnumbered officers attempting to control a hostile crowd may not be able to arrest the instigator safely; however, according to the situation they will likely be able to find him later, since they are aware of his identity. In the other situations, custody arrests are appropriate and more easily accomplished. Although in choice **c** it seems apparent that Antonio knows his cousin's identity, and therefore a warrant could be issued at a later date, the violence of the situation makes immediate action necessary.

**88. a.** Blue pants, sweatshirt, and the color orange are the elements repeated most often by the eyewitnesses and are therefore most likely correct.

**89. b.** The first step is to give the race and sex of the suspect. In this case, the victim has provided that information.

**90. d.** The officer can't give information he doesn't have. The first step he will be able to follow is to give the height and weight description.

**91. c.** The next information the officer can give out is a height and weight description. Since no weapon was seen, choice **d** is not possible.

**92. a.** A burglary can take place in a building; property does not have to be stolen, and a dwelling is a *building*, not *any place*.

**93. c.** Because they remained in a building unlawfully, they were guilty of criminal trespass.

**94. a.** The crime of burglary requires the intent to commit a crime therein; criminal trespass does not mention intent, only knowledge.

**95. c.** Officer Smits is stationed south of Officer Foster. Officer Walters cannot be farthest north, because Foster is north of Walters. Balboa is south of Foster, but may or may not be south of Walters; therefore Balboa may not be farthest south, nor definitely south of Walters.

**96. c.** Step 2 instructs the officer not to move any objects until photos are taken of them as they first appeared when the officer arrived.

**97. b.** Edgar burgled a warehouse before Nelson stole a car. Baker robbed a bank after Nelson stole a car; Mitchell assaulted a police officer after Baker robbed a bank and Nelson stole a car. The order is Edgar, Nelson, Baker, Mitchell.

**98. b.** The first step in the procedure is to move all driveable vehicles, and that should be Officer Gofort's first move.

**99. a.** Three of the witnesses agree that the first number is 9. Three agree that the second number is 2. Three witnesses agree that the third number is 6, and three others agree that the fourth number is also 6. Choice **a** is the best choice because it is made up of the numbers that most of the witnesses agree that they saw.

**100. b.** The suspect described in theft 3 does not match Alfonso's suspect description very closely. The women in 1, 2, and 4 all appear to be the same woman Alfonso saw because of the similarities in height, weight, hair, and eyewear.

## Scoring

Based on the amount of studying you have done, you will hopefully have seen improvement over your score on Practice Exam 2. Regardless of how much your overall score improved, use this practice exam to analyze where you have improved and where you continue to have weaknesses. As you did with the earlier exams, break down your score by section by writing down the number of correct answers for each section. When you add up the sections, remember that each correct answer is worth one point. You should be aiming for a score of at least 70. The better you do on the practice exams, the better your chance of not only passing the real exam, but scoring high enough to be among the first applicants called in for the later steps in the hiring process. If you score is only about 70 or not even at that level, it is particularly important for you to review the individual section scores to see where you need to concentrate your additional study efforts.

CHAPTER

13 ▶ POLICE
OFFICER
PRACTICE
EXAM 6

### CHAPTER SUMMARY

This final practice exam returns to the format of Practice Exam 3.
It tests vocabulary, number and letter recall, and your personal
background.

T he first part of the exam in this chapter includes verbal comprehension and recall questions. You are
given ten minutes to answer 50 vocabulary questions and nine minutes to answer 100 recall questions.
Before you take those two sections, set a timer or stopwatch so that you can time the sections exactly.
Your main task in both of these sections is simply not to get flustered. If you stay calm and focused, you *can* get
the right answers to these questions.

The second part of the official exam consists of 185 personal background questions, which you can take as
much time as you need to answer. There's not much you can or need to do to prepare for these questions, since
they're all about you, your experiences, and your attitudes. The practice exam in this chapter includes 20 personal background questions that will help you get familiar with the format.

After the exam is an answer key for the first part of the exam, the verbal and number and letter recall questions. There is no answer key for the second part, the personal background questions, because those questions
have no correct or incorrect answers.

## Police Officer Practice Exam 6 Part One
### Verbal Section

1. (a) (b) (c) (d)
2. (a) (b) (c) (d)
3. (a) (b) (c) (d)
4. (a) (b) (c) (d)
5. (a) (b) (c) (d)
6. (a) (b) (c) (d)
7. (a) (b) (c) (d)
8. (a) (b) (c) (d)
9. (a) (b) (c) (d)
10. (a) (b) (c) (d)
11. (a) (b) (c) (d)
12. (a) (b) (c) (d)
13. (a) (b) (c) (d)
14. (a) (b) (c) (d)
15. (a) (b) (c) (d)
16. (a) (b) (c) (d)
17. (a) (b) (c) (d)

18. (a) (b) (c) (d)
19. (a) (b) (c) (d)
20. (a) (b) (c) (d)
21. (a) (b) (c) (d)
22. (a) (b) (c) (d)
23. (a) (b) (c) (d)
24. (a) (b) (c) (d)
25. (a) (b) (c) (d)
26. (a) (b) (c) (d)
27. (a) (b) (c) (d)
28. (a) (b) (c) (d)
29. (a) (b) (c) (d)
30. (a) (b) (c) (d)
31. (a) (b) (c) (d)
32. (a) (b) (c) (d)
33. (a) (b) (c) (d)
34. (a) (b) (c) (d)

35. (a) (b) (c) (d)
36. (a) (b) (c) (d)
37. (a) (b) (c) (d)
38. (a) (b) (c) (d)
39. (a) (b) (c) (d)
40. (a) (b) (c) (d)
41. (a) (b) (c) (d)
42. (a) (b) (c) (d)
43. (a) (b) (c) (d)
44. (a) (b) (c) (d)
45. (a) (b) (c) (d)
46. (a) (b) (c) (d)
47. (a) (b) (c) (d)
48. (a) (b) (c) (d)
49. (a) (b) (c) (d)
50. (a) (b) (c) (d)

### Number and Letter Recall Section

1. (a) (b) (c) (d) (e)
2. (a) (b) (c) (d) (e)
3. (a) (b) (c) (d) (e)
4. (a) (b) (c) (d) (e)
5. (a) (b) (c) (d) (e)
6. (a) (b) (c) (d) (e)
7. (a) (b) (c) (d) (e)
8. (a) (b) (c) (d) (e)
9. (a) (b) (c) (d) (e)
10. (a) (b) (c) (d) (e)
11. (a) (b) (c) (d) (e)
12. (a) (b) (c) (d) (e)
13. (a) (b) (c) (d) (e)
14. (a) (b) (c) (d) (e)
15. (a) (b) (c) (d) (e)
16. (a) (b) (c) (d) (e)
17. (a) (b) (c) (d) (e)
18. (a) (b) (c) (d) (e)
19. (a) (b) (c) (d) (e)
20. (a) (b) (c) (d) (e)
21. (a) (b) (c) (d) (e)
22. (a) (b) (c) (d) (e)
23. (a) (b) (c) (d) (e)
24. (a) (b) (c) (d) (e)
25. (a) (b) (c) (d) (e)

26. (a) (b) (c) (d) (e)
27. (a) (b) (c) (d) (e)
28. (a) (b) (c) (d) (e)
29. (a) (b) (c) (d) (e)
30. (a) (b) (c) (d) (e)
31. (a) (b) (c) (d) (e)
32. (a) (b) (c) (d) (e)
33. (a) (b) (c) (d) (e)
34. (a) (b) (c) (d) (e)
35. (a) (b) (c) (d) (e)
36. (a) (b) (c) (d) (e)
37. (a) (b) (c) (d) (e)
38. (a) (b) (c) (d) (e)
39. (a) (b) (c) (d) (e)
40. (a) (b) (c) (d) (e)
41. (a) (b) (c) (d) (e)
42. (a) (b) (c) (d) (e)
43. (a) (b) (c) (d) (e)
44. (a) (b) (c) (d) (e)
45. (a) (b) (c) (d) (e)
46. (a) (b) (c) (d) (e)
47. (a) (b) (c) (d) (e)
48. (a) (b) (c) (d) (e)
49. (a) (b) (c) (d) (e)
50. (a) (b) (c) (d) (e)

51. (a) (b) (c) (d) (e)
52. (a) (b) (c) (d) (e)
53. (a) (b) (c) (d) (e)
54. (a) (b) (c) (d) (e)
55. (a) (b) (c) (d) (e)
56. (a) (b) (c) (d) (e)
57. (a) (b) (c) (d) (e)
58. (a) (b) (c) (d) (e)
59. (a) (b) (c) (d) (e)
60. (a) (b) (c) (d) (e)
61. (a) (b) (c) (d) (e)
62. (a) (b) (c) (d) (e)
63. (a) (b) (c) (d) (e)
64. (a) (b) (c) (d) (e)
65. (a) (b) (c) (d) (e)
66. (a) (b) (c) (d) (e)
67. (a) (b) (c) (d) (e)
68. (a) (b) (c) (d) (e)
69. (a) (b) (c) (d) (e)
70. (a) (b) (c) (d) (e)
71. (a) (b) (c) (d) (e)
72. (a) (b) (c) (d) (e)
73. (a) (b) (c) (d) (e)
74. (a) (b) (c) (d) (e)
75. (a) (b) (c) (d) (e)

## Number and Letter Recall Section (continued)

76. (a) (b) (c) (d) (e)
77. (a) (b) (c) (d) (e)
78. (a) (b) (c) (d) (e)
79. (a) (b) (c) (d) (e)
80. (a) (b) (c) (d) (e)
81. (a) (b) (c) (d) (e)
82. (a) (b) (c) (d) (e)
83. (a) (b) (c) (d) (e)
84. (a) (b) (c) (d) (e)

85. (a) (b) (c) (d) (e)
86. (a) (b) (c) (d) (e)
87. (a) (b) (c) (d) (e)
88. (a) (b) (c) (d) (e)
89. (a) (b) (c) (d) (e)
90. (a) (b) (c) (d) (e)
91. (a) (b) (c) (d) (e)
92. (a) (b) (c) (d) (e)
93. (a) (b) (c) (d) (e)

94. (a) (b) (c) (d) (e)
95. (a) (b) (c) (d) (e)
96. (a) (b) (c) (d) (e)
97. (a) (b) (c) (d) (e)
98. (a) (b) (c) (d) (e)
99. (a) (b) (c) (d) (e)
100. (a) (b) (c) (d) (e)

## Part Two
## Personal Background Section

1. (a) (b) (c) (d) (e) (f)
2. (a) (b)
3. (a) (b) (c) (d) (e)
4. (a) (b) (c) (d) (e) (f)
5. (a) (b) (c) (d) (e) (f)
6. (a) (b) (c) (d) (e) (f)
7. (a) (b) (c) (d) (e)

8. (a) (b) (c) (d)
9. (a) (b) (c) (d)
10. (a) (b) (c) (d) (e) (f) (g) (h)
11. (a) (b) (c)
12. (a) (b) (c) (d)
13. (a) (b) (c) (d) (e) (f)
14. (a) (b) (c) (d)

15. (a) (b) (c) (d) (e) (f) (g) (h)
16. (a) (b) (c) (d) (e) (f) (g)
17. (a) (b) (c) (d)
18. (a) (b) (c) (d) (e) (f) (g) (h)
19. (a) (b) (c) (d) (e) (f)
20. (a) (b) (c) (d) (e) (f) (g)

# Police Officer Practice Exam 6

## Part One: Verbal Section

1. Which word means the *same* as APATHETIC?
   a. eager
   b. indifferent
   c. studious
   d. suspicious

2. Which word means the *same* as SURMISE?
   a. guess
   b. develop
   c. infer
   d. imagine

3. Which word means the *same* as EXPENSIVE?
   a. spacious
   b. out-of-date
   c. modern
   d. costly

4. Which word means the *opposite* of METICULOUS?
   a. careful
   b. delicate
   c. sloppy
   d. painstaking

5. Which words means the *same* as FREQUENT?
   a. rarely
   b. sometimes
   c. never
   d. often

6. Which word means the *same* as DISCLOSE?
   a. confirm
   b. inform
   c. reject
   d. refute

7. Which word means the *opposite* of INTENTIONAL?
   a. premeditated
   b. accidental
   c. cognizant
   d. oblivious

8. Which word means the *same* as AUGMENT?
   a. evaluate
   b. discontinue
   c. expand
   d. critique

9. Which word means the *same* as MALICIOUS?
   a. behaved
   b. methodical
   c. mean
   d. fashionable

10. Which word means the *opposite* of DISTINGUISHED?
    a. inflamed
    b. barbaric
    c. foolish
    d. inconspicuous

11. Which word means the *same* as PREDATOR?
    a. guardian
    b. hunter
    c. alien
    d. prey

12. Which word means the *opposite* of CANDID?
    a. sincere
    b. passive
    c. dishonest
    d. shy

**13.** Which word means the *same* as NEGLIGENCE?
  **a.** prudence
  **b.** pajamas
  **c.** carelessness
  **d.** criminality

**14.** Which word means the *same* as GRATUITY?
  **a.** gift
  **b.** receivable
  **c.** grantor
  **d.** annuity

**15.** Which word means the *same* as UNIVERSAL?
  **a.** limited
  **b.** syndicate
  **c.** synthesized
  **d.** widespread

**16.** Which word means the *same* as FORTIFIED?
  **a.** reinforced
  **b.** altered
  **c.** disputed
  **d.** developed

**17.** Which word means the *opposite* of COVERT?
  **a.** loud
  **b.** unguarded
  **c.** public
  **d.** colorful

**18.** Which word means the *opposite* of MALICE?
  **a.** instinct
  **b.** agitation
  **c.** compassion
  **d.** anger

**19.** Which word means the *opposite* of INCOMPETENCE?
  **a.** ineffectiveness
  **b.** ability
  **c.** insane
  **d.** average

**20.** Which word means the *same* as LIABILITY?
  **a.** responsibility
  **b.** slanderous
  **c.** nuisance
  **d.** reliability

**21.** Which word means the *same* as ACCOMMODATE?
  **a.** constrain
  **b.** disappoint
  **c.** hinder
  **d.** help

**22.** Which word means the *opposite* of NOVICE?
  **a.** adversary
  **b.** resident
  **c.** expert
  **d.** follower

**23.** Which word means the *same* as MINISCULE?
  **a.** immense
  **b.** tiny
  **c.** long
  **d.** short

**24.** Which word means the *opposite* of OBSOLETE?
  **a.** contemporary
  **b.** stubborn
  **c.** perceptive
  **d.** ancient

**25.** Which word means the *opposite* of IRRESISTIBLE?
   **a.** unpredictable
   **b.** unforseen
   **c.** unappealing
   **d.** unnecessary

**26.** Which word means the *same* as PROVOKED?
   **a.** aroused
   **b.** disappointed
   **c.** frightened
   **d.** questioned

**27.** Which word means the *opposite* of ESSENTIAL?
   **a.** useless
   **b.** unnecessary
   **c.** important
   **d.** extra

**28.** Which word means the *opposite* of TESTY?
   **a.** good-natured
   **b.** bad-tempered
   **c.** studious
   **d.** educated

**29.** Which word means the *opposite* of TACTFUL?
   **a.** combative
   **b.** intelligent
   **c.** diplomatic
   **d.** officious

**30.** Which word means the *same* as TENTATIVE?
   **a.** definite
   **b.** enthusiastic
   **c.** unwise
   **d.** provisional

**31.** Which word means the *opposite* of CREDITABLE?
   **a.** unbelievable
   **b.** wealthy
   **c.** believable
   **d.** poor

**32.** Which word means the *same* as ANIMATED?
   **a.** abbreviated
   **b.** civil
   **c.** secret
   **d.** lively

**33.** Which word means the *same* as SUPERSEDE?
   **a.** override
   **b.** strengthen
   **c.** rejuvenate
   **d.** reorder

**34.** Which word means the *opposite* of PROMOTE?
   **a.** explicate
   **b.** curtail
   **c.** concede
   **d.** retain

**35.** Which word means the *opposite* of REASONABLE?
   **a.** irrational
   **b.** awkward
   **c.** realistic
   **d.** acceptable

**36.** Which word means the *same* as COMPLIANT?
   **a.** skeptical
   **b.** obedient
   **c.** forgetful
   **d.** appreciative

**37.** Which word means the *opposite* of SUSPEND?
 a. conceive
 b. trust
 c. delay
 d. sustain

**38.** Which word means the *opposite* of SCANT?
 a. invisible
 b. meager
 c. copious
 d. vocal

**39.** Which word means the *opposite* of WITHHOLD?
 a. deny
 b. bestow
 c. confer
 d. consummate

**40.** Which word means the *same* as AUGMENT?
 a. repeal
 b. evaluate
 c. expand
 d. criticize

**41.** Which word means the *same* as INDISPENSABLE?
 a. determined
 b. experienced
 c. essential
 d. creative

**42.** Which word means the *same* as DESICCATE?
 a. moisten
 b. dry
 c. cool
 d. warm

**43.** Which word means the *same* as EXPEDITE?
 a. accelerate
 b. evaluate
 c. reverse
 d. justify

**44.** Which word means the *opposite* of SUBJECTIVE?
 a. invective
 b. objectionable
 c. unbiased
 d. obedient

**45.** Which word means the *opposite* of SUCCINCT?
 a. distinct
 b. laconic
 c. unpersuasive
 d. verbose

**46.** Which word means the *opposite* of TEDIOUS?
 a. stimulating
 b. alarming
 c. intemperate
 d. tranquil

**47.** Which word means the *same* as PLAUSIBLE?
 a. unbelievable
 b. insufficient
 c. apologetic
 d. credible

**48.** Which word means the *opposite* of UNIFORM?
 a. dissembling
 b. diverse
 c. bizarre
 d. slovenly

**49.** Which word means the *same* as INFERRED?
    **a.** intuited
    **b.** imagined
    **c.** implied
    **d.** surmised

**50.** Which phrase means the *same* as ULTIMATUM?
    **a.** earnest plea
    **b.** formal petition
    **c.** solemn promise
    **d.** non-negotiable demand

## Number and Letter Recall Section

In this section, each set of 25 questions is preceded by a key, which consists of letter sets and numbers. Each question consists of one of the letter sets followed by numbers. Use the key to pick the number that goes with each letter set, and then fill in the appropriate circle on the answer sheet. You have nine minutes for this section.

### KEY 1

| ABT | QXR | RLK | SAB | GTR | DBV | FRE | WRT | QGT |
|-----|-----|-----|-----|-----|-----|-----|-----|-----|
| 27  | 39  | 49  | 43  | 51  | 59  | 66  | 91  | 67  |

| FTB | BEF | POM | QAW | BLU | XRK | YEG | RJT | BJI |
|-----|-----|-----|-----|-----|-----|-----|-----|-----|
| 29  | 82  | 17  | 70  | 82  | 71  | 19  | 37  | 58  |

| NYH | TKG | NAP | ZEF | PTG | MAB | HTD | UGC | KGS |
|-----|-----|-----|-----|-----|-----|-----|-----|-----|
| 43  | 89  | 44  | 18  | 11  | 60  | 15  | 93  | 34  |

| | | a | b | c | d | e | | | a | b | c | d | e |
|---|---|---|---|---|---|---|---|---|---|---|---|---|---|
| 1. | KGS | 34 | 48 | 59 | 92 | 73 | 14. | NAP | 85 | 33 | 44 | 55 | 93 |
| 2. | ZEF | 41 | 18 | 87 | 58 | 33 | 15. | SAB | 92 | 54 | 18 | 43 | 23 |
| 3. | FTB | 62 | 41 | 65 | 13 | 29 | 16. | DBV | 52 | 56 | 71 | 59 | 97 |
| 4. | TKG | 26 | 32 | 41 | 16 | 89 | 17. | UGC | 11 | 91 | 93 | 35 | 26 |
| 5. | QXR | 92 | 47 | 39 | 77 | 10 | 18. | BEF | 75 | 82 | 96 | 33 | 13 |
| 6. | ABT | 11 | 27 | 55 | 41 | 76 | 19. | YEG | 46 | 97 | 28 | 19 | 23 |
| 7. | MAB | 60 | 57 | 49 | 56 | 13 | 20. | PTG | 44 | 71 | 23 | 11 | 17 |
| 8. | POM | 75 | 17 | 55 | 33 | 87 | 21. | RJT | 27 | 73 | 61 | 37 | 40 |
| 9. | BLU | 29 | 12 | 82 | 35 | 63 | 22. | XRK | 65 | 39 | 33 | 92 | 71 |
| 10. | RLK | 63 | 14 | 41 | 93 | 49 | 23. | BJI | 97 | 31 | 58 | 29 | 72 |
| 11. | QGT | 67 | 88 | 23 | 49 | 11 | 24. | FRE | 71 | 42 | 13 | 34 | 66 |
| 12. | NYH | 37 | 43 | 65 | 82 | 95 | 25. | GTR | 44 | 82 | 55 | 51 | 15 |
| 13. | GTR | 95 | 51 | 32 | 94 | 88 | | | | | | | |

## KEY 2

| AOD | ROK | GKS | BRJ | ZQE | GDT | EIR | VID | ANB |
|-----|-----|-----|-----|-----|-----|-----|-----|-----|
| 10 | 80 | 41 | 55 | 87 | 57 | 47 | 26 | 16 |

| RNY | GDJ | RHC | BSW | FVM | DYO | JAT | RXG | NDO |
|-----|-----|-----|-----|-----|-----|-----|-----|-----|
| 73 | 23 | 76 | 50 | 99 | 35 | 32 | 97 | 74 |

| GPH | EAP | LGD | BGS | KRH | YFR | JWD | BFH | QFA |
|-----|-----|-----|-----|-----|-----|-----|-----|-----|
| 12 | 86 | 40 | 54 | 48 | 20 | 64 | 22 | 38 |

|     |     | a | b | c | d | e |     |     | a | b | c | d | e |
|-----|-----|---|---|---|---|---|-----|-----|---|---|---|---|---|
| 26. | EAP | 86 | 59 | 21 | 33 | 65 | 39. | JAT | 61 | 32 | 43 | 14 | 28 |
| 27. | DYO | 78 | 35 | 73 | 93 | 45 | 40. | EIR | 51 | 32 | 47 | 20 | 24 |
| 28. | KRH | 45 | 48 | 43 | 55 | 42 | 41. | BFH | 51 | 43 | 11 | 22 | 58 |
| 29. | QFA | 52 | 64 | 12 | 23 | 38 | 42. | ROK | 24 | 80 | 21 | 14 | 54 |
| 30. | JWD | 15 | 78 | 33 | 64 | 84 | 43. | RNY | 32 | 73 | 38 | 62 | 24 |
| 31. | GDJ | 54 | 23 | 98 | 32 | 35 | 44. | VID | 52 | 26 | 84 | 27 | 83 |
| 32. | ZQE | 87 | 62 | 13 | 51 | 34 | 45. | ANB | 35 | 48 | 23 | 34 | 16 |
| 33. | AOD | 72 | 43 | 10 | 24 | 37 | 46. | RHC | 93 | 11 | 23 | 76 | 52 |
| 34. | NDO | 52 | 43 | 74 | 39 | 63 | 47. | BRJ | 55 | 25 | 90 | 31 | 28 |
| 35. | GKS | 41 | 24 | 68 | 53 | 54 | 48. | YFR | 42 | 36 | 74 | 42 | 20 |
| 36. | FVM | 99 | 36 | 45 | 48 | 23 | 49. | GDT | 31 | 57 | 23 | 38 | 75 |
| 37. | BGS | 54 | 88 | 13 | 43 | 86 | 50. | RXG | 98 | 35 | 55 | 64 | 97 |
| 38. | GPH | 52 | 46 | 85 | 23 | 12 |     |     |    |    |    |    |    |

## KEY 3

| UHJ | BKR | PJD | ABD | LBC | PRT | QAS | MNC | GKX |
|-----|-----|-----|-----|-----|-----|-----|-----|-----|
| 21  | 13  | 30  | 84  | 96  | 45  | 63  | 61  | 72  |

| ASW | CPA | WQH | LDM | MAM | NAN | ANZ | IXD | BQC |
|-----|-----|-----|-----|-----|-----|-----|-----|-----|
| 88  | 90  | 42  | 62  | 81  | 77  | 53  | 79  | 10  |

| DPB | QRT | MNA | UGL | XYZ | DAL | IYP | KUB | ASF |
|-----|-----|-----|-----|-----|-----|-----|-----|-----|
| 64  | 26  | 44  | 56  | 52  | 24  | 65  | 28  | 55  |

|     |     | a  | b  | c  | d  | e  |     |     | a  | b  | c  | d  | e  |
|-----|-----|----|----|----|----|----|-----|-----|----|----|----|----|----|
| 51. | PJD | 30 | 44 | 55 | 95 | 68 | 64. | ANZ | 21 | 76 | 84 | 53 | 44 |
| 52. | QAS | 63 | 84 | 22 | 12 | 69 | 65. | NAN | 41 | 77 | 63 | 58 | 14 |
| 53. | UHJ | 65 | 68 | 21 | 15 | 69 | 66. | IXD | 22 | 66 | 25 | 79 | 27 |
| 54. | ABD | 65 | 84 | 14 | 62 | 79 | 67. | MAM | 37 | 65 | 81 | 84 | 34 |
| 55. | GKX | 25 | 68 | 35 | 61 | 72 | 68. | XYZ | 52 | 54 | 35 | 93 | 14 |
| 56. | BKR | 72 | 13 | 64 | 34 | 25 | 69. | DPB | 39 | 57 | 94 | 62 | 64 |
| 57. | MNC | 61 | 35 | 53 | 79 | 29 | 70. | IYP | 25 | 65 | 62 | 59 | 54 |
| 58. | LBC | 54 | 74 | 96 | 57 | 90 | 71. | DAL | 75 | 85 | 25 | 24 | 12 |
| 59. | ASF | 55 | 95 | 35 | 21 | 14 | 72. | BQC | 15 | 62 | 10 | 25 | 92 |
| 60. | ASW | 55 | 34 | 28 | 61 | 88 | 73. | UGL | 71 | 56 | 61 | 24 | 18 |
| 61. | PRT | 45 | 21 | 68 | 35 | 24 | 74. | MNA | 61 | 70 | 35 | 18 | 44 |
| 62. | WQH | 42 | 98 | 61 | 52 | 96 | 75. | QRT | 63 | 26 | 25 | 15 | 89 |
| 63. | LDM | 18 | 59 | 85 | 62 | 76 |     |     |    |    |    |    |    |

**KEY 4**

| BGR | MDV | LRW | BLE | NRW | GBY | VDJ | XAQ | MUP |
|-----|-----|-----|-----|-----|-----|-----|-----|-----|
| 55 | 85 | 53 | 66 | 45 | 21 | 15 | 45 | 65 |

| HTF | SQN | QLU | NHT | MJY | LOK | PLM | QAZ | WSX |
|-----|-----|-----|-----|-----|-----|-----|-----|-----|
| 61 | 68 | 64 | 84 | 94 | 25 | 54 | 95 | 12 |

| CDE | VFR | BGR | NHT | MJY | XDW | CDM | OZP | QMI |
|-----|-----|-----|-----|-----|-----|-----|-----|-----|
| 37 | 98 | 34 | 85 | 19 | 69 | 24 | 62 | 51 |

| | | a | b | c | d | e | | | a | b | c | d | e |
|---|---|---|---|---|---|---|---|---|---|---|---|---|---|
| 76. | QMI | 36 | 88 | 14 | 51 | 43 | 89. | MJY | 85 | 94 | 73 | 55 | 19 |
| 77. | NHT | 85 | 54 | 84 | 28 | 73 | 90. | MUP | 17 | 47 | 71 | 41 | 65 |
| 78. | BGR | 82 | 81 | 55 | 33 | 27 | 91. | BLE | 85 | 52 | 66 | 71 | 83 |
| 79. | HTF | 16 | 32 | 98 | 23 | 61 | 92. | MDV | 12 | 85 | 43 | 24 | 36 |
| 80. | PLM | 61 | 83 | 49 | 54 | 22 | 93. | NHT | 75 | 42 | 85 | 84 | 28 |
| 81. | VDJ | 15 | 12 | 45 | 57 | 80 | 94. | GBY | 46 | 62 | 28 | 21 | 99 |
| 82. | NRW | 29 | 53 | 35 | 45 | 29 | 95. | SQN | 68 | 91 | 45 | 22 | 21 |
| 83. | LRW | 47 | 53 | 51 | 75 | 85 | 96. | OZP | 81 | 46 | 55 | 62 | 40 |
| 84. | WSX | 39 | 51 | 12 | 63 | 46 | 97. | MJY | 54 | 82 | 33 | 38 | 94 |
| 85. | QLU | 64 | 98 | 43 | 59 | 12 | 98. | XDW | 97 | 32 | 69 | 65 | 36 |
| 86. | BGR | 85 | 89 | 65 | 34 | 88 | 99. | LOK | 25 | 35 | 49 | 14 | 73 |
| 87. | CDE | 37 | 21 | 85 | 59 | 98 | 100. | QAZ | 44 | 37 | 64 | 95 | 69 |
| 88. | VFR | 73 | 24 | 64 | 98 | 52 | | | | | | | |

## Part Two:
## Personal Background Section

Answer each question honestly. Mark only one answer unless the question states otherwise. There is no time limit for this section.

1. If I were struggling with a course in school, the last thing I would do would be to
   a. put in extra time on my own.
   b. seek help from the teacher.
   c. do extra research in the library.
   d. request a tutor.
   e. seek help from family or friends.
   f. drop the course.

2. At work, I prefer to
   a. work on one project at a time.
   b. work on many projects simultaneously.

3. I exercise strenuously
   a. daily.
   b. every other day.
   c. two or three times a week.
   d. whenever I can fit it into my schedule.
   e. rarely or never.

4. In school, I learned the most from
   a. lectures by teachers.
   b. guest lectures.
   c. field trips.
   d. visual presentations.
   e. independent research.
   f. participation in class discussions.

5. The main reason I accepted my most recent employment position was because it
   a. offered a challenge.
   b. provided a good income and benefits.
   c. offered career advancement.
   d. gave me a lot of responsibility.
   e. allowed me to provide for myself and/or my family.
   f. was conveniently located.

6. I prefer to meet with my supervisor
   a. daily.
   b. weekly.
   c. every other day.
   d. every other week.
   e. as often as problems materialize.
   f. infrequently.

7. I work late
   a. on a regular basis.
   b. whenever I need to catch up.
   c. in order to meet deadlines.
   d. when asked to do so.
   e. never.

8. I enjoy myself the most when I spend time
   a. alone.
   b. with one or two other people.
   c. with a group of three or four people.
   d. in larger groups of people.

9. I prefer tasks that are
   a. physically demanding.
   b. mentally demanding.
   c. both physically and mentally demanding.
   d. neither physically nor mentally demanding.

**10.** Of the following hobbies, the ones I engage in at least once a year are (Mark all that apply)
a. reading a book.
b. watching a movie.
c. golfing.
d. hunting.
e. skiing (water or snow).
f. home improvement projects.
g. attending cultural events.
h. hiking.

**11.** If I get lost while driving, I am most likely to
a. ask for directions.
b. refer to a map.
c. continue driving until I find my way.

**12.** If my supervisor needs to discipline me at work, I would prefer that my supervisor
a. speak with me directly.
b. issue me a memo.
c. show me what I should have done.
d. call the staff together to discuss the problem.

**13.** I consider an appropriate length of commitment for a new professional position to be
a. six months.
b. one year.
c. two years.
d. three years.
e. five years.
f. more than five years.

**14.** I have shoplifted
a. never.
b. once or a few times, when I was young.
c. once or a few times, but only inexpensive items.
d. several times.

**15.** The most important consideration for me when I am deciding whether to take a new position is
a. the hours.
b. the pay.
c. the health benefits.
d. the retirement/investment benefits.
e. my coworkers.
f. my supervisor.
g. the work itself.
h. other.

**16.** The most important thing I have gained from my family is a sense of
a. trust.
b. cooperation.
c. responsibility.
d. caring.
e. commitment.
f. self-sufficiency.
g. other.

**17.** My free time is mostly spent
a. alone.
b. with family.
c. with friends.
d. with colleagues from work.

**18.** My coworkers would describe me as (Mark all that apply)
a. motivated.
b. laid-back.
c. professional.
d. driven.
e. intelligent.
f. fearless.
g. focused.
h. flexible.

**19.** If criticized at work, my first reaction is to
   **a.** use the criticism to improve my skills.
   **b.** defend myself to the person making the critical comments.
   **c.** consider the criticism irrelevant.
   **d.** get upset with myself.
   **e.** lose focus.
   **f.** sharpen my focus.

**20.** The main reason I enjoy being with my friends is being able to
   **a.** confide in them.
   **b.** have fun times together.
   **c.** engage in serious discussions.
   **d.** learn from them.
   **e.** take my mind off concerns I may have.
   **f.** engage in activities I can't do alone.
   **g.** some other reason.

# Answer Key

*Verbal*

1. b.
2. c.
3. d.
4. c.
5. d.
6. b.
7. b.
8. c.
9. c.
10. d.
11. b.
12. c.
13. c.
14. a.
15. d.
16. a.
17. c.
18. c.
19. b.
20. a.
21. d.
22. c.
23. b.
24. a.
25. c.
26. a.
27. b.
28. a.
29. a.
30. d.

31. a.
32. d.
33. a.
34. b.
35. a.
36. b.
37. d.
38. c.
39. b.
40. c.
41. c.
42. b.
43. a.
44. c.
45. d.
46. a.
47. d.
48. b.
49. d.
50. d.

*Number and Letter Recall*

1. a.
2. b.
3. e.
4. e.
5. c.
6. b.
7. a.
8. b.

9. c.
10. e.
11. a.
12. b.
13. b.
14. c.
15. d.
16. d.
17. c.
18. b.
19. d.
20. d.
21. d.
22. e.
23. c.
24. e.
25. d.
26. a.
27. b.
28. b.
29. e.
30. d.
31. b.
32. a.
33. c.
34. c.
35. a.
36. a.
37. a.
38. e.
39. b.

40. c.
41. d.
42. b.
43. b.
44. b.
45. e.
46. d.
47. a.
48. e.
49. b.
50. e.
51. a.
52. a.
53. c.
54. b.
55. e.
56. b.
57. a.
58. c.
59. a.
60. e.
61. a.
62. a.
63. d.
64. d.
65. b.
66. d.
67. c.
68. a.
69. e.
70. b.

71. d.
72. c.
73. b.
74. e.
75. b.
76. d.
77. a.
78. c.
79. e.
80. d.
81. a.
82. d.
83. b.
84. c.
85. a.
86. d.
87. a.
88. d.
89. b.
90. e.
91. c.
92. b.
93. c.
94. d.
95. a.
96. d.
97. e.
98. c.
99. a.
100. d.

# Scoring

The exam score is computed using a formula that subtracts for incorrect answers on Part One, the verbal and number and letter recall sections. Scoring on the personal background section varies by department, so there's no way to estimate how you would score on that section. Here's a method for computing a rough score for Part One.

## Verbal Score

First, count the number of questions you answered correctly. Then, count the number of questions you answered incorrectly and divide by four. Subtract the results of the division from the number you got correct for your raw score. Questions you didn't answer don't count either way.

1. Number of questions correct:_____
2. Number of questions incorrect:_____
3. Divide number **2** by 4:_____
4. Subtract number **3** from number **1**:_____

The result of number **4** above is your raw score on the verbal section.

## Number and Letter Recall Score

Count the number and letter recall questions you answered correctly. Then, count the number of questions you answered incorrectly and divide by five. Subtract the results of the division from the number you got correct, and that's your score. Questions you didn't answer don't count.

1. Number of questions correct:_____
2. Number of questions incorrect:_____
3. Divide number **2** by 5:_____
4. Subtract number **3** from number **1**:_____

The result of number **4** is your raw score on the number and letter recall section.

## What the Scores Mean

In general, a score of at least 70% is enough to pass. That would mean a score of at least 35 on the verbal section and 70 on the recall section. The personal background section will also be factored into your final score, but you can't predict how that section will be scored.

Your goal is to score as high as possible on the written exam, because that score in part determines your rank on the eligibility list. You've probably already seen an improvement in your score between the exam in Chapter 6 and this exam. If you want to score even higher, the best place to put your energy is the vocabulary section, because that's the one part of the exam you can really study for. Use the tips in Chapter 9 to help you continue to improve your vocabulary.

As exam day draws near, the biggest thing you can do to continue to improve is to practice your self-confidence. Remember, the key to doing well on this exam, in which timing counts so much, is to stay calm and focus.

Practice your self-confidence in front of the mirror every morning. Say to yourself: *I can beat this exam. It's not really that hard. I just have to focus and answer one question at a time. I can find the right answer. I can score well.* Armed with self-confidence, and knowing that you've practiced the kinds of questions on the exam, you can do your best on exam day.

# GLOSSARY ▶

**Americans with Disabilities Act**   this law, which came into effect in 1990, prohibits discrimination against those with disabilities in a number of areas, including employment. It has had a major impact on the order in which police departments administer portions of their entry requirements, particularly the medical exam and physical agility tests.

**arraignment**   a hearing before a court having jurisdiction in a criminal case at which the defendant is identified, informed of his or her rights, and required to enter a plea

**arrest**   an arrest occurs when any sworn officer deprives a person of his/her liberty by taking that person into custody to answer for a criminal offense or a violation of a code or ordinance that the officer's jurisdiction is authorized to enforce. Most arrests are made by police officers, peace officers, troopers, or sheriff's deputies, but depending on the jurisdiction or circumstances, probation, parole, or court officers may be authorized to arrest all or certain categories of people.

**auxiliary/reserve/part-time police officer**   designations that refer to different types of officers in different areas of the United States; regardless of title, they are found in many police departments and sheriffs' offices but rarely in state police agencies. Depending on local usage, these officers may be volunteers or may be paid; they generally perform in uniform a certain number of hours per week or per month, supplementing regular officers during certain times of the year (such as in resort communities when populations increase substantially), or for certain events, including traffic control or work at fairs or civic or cultural events; in other jurisdictions, they have the same duties as fully-sworn, full-time officers. Many officers employed in these positions are interested in employment as full-time law enforcement officers. In some jurisdictions, this type of employment is viewed as a stepping-stone to full-time employment, offered first to those who are Police Explorers or others involved in similar programs, or to those who are on the civil service eligibility list and are awaiting being called for full-time police employment.

**background investigation**   a key element in the hiring process, it delves into a candidate's past life, including education, employment, military service, criminal history, credit and driving records, and past associations. A candidate must provide information which is verified by the hiring agency to help in determining whether the candidate is suitable for law enforcement employment. Deliberate falsehoods are automatic grounds for a candidate to be dropped from further consideration for employment.

**beat**   the smallest geographical area that an officer is assigned to patrol. In large cities and in high-density jurisdictions (e.g., airports, large rail stations), an officer will likely be assigned to walk the beat; in rural areas or agencies that cover a large geographical area (state police, suburban agencies) an officer will likely be assigned to patrol the beat from a vehicle. Some departments rely on other motorized vehicles, such as scooters or three-wheeled carts, and some assign officers to patrol beats in parks and recreation areas on bicycles.

**booking**   the process of fingerprinting, processing, and photographing a suspect who has been taken into custody by a police officer and placed under arrest

**bureaucracy**   any organization with a strictly-defined hierarchy; a defined promotion policy generally based on written tests; a career path; reliance on rules and regulations, and a formal and impersonal style of management. Police agencies, regardless of size, are considered to be bureaucracies.

**burnout**   a form of stress associated with policing and many other emergency service positions that involve constant interaction with members of the public. Burnout manifests in feelings of fatigue, frustration, and cynicism, all of which may ultimately end in depression and extremely negative attitudes toward the employing agency or the public. See also: police cynicism.

**chain of command**   each person in the organization is supervised and reports to one person, generally one or two ranks above him or her. For example, a police officer reports to a sergeant in most agencies, sometimes to a lieutenant, but almost never to a captain. A lieutenant reports to a captain or higher rank, never to a sergeant or police officer, both of whom are lower in the chain of command than the lieutenant.

**chain of custody**   the witnessed, unbroken, written chronological history of who had any piece of evidence at any time

**civil service system**   a system of hiring and promoting employees that is designed to eliminate political influence, nepotism, and bias, generally involving a written examination on factual material, and sometimes combining interviews and other criteria as part of the process of hiring or promoting personnel. Most municipal, county, and state police departments and most federal law enforcement agencies are covered by civil service regulations; some sheriffs' and special-jurisdiction departments are not.

**civilianization**   the trend of agencies hiring non-sworn employees (civilians) to fill positions that were once filled by police officers. Among these jobs have been answering non-emergency and emergency phones, dispatching beat officers, investigating traffic accidents and civil infractions, and media relations. In recent decades, civilians have been hired to provide computer services and web design; crime and crime scene analysis and technical services, and budget, legal, and financial expertise. Departments may also call upon civilians who are multilingual for interpreting services.

**collective bargaining**   an employer and its employees, represented by their union, negotiate a formal agreement over salaries, hours, benefits, and other conditions of employment

**community policing**   a philosophy of policing that gained public attention beginning in the 1970s. Also called community-oriented policing or COP, it is based on police agencies developing close relationships with civilian populations and developing partnerships with the community to develop solutions to persistent crime problems.

**confession**   a formal, written document in which a person admits to having been involved in specific criminal activity

**conditional offer of employment**   a job offer from a police agency to an applicant, extended with the understanding that there are still steps in the employment process that the applicant must complete, and that if these are completed successfully, the agency intends to hire the applicant

**consent decree**   an agreement that requires an agency to take specific actions involving hiring and promoting minority group members and/or women. A law enforcement agency that is operating under a consent decree will often hire or promote individuals on a basis other than strict test scores.

**crime (criminal offense)**   legal definition of an act that the government (local, state, federal) has declared to be unlawful; a crime is defined by law (statute) and is prosecuted in a criminal proceeding

**crime prevention**   activities undertaken by police officers and agencies to help the community reduce crime and support community safety. Crime prevention efforts by police might include such activities as patrol or community outreach efforts; efforts by companies or institutions might include developing access control polices, installing surveillance cameras or video systems, and using landscaping and building placements to minimize areas that are dark, unattended, or unobserved.

**crime scene/crime scene investigators**   the location where a crime has occurred; over the past decade, the emergence of television programs that feature crime scene investigators has led the public to focus on crime scenes and evidence obtained at them in greater detail than in the past. The expectation of jurors that there will always be physical evidence of a crime has led to what has become known as the *CSI effect*, which has resulted in juries failing to convict defendants without the types of evidence they have come to expect via television. In most large city police departments, crime scene investigators are sworn police officers selected for the job on a number of criteria. In this regard, they differ from detectives, who may or may not gather physical evidence but who are also responsible for interviewing victims, witnesses, and suspects and following up on various aspects of the crime. In some police and investigative agencies those who collect and analyze certain types of evidence may be civilians hired specifically for these tasks. See also: detective.

**crime-fighter style**   a philosophy of policing popular particularly from the 1930s to the 1970s, that focused almost solely on the police role fighting crime and enforcing the law rather than also providing community services. This is the police role featured most frequently in fictional portrayals of the police and which many police candidates incorrectly believe will form the largest portion of their job responsibilities.

**criminal justice system**   the term used to encompass the police, the judicial system, and correctional facilities and to show their interrelatedness. The police are viewed as the gatekeepers to the system because they make the initial contact with law-breakers and, through the arrest process, determine who will enter into the system. The judicial system is the middle phase, where guilt or innocence is determined, and correctional institutions are viewed as the final phase, where punishment is meted out. A broader description might also include probation and parole as alternatives to correctional institutions or post-correctional oversight of an offender.

**custody**    legal or physical control of a person or thing

**deadly physical force**    physical force which, under the circumstances in which it is used, is readily capable of causing death or other serious physical injury. Police officers are among the few government employees who are authorized to use deadly force under certain circumstances determined by department policies and court decisions.

**decoy operations**    a non-uniformed (plainclothes) assignment during which officers are assigned to play the role of potential victims with the goal of attracting and catching a criminal. Decoy operations can be very dangerous because the decoy is often unarmed and carries no police identification, which results in the decoy being totally dependent on the back-up team (officers observing and positioned to assist) should the decoy be attacked or mistaken by other police or members of the public for an actual criminal.

**detective**    generally an experienced police officer who is assigned to investigate serious crimes by following up on initial information obtained at the crime scene by the patrol officers. In many police agencies, detectives are selected and appointed based on their active arrest records while police officers or having worked in plainclothes assignments; in some agencies, detective is a civil service rank for which police officers must take and pass a written test to be selected from a list. The position of detective is highly sought-after because it means working out of uniform, provides more freedom than is provided to uniformed police officers, and carries prestige, particularly based on the media portrayal of what has come to be known as the *detective mystique*, a view that detective work is glamorous and dangerous and that only detectives ever have the opportunity to arrest criminals accused of serious crimes (felonies).

**directed patrol**    an assignment for officers to concentrate on areas where certain crimes have been known to occur and are a significant community problem

**discretion**    freedom to act on one's own and make decisions from a wide range of choices. Although police officers are expected to act according to department rules and procedures, police work entails considerable discretion by officers because situations may develop or change in ways that cannot be predicted in advance. Policing is often singled out as a profession is which the most important discretionary decisions are made by the lowest ranking personnel; this view is based on the understanding that the officer who arrives on the scene of an event who almost always makes decisions that more senior or higher-ranking personnel are not involved in until after the fact.

**domestic (or family) violence**    incidents of violence between spouses or partners or between family members; these calls are disliked by many police officers because they are often unpredictable and may turn violent when family members had intended for the police to simply defuse a situation, rather than possibly having to use force or make an arrest

**drug testing (or screening)**    analysis of employees or applicants for use of illegal drugs or substances. Most agencies screen candidates at the time of hiring, and many also have policies for random testing of officers or for testing after a vehicle accident, shooting, or any situation in which impairment may have influenced the event. Drug screening is usually done via urinalysis, but some agencies also use hair analysis tests.

**evidence**    anything that tends to prove or disprove an alleged act (crime) or a fact or action pertaining to a crime. Direct evidence is generally defined as an eyewitness account, a confession, or a tangible link to the act; indirect evidence (or circumstantial evidence) is the deductive process of inferring an unknown fact from a known or proven fact; and physical evidence is anything tangible that links a person to the act under investigation.

**field training (field training officer)**   on-the-job training that generally occurs immediately after completion of the police academy when a new officer ("rookie") is assigned to work with an experienced officer (the field training officer). Depending on the agency, this period may be few weeks and may be informal; in some agencies, field training may be a formalized program up to a year long, during which rookies are assigned sequentially to a number of training officers and the trainers file formal reports on the rookies' performance of particular tasks. In some agencies, failure of the rookie to be positively appraised by the training officer may result in termination during the probationary period.

**foot patrol**   the historical method of patrolling, particularly in large cities, that lost ground to patrolling in marked police cars in the 1930s but re-emerged in the 1960s as a way to combat disorder. It gained additional attention in the 1970s and 1980s as a community policing technique to make officers more visible and accessible to members of the community. In many large cities, recent graduates of the police academy are often assigned to foot patrol as a way for them to gain experience interacting with the public.

**hot spot**   defines an area that is known for significant criminal activity, such as a storefront where drug sales or prostitution solicitations are common. A *hot time* is a period of day or the week when crime is a problem, such as a storefront on Saturday nights after 11 P.M.

**incident report**   the first recorded, official report prepared by an officer after responding to events. Some incident reports are not followed up but others may be referred to detectives or investigators assigned to learn more about the event (generally referred to as a follow-up investigation).

**informant**   any civilian who brings information about a past or potential crime to the police. Informants may be individuals who are not involved in a crime but have knowledge of it and have no other involvement with the police, or they may be individuals who have been involved in criminal activity who assist the police in investigations, often for considerations of leniency in their cases. Although many types of enforcement (such as the purchase of narcotics or guns by police officers) depend on informants, police prefer not to rely on the testimony of informants in court and to verify information from informants through independent sources.

**in-service training**   general term used to describe training that occurs after a police officer graduates from the academy; it might occur on a regular basis or be scheduled occasionally to instruct officers in new techniques, policies, or laws. In some states, in-service training is mandated for officers to retain their commissions (legal status as officers empowered to make arrests).

**job analysis**   a scientific or quasi-scientific method to identify the tasks that police officers perform and the knowledge, skills, and abilities (often abbreviated as KSAs) required to perform those tasks. A job analysis is often performed by consultants who ride along with officers to observe their activities or who ask officers to list the KSAs they believe are needed to perform their jobs as a means of validating the requirements for employment. Agencies rely on these studies to create applicant tests that reflect the reality of police work.

**jurisdiction**   authority of a law enforcement agency to enforce particular laws in specific political and/or geographic boundaries. United States law enforcement is highly decentralized; no one law enforcement agency has total jurisdiction, which means that no one single agency has the authority to enforce all the laws in all places.

**lateral transfer**   the ability of an officer to transfer from one police agency to another while retaining rank or seniority gained in the original agency; these transfers are rare in the United States, where it is traditional that officers begin their careers at the lowest rank in a one agency and remain there for their entire careers. The inability to transfer laterally is one reason that is important that candidates consider carefully the agencies to which they apply, since quitting one and joining another will often require the officer to begin as a rookie in the new agency.

**mentor**   a person who fulfills the role of teacher, model, motivator, or advisor; often a more senior member of the agency who takes an interest in the career of a new officer. The importance of mentors has been debated in leadership literature, but it is generally agreed that new officers benefit from having a senior person to whom they can turn for advice. Mentors can also come from outside the agency; they may be family members, teachers, or anyone who inspires or assists a person in setting and reaching goals.

**misdemeanor**   class of criminal activity below a felony. Although the exact definitions differ by state, this class of crime is generally punishable by a fine of from $1,000 to $5,000, depending on jurisdiction, and a maximum of up to one year in a county or city correctional facility rather than a state prison.

**moonlight**   term used to describe the act of police officers working non-police jobs during their off-duty hours. In some parts of the country, it implies that the second job is in private security, but it may refer to any non-police work; regardless of the type of work, many agencies restrict the hours and types of jobs police officers may hold while off-duty.

**nonsworn (civilian) employees**   members of a law enforcement agency who do not have traditional police powers and are generally assigned to a wide variety of non-enforcement tasks. See also: civilianization.

**omnipresence**   a concept associated with patrol that suggests that visibly patrolling on foot, in motorized vehicles, or on bicycles or horses will create the appearance that uniformed officers are always present. The officers' visibility will deter criminals from committing crimes and reassure citizens of their safety.

**order maintenance**   expands the police role beyond the crime-fighter by emphasizing that officers are assigned to keep the peace and provide social services, not only to prevent crimes

**ordinance/infraction/violation**   although not identical, these terms each refer to the least serious category of offense, generally punishable by a small fine, no more than a few days in jail if any, and may not permit the right to trial because a conviction may not result in a permanent record

**physical agility test**   portion of the entrance requirements for most police agencies that requires an applicant to complete strength and endurance activities required to perform police tasks; tests might include running a particular distance within a designated time or completing specific physical activities (such as sit-ups or push-ups) within a designated time

**police academy**   the formal training that a newly hired officer receives. When officers refer to the police academy, they may be speaking about their training or about an actual, physical place. Police academies differ among agencies; you may commute from home or live at the facility, or you may attend only with members of your agency or at a regional academy where new officers from many departments attend classes together.

**police cynicism** cynicism means seeing the worst in situations or in people, and the belief that events or actions that appear positive will soon become negative. Police cynicism has been identified by sociologists as a belief that there is no hope for society and that people will always behave badly; it has been suggested that because police are often faced with negative situations, they are more cynical than other members of society. See also: burnout.

**police cadet** a position that differs in agencies around the country; in most agencies it a non-sworn position for teenagers and young adults who are interested in a police career. Other agencies employ only cadets who are high-school or college students who receive school credits or a financial stipend rather than a salary. In some agencies, if you are employed as a cadet and you pass the department's entry exam, you will be given certain preferences in the hiring process.

**Police Explorers** a structured career and educational program that grew out of the Boy Scouts of America for young men, but that now enrolls both men and women between the ages of 14 and 20 and allows them to explore policing through volunteer or work experiences in police agencies. Some Explorer programs provide accelerated entry into a department, making Explorers and similar internship, volunteer, or cadet programs popular with young people interested in police careers.

**police officer** member of a police agency who is sworn to make arrests and in most departments carries handcuffs and various defensive weapons, including a firearm. The term *police officer* is most often used to denote the entry-level rank of sworn officers, but is also used more broadly to define the status of anyone employed in a police department without an indication of rank. Thus, police officers are sworn members of the department, but not all sworn members are police officers since they may hold higher ranks. In state police and in some county police departments, the entry-level rank of police officer is called a trooper; in federal law enforcement, particularly if the individual does not work in uniform, the entry-level position is usually called a special agent or an investigator.

**police subculture** a subculture is a combination of norms, values, goals, career patterns, lifestyles, and roles that define a group. Of the many professional subcultures that exist, sociologists have found the police subculture to be among the strongest; suggested reasons include the belief that people who are similar are attracted to police work; the structured style of training and operations; the reliance on other officers that the job tasks engender; the potential danger the occupation presents; and the fear of being isolated from peers if officers do not adhere to the subculture's norms, which are viewed as secretive and as separating officers from civilians.

**polygraph (or lie detector) test** test that relies on a polygraph machine to determine whether the person being tested is telling the truth; the machine measures physiological responses (such as perspiration and pulse) to psychological stimuli (the questions). Although many people question the validity of these tests, some police agencies use them in the hiring process to verify the truthfulness of an applicant's claims.

**precinct/district/stationhouse** depending on local usage, these terms may refer to the collection of beats within a given geographic area, or to the organizational substations of a law enforcement agency; generally, not all officers report to headquarters but to a building that is located within the area they patrol and that houses that area's equipment and supervisory personnel

**private security**   the industry that provides uniformed or investigative functions by non-governmental agencies. Private security officers (sometimes called private police) are paid from private funds, and may work directly for a company (termed proprietary officers) or may work for an outside provider (termed contract officers). The number of private security personnel far exceeds the number of police personnel in the United States; in 2000, the Department of Justice estimated that two million people were employed in private security, compared to approximately 600,000 police officers. Opinion differs as to whether working in private security provides experience helpful to a police career, or whether the duties and legal responsibilities are too dissimilar to be helpful.

**probationary period**   the time from when an officer begins the academy until the officer becomes covered by civil service or other tenure regulations. During the probationary period (generally from six months to as long as two years depending on local law or union contract) an officer may be fired without a hearing or without the protections afforded by civil service law. Common reasons for termination during this period include conduct on- or off-duty that does not meet the department's standards, or an issue in the candidate's background that was not uncovered prior to hiring or during academy training.

**random patrol**   tactic of having an officer walk or drive around a designated geographic area in what seems to the public to be a random manner but may be pre-determined by patrol supervisors. The theory behind random patrol is that officers create a sense of omnipresence by appearing at unpredictable intervals; the tactic is based on the belief that the surprise presence of officers creates a fear of detection in criminals, and for that reason creates a sense of security in members of the public who feel safer knowing officers may be in the area.

**reserve officer**   usually a part-time employee who is a sworn police officer, often employed in communities with large population shifts during certain times of the year. In some parts of the country, reserve officers are not sworn and assist primarily with such non-enforcement duties as patrol at parades, fairs, and civic events or with traffic enforcement at major events. Not all reserve officers are interested in a full-time law enforcement career, but many who are consider this an excellent way to learn about the field and to establish positive relationships with their local police departments.

**residency requirement**   a requirement that officers must reside within the community they serve as a condition of employment; the community may defined as within the city or town limits, within the county, or within jurisdiction(s) that are specified in the collective bargaining agreement

**squad**   a group of officers who work together for a certain length of time under the supervision of the same sergeant or lieutenant. Police officers will often refer to themselves as part of a particular squad, identifying it by name or by tour of duty (such as "I work the 4 to 12 squad," which means the officer works the 4 P.M. to midnight shift, or "I work the burglary squad," which means the speaker is assigned to a group of officers that investigates past burglaries).

**sting operations**   an undercover operation where officers pose as something they are not to surprise and arrest criminals. In some cases the police may pose as criminals by, for instance, setting up a store to purchase stolen goods or to pretend to be looking for someone to commit a crime for them. Other types of stings have used a different element of surprise; for example, an officer may invite criminals with warrants for arrest to a party or event, at which they attend with no expectation of being arrested.

**SWAT**    Special Weapons and Tactics (SWAT) teams began in the 1960s; the term is used to describe teams of officers who are specially trained and equipped to deal with situations that present a higher-than-usual level of danger, such as hostage-taking, or situations in which it appears there are multiple aggressors. SWAT training varies across jurisdictions but generally ranges from hostage negotiation to special weapons training, including training as sharpshooters. In large agencies, SWAT members are permanently assigned to this team, in smaller agencies, they are likely to maintain their regular assignments but are called upon when a situation occurs in which their skills are determined appropriate. There has been criticism of dedicated SWAT teams in smaller agencies because there are often few situations for which their skills are truly required, leading to their use at times at which it is perceived as an over-reaction to the event.

**testimonial evidence**    verbal testimony given by a witness at trial, including police officers who testify about their observations or actions

**undercover operations or investigations**    activity undertaken by police which is covert (hidden) and during which officers work in plainclothes (out of uniform and either in business attire or in clothing appropriate to the undercover situation). For instance, officers attempting to observe the purchase of guns or narcotics or pretending to be gun purchasers or drug dealers would dress differently than officers pretending to be businessmen attempting to purchase a restaurant to use as a front for money laundering. Undercover operations are seen as among the most dangerous in police work; officers must convince others that they are authentic in the roles they are portraying, must often work without their police identification and firearms, and in some undercover situations must position themselves to become crime victims while depending on a hidden, backup team of officers to come to their aid as the situation develops.

**union**    an organization that represents dues-paying officers for the purpose of negotiating a collective bargaining agreement (contract) with employers

# ADDITIONAL ONLINE PRACTICE

Whether you need help building basic skills or preparing for an exam, visit the LearningExpress Practice Center! On this site, you can access additional practice materials. Using the code below, you'll be able to log in and take a practice police officer exam modeled on the official exam. This online practice exam will also provide you with:

- **Immediate scoring**
- **Detailed answer explanations**
- **Personalized recommendations for further practice and study**

Log in to the LearningExpress Practice Center by using the URL: **www.learnatest.com/practice**

This is your Access Code: **7403**

Follow the steps online to redeem your access code. After you've used your access code to register with the site, you will be prompted to create a username and password. For easy reference, record them here:

**Username:** _____ **Password:** _____

With your username and password, you can log in and access your additional practice exam. If you have any questions or problems, please contact LearningExpress customer service at 1-800-295-9556 ext. 2, or e-mail us at **customerservice@learningexpressllc.com**

# NOTES

**NOTES**

# NOTES

# NOTES

**NOTES**

# NOTES

# NOTES

**NOTES**

# NOTES